(above) Barbara La Marr in Heart of a Siren (LeMaire),
(preceding pages) scene from On Your Back (Wachner)

COSTUME DESIGN
IN THE MOVIES

An Illustrated Guide to the Work of 157 Great Designers

ELIZABETH LEESE

DOVER PUBLICATIONS, INC.
New York

Acknowledgments

The author gratefully acknowledges the help, advice and encouragement of the following people and organisations:

Academy of Motion Picture Arts & Sciences
    (Mildred Simpson and her staff)
David Badder
Bob Baker
DeWitt Bodeen
Eddie Brandt
British Academy of Film & Television Arts
    (Doreen Dean)
British Film Institute
    (Brenda Davies and the staff of the
    Information and Documentation Department)
Kevin Brownlow
Bonnie Cashin
Costumer Designers' Guild
Donfeld
Leslie Flint
Robert Florey
Vernon Harbin (RKO)
Julie Harris
Elois Jenssen
Celia John
Philip Kendal
Kodak Museum (Brian Coe)
Bert Langdon
Peter Miles
Museum of Modern Art Film Library,
    New York
National Film Archive, London
    (Harold Brown)
National Film Archive, London
    (Michele Snapes and the staff of the Stills Library)
Dame Anna Neagle
New York Public Library, Lincoln Center
    (Paul Myers and his staff)
Sheila O'Brien
Al Reuter
Shirley Russell
Markuu Salmi
Alan Sawford-Dye
Anthony Slide
Wisconsin Center for Theatre Research
    at the University of Wisconsin
    (Susan Dalton, Todd Luspinski, Steve Masar)

Published in Canada by General Publishing Company, Ltd., 30 Lesmill Road, Don Mills, Toronto, Ontario.

Published in the United Kingdom by Constable and Company, Ltd., 3 The Lanchesters, 162–164 Fulham Palace Road, London W6 9ER.

This Dover edition, first published in 1991, is a revised republication of the work originally published in England by BCW in 1976 and in the U.S. by Frederick Ungar Publishing Co., N.Y., in 1977. The "Publisher's Note, 1991" indicates the extent and nature of the revision.

Manufactured in the United States of America
Dover Publications, Inc., 31 East 2nd Street, Mineola, N.Y. 11501.

Library of Congress Cataloging-in-Publication Data

Leese, Elizabeth, 1937–
    Costume design in the movies : an illustrated guide to the work of 157 great designers / Elizabeth Leese.
        p.   cm.
    "Revised republication of the work originally published in England by BCW in 1976 and in the U.S. by Frederick Ungar Publishing Co., N.Y., in 1977"—T.p. verso.
    Includes indexes.
    ISBN 0-486-26548-X (pbk.)
    1. Costume   design.   2. Costume   designers.   3. Costume.   I. Title.
TT507.L42   1990
791.43′026′0922—dc20
[B]   90-44762
                                                        CIP

The illustrations have been researched and assembled by the author with the specific help of some of the people and organisations acknowledged opposite. For permission to reproduce some of these illustrations, we are grateful to: AIP, Anglo-Amalgamated, Avco-Embassy, British Lion, CIC, Columbia Pictures, Columbia-Warner, Ealing Studios, Fox-Rank, M-G-M, Paramount, The Rank Organisation, Screen Gems, 20th Century-Fox, United Artists, Universal, Walt Disney and Warner Brothers

Contents

Publisher's Note, (1991)

The number of designers covered in the present edition remains the same as in the first edition (except for the deletion of Motley), but over 400 film credits through 1987 have been added in the body of the text, and a number of rectifications made to credits already given. Films mentioned in the body of the book for the first time have been listed in a Supplement to the Index, while rectifications to existing credits have been reflected tacitly in the original part of the Index. Death dates have been added to the biographical statements wherever necessary. The lists of Oscar and BAFTA* nominations have been extended through 1988, with the appropriate additions made to the individual designer entries in the body of the text. Twenty-seven picture substitutions have been made, and only one omission; all but six of the illustrations (one of which was formerly in color) have been newly reshot from glossy photographs. The original endpaper illustrations (omitted in the Ungar paperback printing of 1978) now appear within the book (on pages ii/iii and iv).

*In many areas of the book, BAFTA is still referred to by its former designation SFTA (see page 169).

Foreword

Last year it was my privilege to design the costumes for the Bryan Forbes production *The Slipper and the Rose* which was a happy climax to my thirty years in the business. A Royal Film Performance choice, a lavish budget and a film in which every single extra had to be "dressed." It also gave me the chance to work again with a director for whom I have a great respect and with whom I have had a thoroughly enjoyable working relationship, dating back to *The Wrong Box*.

The Slipper and the Rose was a wonderful assignment because a period film is always so showy and spectacular. The costumes are centre-screen and the designers get their share of the applause along with all the other craftsmen and technicians whose work is increasingly appreciated by the filmgoing public.

But not all films are as inviting, as tempting or (and I use the word cautiously) as "easy" as *The Slipper and the Rose*. More difficult, and far less likely to win any applause, are the films that require dressing down, rather than dressing up. The designer's job is not only to dress a picture beautifully, if the subject so requires, but to help create character, be it rich or poor, rough or smart. Shopping around for off-the-peg costumes is not quite as glamorous as some people seem to think. I remember that, in *The Whisperers*, I was set the daunting task of transforming Dame Edith Evans into a shabby, pathetic old-age pensioner. This is even more difficult than it sounds, because there are some people who simply rise above whatever you put them in. I found a dreadful old fur coat for £1 in the Portobello Road, but when Dame Edith put it on, she still looked like Lady Bracknell.

These are the things that the public does not realise. Nor should they for, like all departments of film-making, this is the art that conceals art. It is all part of the alchemy we call the cinema.

But, even within the film business, the costume designer has been a long time winning proper rec-ognition. It was as late as 1948 before the American Academy Awards recognised us with our own Oscars. The wardrobe department and all it encompasses was taken for granted far too long.

As a child, I always dreamed of becoming a film star. I was raised on a diet of Carole Lombard, Joan Crawford and Irene Dunne gliding down a staircase singing "Smoke Gets in Your Eyes" swathed in white fox. But my parents disapproved of my becoming an actress, so I went to art school instead, and later went to work for a court dressmaker. When I was demobbed from the ATS, I sent sketches round to the studios and they politely sent them back until one day, thanks to the right introduction, I went to work at Gainsborough to help in the Design Department under the late Elizabeth Haffenden. If I had any illusions about the life, they were soon dispelled by my first solo assignment. It was Ken Annakin's first film as director, it was called *Holiday Camp,* and we went on location to a holiday camp in Filey, Yorkshire! Luckily, more exotic locations were to come in later years.

Today the costume designer has won a degree more respectability within the business. We even merit our own solo credit in among the titles of a film, instead of being hidden away among the minor technical acknowledgments. There were two Oscar categories open to us (one for design in colour films, one for black and white). But, as black and white films became scarcer, these merged into one award in 1967. I was fortunate enough to win the penultimate black and white Oscar for my designs for *Darling . . .* in 1965. I can't help thinking that, had the awards merged two years earlier, I should have lost that valued statuette to my distinguished British colleague, Phyllis Dalton, whose designs for David Lean's *Doctor Zhivago* were honoured the same year.

At the time of the ceremony, I was hard at work on *Casino Royale,* and it would have been difficult to attend in such an uncertain situation. Retrospectively, I wish I *had* gone – I may not get the chance again. My Oscar has a special place in my home and I see no reason to be *blasé* about it. Any recognition of the work done by any of us in the field of costume design is welcome. That is why I am particularly happy to welcome this book which, I feel, corrects a long-standing imbalance.

Julie Harris

Opposite: Richard Chamberlain and Gemma Craven in The Slipper and the Rose

Introduction

In the past decade, an enormous number of books have appeared on virtually all aspects of world cinema. Why, then, has nobody previously produced a factual book on costume design in the movies? Two of the designers themselves have written autobiographies (Edith Head's "The Dress Doctor" and Howard Greer's "Designing Male") but no standard reference work has been published. Those that were announced never came to fruition.

From my own researches, I can understand why. It is a desperately time-consuming operation (even with access to the considerable amount of material held by the National Film Archive in London) and it would be impossible for a freelance writer to survive financially while sifting through the necessary quantities of leads and sources. It is uncommonly difficult to *confirm* factual information about costume designers and their work. The contribution of the actor, the director, or almost any of the technicians is capable of being confirmed. But in the days of silent films, the costume designer received no screen credit at all, and contemporary film magazines are the only reliable source. Later, contemporary campaign books and press books apportioned credit fairly. But, with the financial recessions of the late '50s and '60s, even these became less useful in research. Today the studio publicity department gives only the most basic information and a minimum of credits.

As the Hollywood studios moved over to television production, irreplacable records were destroyed. Existing reference books for the film industry have ignored almost all costume designers or, perhaps worse, appended the entry with a list of films that is completely inadequate. I would never presume to suggest that the biographical entries and filmographies in this book are complete. That is perhaps an impossibility, because designers worked so often without credit in the Wardrobe Department before they were given acknowledgment for a film, or a part of a film. The credits in this book have been compiled, wherever possible, from contemporary studio material, but a common difficulty arises when pictorial evidence exists that a designer did sketches for a film, yet is omitted from the final screen credits.

Illustration has presented problems of its own. In the '30s and '40s, Hollywood studios did provide posed stills showing what the stars would be wearing in forthcoming films, but these were dis-continued when publicity budgets were drastically reduced. The basic set of stills issued subsequently could seldom be relied upon to show a designer's work to even tolerable advantage.

I have traced and contacted costume designers, both in England and abroad, and all have shared a common dismay at the wanton destruction by the studios of records of their work. Some of the illustrations used in this book have been supplied from their private collections, some have been bought in auctions, the rest have been culled from archives and libraries throughout the world.

In writing this book, I had two basic aims. One was to publish a record of the couturiers' contribution to the cinema, for only through these occasional film assignments might their work be recorded for the future. The other aim was to document the achievements of the costume designers in the cinema, achievements that are rarely acknowledged and never published.

In film research, the question of a film's official year is always a hotly argued one. In Britain we favour the year of production, in America the year of release. Other researchers prefer the year of copyright. The year I have chosen is, as far as can be ascertained, the year that the film was in production and therefore the designer, one of the first people to start work on a film, was active at the studio. To cite an extreme instance, George Stevens' *The Greatest Story Ever Told* is given as 1959/1965. Vittorio Nino Novarese and Marjorie Best began their epic task in 1959, although the film was not released in the USA until March, 1965. In the listings of Award nominations, winners are indicated by an asterisk. The Oscar Awards are for colour unless otherwise indicated.

I hope that this book will provide a basis of research for the people whose interest in the subject has always been frustrated by the inadequate coverage it has been given. If they have any additions or corrections to make, I shall be more than glad to hear of them. More importantly, I hope the book is instrumental, in no matter how small a way, in giving some long-delayed credit to the designers for their contribution to the cinema.

ELIZABETH LEESE
London, July 1976

Opposite: Joan Crawford in the famous "Letty Lynton" dress from the film of the same name. Designed by Adrian

VOGUE

GOWN BY

NORMAN HARTNELL

Couture on the Screen

The first films ever made were records of everyday events and were shot in the open air. They were not unlike the first attempts of someone experimenting with one of today's 8 mm movie cameras and, because the filming had to be done outside, it is possible for us to know what ordinary people of the time really looked like – not as stiff figures in photographs, but as living, moving people. Before the advent of the cinema, the average woman could keep in touch with society fashions by studying newspapers, magazines or the limited number of fashion publications available. Probably the most accessible source of this information was the series of picture postcards of famous beauties.

When halls in every town and village were converted into cinemas, then high fashion could be seen by everyone. The cameras took audiences into the salons of exclusive dress designers and showed them the very latest fashions being paraded before them. It is slightly surprising that designers and rather exclusive dress shops were willing to allow this invasion of their privacy, as it could hardly have increased their clientele, but many fashion houses and shops, such as Liberty and Swan & Edgar, seemed only too pleased to co-operate with the film companies.

The earliest fashion film I have discovered was shown in London in February 1910, and was probably filmed at the end of 1909. It was called *Fifty Years of Paris Fashions 1859–1909*, and the trade paper, "The Bioscope," described it as showing:

> "... magnificent examples of the art of the dressmaker and milliner, and a lady sitting in the picture theatre where this is being shown can imagine that she is in the showroom of a fashionable modiste with the mannequins walking round for her inspection ..."

So the invention of moving pictures brought high fashion to an even wider audience.

In 1911 the *All-British Fashions Exhibition at Kensington Gore* was recorded on film, and the following description of the event appeared in the Kinemacolor Film Catalogue of 1912:

> "... remarkable as showing the styles of costume fashionable in the year of grace 1911, and also as proving that the skill of British designers is not so far behind that of our French cousins as is sometimes supposed. The film was secured in co-operation with Messrs. Liberty & Co. and consists of photographs of mannequins parading in gowns of the latest, and sometimes ultra fashionable design. The harem skirt, the fashion sensation of the year finds a place in the array."

By 1910 newsreel companies such as Pathé and Gaumont were producing films that contained two or three subjects on each reel, and the footage showing the latest creations from Paris was a very small part of a film, running only a few minutes. However, at the end of 1911, Pathé decided to expand their coverage of the subject by producing a series of short films entirely devoted to forthcoming fashions. The review for the first of the series appeared in "The Bioscope" in October 1911:

> Parisian Modes
> "The delight with which the coloured fashions in Pathé's Animated Gazette have been viewed by thousands of feminine spectators every week has been the precursor of a frequently expressed desire for films giving a greater number of pictures showing the changes foreshadowed by Dame Fashion. To meet this desire and demand for fashion films, Messrs. Pathé are commencing a series showing the coming models from Paris. The present one gives coloured pictures of hats, dinner gowns, tailor-made costumes, walking dresses, negligees and teagowns."

Even at this early date, "coloured pictures" were not a novelty. Early experiments in colour film have a strong bearing on fashion in the cinema. Such experiments date back to the infancy of films. The French pioneer, George Méliès, had a factory for hand-colouring each frame of his film. In the early part of this century, film-makers tried cheaper and quicker methods, sometimes tinting sections of the film with a colour wash, and producing in 1908 a process called Kinemacolor which gave a fairly good effect of colour by alternating green and red. The short interest films were very suitable for these colour experiments and a parade of the latest fashions was an ideal subject for a cinemagazine. In those days feature films were very short, and the programme had to be filled out with four or five other items. In 1913 a very ambitious project was devised by an enterprising fashion journalist called Miss Abbey Meehan. In conjunction with the Natural Colour Kinematograph Co. she produced the *Kinemacolor Fashion Gazette*. The film played at the Scala Theatre in London (and also at several provincial theatres) in November 1913 and showed all the latest fashions, which were modelled by actresses and society ladies. Miss Meehan managed to recruit as models the Princess Bariatinsky, Miss Joy Chatwyn, Miss Dorothy Minto, Miss Sybil de Bray, Miss Violet Essex, Miss June Ford, Miss Elsa Collins and Madame Bonita. The clothes were modelled in natural outdoor settings and there was a carefully chosen musical accompaniment for each gown. Several London West End and Parisian costumiers and milliners permitted their creations to be photographed, and one of the highlights was the

Opposite: Anna Neagle in Maytime in Mayfair

appearance of the tango dress, shown by two dancers who gave an exhibition of London's newest dance craze.

This production was also shown at the "Evening News" Review of Fashion at the West End Cinema Theatre in Coventry Street. The "Evening News" invited a great many dressmakers and milliners, as well as celebrities, to the performance.

The great French designer, Paul Poiret, made a number of films in 1913, but I can find no evidence to show that they were ever released in Britain. He did, however, take some of his film footage over to the USA and was amazed to find his film seized by Customs and, after examination, declared obscene. All it showed was a few of the Poiret models parading in his garden in skirts that stopped just above the ankle. One of his films, *Winter Fashion Show of Paris Styles*, was registered with the Library of Congress in Washington in 1914. It may well have been that the Customs authorities changed their minds about allowing the film into the country, and that this was the allegedly obscene film.

When World War I started, newsreel companies obviously had more serious events to cover, although Pathé Animated Gazette were still showing news items from the Paris fashion world as late as 1915 with the slogan: "Despite the War, Paris still leads the world of dress". Europeans were too involved with the war effort to devote much time to fashion coverage but, as America did not enter the war until 1917, American film companies took over the fashion coverage.

In 1915 a lady called Mrs Armstrong Whitney organised a fashion tour of the USA which included three shows at the Casino Theatre in New York. While the tour was in New York, they went to the Peerless Fort Lee Studio (very near to New Jersey) and the event was captured on film by an enterprising producer called Jacob Wilk of World Film Productions. This differed from previous films by having a definite story line:

> "An innocent miss fears that her fiancé is being captured by an Indian princess so quite sensibly she decides to enhance her charms by wearing the most becoming costumes money can buy. In this way her uncertain lover is to be held. Visiting a society modiste she watches a parade of beautiful gowns and takes her pick. She chooses so wisely that her fiancé forgets all about his Indian princess. Moral: 'Clothes make the woman'."

This description was taken from "The Moving Picture World", an American trade paper for the film industry. In this way, Mrs Whitney's fashion show could be seen in many more cities and, to get the maximum publicity, Mr Wilk arranged for a number of journalists to go to the studio and see the filming. The gowns were from Paris and were from Worth, Paquin etcetera, plus a few American designs.

Apart from the fashion news in the supporting programmes, filmgoers were often treated to a display of ultra fashionable gowns in early serials, as many stars from New York worked at the East Coast studios and would frequently provide dres-

Frame enlargements from a fashion newsreel c.1928

ses from their private wardrobes to use in film production.

During the late 'teens and '20s, every programme boasted such an attraction, starring a popular serial queen. Pearl White, though perhaps the best remembered, was only one of many actresses (their names quite forgotten today) who appeared in some extremely stylish outfits.

Pearl White, although American, was a frequent visitor to the Continent, especially France, and bought a lot of her clothes in Paris fashion houses. That the serial stars spent most of their screen time jumping along the tops of trains in jodhpurs and

Frame enlargement from a Gaumont newsreel c.1910

*Left: an
advertisement in a
film trade paper for
a 1916 Essanay
serial. Far left: an
advertisement for a
dress shop, aimed at
the film trade,
c.1928*

riding boots is a popular misconception. In 1915 another of the serial stars, Eleanor Woodruff, was engaged for a five-part film called *Colton, USN*, in which she played the part of a leader of fashion in Newport. The advance publicity was published in a magazine called "News of Photoplays and Photoplayer":

> "Gowns valued at £10,000 and designed by M Maurice of Maison Maurice will be worn by Eleanor Woodruff in a New Vitagraph five-part feature. Miss Woodruff will pose so as to display the costumes to their best advantage. Those who have seen the collection describe them as exquisite creations and will include all necessary apparel from negligée to opera cloak."

Posing to show the costumes must have had a disastrous effect on Miss Woodruff's acting.

1916 saw a very curious experiment in serials. It was called *The Adventures of Dorothy Dare* and once again was made in the USA. Fashion films had started out by being simple displays of gowns, then progressed to a storyline built round the display. *The Adventures of Dorothy Dare* tried to combine a plot more suited to a feature film, with a series of fashionable outfits which were "described" in the title card. The plot is very difficult to believe. A young lady in the clutches of a villain is saved from a fate worse than death by the intrepid heroine, Dorothy Dare, and the victim's impecunious sweetheart. Much of the action took the form of a complicated car and train chase to save the victim. If a contemporary reviewer is to be believed, the action was stopped at intervals to describe the gowns. A rather caustic review of the film was written by Thomas C Kennedy who said that he was not much taken with any of the gowns, but supposed that this was the highest compliment the creations could possibly receive. I imagine that this idea of endeavouring to tell an exciting story

while also describing the lavish gowns of the female players proved unsatisfactory, because it appears that no further Dorothy Dare stories were released.

In 1917 the American side of the Pathé company made a series of films called *Florence Rose Fashions*, which were directed by the fashion page editor of the "New York Evening Mail", Florence Rose. Thirty-one of these shorts were issued between 1916 and 1917 and these also have a simple storyline, but the series was promoted with far more care than any previous efforts.

The idea was to release a film every fortnight with a tie-up between a dozen of the leading American newspapers such as the "Chicago Daily News", the "Boston Traveller", "Pittsburgh Dispatch" etcetera, and articles appeared in the relevant papers for twelve days before the film was to be shown at the local cinema. The articles were written by Mrs Radnor-Lewis, formerly managing editor of "Harper's Bazaar", and were illustrated by Winifred I Messer. So, for the first time, the ordinary fashion-conscious woman in America could read the fashion page in her local paper and then go along to the cinema to see the styles modelled. The newspapers must have given all the details of where the reader could buy the clothes, because no advertising was done on the screen.

All clothes used in the *Florence Rose Fashions* films were American, and reference was constantly made to the manufacturers, not designers, so it seems that the clothes were more accessible than in the earlier examples of fashion films. The titles used at the beginning of the series indicate what sort of simple plots were used. *The Beginning of the Social Season, Weekend House Party, Preparing For*

one or two outfits for the star. The publicity books for this film described each outfit in detail so the usual problem of trying to identify each designer's work doesn't arise. The same studio also arranged for six top designers to provide clothes for Frances Drake in a 1936 film called *I'd Give My Life*. They were Lucille Toray, Schiaparelli, Lanvin, Morgaleau, Charles Creed and Victor Stiebel. There is nothing unusual about using other designers, but it is slightly odd that this was done in 1936, particularly at Paramount, who had the estimable Travis Banton under contract. It would have passed without comment if the films had been made at a low budget studio without a contract designer.

Lucille was one of the first designers to gain the maximum amount of publicity from her work in films. Apart from the newsreel films mentioned earlier, she was very busy during the time her New York house was active. In 1916 an actress called Edna Mayo appeared in two serials – *The Strange Case of Mary Page* and *The Misleading Lady*. In both she was dressed by Lucille, and this fact was publicised as a strong selling point in the film trade papers. Several costumes for the five-part serial, *The Misleading Lady*, were supplied, but *The Strange Case of Mary Page* was a fifteen-part serial in which Miss Mayo appeared in no less than thirty-three Lucille outfits. The actress Hedda Hopper (who later became a gossip writer) was reputed to have worn $25,000 worth of Lucille clothes in a 1918 film called *Virtuous Wives*, but it is probable that the sum is slightly exaggerated.

The famous D W Griffith picture, *Way Down East*, had a rural setting, but the prologue gowns (excluding those worn by Lillian Gish) were designed by Lady Duff Gordon. Schiaparelli worked on a number of British films in the '30s when she had a salon in Upper Grosvenor Street. She worked on *Brewster's Millions* (with Motley and Norman Hartnell Ltd.), did Valerie Hobson's clothes for *Jump for Glory* (also with Hartnell) and some of Wendy Hiller's clothes for *Pygmalion* (a version that was updated to the '30s).

Her strangest assignment was when she was asked to design for a Mae West picture called *Every Day's a Holiday*. Miss West travelled to Paris for discussions, but didn't stay long enough for the fittings. Instead she sent over a life-size plaster statue of herself in the pose of the Venus de Milo. Schiaparelli is rumoured to have based the design of her Shocking perfume bottle on this shape. She also designed for an American actress called Helen Vinson in two British films, *Love in Exile* and *King of the Damned*. Her last film credit was for the costumes worn by Zsa Zsa Gabor in *Moulin Rouge*.

Chanel was signed up by Samuel Goldwyn in an effort to overcome the problems of shifting waistlines and hemlines that occurred in the '20s and early '30s. These changes had cost him a lot of money. His company had been forced to discard thousands of feet of film, because a change in hemline could make a film out of date in the interval between finishing a production and its actual release. Mr Goldwyn blamed Paris for this, and decided he could beat them at their own game by hiring a French designer to predict the styles, and not leave him high and dry with a dated film. Chanel travelled to Hollywood in 1931 and Goldwyn set up a special department for her with facilities for dyeing fabrics, cutting and fitting. The department employed over 100 workers and was supervised by Chanel's representative, Jane Courtois. The film she was to work on was *The Greeks Had A Word For It*, which was changed to *The Greeks Had A Word For Them* to satisfy the sensitive censorship authorities. Chanel did the original sketches in Hollywood and returned to Paris to supervise the making up. All the dresses were made in plain white silk and were sent back to America, with the appropriate jewellery and accessories, along with instructions about fabrics. The actual making of the gowns was supervised by Miss Courtois in Hollywood.

The first film Chanel designed for in Hollywood was an Eddie Cantor musical called *Palmy Days*. She made one dress for Barbara Weeks and this gave her an opportunity to experiment with a new idea. Chanel realised that an actress on the stage wore a particular dress for sitting, standing or lounging, and a designer had to produce an outfit that looked attractive in all these stances. But filming was quite different, being done in short takes. She decided to make at least four versions of each dress. They would seem identical, but each would have been cut to be seen at its best for a specific movement or action.

It was after *Palmy Days* that Chanel worked on *The Greeks Had A Word For Them*, a subject worthy of her talent, which starred Ina Claire, Joan Blondell and Madge Evans. Thirty complete outfits (which cost Goldwyn over $100,000) were supplied for the three leading ladies, who were playing Park Avenue adventuresses. The studio kept the details of what they were wearing secret until the film was released.

Chanel's next assignment was a Gloria Swanson picture called *Tonight or Never*, but Miss Swanson and Chanel just couldn't seem to work well together. Gloria Swanson had been in pictures for years and, after a very bad start as a hopelessly overdressed star of Cecil B DeMille society dramas, had managed to acquire a reputation as one of the best dressed stars in Hollywood. She always had complete control over her screen wardrobe and insisted that Chanel knew nothing about designing for films. It was unfortunate for Chanel that most of the stars she worked with in Hollywood seemed unimpressed by her reputation and were unappreciative of her beautiful designs. Perhaps they resented being fitted by Chanel's representative and wanted the designer actually there to discuss any problems that arose. But actresses

Opposite: Audrey Hepburn in Funny Face

Sarah Miles in The Hireling, *for which the costumes were designed by Phyllis Dalton. The film was made in the '70s but set in the '20s: had it been made in the '40s, when the novel was published, the authenticity of dress would not have been acceptable*

were used to getting their own way about their screen wardrobes and probably found that Chanel was not prepared to compromise. A special display of the clothes for *The Greeks Had A Word For Them* took place in New York and was supervised by the designer. Apart from supplying clothes to actresses who bought from her for their off-screen wardrobes, she was never again to work so closely with films. Chanel simply didn't need Hollywood.

Norman Hartnell has been steadily supplying clothes for British films for about forty-five years, sometimes just one or two special dresses, but in many cases responsible for all clothes worn by the leading ladies, and often getting screen credits. His first film appears to have been *Such Is The Law* in 1930, which had a credit for Reville Ltd., Hartnell and Elspeth Fox-Pitt. Following this was *That's a Good Girl*, made in 1933. Hartnell worked with Eileen Idare Ltd. on this film. During the late '20s and '30s the British studios were rather short of outstanding fashion designers, but this gave opportunities for British couture houses to supply fashionable clothes.

Anna Neagle has often used Norman Hartnell for her films. The best example is the musical *Maytime in Mayfair*, because it came at the end of a long period of austerity, and audiences were slightly surprised to find that British film studios could, when required, produce a lavish film. The big production number took place on a set decorated with enlargements of covers from "Vogue" and "Harper's". Each one had in front of it a model showing a dress or outfit designed by one of the top ten designers of 1947. They were Molyneux, Norman Hartnell, Charles Creed, Peter Russell, Hardy Amies, Mattli, Victor Stiebel, Worth, Bianca Mosca and Digby Morton.

In 1941 a British film called *Ships With Wings* was made at Ealing Studios and the dresses for the women stars were designed by Digby Morton, Lachasse, Maison Arthur, Molyneux, Hartnell, Peter Russell and Victor Stiebel. During the war, the British studios were having great difficulty with the wardrobe department because of restrictions and clothing coupons, so it made sense to use the facilities of the couture houses.

Just after the war, Norman Hartnell was involved in a film which could show future costume researchers how a top salon looked in 1946. The film was called *Fashion Fantasy* and the plot was of a newly-demobbed WREN reading a fashion magazine and dreaming of the models' glamorous life. She falls asleep and dreams that she is going to be a model, is interviewed by Mr Hartnell who engages her for his salon. He is then seen at work and the audience can see an evening gown being created from its first rough design to the appearance at the fashion show. The final sequence is a parade of Hartnell gowns. With a running time of thirty-five minutes, the film is unusually long for this type of supporting programme.

Another British film that utilised the Incorporated Society of London Fashion Designers was *The Demi-Paradise*, made in 1943. In this film, Penelope Ward's clothes were done by Hartnell, Molyneux, Digby Morton, Bianca Mosca, Charles Creed and Peter Russell. The producer was Anatole de Grunwald who wanted to show the world what we could do under wartime restrictions. A sad little footnote in the publicity material points out that each dress or suit had been cut so as to economise on material and save on coupons. Only stock materials were used.

Christian Dior has, of course, contributed clothes to many French films, but his work is also to be seen in British and American pictures, as many stars who were dressed by Dior in their private life were only too happy to have their film wardrobes supplied by his house. In this way, they could keep the clothes and have the film company foot the bill. He dressed Ingrid Bergman in *Indiscreet* and *Goodbye Again*, Olivia de Havilland in *Libel*, *Light in the Piazza* and *The Ambassador's Daughter* (including a fashion show in the latter film), and supplied a very glamorous wardrobe for Marlene Dietrich in *Stage Fright*.

If a continental actress is signed up for a British film, she will often ask for the clothes to be done by a French or Italian house. For example, Gina Lollobrigida's wardrobe in *Woman of Straw* was by Dior. In some cases an actress will accept a part in a fairly mediocre production if, when the film is finished and forgotten, she will at least have acquired some outfits from a world famous designer.

This is best illustrated by giving some titles of films for which Pierre Balmain designed the clothes. *The Happy Road* (for Barbara Laage), *Fire Down Below* (for Rita Hayworth), *Drop Dead Darling* (for Rosanna Schiaffino), *Come Fly With Me* (for Dawn Addams), *Betrayed* (for Lana Turner), *Two Weeks in Another Town* (for Cyd Charisse) and *Night Without Stars* and *Mr Topaze* (for Nadia Gray). Balmain had much better luck with the clothes for Sophia Loren in *The Millionairess* and Kay Kendall in *The Reluctant Debutante*.

Givenchy has been luckier than most because he is the favourite designer of Audrey Hepburn, who always looks extremely elegant on the screen. He was responsible for her wardrobe in *How to Steal a Million, Funny Face, Charade, Breakfast at Tiffany's, Love in the Afternoon* and *Paris When it Sizzles*. But the most rewarding film for them both must have been *Funny Face* as it was set in the fashion world. He also dressed Elizabeth Taylor in *The VIPs*, but she hasn't Miss Hepburn's model girl figure, and it is very difficult to make Elizabeth Taylor look elegant.

The '60s produced a new type of designer who seemed to be running their own business within hours of leaving the Royal College of Art. Mary Quant is the most famous example and she did the clothes for Charlotte Rampling in *Georgy Girl*. The old studio system had almost finished and production companies either used freelance designers who could have their work executed by such theatrical costumers as Nathan's and Berman's, or use a newsworthy young designer who had her own workroom. Which really brings the wheel full circle. Mary Quant contributed to Audrey Hepburn's wardrobe in *Two For the Road* as Miss Hepburn had temporarily abandoned her favourite, Givenchy. Foale and Tuffin also supplied outfits for *Two For the Road* and an extensive wardrobe for Susannah York in *Kaleidoscope*. Mia Fonssagrives and Vicky Tiel worked on *Candy,* and dressed Elizabeth Taylor in *The Only Game in Town*. This was quite a privilege for them since Miss Taylor usually favours Italian designers like Tiziani of Rome who did the incredibly outrageous costumes for *Boom!*

Most of the popular films of the '70s have featured clothes from previous decades, and these have often influenced young people's own fashion tastes. Within the last few years the top money-making films have been set in times that look more romantic and exciting than the present day – *Bonnie and Clyde, The Go-Between, The Great Gatsby, The Hireling, Funny Lady, The Way We Were, At Long Last Love, The Sting, Death in Venice, The Damned*, have all been featured heavily in film or fashion magazines. Years ago, film-makers were worried about keeping up with fashion or better still, being in advance of it. Today the exact reverse is true and although the taste for nostalgia recalls attractive and elegant fashions, it does sadly leave little room for original work.

The Designers

ABBEY, ELEANOR

British designer, often worked as assistant to Oliver Messel, but also some solo film credits. Assistant to Cecil Beaton on *My Fair Lady*.

FILMS:

1946: *Hungry Hill*. 1947: *The Mark of Cain*. 1948: *It's Hard to be Good; Cardboard Cavalier; Woman Hater*. 1949: *The Chiltern Hundreds* (US *The Amazing Mr Beecham*); *The Romantic Age* (US *Naughty Arlette*). 1950: *Tony Draws a Horse*. 1956: *Jacqueline*. 1958: *Sea Fury; Dangerous Exile*. 1959: *Operation Amsterdam*. 1960: *The Three Worlds of Gulliver*.

ADRIAN

Born Gilbert Adrian, Connecticut 1903. Died 1959. Studied at the School for Fine and Applied Arts. First professional job was designing costumes for a sketch in George White's Scandals. Irving Berlin was impressed by some of his costumes at the Grand Prix Ball and commissioned him to design for the Music Box Revue. Mrs Rudolph Valentino (Natasha Rambova) asked Adrian to do costumes for an unrealised Valentino film called *The Hooded Falcon*. He also worked on two other Valentino films – *The Eagle* and *Cobra*. This was followed by a contract at the Demille Studios from 1926 to 1928.

. Adrian moved to M-G-M in 1928 and remained there until 1942. It was at M-G-M that his talents really developed and he was one of the few top designers that could do both exquisite period costume and also provide the elegant M-G-M stars such as Joan Crawford and Norma Shearer with fashionable wardrobes. The rag trade were always interested in Joan Crawford's clothes and with the full co-operation of the studio's vast publicity machine, would copy the clothes quickly enough to get them into the shops for the film's release. M-G-M contract players were quite happy to co-operate with the Publicity Departments in order to get the maximum publicity for all. One of the best examples of this was the famous Letty Lynton dress worn by Joan Crawford in the film of the same name. Macys in New York claimed to have sold over 500,000 copies of the dress.

Adrian left M-G-M to open his own shop in Beverly Hills. Like other designers who opened their own retail businesses, Adrian continued to supply clothes for films and returned to M-G-M in 1952 for one film, *Lovely to Look At* (a remake of *Roberta*). Adrian designed the costumes for the leading players for this film and also for the fashion show.

FILMS:

1925: *Her Sister from Paris; The Eagle; Cobra*. 1926: *The Volga Boatman; Fig Leaves; For Alimony Only; Gigolo; Young April*. 1927: *King of Kings* (+Earl Luick, Gwen Wakeling); *The Little Adventuress; Vanity; The Fighting Eagle; His Dog; The Country Doctor; The Angel of Broadway; Dress Parade; The Forbidden Woman; The Main Event; The Wise Wife; Almost Human; The Wreck of the Hesperus; Chicago; Let 'er Go Gallagher*. 1928: *Skyscraper; Stand and Deliver; My Friend from India; Walking Back; The Blue Danube; A Ship Comes In; Midnight Madness; Manmade Woman; Dream of Love; Masks of the Devil; A Lady of Chance; A Single Man; A Woman of Affairs; The Godless Girl; The Trial of Mary Dugan*. 1929: *The Bridge of San Luis Rey; Wild Orchids; The Last of Mrs Cheyney; A Single Standard; Our Modern Maidens; Marianne; Olympia* (French-language version of *His Glorious Night*); *The Thirteenth Chair; The Unholy Night;*

Opposite: Helen Mack in Kiss and Make Up (Banton)

The Kiss; Untamed; Devil-may-care; Dynamite; Their Own Desire; Anna Christie; Not So Dumb; The Rogue Song; A Lady to Love.

1930: *The Divorcee; Montana Moon; Redemption; The Floradora Girl; In Gay Madrid; A Lady of Scandal; Let us be Gay; Romance; This Mad World; Our Blushing Brides; Madam Satan; A Lady's Morals; The Passion Flower; Paid; Inspiration*. 1931: *Dance, Fools, Dance; Polly of the Circus; Strangers May Kiss; A Free Soul; The Guardsman; This Modern Age; Susan Lenox, Her Fall and Rise; The Sin of Madelon Claudet* (GB *Lullaby*); *Private Lives; Emma; Mata Hari*. 1932: *Men Must Fight; Secrets; Grand Hotel; Letty Lynton; As You Desire Me; Blondie of the Follies; Smilin' Through; Faithless; Payment Deferred; Fast Life; The Mask of Fu Manchu; Rasputin and the Empress; Red Dust; Strange Interlude* (GB *Strange Interval*). 1933: *Looking Forward; Today We Live; Made on Broadway; Hold Your Man; When Ladies Meet; Midnight Mary; Storm at Daybreak; The Stranger's Return; Another Language; Dinner at Eight; Turn Back the Clock; Beauty for Sale; Penthouse; The Solitaire Man; Stage Mother; Bombshell; Dancing Lady; Going Hollywood; Queen Christina; Should Ladies Behave?; The Women in His Life; The Cat and the Fiddle; Mystery of Mr X; Men in White; Riptide; Nana* (+Banton, Harkrider). 1934: *Hollywood Party; Sadie McKee; Operator 13; Paris Interlude; Chained; The Girl from Missouri; The Barretts of Wimpole Street; The Merry Widow; What Every Woman Knows; Outcast Lady; The Painted Veil; Forsaking All Others; Biography of a Bachelor Girl; After Office Hours; Naughty Marietta; Mark of the Vampire*.

1935: *Reckless; No More Ladies; China Seas; Anna Karenina; Broadway Melody of 1936; I Live My Life; Rose Marie*. 1936: *The Great Ziegfeld; San Francisco; Romeo and Juliet; The Gorgeous Hussy; Born to Dance; Love on the Run; Camille; Last of Mrs Cheyney; Maytime*. 1937: *Between Two Women; The Emperor's Candlesticks; Parnell; Broadway Melody of 1938; Double Wedding; The Firefly; The Bride Wore Red; Conquest* (GB *Marie Walewska*); *The Last Ganster; Mannequin; Tovarich* (+Orry-Kelly); *Love is a Headache; The Girl of the Golden West*. 1938: *The Shopworn Angel; The Toy Wife* (+Gile Steele); *Marie Antoinette* (+Gile Steele); *Three Loves Has Nancy; The Great Waltz; The Shining Hour; Vacation from Love; Dramatic School; Sweethearts; Idiot's Delight; Honolulu; Ice Follies of 1939* (+Dolly Tree). 1939: *Lady of the Tropics* (+Valles); *Ninotchka; The Wizard of Oz; The Women; Balalaika* (+Valles); *I Take this Woman; Broadway Melody of 1940; Strange Cargo; Its a Wonderful World*.

1940: *Florian* (+Gile Steele); *Waterloo Bridge* (+Gile Steele); *Susan and God* (GB *The Gay Mrs Trexel*); *The Mortal Storm* (+Gile Steele); *New Moon* (+Gile Steele); *Pride and Prejudice* (+Gile Steele); *Rage; Boom Town* (+Gile Steele); *Bitter Sweet* (+Gile Steele); *Dulcy; Escape* (+Gile Steele); *The Philadelphia Story; Comrade X; Gallant Sons; Come Live with Me*. 1941: *Ziegfield Girl; A Woman's Face* (+Gile Steele); *They Met in Bombay; Blossoms in the Dust* (+Gile Steele); *Dr Jekyll and Mr Hyde* (+Gile Steele); *Lady be Good; The Chocolate Soldier* (+Gile Steele); *Two-faced Woman; Woman of the Year; We Were Dancing* (+Kalloch); *Smilin' Through* (+Steele). 1942: *Keeper of the Flame; The Powers Girl* (GB *Hello Beautiful*) (+Rene Hubert); *Shadow of a Doubt* (+Vera West); *They Got Me Covered* (+Edith Head); *Flight for Freedom*. 1943: *Hers to Hold* (+Vera West); *Hi Diddle Diddle; His Butler's Sister* (+Vera West).

1946: *Without Reservations; Humoresque* (+Bernard Newman). 1947: *Possessed* (+Bernard Newman); *The Bishop's Wife* (+Irene Sharaff); *Smart Woman*. 1948: *Rope*.

1952: *Lovely to Look At* (+Tony Duquette).

AGHAYAN, RAY

Born in Teheran and went to Los Angeles to study architecture. Has often designed costumes for American TV specials, also for stage and night club performances by Marlene Dietrich, Judy Garland, Carol Channing and many other American stars. Often worked with Bob Mackie.

ACADEMY AWARD NOMINATIONS:
1970: *Gaily, Gaily* (GB *Chicago, Chicago*). 1972: *Lady Sings the Blues* (+Bob Mackie, Norma Koch). 1975: *Funny Lady* (+Bob Mackie).

FILMS:
1964: *Father Goose; John Goldfarb, Please Come Home; The Art of Love.* 1965: *Do Not Disturb; Our Man Flint; The Glass Bottom Boat.* 1966: *Dr Dolittle; Caprice; In Like Flint.* 1969: *Gaily, Gaily* (GB *Chicago, Chicago*). 1971: *Hannie Caulder.* 1972: *Lady Sings the Blues* (+Bob Mackie, Norma Koch). 1974: *Funny Lady* (+Bob Mackie).

ALDREDGE, THEONI V.

Greek-born costume designer working in America. Theatre work from 1950. Her most important film to date is *The Great Gatsby*, for which she won an Academy Award.

ACADEMY AWARD NOMINATION:
1974: **The Great Gatsby.*

SFTA NOMINATION:
1974: **The Great Gatsby.*

FILMS:
1960: *Girl of the Night.* 1966: *You're a Big Boy Now.* 1967: *No Way to Treat a Lady.* 1968: *Uptight!* 1969: *Last Summer; I Never Sang for My Father.* 1970: *Promise at Dawn.* 1973: *The Great Gatsby.* 1976: *Harry and Walter Go to New York; Network.* 1977: *Semi-Tough.* 1978: *The Cheap Detective; Eyes of Laura Mars; The Fury.* 1979: *The Champ; The Rose.* 1980: *Can't Stop the Music.* 1981: *Rich and Famous.* 1982: *Annie; Monsignor.*

Mia Farrow and Robert Redford in The Great Gatsby
(Theoni V Aldredge)

ANDERSON, MILO

Born Milo Leon Anderson, Chicago, 1912. Educated in Los Angeles. Started his career as a designer for Goldwyn Pictures in 1932, but the major part of his career in films was at the Warner Brothers–First National Studio where he worked from 1933 to 1952. After leaving Warners he became a highly successful interior decorator in Los Angeles. Died 1984.

FILMS:
1932: *Cynara; The Kid From Spain; Hallelujah, I'm a Bum* (GB *Hallelujah, I'm a Tramp*); *The Masquerader.* 1933: *Footlight Parade; Goodbye Again.* 1935: *Don't Bet on Blondes; Front Page Woman; The Story of Louis Pasteur; Captain Blood.* 1936:

Anthony Adverse; Green Pastures; Charge of the Light Brigade; Trailin' West; Down the Stretch; Smart Blonde; Black Legion; The Case of the Black Cat; Sing Me a Love Song; The Captain's Kid; Fugitive in the Sky; Melody for Two; Midnight Court; Once a Doctor; The Great O'Malley. 1937: *The Prince and the Pauper; Draegerman Courage; Mountain Justice; Life of Emile Zola; Mr Dodd Takes the Air; The Great Garrick; Gold is Where You Find It; Fools for Scandal* (+Travis Banton). 1938: *You Can't Get*

Joan Crawford in When Ladies Meet *(Adrian)*

(above) Joan Crawford in This Modern Age *(Adrian),*
(opposite) Alexis Smith in Night and Day *(Anderson)*

Away With Murder; The Adventures of Robin Hood; The Amazing Dr Clitterhouse; Cowboy From Brooklyn; White Banners; Boy Meets Girl; Valley of the Giants; Brother Rat; Hard to Get; Heart of the North; Nancy Drew, Detective; They Made Me a Criminal; The Adventures of Jane Arden. 1939: Confessions of a Nazi Spy; Dodge City; Hell's Kitchen; Waterfront; Angels Wash Their Faces; Dust Be My Destiny; The Roaring Twenties; Smashing the Money Ring; We Are Not Alone; Cowboy Quarterback; Kid Nightingale; Granny Get Your Gun; A Child is Born; Invisible Stripes; Three Cheers for the Irish; The Return of Dr. X.

1940: King of the Lumberjacks; Saturday's Children; They Drive By Night; Santa Fe Trail; High Sierra; Father's Son; The Lady with Red Hair. 1941: The Wagons Roll at Night; A Shot in the Dark; Manpower; Bad Men of Missouri; One Foot in Heaven; They Died With Their Boots On; The Body Disappears. 1942: The Big Shot: Escape From Crime; Spy Ship; Wings for the Eagle; Yankee Doodle Dandy; Across the Pacific; Desperate Journey; Secret Enemies; The Hidden Hand; You Can't Escape For Ever; Gentleman Jim; Truck Busters. 1943: The Mysterious Doctor; Shine on Harvest Moon; Action in the North Atlantic; Thank Your Lucky Stars. 1944: Make Your Own Bed; The Doughgirls; To Have and Have Not; The Very Thought of You; Hollywood Canteen.

1945: Escape in the Desert; Pillow to Post; Christmas in Connecticut (+ Edith Head); Pride of the Marines; Mildred Pierce; Danger Signal; San Antonio; Three Strangers; Conflict. 1946: Devotion; One More Tomorrow; Night and Day (+ Travilla); Of Human Bondage; Nobody Lives Forever; The Man I Love. 1947: Stallion Road (+ Leah Rhodes); Cheyenne; The Two Mrs Carrolls (+ Edith Head); Life With Father; Magic Town; The Unsuspected; To the Victor. 1948: The Woman in White; Romance on the High Seas (GB It's Magic); Johnny Belinda; The Decision of Christopher Blake; Whiplash; John Loves Mary; South of St. Louis; A Kiss in the Dark; My Dream is Yours. 1949: The Fountainhead; Look for the Silver Lining; One Last Fling; It's a Great Feeling: The Lady Takes a Sailor; Montana (+ Marjorie Best); Stage Fright (+ Christian Dior), Young Man with a Horn (GB Young Man of Music); Perfect Strangers (GB Dangerous to Love). 1950: The West Point Story (GB Fine and Dandy) (+ Marjorie Best); The Lullaby of Broadway; Storm Warning. 1951: The Blue Veil; Tomorrow is Another Day; Painting the Clouds with Sunshine; Jim Thorpe—All American (GB Man of Bronze); On Moonlight Bay. 1952: Mara Maru; The Story of Will Rogers; The Man Behind the Gun. 1955: Miracle in the Rain.

Adrian design for Hedy Lamarr
in I Take This Woman

Milo Anderson, Lauren Bacall and Michael Curtiz
on the set of Young Man With a Horn

ANDRE-ANI

Born Clement Andre-Ani, California. Worked at M-G-M from 1925 to 1928. M-G-M has always lavished money on the

Opposite: Joan Crawford in The Women *(Adrian)*

wardrobes of its female stars and Andre-Ani designed for the most important leading ladies at the studio. Under contract were Greta Garbo, Norma Shearer, Claire Windsor, Mae Murray, Marion Davies and Carmel Myers: almost all of them required Andre-Ani to provide clothes for their personal wardrobes as well as on the screen.

In 1925 Andre-Ani worked with Erte, who was put under contract to M-G-M, on *Dance Madness, Paris* and *The Mystic*. Andre-Ani worked at Universal in 1930.

Mary Duncan in The Boudoir Diplomat *(Andre-Ani)*

FILMS:
1925: *If Marriage Fails*; *The Mystic* (+Erte); *His Secretary*; *Soul Mates*; *The Black Bird*; *Dance Madness* (+Erte, Kathleen Kay, Maude Marsh); *The Torrent* (+Kathleen Kay,Maude Marsh, Max Ree); *The Exquisite Sinner*; *Monte Carlo* (+ Kathleen Kay, Maude Marsh); *Money Talks* (+Kathleen Kay, Maude Marsh).
 1926: *Beverly of Graustark* (+Kathleen Kay, Maude Marsh); *The Boy Friend* (+Kathleen Kay, Maude Marsh); *The Gay Deceiver* (+Kathleen Kay, Maude Marsh); *The Waning Sex* (+Kathleen Kay, Maude Marsh); *Bardelys the Magnificent* (+Lucia Coulter); *Blarney*; *Love's Blindness* (+Kathleen Kay, Maude Marsh); *The Temptress* (+Max Ree); *Exit Smiling*; *The Flaming Forest*; *Upstage* (+Kathleen Kay, Maude Marsh); *Tin Hats*; *The Fire Brigade* (+Kathleen Kay, Maude Marsh); *Flesh and the Devil*; *A Little Journey*; *Valencia*; *The Red Mill*; *The Taxi Dancer*.
 1927: *The Demi-Bride*; *Slide, Kelly, Slide*; *Women Love Diamonds*; *Altars of Desire* (+Kathleen Kay, Maude Marsh); *Lovers?*; *Rookies*; *The Understanding Heart*; *Annie Laurie*; *Heaven On Earth* (+Kathleen Kay, Maude Marsh); *Tillie the Toiler*; *California*; *Captain Salvation*; *The Bugle Call*; *Becky*; *The Frontiersman*.
 1928: *The Wind*. 1929: *The Great Gabbo*.
 1930: *The Cat Creeps*; *The Boudoir Diplomat*.

ANTHONY, LON

Costume designer, mainly at Columbia Pictures.

FILMS:
1936: *Counterfeit*; *Meet Nero Wolf*; *Two Fisted Gentleman*; *They Met in a Taxi*; *Craig's Wife*; *Hats Off*. 1948: *Shed No Tears*.

ARMSTRONG, JOHN

British artist and designer, under contract to Alexander Korda's London Films.

FILMS:
1933: *The Private Life of Henry VIII*; *Catherine the Great*; *The*

Opposite: Greta Garbo in Susan Lenox, Her Fall and Rise *(Adrian)*

Scarlet Pimpernel (+Oliver Messel). 1935: *Things to Come* (+Rene Hubert and The Marchioness of Queensberry); *The Ghost Goes West* (+ Rene Hubert); *Moscow Nights* (US *I Stand Condemned*). 1936: *The Man Who Could Work Miracles*; *As You Like It* (+Joe Strassner); *Rembrandt*. 1937: *Saint Martin's Lane* (US *Sidewalks of London*). 1940: *The Thief of Bagdad* (+ Oliver Messel, Marcel Vertes). 1953: *Hobson's Choice* (+Julia Squire).

BALKAN, ADELE

Designer at RKO 1947/1952 and at Fox 1955/1960.

FILMS:
1947: *Arizona Ranger*; *Fighting Father Dunne*. 1948: *They Live By Night*; *The Boy With Green Hair*. 1949: *Mighty Joe Young*. 1951: *Two Tickets to Broadway* (+ Woulfe). 1952: *The Narrow Margin*. 1955: *Seven Cities of Gold* (+ Charles LeMaire). 1956: *Three Brave Men* (+ Charles LeMaire). 1957: *The Way To the Gold* (+ Charles LeMaire). 1958: *The Young Lions* (+ Charles LeMaire). 1959: *Blue Denim* (GB *Blue Jeans*). 1960: *Flaming Star*.

BALLARD, LUCINDA

Born 1908. Costume and scenic designer. Extensive theatre and ballet credits in USA since 1937.

Shine on Harvest Moon (Milo Anderson)

Alexis Smith in One More Tomorrow *(Anderson)*

ACADEMY AWARD NOMINATION:
1951: *A Streetcar Named Desire* (b&w).

FILMS:
1948: *Portrait of Jennie* (GB *Jennie*) (+Anna Hill Johnstone).
1951: *A Streetcar Named Desire*.

BALMAIN, PIERRE

French couturier with fashion house in Paris.

FILMS:

1951: *Night Without Stars* (+Julie Harris). 1954: *Betrayed*. 1955: *The Deep Blue Sea* (+Duse). 1956: *Foreign Intrigue*; *The Happy Road*. 1957: *Fire Down Below*; *Paris Holiday*. 1958: *The Reluctant Debutante* (+Helen Rose). 1961: *Mr Topaz*; *Tender Is the Night*; *The Roman Spring of Mrs Stone* (+Beatrice Dawson). 1962: *Two Weeks in Another Town* (+Plunkett); *The Happy Thieves*. 1963: *In the Cool of the Day* (+Orry-Kelly); *Come Fly with Me*. 1966: *Arrivederci, Baby* (GB *Drop Dead Darling*) (+Elizabeth Haffenden, Joan Bridge). 1972: *Tamlin* (US *The Devil's Widow*) (+Dawson).

Mae West in Goin' To Town *(Travis Banton)*

Adrienne Ames and Carole Lombard in
Sinners in the Sun *(Banton)*

BANTON, TRAVIS

Born Waco, Texas, 1894. Educated at Columbia University and the Art Students' League of Fine and Applied Arts in New York. While still an art student, Travis Banton met Norma Talmadge who was in New York making *Poppy* (1917). She commissioned him to design one of her costumes for this production but, apart from one Alice Joyce film, it was another seven years before he designed for the cinema. His first job was with the New York couture house of Madame Frances and it was there that Mary Pickford chose one of his designs for a wedding dress when she married Douglas Fairbanks.

In 1924 a summons from the West Coast Studio of Paramount Pictures took Travis Banton to Hollywood and his career began with a Leatrice Joy picture called *The Dressmaker From Paris*. No designer could have wished for a better start: dozens of fashionable outfits were needed for the star and for the fashion show and, naturally, there was plenty of publicity in the fan magazines. The studio publicity department insisted that their new designer was from Paris, but they need not have bothered for, within the next few years, Travis Banton's designs reached a far larger audience than those of any French dress designer. He created lavish screen wardrobes in the '20s for Florence Vidor, Bebe Daniels, Pola Negri, Clara Bow and Evelyn Brent, but it was in the '30s that Banton reached his peak.

During those years Paramount had under contract some of the most beautiful and elegant stars in the world – Carole Lombard, Marlene Dietrich, Kay Francis, Lilyan Tashman, Claudette Colbert, Sylvia Sidney, Gail Patrick and Helen Vinson. Many of the stars he worked with demanded that he design the clothes they wore for the films made when loaned to other studios; Carole Lombard's costumes for *My Man Godfrey* and *Love Before Breakfast* (made at Universal), *Nothing Sacred* (David Selznick Productions) and *Fools for Scandal* (Warners) were all done by Travis Banton.

In 1932 Mae West came to Hollywood to film *Night after Night* and *She Done Him Wrong*, based on her stage success "Diamond Lil." Travis Banton's uncle was Joab Banton, the New York District Attorney who had prosecuted the cast of Mae West's play "Sex" for corrupting the morals of the young. Miss West graciously overlooked the whole incident and Banton created several new styles for *She Done Him Wrong*. Dorothy Tree had done the original Broadway production and had based her designs on the clothes worn by Lillian Russell and Mrs John Jacob Astor.

After fourteen years with Paramount he left to open his own business, but worked for Fox from 1939–1941, and at Universal Studios from 1945–1948 as Head Stylist. Died 1958.

FILMS:
1917: *Poppy*. 1924: *Dressmaker From Paris*. 1925: *Grounds for Divorce*; *Grand Duchess and the Waiter*. 1926: *Miss Brewster's Millions*. 1927: *Doomsday*; *The Fifty-Fifty Girl*; *Fashions for Women*; *Wings* (+Head). 1928: *Three Sinners*; *Red Hair*; *Dragnet*; *His Tiger Lady*; *The Canary Murder Case*; *The Wild Party*; *The Man I Love*. 1929: *The Dance of Life*; *The Love Parade*.
1930: *Street of Chance*; *The Vagabond King*; *Safety in Numbers*; *Follow Through*; *Morocco*; *Monte Carlo*. 1931: *Dishonoured*; *Girls About Town*; *Dr Jekyll and Mr Hyde*; *One Hour With You*; *I Take This Woman*. 1932: *No One Man*; *Shanghai Express*; *The Sign of the Cross*; *Trouble in Paradise*; *Luxury Liner*; *Sinners in the Sun*; *Man From Yesterday*; *Love Me Tonight*; *Blonde Venus*; *Evenings for Sale*; *No Man of Her Own*; *A Farewell to Arms*; *Crime of the Century*; *He Learned About Women*; *The Devil and the Deep*. 1933: *From Hell to Heaven*; *A Lady's Profession*; *Tonight Is Ours*; *A Bedtime Story*; *Supernatural*; *International House*; *College Humor*; *Disgraced*; *Midnight Club*; *Song of Songs*; *Terror Aboard*; *Brief Moment*; *Three Cornered Moon*; *I'm No Angel*; *Torch Singer* (GB *Broadway Singer*); *Cradle Song*; *Design for Living*; *Girl Without a Room*; *All of Me*; *Death Takes a Holiday*; *Search for Beauty*; *Bolero*; *One Sunday Afternoon*; *Sitting Pretty*; *Nana* (+Adrian, Harkrider). 1934: *You're Telling Me*; *We're Not Dressing*; *Belle of the Nineties*; *Mrs Wiggs of the Cabbage Patch*; *Private Worlds*; *The Great Flirtation*; *Kiss and Make Up*; *The Notorious Sophie Lang*; *The Scarlet Empress*; *Menace*; *Imitation of Life*; *Here is My Heart*; *The Lives of a Bengal Lancer*; *Enter Madam*; *Ruggles of Red Gap*; *Rumba*; *All the King's Horses*; *The Gilded Lily*; *Now and Forever*.
1935: *The Devil Is a Woman*; *Goin' to Town*; *The Crusades*;

Opposite: Norma Shearer in The Waning Sex *(Andre-Ani)*

From left: design by Banton for Claudette Colbert in The Bride Comes Home; *Banton design for* Sinners in the Sun; *gown designed by Banton for Miriam Hopkins in* Design For Living

Hands Across the Table; Two Fisted; So Red the Rose; The Bride Comes Home; Rose of the Rancho; Desire; Anything Goes. 1936: *Love Before Breakfast* (+Brymer); *Ladies Love Brutes; The Princess Comes Across; My Man Godfrey* (+Brymer); *My American Wife; Yours For The Asking; The General Died at Dawn; Wives Never Know; Valiant Is the Word for Carrie; Big Broadcast of 1937; Maid of Salem; Swing High, Swing Low; Her Husband Lies* (+Edith Head). 1937: *Sophie Lang Goes West* (+Edith Head); *Clarence; Interns Can't Take Money* (GB *You Can't Take Money*); *I Met Him in Paris; High, Wide and Handsome; Easy Living; Artists and Models; Angel; True Confession; Nothing Sacred* (+Walter Plunkett); *Romance in the Dark.* 1938: *Fools for Scandal* (+Milo Anderson); *Bluebeard's Eighth Wife; Made for Each Other.* 1939: *Eternally Yours* (+Irene); *Intermezzo, A Love Story* (GB *Escape to Happiness*) (+Irene); *Slightly Honorable; Lillian Russell.*

1940: *Four Sons; The Man I Married; Maryland; The Return of Frank James; Down Argentine Way; The Mark of Zorro; Tin Pan Alley; Hudson's Bay; Chad Hanna; Tall, Dark and Handsome;* *Western Union.* 1941: *That Night In Rio; The Great American Broadcast; Sun Valley Serenade; Blood and Sand; Manhunt; Charley's Aunt* (GB *Charley's American Aunt*); *Wild Geese Calling; Belle Starr.* 1943: *What a Woman* (GB *The Beautiful Cheat*); *Cover Girl* (+Gwen Wakeling, Muriel King). 1944: *A Song To Remember* (+Walter Plunkett); *Roughly Speaking.*

1945: *The Strange Affair of Uncle Harry; Paris Underground* (GB *Madame Pimpernel*); *This Love of Ours* (+Vera West); *Scarlet Street; Because of Him.* 1946: *Tangier; Night in Paradise; Lover Come Back; The Runaround; Canyon Passage; Sister Kenny; Magnificent Doll* (+Vera West); *I'll Be Yours; The Guilt of Janet Ames* (+Jean Louis); *The Egg and I.* 1947: *Time Out of Mind; The Lost Moment; Pirates of Monterey* (+Vera West); *Mourning Becomes Electra; Secret Beyond the Door; The Paradine Case; A Double Life* (+Yvonne Wood). 1948: *Letter from an Unknown Woman; The Velvet Touch.*

1950: *Valentino* (+Gwen Wakeling).

Opposite: Eleanor Whitney in The Big Broadcast of 1937 *(Travis Banton)*

BARKER, SHIRLEY

Dress designer trained at the New York branch of Lucille Ltd. Worked as assistant to Irene at M-G-M in 1947.

FILMS:

1947: *Living in a Big Way* (+Irene): *Song of the Thin Man* (+Irene); *Three Daring Daughters* (GB *The Birds and the Bees*) (+Irene).

BEATON, CECIL

Born 1904. Distinguished theatrical designer with occasional film work from 1941. Did costumes for both stage and film version of *My Fair Lady*. Died 1980.

ACADEMY AWARD NOMINATIONS:

1958: **Gigi*. 1964: **My Fair Lady*.

FILMS:

1941: *Kipps* (US *The Remarkable Mr Kipps*); *Major Barbara*; *Dangerous Moonlight* (US *Suicide Squadron*). 1942: *The Young Mr Pitt* (+Elizabeth Haffenden). 1943: *On Approval*. 1946: *Beware of Pity*. 1947: *An Ideal Husband*; *Anna Karenina*; *The Truth About Women*. 1957: *Gigi*. 1959: *The Doctor's Dilemma*. 1964: *My Fair Lady*. 1970: *On a Clear Day You Can See Forever* (+Arnold Scaasi).

Cecil Beaton drawing for The Doctor's Dilemma

BEHM, ELEANOR

Designer at Fox 1942/47, also some films for independent production companies.

FILMS:

1942: *Hangmen Also Die!* (for Anna Lee). 1944: *Sensations of 1945*. 1946: *It Shouldn't Happen to a Dog*; *If I'm Lucky* (+Sascha Brastoff). 1947: *The Brasher Doubloon* (GB *The High Window*); *The Ghost and Mrs Muir* (+Charles LeMaire); *Thunder in the Valley* (+Charles LeMaire).

BENDA, GEORGES

Born in Paris and educated at the Beaux Arts. Entered films in France in 1930 as costume designer and period adviser. Designed costumes for many London revues and occasional films for Alexander Korda's London Films.

FILMS:

1937: *Knight Without Armour*. 1947: *A Man About the House*. 1948: *Bonnie Prince Charlie*; *Britannia Mews* (US *Forbidden Street*); *Saraband For Dead Lovers*.

Beaton with a design for My Fair Lady

ACADEMY AWARD NOMINATIONS:

1949: **The Adventures of Don Juan* (+Travilla, Leah Rhodes). 1956: *Giant* (+Moss Mabry). 1960: *Sunrise at Campobello*. 1965: *The Greatest Story Every Told* (+Vittorio Nino Novarese).

FILMS:

1943: *The Desert Song* (+Leah Rhodes). 1948: *The Adventures of Don Juan* (+Travilla, Leah Rhodes). 1949: *Look For the Silver Lining* (+Travilla); *Montana* (+Milo Anderson). 1950: *The Daughter of Rosie O'Grady* (+Travilla); *Bright Leaf* (+Leah Rhodes); *Rocky Mountain*; *Dallas*; *The West Point Story* (GB *Fine and Dandy*); *Along the Great Divide*. 1951: *Carson City*; *Distant Drums*; *I'll See You in My Dreams* (+Leah Rhodes). 1952: *Room For One More* (+Leah Rhodes); *She's Working Her Way Through College* (+Travilla); *His Majesty O'Keefe*. 1953: *The Charge at Feather River*; *Blowing Wild* (+Kay Nelson). 1954: *King Richard and the Crusaders*. 1956: *Santiago* (GB *The Gun Runners*); *The Burning Hills*; *Giant* (+Moss Mabry); *Shoot-out at Medicine Bend*. 1957: *The Nun's Story*; *Band of Angels*; *The Story of Mankind*; *Darby's Rangers*; *Fort Dobbs*; *Lafayette Escadrilles* (GB *Hell Bent for Glory*). 1958: *The Left-Handed Gun*; *The Hanging Tree* (+Orry-Kelly); *Rio Bravo*; *Born Reckless*. 1959: *Yellowstone Kelly*; *The Miracle*; *Guns of the Timberland*; *The Greatest Story Ever Told* (+Vittorio Nino Novarese). 1960: *Sergeant Rutledge*; *The Dark at the Top of the Stairs*; *Sunrise at Campobello*; *The Sins of Rachel Cade*. 1961: *The Comancheros*; *Tender is the Night* (+Pierre Balmain); *State Fair*.

BERNSTEIN, ALINE

Born Aline Frankstein, New York, 1881. Died 1955. Distinguished set and costume designer associated with the Theatre Guild in New York. Worked on two RKO films in 1935.

FILMS:

1935: *She* (+Harold Miles); *The Last Days of Pompeii*.

BEST, MARJORIE

Studied art at the Chouinard School of Art in Los Angeles, then worked at the United Costume Company. Warner Brothers bought out United Costume and offered several of their designers jobs in the Wardrobe Department at the studio. Majorie Best specialises in men's costume and period films.

Opposite: Vivien Leigh in The Deep Blue Sea *(Balmain)*

BLAKE, YVONNE

British designer, in films since 1966.

ACADEMY AWARD NOMINATIONS:
1971: *Nicholas and Alexandra (+Antonio Castillo). 1975: *The Four Musketeers* (+Ron Talsky).

SFTA NOMINATIONS:
1971: *Nicholas and Alexandra* (+Antonio Castillo). 1973: *Jesus Christ Superstar*. 1974: *The Three Musketeers*. 1975: *The Four Musketeers* (+Ron Talsky).

FILMS:
1966: *The Idol*; *The Spy with a Cold Nose*; *Judith*; *Charlie Bubbles*; *Fahrenheit 451*. 1967: *Assignment K*. 1968: *Duffy*. 1969: *The Best House in London*; *Country Dance* (US *Brotherly Love*). 1970: *The Last Valley*; *Puppet on a Chain*. 1971: *Nicholas and Alexandra* (+Antonio Castillo, Anthony Powell). 1973: *Jesus Christ Superstar*. 1974: *The Three Musketeers* (+Ron Talsky). 1975: *The Four Musketeers* (+Ron Talsky). 1976: *Crime and Passion*; *The Eagle Has Landed*; *Robin and Marian*. 1978: *Superman*. 1979: *Escape to Athena*. 1980: *Superman II* (+Sue Yelland). 1981: *Green Ice*. 1985: *Flesh and Blood*.

BRIDGEHOUSE, WILLIAM

Head of Edward Small Productions' Wardrobe Department.

FILMS:
1936: *Doctor's Diary*; *John Meade's Woman* (+Edith Head). 1938: *King of the Turf*. 1939: *The Man in the Iron Mask*. 1940: *Courageous Dr Christian*; *Isle of Destiny*; *My Son, My Son* (+Helen Taylor).

BRIERLEY, EVELYN

Born in Paris and worked at the French couture house of Premet in the Place Vendôme. Also worked at Worth in London. On the stage for many years but worked as costume designer at Pinewood Studios 1948/49.

FILMS:
1948: *Once a Jolly Swagman* (US *Maniacs on Wheels*) (+Terry Morgan); *All Over Town*. 1949: *Dear Mr Prohack* (+Beatrice Dawson); *Give Us This Day* (US *Salt to the Devil*). 1950: *Hell is Sold Out* (+Nina Margo).

BROOKS, DONALD

American fashion designer often used by Julie Andrews.

ACADEMY AWARD NOMINATIONS:
1963: *The Cardinal*. 1968: *Star!* 1970: *Darling Lili* (+Jack Bear).

FILMS:
1963: *The Cardinal*. 1965: *The Third Day*. 1968: *Star!* 1970: *Darling Lili* (+Jack Bear). 1975: *The Drowning Pool*. 1979: *The Bell Jar*.

BRYMER

Costume designer who worked on over 100 New York stage productions. Worked at Universal Studios in the mid-'30s, often as assistant to Vera West.

FILMS:
1933: *Moonlight and Pretzels* (GB *Moonlight and Melody*). 1934: *His Night Out*. 1935: *The Great Impersonation* (+Vera West); *Magnificent Obsession* (+Vera West); *The Invisible Ray*. 1936: *My Man Godfrey* (+Travis Banton); *Love Before Breakfast* (+Travis Banton); *Crash Donovan*. 1937: *Make a Wish*.

Bonnie Cashin design for Gene Tierney in Laura

CAFFIN, YVONNE

Born in South Africa and educated at Johannesburg University. Entered film industry in 1934 and worked in the Wardrobe Department at Gaumont-British and the Gainsborough Studios at Islington.

FILMS:
1944: *Waterloo Road*. 1945: *They Were Sisters*; *The Rake's Progress* (US *The Notorious Gentleman*). 1946: *The Root of All Evil* (+Dorothy Broomham); *Dear Murderer*. 1947: *Miranda*; *When the Bough Breaks*. 1948: *The Huggetts Abroad*; *The Blind Goddess*; *Vote for Huggett*; *It's Not Cricket*. 1949: *Boys in Brown*; *The Astonished Heart* (+Molyneux, Digby Morton). 1950: *The Woman in Question* (US *Five Angles on Murder*); *Blackmailed*; *The Browning Version*; *White Corridors*. 1951: *The Story of Robin Hood and His Merry Men* (+Michael Whittaker). 1953: *Doctor in the House*; *A Day to Remember*; *Trouble in Store*. 1954: *Young Lovers* (US *Chance Meeting*); *As Long As They're Happy*; *To Paris With Love*. 1955: *An Alligator Named Daisy*; *Lost* (US *Tears for Simon*). 1956: *The Iron Petticoat*; *Doctor at Large*. 1958: *A Night to Remember*; *Rockets Galore* (US *Mad Little Island*); *The Square Peg*; *The Thirty Nine Steps*. 1959: *North-West Frontier* (US *Flame Over India*) (+Julie Harris); *Conspiracy of Hearts*. 1960: *No Love for Johnnie*; *The Singer Not the Song*; *Carry on Constable*. 1961: *Flame in the Streets*; *No, My Darling Daughter*. 1962: *A Pair of Briefs*; *Tiara Tahiti*; *The Wild and the Willing* (US *Young and Willing*); *This Sporting Life*. 1963: *Doctor in Distress*; *The Informers*; *This Is My Street*; *Hot Enough for June* (US *Agent 8¾*). 1964: *The High Bright Sun* (US *McGuire Go Home!*). 1965: *Three Hats for Lisa*; *The Big Job*; *Doctor in Clover*; *Sky West and Crooked* (US *Gypsy Girl*). 1967: *Danger Route*; *Bedazzled*. 1968: *Nobody Runs Forever*. 1968: *Some Girls Do* (+Clive of London); *Carry on Camping*. 1969: *The Southern Star*. 1970: *The Executioner*.

CASHIN, BONNIE

Born in California, Bonnie Cashin started with two great assets – a mother in the fashion business and an enormous amount of talent. Her career began in New York in the '30s when she began as a designer at the Roxy Theatre, at the same time studying at the Art Student's League. To earn extra money, she designed some sports clothes for a manufacturer, and from then on continued to divide her time very successfully between showbusiness and the rag trade. At the end of

Robert Redford and Mia Farrow in The Great Gatsby *(Aldredge)*

1943, she was invited to work at the Twentieth Century–Fox Studio in California. It was fortunate that one of her early assignments was *Laura* (1944) which starred one of the most beautiful and elegant actresses in Hollywood, Gene Tierney. The wardrobe Miss Cashin created for Gene Tierney in this film was in marked contrast to the over-dressing so common in American films of the '40s. This was a natural antidote to war-time austerity, but it meant that the films often looked ludicrous in retrospect. Bonnie Cashin never fell into this trap and the clothes for *Laura* do not look out of place today.

The training at the Roxy Theatre proved very useful, as Fox were at that time making some rather gaudy musicals with Betty Grable and June Haver. In 1950 Miss Cashin returned to New York and opened her own design studio in 1953. She is one of the most original and successful dress designers in America and has won countless awards and citations from the fashion critics. Perhaps the greatest compliment to her work is that the Brooklyn Museum has been collecting Bonnie Cashin originals for many years.

FILMS:
1943: *Claudia*. 1944: *Ladies of Washington; The Eve of St Mark; Home in Indiana; In the Meantime, Darling; Laura; Keys of the Kingdom; A Tree Grows in Brooklyn*. 1945: *The Bullfighters; Billy Rose's Diamond Horseshoe* (GB *Diamond Horseshoe*); *Where Do We Go From Here?; Junior Miss; The Caribbean Mystery; The House on 92nd Street; Fallen Angel*. 1946: *Do You Love Me?; Cluny Brown; Anna and the King of Siam; Claudia and David; Three Little Girls in Blue*. 1947: *I Wonder Who's Kissing Her Now?* (+Charles LeMaire); *Nightmare Alley* (+Charles LeMaire). 1948: *Scudda Hoo! Scudda Hay!* (+Charles LeMaire); *Give My Regards to Broadway* (+Charles LeMaire); *The Iron Curtain* (+Charles LeMaire); *Cry of the City* (+Charles LeMaire); *The Luck of the Irish* (+Charles LeMaire); *Unfaithfully Yours* (+Charles LeMaire); *The Snake Pit* (+Charles LeMaire). 1949: *Mr Belvedere Goes to College* (+Charles LeMaire); *It Happens Every Spring* (+Charles LeMaire); *You're My Everything* (+Charles LeMaire).

CASSINI, OLEG

Designer married (1941–52) to Gene Tierney. Designed her costumes for *The Shanghai Gesture, The Razor's Edge, That Wonderful Urge, Whirlpool, Where the Sidewalk Ends, The Mating Season* and *On the Riviera*.

FILMS:
1941: *The Shanghai Gesture* (+Royer). 1942: *Tales of Manhattan* (+Irene, Tree, B Newman, Wakeling). 1946: *The Razor's Edge* (+Charles LeMaire); *Born to Speed; It's a Joke, Son*. 1947: *Repeat Performance*. 1948: *That Wonderful Urge* (+Charles LeMaire). 1949: *Whirlpool* (+Charles LeMaire). 1950: *Where the Sidewalk Ends* (+Charles LeMaire). 1951: *The Mating Season; On the Riviera* (+Charles LeMaire, Travilla). 1962: *Rampage*. 1967: *The Ambushers*.

CHAFFIN, ETHEL

Head of Wardrobe Department at Famous Players-Lasky from 1919. Designed clothes for all the Famous Players-Lasky stars – Pola Negri, Gloria Swanson, Nita Naldi, Agnes Ayres, Bebe Daniels and Betty Compson, but most of her film work was uncredited. In 1925 she worked at M-G-M and received some screen credits.

FILMS:
1924: *Bluff*. 1925: *The Big Parade; Confessions of a Queen; The Sporting Venus; The Circle; Lights of Old Broadway* (GB *The Merry Wives of Gotham*).

CLARK, GILBERT

British designer who worked at M-G-M in 1927/28.

FILMS:
1925: *The American Venus*. 1927: *Mockery; The Road to Romance* (GB *Romance*); *The Fair Co-Ed; In Old Kentucky; Tea for Three;*

Opposite: Nancy Coleman wearing a Milo Anderson design

Love (GB *Anna Karenina*); *Lovelorn; Man, Woman and Sin; Baby Mine; The Enemy; West Point; Wickedness Preferred; Bringing Up Father*. 1928: *The Patsy; A Certain Young Man; Laugh, Clown, Laugh; The Actress; Telling the World; Beau Broadway; The Mysterious Lady; The Baby Cyclone; While the City Sleeps; The Bellamy Trial; Buttons; The Iron Mask* (+Maurice Leloir). 1935: *Her Last Affaire*.

COFFIN, GENE

American costume designer.

FILMS:
1961: *Lolita*. 1963: *Act One*. 1964: *The Yellow Rolls Royce* (+Mendleson, Castillo of Paris, Head, Pierre Cardin). 1966: *The Happening* (+Jason Silverstein). 1967: *The Producers*. 1968: *Goodbye Columbus*. 1969: *Don't Drink the Water*. 1970: *Bananas*. 1971: *The Anderson Tapes*. 1975: *The Education of Sonny Carson*.

COLT, ALVIN

Costume and set designer. Born Louisville, Kentucky, 1915. Has worked in the theatre in the USA since 1941. Two shows for which he designed costumes were later filmed, "Top Banana" and "Li'l Abner", and Colt also did the costumes for the screen versions.

FILMS:
1953: *Top Banana*. 1959: *Li'l Abner*. 1969: *Stiletto* (+Stavropoulos).

COLVIG, HELEN

American designer, mainly at Universal.

FILMS:
1960: *Psycho*. 1964: *The Killers; McHale's Navy; The Night Walker*. 1965: *The Trouble With Angels* (+Sybil Connolly); *Incident at Phantom Hill; The Sword of Ali Baba*. 1966: *The Plainsman; Texas Across the River* (+Rosemary Odell); *Out of Sight*. 1967: *Gunfight in Abilene; Rough Night in Jericho* (+Odell). 1968: *Deadly Roulette; Coogan's Bluff; Sam Whiskey; Death of a Gunfighter*. 1969: *A Man Called Gannon; The Love God?; A Change of Habit; Two Mules for Sister Sara*. 1970: *I Love My Wife; The Beguiled; Willy Wonka and the Chocolate Factory; Cockeyed Cowboys of Calico County*. 1971: *Play Misty For Me; Minnie and Moskovitch; The Great Northfield Minnesota Raid; How to Frame a Figg*. 1973: *Charley Varrick*.

CONWAY, GORDON

American designer in British films 1929/1933. Also costumes for theatre productions.

FILMS:
1929: *High Treason*. 1931: *Michael and Mary; Sunshine Susie* (US *Office Girl*). 1932: *Faithful Heart; Love on Wheels; The Good Companions; After the Ball; Rome Express*. 1933: *Falling for You; It's a Boy; Orders is Orders; The Lucky Number; I Was a Spy; Just Smith; The Firerakers; Friday the Thirteenth; Britannia of Billingsgate; Cuckoo in the Nest; The Constant Nymph; Red Ensign; Aunt Sally* (+Norman Hartnell).

CORSO, MARJORIE

American designer, first screen credit 1958. Many films for Roger Corman's production company.

FILMS:
1958: *Teenage Caveman* (GB *Out of the Darkness*); *High School Hellcats* (GB *School for Violence*); *I, Mobster; Missile to the Moon*. 1960: *The Fall of the House of Usher; Why Must I Die?*. 1961: *Angel Baby; The Pit and the Pendulum; The Premature Burial*. 1962: *Panic in the Year Zero; The Nun and the Sergeant; The Raven*. 1963: *Diary of a Madman; Beach Party; The Haunted Palace; The Terror; Twice Told Tales; The Comedy of Terrors*. 1964: *Muscle Beach Party; Bikini Beach; The Pajama Party*. 1965: *Beach Blanket Bingo*. 1966: *Boy, Did I Get a Wrong Number*. 1967: *The Wicked Dreams of Paula Schultz*.

COULTER, LUCIA

Wardrobe mistress at the M-G-M West Coast studio in the late '20s.

FILMS:

1926: *Lovey Mary*; *Bardelys the Magnificent* (+Andre-Ani). 1927: *The Show*; *Mr Wu*; *The Unknown*; *London After Midnight*; *Spoilers of the West*; *The Big City*; *The Trail of '98*. 1928: *The Law of the Range*; *Under the Black Eagle*; *Riders of the Dark*; *Wyoming*; *The Adventurer*; *Shadows of the Night*; *Behind the Sierras*; *The Bushranger*; *Morgan's Last Raid*; *The Overland Telegraph*. 1929: *The Desert Rider*; *Sioux Blood*.

COX, DAVID

Born James David Cox, New York, 1906. Educated at Rutgers College and New York School of Fine And Applied Arts. Joined Paramount's East Coast Studios at Long Island. Under contract to M-G-M in 1927 and then to Fox in 1931.

FILMS:

1927: *Spring Fever*; *Rose-Marie*; *The Smart Set*. 1928: *The Man Who Laughs* (+Vera West); *Circus Rookies*; *Across to Singapore*; *Diamond Handcuffs*; *The Cossacks*; *Four Walls*; *Excess Baggage*; *Detectives*; *Our Dancing Daughters*; *Alias Jimmy Valentine*; *West of Zanzibar*; *Broadway Melody*; *The Flying Fleet*; *Spite Marriage*; *Tide of Empire*. 1929: *The Duke Steps Out*; *Madame X*; *The Idle Rich*; *A Man's Man*; *Where East Is East*; *China Bound*; *Wonder of Women* (+Howard Greer); *The Hollywood Revue of 1929* (+Henrietta Frazer, Joe Rapf); *Speedway*; *His Glorious Night*; *It's a Great Life*; *Navy Blues*; *Chasing Rainbows*; *Lord Byron of Broadway* (GB *What Price Melody*); *Wise Girls*.
1930: *Free and Easy*; *The Girl in the Show*; *The Girl Said No*; *The Woman Racket* (GB *Lights and Shadows*); *Sins of the Children* (GB *Richest Man in the World*); *Strictly Unconventional*; *They Learned About Women*; *The Unholy Three*; *Children of Pleasure*; *Way Out West*; *Call of the Flesh*; *Good News*; *Love in the Rough*; *Billy the Kid*; *Reaching for the Moon*. 1931: *Cheaters at Play*. 1932: *Man About Town*; *The Woman in Room 13*; *Bachelor's Affairs*; *Society Girl*; *Mystery Ranch*; *The First Year*; *Six Hours To Live*; *Call Her Savage* (+Rita Kaufman); *Rackety Rex*; *Tess of the Storm Country*; *Second Hand Wife* (GB *Illegal Divorce*); *Face in the Sky*; *The Trial of Vivienne Ware*.

DALTON, PHYLLIS

British designer, trained at Ealing Art School. Began her film career in 1946 at the Gainsborough Studios in Shepherds Bush, where she worked as assistant to Yvonne Caffin.

ACADEMY AWARD NOMINATIONS:

1965: *Doctor Zhivago. 1968: Oliver!

SFTA NOMINATIONS:

1968: Oliver! 1973: *The Hireling.

FILMS:

1949: *Your Witness* (US *Eye Witness*). 1951: *Circle of Danger*; *Scrooge*. 1953: *Rob Roy, the Highland Rogue*. 1954: *One Good Turn*. 1955: *Passage Home*. 1956: *Zarak*; *The Man Who Knew Too Much*. 1957: *Island in the Sun*. 1958: *John Paul Jones*; *Carve Her Name With Pride*. 1959: *Our Man in Havana*. 1960: *The World of Suzie Wong*. 1961: *Fury at Smuggler's Bay*; *Man Detained*. 1962: *Lawrence of Arabia*. 1964: *Lord Jim*. 1965: *Doctor Zhivago*. 1968: *Oliver!* 1970: *Fragment of Fear*. 1973: *The Hireling*. 1975: *The Message*. 1976: *Voyage of the Damned*. 1979: *The Spaceman and King Arthur* (US *The Unidentified Flying Oddball*); *The Water Babies*. 1980: *The Awakening*; *The Mirror Crack'd*. 1985: *A Private Function*. 1987: *The Princess Bride*.

DAWSON, BEATRICE

Born Lincoln, England 1908. Died 1976. Educated at the Slade School of Art and Chelsea Polytechnic. Her first professional work in the theatre was for "The Duchess of Malfi" at the Haymarket Theatre in 1945.

Opposite: Audrey Hepburn in My Fair Lady *(Cecil Beaton)*

Agnes Ayres in Bluff *(Ethel Chaffin)*

Selection of sketches by Gordon Conway

Bebe Daniels in Reaching For the Moon *(David Cox)*

ACADEMY AWARD NOMINATION:

1955: *The Pickwick Papers* (b&w)

SFTA NOMINATIONS:

1964: *Of Human Bondage* (b&w); *Woman of Straw*. 1973: *A Doll's House* (Dir/Garland).

FILMS:

1947: *Night Beat*. 1949: *Dear Mr Prohack*; *Trottie True* (US *Gay Lady*); *The Reluctant Widow*; *State Secret* (US *The Great Manhunt*). 1950: *Pandora and the Flying Dutchman* (+Julia Squire). 1951: *Tom Brown's Schooldays*. 1952: *The Importance of Being Earnest*; *Penny Princess*; *The Pickwick Papers*. 1953: *Grand National Night* (US *Wicked Wife*). 1954: *The Black Knight*. 1955: *Footsteps in the Fog* (+Haffenden); *Svengali*. 1956: *The Black Tent*. 1957: *The Prince and the Showgirl*; *Manuela* (US *Stowaway Girl*). 1958: *The Wind Cannot Read*; *The Key*; *Life is a Circus*; *A Tale of Two Cities*. 1959: *Expresso Bongo* (+Balmain); *Faces in the Dark*. 1960: *The Full Treatment* (US *Stop Me Before I Kill You*). 1961: *The Day the Earth Caught Fire*; *Waltz of the Toreadors*; *Macbeth*. 1962: *Term of Trial*; *The L-Shaped Room*; *I Could Go On Singing*. 1963: *Stolen Hours* (+Fabiana); *The Servant*; *Woman of Straw* (+Christian Dior). 1964: *The Beauty Jungle* (US *Contest Girl*) (+Christian Dior); *Of Human Bondage*; *Masquerade*; *The Intel-*

ligence Men (US *Spylarks*). 1965: *Where the Spies Are*; *Life at the Top*; *Promise Her Anything*. 1966: *Modesty Blaise*; *Accident* (+De Luca of Rome). 1968: *Only When I Larf*; *The Assassination Bureau*; *Mrs. Brown, You've Got a Lovely Daughter*. 1969: *The Man Who Haunted Himself*. 1970: *Zee & Co*; *Three Sisters*; *The Last Grenade*. 1972: *Tamlin* (US *The Devil's Widow*) (+Balmain). 1973: *A Doll's House*. 1974: *Brief Encounter*.

DEAN, KAY

Designer at M-G-M 1944/45, associate to Irene.

FILMS:

1944: *Two Girls and a Sailor* (+Irene); *Bathing Beauty* (+Irene; water ballet costumes by Irene Sharaff); *Lost in a Harem* (+Irene, Valles); *Music For Millions* (+Irene); *This Man's Navy* (+Irene). 1945: *Thrill of a Romance* (+Irene); *Anchors Aweigh*.

Opposite: Marlene Dietrich in Desire *(Travis Banton)*

Adaptations by Dryden of his Lost Horizon *costumes*

DE LIMA, JOSETTE

Designer at RKO in 1932.

FILMS:

1932: *Westward Passage* (+Mrs Brock Pemberton); *A Bill of Divorcement*; *The Conquerors.*

DIOR, CHRISTIAN

Paris fashion house which continues to use the name after Dior's death.

ACADEMY AWARD NOMINATION:

1954: **Stazione Termini* (=*Indiscretion of an American Wife*) (b&w).

SFTA NOMINATION:

1966: *Arabesque.*

FILMS:

1949: *Stagefright* (+ Milo Anderson). 1951: *No Highway* (for Marlene Dietrich). 1952: *Don't Bother to Knock* (+Michael). 1953: *Stazione Termini* (= *Indiscretion of an American Wife*). 1955: *Gentlemen Marry Brunettes* (+Travilla). 1956: *The Little Hut; The Ambassador's Daughter.* 1958: *Indiscreet.* 1959: *Libel.* 1961: *The Grass is Greener* (+Hardy Amies); *Goodbye Again; The Light in the Piazza.* 1963: *Woman of Straw* (+ Beatrice Dawson); *Paris When It Sizzles* (+Givenchy). 1964: *The Beauty Jungle* (+ Beatrice Dawson). 1966: *Arabesque.* 1967: *The Double Man* (+Courtney Elliott). 1968: *Secret Ceremony.* 1970: *Lady in the Car with Glasses and Gun* (for Samantha Eggar and Stéphane Audran, designed by Marc Bohan).

DODSON, MARY KAY

Designer at Paramount 1944/1949. Also some films for Universal.

Opposite: Leatrice Joy in The Dressmaker
From Paris, *Travis Banton's first film*

FILMS:

1944: *Our Hearts Were Growing Up.* 1945: *On Stage Everybody* (+Vera West); *Duffy's Tavern* (+Edith Head). 1946: *Monsieur Beaucaire; Ladies Man; Suddenly It's Spring.* 1947: *Golden Earrings.* 1948: *The Saxon Charm; Sealed Verdict; The Paleface* (+Gile Steele); *Whispering Smith; Alias Nick Beal* (GB *Contact Man*); *A Connecticut Yankee in King Arthur's Court* (GB *A Yankee in King Arthur's Court*) (+ Head, Steele); *Sorrowful Jones.* 1949: *Chicago Deadline; Top o' the Morning; Dear Wife; Captain Carey, USA.*

DONFELD

American designer in films from 1960. Has designed costumes for television programmes and the cabaret appearances of Barbra Streisand, Nancy Sinatra etcetera. Special consultant to Michelangelo Antonioni on *Zabriskie Point* (1971). At Fox from 1960 to 1962, also films for M-G-M and Warners.

ACADEMY AWARD NOMINATIONS:

1962: *Days of Wine and Roses* (b&w). 1969: *They Shoot Horses, Don't They?* 1973: *Tom Sawyer.* 1985: *Prizzi's Honor.*

FILMS:

1960: *Sanctuary.* 1961: *Return to Peyton Place; Wild in the Country; The Second Time Around; Bachelor Flat.* 1962: *Mr Hobbs Takes a Vacation; Hemingway's Adventures of a Young Man; Days of Wine and Roses.* 1963: *Island of Love; Under the Yum-Yum Tree; Dead Ringer* (GB *Dead Image*). 1964: *Viva Las Vegas* (GB *Love in Las Vegas*); *Robin and the Seven Hoods; The Outrage; Dear Heart; Joy in the Morning.* 1965: *The Great Race* (+Edith Head); *The Cincinnati Kid; The Chase.* 1966: *Hombre; Double Trouble.* 1967: *Don't Make Waves; Luv; Fitzwilly* (GB *Fitzwilly Strikes Back*). 1969: *They Shoot Horses, Don't They?; The April Fools.* 1970: *A Walk in the Spring Rain; The Grasshopper.* 1971: *Diamonds Are Forever* (+ Ted Tetrick, Elsa Fennell). 1973: *Lady Ice; Tom Sawyer.* 1974: *Huckleberry Finn.* 1975: *Rafferty and the Gold Dust Twins.* 1976: *Lipstick.* 1977: *Fun with Dick and Jane; One on One.* 1979: *The China Syndrome.* 1983: *Brainstorm; Class.* 1985: *Prizzi's Honor.* 1987: *Spaceballs.*

DRYDEN, ERNEST

Dress designer who worked at Columbia for two years between 1935 and 1937.

FILMS:

1935: *Remember Last Night?* (+Vera West); *Lost Horizon; The King Steps Out; The Final Hour; The Garden of Allah; Come Closer, Folks; Lady from Nowhere; Devil's Playground.* 1937: *The Prisoner of Zenda.*

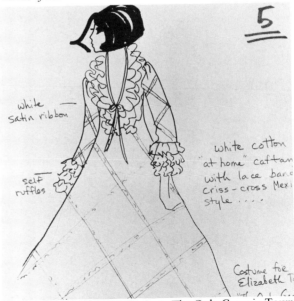

Design for Elizabeth Taylor in The Only Game in Town
by Mia Fonssagrives and Vicky Tiel

DUSE, ANNA

British designer active in films 1948 to 1969.

FILMS:
1948: *Noose* (US *The Silk Noose*). 1950: *Happy Go Lovely*. 1951: *Lady Godiva Rides Again*. 1952: *Folly to Be Wise*. 1953: *Isn't Life Wonderful!* 1954: *The Belles of St Trinians*. 1955: *The Constant Husband*; *A Kid for Two Farthings*; *Geordie* (US *Wee Geordie*); *The Deep Blue Sea* (+ Balmain for Vivien Leigh). 1956: *The Green Man*. 1957: *No Time for Tears*; *Tarzan and the Lost Safari*; *Blue Murder at St Trinians*; *Let's Be Happy*. 1958: *Alive and Kicking*. 1966: *That Riviera Touch*; *The Magnificent Two*. 1967: *Decline and Fall . . . of a Birdwatcher!* 1969: *Carry on Again, Doctor*; *The Chairman* (GB *The Most Dangerous Man in the World*).

DUTY, GUY

Born Cleveland, Ohio, 1886. Dress designer for George C Heimendinger & Co. and Milgrim's. Under contract to Fox 1931/32 as fashion creator and designer.

FILMS:
1931: *Ambassador Bill*; *Surrender*; *Delicious*; *The Silent Witness*; *After Tomorrow*. 1932: *Careless Lady*; *Disorderly Conduct*; *While Paris Sleeps*.

EHREN, FRANCES

Costume supervisor for Eagle-Lion in the late '40s.

FILMS:
1947: *T Men*; *Railroaded*. 1948: *Assigned to Danger*; *Canon City*; *Mickey*; *Northwest Stampede*; *The Spiritualist*; *In This Corner*; *Behind Locked Doors*.

ELLACOTT, JOAN

Born London 1920 and educated in the USA. Studied dress design at Birmingham, Northampton and Bromley School of Arts and Crafts. Entered the film industry in 1946 as assistant to Elizabeth Haffenden on *Jassy*.

FILMS:
1947: *Snowbound*. 1948: *Easy Money*; *Portrait From Life* (US *Girl In the Painting*). 1949: *Don't Ever Leave Me*; *Helter Skelter*; *The Happiest Days of Your Life*; *Christopher Columbus* (+ Elizabeth Haffenden). 1950: *The Adventurers* (US *The Great Adventure*); *The Galloping Major*. 1951: *Madame Louise*; *Appointment With Venus* (US *Island Rescue*). 1952: *Top of the Form*; *The Long Memory*. 1953: *Personal Affair*; *The Kidnappers* (US *The Little Kidnappers*); *Fast and Loose*; *Forbidden Cargo*. 1954: *Up To His Neck*; *To Dorothy a Son* (US *Cash on Delivery*); *Mad About Men*. 1955: *Above Us the Waves*; *Doctor at Sea*; *Man of the Moment*; *All for Mary*; *Jumping for Joy*. 1956: *Tiger in the Smoke*; *High Tide at Noon*. 1957: *Across the Bridge*. 1958: *Carry on Sergeant*; *Floods of Fear*; *The Captain's Table*. 1959: *Upstairs and Downstairs*. 1960: *Suddenly Last Summer* (+ Messel, Louis, Hartnell); *Piccadilly Third Stop*; *Watch Your Stern*; *Circle of Deception*; *No Kidding* (US *Beware of Children*); *The League of Gentlemen*. 1961: *Carry on Regardless*; *In the Doghouse*. 1962: *Carry on Cruising*; *Bitter Harvest*; *Carry on Cabby*; *The Iron Maiden* (US *Swingin' Maiden*). 1963: *Nurse on Wheels*; *A Stitch in Time*. 1964: *Carry on Jack*.

ELOISE

Designer at the Republic Studios 1936/37.

FILMS:
1936: *Follow Your Heart*; *The President's Mystery* (GB *One for All*); *The Country Gentlemen*; *The Bold Caballero*; *Happy Go Lucky*; *Beware of Ladies*; *Join the Marines*; *Larceny on the Air*; *A Man Betrayed*; *The Chorus Girl*; *Two Wise Maids*; *Bill Cracks*

Opposite: Agnes Ayres in Bluff *(Ethel Chaffin)*

Down; *Navy Blues*; *Paradise Express*. 1937: *The Hit Parade*; *The Affair of Cappy Ricks*; *Jim Hanvey, Detective*; *Michael O'Halloran*; *Dangerous Holiday*; *The Mandarin Mystery*; *Meet the Boyfriend*; *All Over Town*; *Escape by Night*; *It Could Happen to You*; *Sea Racketeers*; *The Wrong Road*; *Youth on Parole*; *Manhattan Merry-Go-Round* (GB *Manhattan Music Box*) (+ Muriel King); *Portia on Trial* (GB *The Trial of Portia Merriman*); *The Duke Comes Back* (GB *The Call of the Ring*).

ERTE

Born Romain de Tirtoff, Petrograd, 1892. Erte's extraordinarily long and varied career has been the subject of several books but he worked for only one year in Hollywood before becoming completely disillusioned with the film world. M-G-M must have been extremely proud to have secured the services of such a talented designer and issued publicity stills of Erte surrounded by the top stars of the studio before he had been given an assignment. The first film he worked on was an Aileen Pringle picture called *The Mystic*. He also worked on a Pauline Starke film called *Paris* and designed a Mask Ballet for *Dance Madness*. It was on the film *La Boheme* that a clash of personalities occurred. Lillian Gish refused to wear the costumes Erte had designed for her role as Mimi and tried to persuade Renee Adoree (who was playing the role of Musetta) to refuse them as well. Miss Adoree wore the Erte clothes in the film but Lillian Gish redesigned all of Mimi's costumes with the help of the M-G-M wardrobe mistress Lucia Coulter, and Erte's name did not appear in the publicity material for *La Boheme*.

It is impossible to analyse why M-G-M failed to use Erte's unique talents for costume and set design. It is true that his work is exotic and theatrical but certainly no more outlandish than Clare West's costumes used in the Cecil B DeMille pictures, or anything worn by stars like Barbara LaMarr, Mae Murray or Pola Negri. His contract at M-G-M was not the first attempt he made at designing for films – in 1919 William Randolph Hearst commissioned him to do sets and costumes for *Bal des Arts* but the project was never realised and very little of Erte's work ever reached the screen. Died 1990.

FILMS:
1925: *The Mystic* (+ Andre-Ani); *Bright Lights*; *Time, the Comedian*; *Dance Madness* (+ Andre-Ani, Kathleen Kay, Maude Marsh); *La Boheme*; *Paris* (+ Andre-Ani, Kathleen Kay, Maude Marsh).

FONSSAGRIVES, MIA and TIEL, VICKY

British Fashion designers who worked in partnership during the '60s.

FILMS:
1965: *What's New, Pussycat?* 1968: *Candy* (+ Enrico Sabbatine). 1969: *The Only Game in Town*. 1970: *The Walking Stick* (+ Sue Yelland).

FRAZER, HENRIETTA

Wardrobe department at M-G-M 1928/30.

FILMS:
1928: *Show People*; *Brotherly Love*. 1929: *Desert Nights*; *All at Sea*; *Hallelujah!*; *The Hollywood Revue of 1929* (+ David Cox, Joe Rapf); *Honeymoon*; *So This is College?*; *The Bishop Murder Case*. 1930: *Caught Short*.

FURNESS, JOHN

British designer, in films since 1966.

ACADEMY AWARD NOMINATION:
1974: *Daisy Miller*.

1966: *The Blue Max*. 1971: *The Go-Between*.

FILMS:
1966: *The Blue Max*; *Eye of the Devil* (+Julie Harris); *The Long Duel*; *The Viking Queen*. 1969: *Monte Carlo or Bust* (US *Those Daring Young Men in Their Jaunty Jalopies*) (+Orietta Nasalli-Rocca); *The Valley of Gwangi*; *The Kremlin Letter*. 1970: *The Go-Between*. 1971: *Endless Night*. 1973: *England Made Me*; *Sleuth*; *A Doll's House* (Dir/Losey) (+Edith Head). 1974: *Soft Beds, Hard Battles*; *Daisy Miller*. 1978: *International Velvet*.

FURSE, MARGARET

Born 1911, died 1974. Studied at the Central School of Art under Jeanetta Cochrane. Joined Gaumont-British Studios as an assistant designer. Married to Roger Furse and worked as his assistant on *Henry V*.

ACADEMY AWARD NOMINATIONS:
1951: *The Mudlark* (+Edward Stevenson)(b&w). 1964: *Becket*. 1968: *The Lion in Winter*. 1969: **Anne of the Thousand Days*. 1970: *Scrooge*. 1971: *Mary, Queen of Scots*.

SFTA NOMINATIONS:
1964: **Becket*. 1965: *A Shot in the Dark*; *Young Cassidy*. 1968: *The Lion in Winter*. 1970: *Anne of the Thousand Days*.

FILMS:
1944: *Henry V* (+Roger Furse). 1946: *Great Expectations* (+Sophie Harris of Motley); 1947: *Blanche Fury* (+Sophie Harris). 1948: *Oliver Twist*; *The Passionate Friends* (US *One Woman's Story*). 1949: *Madeleine*. 1950: *Night and the City* (+Oleg Cassini); *The Mudlark* (+Edward Stevenson). 1951: *No Highway* (US *No Highway in the Sky*); *The House in the Square* (US *I'll Never Forget You*). 1952: *Meet Me Tonight*; *The Crimson Pirate*; 1953: *Master of Ballantrae*; *The Million Pound Note* (US *Man With a Million*). 1956: *The Spanish Gardener*. 1958: *Inn of the Sixth Happiness* (+Olga Lehmann). 1960: *Kidnapped*; *Sons and Lovers*; *Greyfriars Bobby*; *The Horsemasters*. 1962: *The Prince and the Pauper*; *In Search of the Castaways*. 1963: *Becket*. 1964: *A Shot in the Dark*; *Young Cassidy*; *The Three Lives of Thomasina*. 1965: *Return From the Ashes*; *Cast a Giant Shadow*. 1966: *The Trap*. 1967: *The Lion in Winter*; *Great Catherine*. 1968: *Sinful Davy*. 1969: *Anne of the Thousand Days*; *Scrooge*. 1971: *Mary, Queen of Scots*. 1973: *A Delicate Balance*.

FURSE, ROGER

Born 1903. Artist and set designer. Studied at the Slade School, then worked for several years as a commercial artist in America. From 1936 to 1939 designed theatre productions in London including Laurence Olivier's "Othello".

ACADEMY AWARD NOMINATION:
1948: **Hamlet* (b&w)

FILMS:
1944: *Henry V* (+Margaret Furse). 1947: *Hamlet*. 1949: *The Angel With the Trumpet*; *Under Capricorn* (+Julia Squire). 1952: *Ivanhoe*. 1954: *Knights of the Round Table*.

GIVENCHY, HUBERT DE

French couturier, often used to design for Audrey Hepburn films of the '50s and '60s.

ACADEMY AWARD NOMINATION:
1957: *Funny Face* (+Edith Head).

FILMS:
1956: *Funny Face* (+Edith Head). 1957: *Love in the Afternoon*;

*Opposite: Howard Greer design for
Sylvia Sidney in* Thirty Day Princess

Bonjour Tristesse. 1959: *Once More, with Feeling*. 1960: *Crack in the Mirror*. 1961: *Breakfast at Tiffanys* (+Edith Head, Pauline Trigere). 1963: *The VIPs* (+Pierre Cardin); *Charade*; *Paris When It Sizzles* (+Dior). 1966: *How to Steal a Million*.

GRANT, MARY

Designer at Paramount, also freelance work at Universal and RKO.

FILMS:
1944: *The Princess and the Pirate*. 1948: *Up in Central Park*; *Bride of Vengeance* (+Mitchell Leisen). 1955: *We're No Angels*; *The Vagabond King*. 1957: *The Bachelor Party*; *Sweet Smell of Success*. 1958: *The Devil's Disciple*.

GREER, HOWARD

Born Nebraska, died Los Angeles, 1974. Started his career at the Chicago fashion house of Lucille Ltd in 1916. He worked at both the Chicago and New York branches of Lady Duff Gordon's house but left to serve in France during World War I. Greer was demobilised in Paris and worked once again for Lucille, and also Paul Poiret and Molyneux. For the next three years he worked in Europe, designing clothes for the theatre in London and Paris, writing monthly newsletters on fashion for the "Theatre Magazine" and illustrating fashion articles written by Mary Brush Williams in the Chicago Tribune syndicate of newspapers. In 1921 he returned to America and was associated with Hickson Inc until commissioned to do costumes for the "Greenwich Village Follies". Through his work on this revue Greer was engaged to act as Chief Designer at the West Coast Studios of Famous Players-Lasky, which later became Paramount Pictures Corporation.

Howard Greer worked for several years at the studio but left to open his own couture house. Greer Inc was situated just off Sunset Boulevard and opened on 27 December 1927 (the decor was by Harold Grieve) and although he later turned to mass merchandising, Greer remained in the couture business until his retirement in 1962. Although he was under contract to a studio for only a few years, he continued to supply clothes for films. Many studios without a resident designer or proper wardrobe facilities would get the star's costumes from a commercial fashion house and his designs could still be seen up to the mid-'50s.

During his time at Famous Players-Lasky (1923–1928) he attracted a great deal of publicity for the clothes he designed for Pola Negri, Agnes Ayres, Betty Compson, Bebe Daniels, Nita Naldi, Anna Q Nilsson and others. Many of the stars he worked with at the studio were customers of Greer Inc and remained faithful for years to come.

The latter part of Howard Greer's retirement was spent in London. His autobiography "Designing Male" was published in 1951.

FILMS:
1923: *The Spanish Dancer*. 1924: *Forbidden Paradise*; *Locked Doors*; *Are Parents People?* 1925: *The Trouble With Wives* (GB *Ten Modern Commandments*). 1929: *Coquette*; *Wonder of Women* (+David Cox).
1930: *The Ship From Shanghai*; *Hell's Angels*. 1932: *Hollywood Speaks*; *The Animal Kingdom* (GB *The Woman in His House*). 1933: *Christopher Strong*. 1934: *Thirty Day Princess*. 1935: *Dressed to Thrill*. 1938: *Bringing Up Baby*; *Merrily We Live* (+Irene); *Carefree* (+Edward Stevenson). 1939: *Love Affair*; *Fifth Avenue Girl*.
1940: *My Favourite Wife*. 1941: *Unfinished Business* (+Vera West). 1944: *Follow the Boys* (+Vera West); *Christmas Holiday* (+Muriel King, Vera West); *Practically Yours*. 1945: *Lady On a Train*; *Spellbound*. 1946: *The Madonna's Secret* (+Adele Palmer); *Heartbeat*. 1949: *Holiday Affair*.
1951: *His Kind of Woman* (for Jane Russell); *The Las Vegas Story*. 1953: *The French Line* (+Michael Woulfe).

HAACK, MORTON

American costume designer active in films 1959 to 1971. Also visual consultant on *Games* (1967). Died 1987.

Two sketches by Morton Haack for Debbie Reynolds in The Unsinkable Molly Brown

ACADEMY AWARD NOMINATIONS:

1964: *The Unsinkable Molly Brown*. 1968: *Planet of the Apes.* 1971: *What's the Matter With Helen?*

FILMS:

1959: *Please Don't Eat the Daisies*. 1961: *Come September*. 1962: *Billy Rose's Jumbo (GB Jumbo)*. 1963: *The Unsinkable Molly Brown*. 1966: *Walk, Don't Run*. 1967: *Planet of the Apes*. 1968: *Buona Sera, Mrs Campbell*. 1970: *Beneath the Planet of the Apes*. 1971: *What's the Matter with Helen?*

HAFFENDEN, ELIZABETH

Born Croydon 1906, died 1976. Educated at the Croydon School of Art. First job in the film industry was with Sound City in 1933. Later in charge of costume department at Gainsborough Studios. Often worked in association with Joan Bridge, a colour consultant on many British pictures.

ACADEMY AWARD NOMINATIONS:

1959: **Ben Hur*. 1966: **A Man For All Seasons* (+Joan Bridge).

SFTA NOMINATIONS:

1965: *The Amorous Adventures of Moll Flanders* (+Joan Bridge). 1967: *Half a Sixpence* (+Joan Bridge); **A Man for All Seasons* (+Joan Bridge).

FILMS:

1936: *Wedding Group (US Wrath of Jealousy)*. 1942: *The Young Mr Pitt* (+Cecil Beaton). 1944: *Fanny by Gaslight*; *Love Story*

Opposite: Jessie Matthews in Friday the 13th *(Conway)*

(US *A Lady Surrenders*); *A Place of One's Own*. 1945: *The Wicked Lady*; *Caravan* (+Ernst Stern). 1946: *Bedelia*; *The Magic Bow*. 1947: *The Man Within (US The Smugglers)*; *Jassy*; *Call of the Blood*; *The First Gentleman (US Affairs of a Rogue)*. 1949: *The Bad Lord Byron*; *Christopher Columbus* (+Joan Ellacott); *The Spider and the Fly*. 1950: *So Long at the Fair*; *Portrait of Clare*; *The Late Edwina Black (US Obsessed)*. 1953: *Laughing Anne*. 1954: *Beau Brummel*. 1955: *The Dark Avengers (US The Warriors)*; *The Adventures of Quentin Durward*; *Footsteps in the Fog* (+Dawson). 1956: *Invitation to the Dance* (+Rolf Gerard); *Bhowani Junction*; *Moby Dick*; *The Barretts of Wimpole Street*; *The Shiralee*. 1957: *Heaven Knows, Mr Allison*; *Davy*; *I Accuse!* 1959: *Ben-Hur*.

1960: *The Sundowners* (+ Joan Bridge). 1961: *Village of Daughters*. 1962: *I Thank a Fool*; *Kill or Cure* (+Joan Bridge). 1964: *Behold a Pale Horse* (+Joan Bridge). 1965: *The Amorous Adventures of Moll Flanders* (+Joan Bridge); *The Liquidator* (+Joan Bridge). 1966: *A Man For All Seasons* (+Joan Bridge); *Drop Dead Darling (US Arriverderci Baby)* (+Pierre Balmain, Joan Bridge). 1967: *Half a Sixpence* (+Joan Bridge). 1968: *Chitty Chitty Bang Bang* (+Joan Bridge); *The Prime of Miss Jean Brodie* (+Joan Bridge). 1971: *Fiddler on the Roof* (+Joan Bridge). 1972: *Pope Joan* (+Joan Bridge). 1973: *The Day of the Jackal* (+Joan Bridge, Rosine Delamare); *The Homecoming* (+Joan Bridge). 1974: *Luther*. 1975: *Conduct Unbecoming* (+Joan Bridge).

HARKRIDER, JOHN

American theatrical designer under contract to Florenz Ziegfeld. Supervising Art Director at the Universal Studios.

FILMS:

1929: *Glorifying the American Girl*. 1930: *Whoopee*. 1933: *Roman Scandals*; *Nana* (+Adrian, Banton). 1936: *Swingtime* (+Bernard Newman); *Three Smart Girls*; *As Good as Married* (+Vera West).

HARRIS, JULIE

Born London, 1921. Studied art at the Chelsea Polytechnic. Worked at the court dressmaker Reville. First job in the film industry was in 1945 as assistant designer at Gainsborough Studios under Elizabeth Haffenden. First film was *Holiday Camp* in 1947.

ACADEMY AWARD NOMINATION:

1965: *Darling . . .* (b&w).

SFTA NOMINATIONS:

1964: *Psyche 59* (b&w). 1965: *Help!* 1966: ★ *The Wrong Box*. 1967: *Casino Royale*. 1976: *The Slipper and the Rose*.

FILMS:

1947: *Holiday Camp*; *Once Upon a Dream*. 1948: *Broken Journey*; *Good Time Girl*; *The Calendar*: *My Brother's Keeper*; *Quartet*. 1949: *Under Capricorn* (+Roger Furse). 1950: *Trio*; *The Clouded Yellow*; *Highly Dangerous*; *Traveller's Joy*; *Mr Drake's Duck*. 1951: *Night Without Stars* (+Balmain); *Hotel Sahara*; *Another*

Harris sketch for Hotel Sahara

Man's Poison; *Encore*; *So Little Time*. 1952: *Something Money Can't Buy*; *South of Algiers* (US *The Golden Mask*); *Made in Heaven*; *Desperate Moment*. 1953: *Turn the Key Softly*; *Always a Bride*; *The Red Beret* (US *Paratrooper*); *You Know What Sailors Are*. 1954: *The Seekers* (US *Land of Fury*). 1955: *Value For Money*; *Cast a Dark Shadow*; *Simon and Laura*. 1956: *The March Hare*; *Reach for the Sky*; *It's a Wonderful World*; *House of Secrets* (US *Triple Deception*). 1957: *Miracle in Soho*; *The Story of Esther Costello* (+Jean Louis); *Seven Thunders* (US *The Beast of Marseilles*); *The Gypsy and the Gentleman*. 1958: *The Sheriff of Fractured Jaw*; *Whirlpool*. 1959: *Sapphire*; *North West Frontier* (US *Flame Over India*) (+Yvonne Caffin).
1960: *The Greengage Summer* (US *Loss of Innocence*). 1961: *All Night Long*. 1962: *We Joined the Navy*; *The Fast Lady*. 1963: *Tamahine* (+Guy Laroche); *The Chalk Garden*; *Father Came Too*; *Psyche 59*. 1964: *A Hard Day's Night*; *Carry on Cleo*. 1965: *Help!*; *Darling . . .*; 1966: *The Wrong Box*; *Eye of the Devil* (+John Furness); *Casino Royale* (+Guy Laroche, Paco Rabanne). 1967: *Deadfall*; *The Whisperers*. 1968: *Decline and Fall . . . of a Bird-watcher!* (+Duse); *Prudence and the Pill*. 1969: *Goodbye Mr. Chips*. 1970: *The Private Life of Sherlock Holmes*. 1972: *Follow Me* (US *The Public Eye*). 1973: *Live and Let Die*. 1975: *The Slipper and the Rose*. 1976: *Candleshoe*.

Opposite: Dietrich wardrobe test for
The Garden of Allah *(Ernest Dryden)*

Haffenden sketch for The Adventures of Quentin Durward

Haffenden sketch for Beau Brummell

HARTNELL, NORMAN

British fashion designer whose couture house, Norman Hartnell Ltd, has supplied clothes for British films from 1930.

FILMS:

1930: *Such is the Law* (+Reville, Elspeth Fox-Pitt). 1933: *That's a Good Girl* (+Eileen Idare Ltd); *A Southern Maid.* 1934: *Princess Charming; The Church Mouse; The Return of Bulldog Drummond; Give Her a Ring; Brewster's Millions* (+Motley, Schiaparelli). 1936: *Once In a Million* (US *Weekend Millionaire*); *Two's Company.* 1937: *Jump for Glory* (+Schiaparelli); *Non-Stop New York; Sailing Along.* 1938: *Climbing High.* 1941: *He Found a Star* (+Joe Strassner). 1941: *Ships With Wings* (+Digby Morton, Lachasse, Maison Arthur, Molyneux, Peter Russell, Victor Stiebel, Dorothy Broomham). 1943: *The Demi-Paradise* (+Molyneux, Digby Morton, Bianca Mosca, Charles Creed, Peter Russell). 1956: *The Passionate Stranger* (US *A Novel Affair*). 1958: *Nowhere To Go.* 1960: *Suddenly, Last Summer* (+Messel, Louis, Ellacott). 1963: *Never Put it in Writing.*

HEAD, EDITH

Studied art at the Otis Art Institute and Chouinard School of Art. When Howard Greer (who was Head Designer at Paramount) advertised for a sketch artist, Edith Head went for an interview, taking a selection of drawings from all the students in her class at Chouinard. Howard Greer was suitably impressed and hired her on the spot – he also kept her on when she confessed that she couldn't draw and trained her as a sketch artist. When Travis Banton took over from Howard Greer, Edith Head worked with him until he left in 1938 and she then became Head Designer at Paramount until 1967. Then she went to Universal, but has also worked on films for M-G-M, Warners, Columbia and Fox. Edith Head has had an extraordinarily long career in films and has involved herself in many allied activities, lecturing extensively on dress to clubs all over the United States. A former fashion editor of "Holiday" magazine, she has made many radio and television appearances and is the author of two books, "The Dress Doctor" and "How to Dress for Success". Edith Head appeared as herself in the films *Lucy Gallant* and *The Oscar.* Died 1981.

ACADEMY AWARD NOMINATIONS:

1948: *The Emperor Waltz.* 1949: **The Heiress* (b&w) (+Gile Steele). 1950: **All About Eve* (b&w) (+Charles LeMaire); **Samson and Delilah* (+Dorothy Jeakins, Elois Jenssen, Gile Steele, Gwen Wakeling). 1951: **A Place in the Sun* (b&w). 1952: *Carrie* (b&w); *The Greatest Show on Earth* (Dorothy Jeakins, Miles White). 1953: **Roman Holiday* (b&w). 1954: **Sabrina* (b&w). 1955: *The Rose Tattoo* (b&w); *To Catch a Thief.* 1956: *The Proud and the Profane* (b&w); *The Ten Commandments* (+Ralph Jester, John Jensen, Dorothy Jeakins, Arnold Friberg). 1957: *Funny Face* (+Hubert de Givenchy). 1958: *The Buccaneer* (+Ralph Jester, John Jensen). 1959: *Career* (b&w); *The Five Pennies.*

1960: **The Facts of Life* (b&w) (+Edward Stevenson); *Pepe.* 1961: *Pocketful of Miracles.* 1962: *The Man Who Shot Liberty Valance* (b&w); *My Geisha.* 1963: *Love With the Proper Stranger* (b&w); *A New Kind of Love; Wives and Lovers* (b&w). 1964: *A House is Not a Home* (b&w); *What a Way To Go* (+Moss Mabry). 1965: *The Slender Thread* (b&w); *Inside Daisy Clover* (+Bill Thomas). 1966: *The Oscar.* 1969: *Sweet Charity.*

1970: *Airport.* 1973: **The Sting.* 1975: *The Man Who Would Be King.* 1977: *Airport 77* (+Burton Miller).

SFTA NOMINATION:

1975: *The Man Who Would Be King.*

FILMS:

1927: *Wings* (+Banton). 1932: *She Done Him Wrong.* 1934: *She Loves Me Not; You Belong to Me.* 1936: *Poppy; Rhythm on the Range; Murder with Pictures; College Holiday; John Meade's Woman* (+William Bridgehouse); *Waikiki Wedding; Her Husband Lies* (+Travis Banton). 1937: *Souls at Sea; Sophie Lang Goes West* (+Travis Banton); *This Way, Please; Ebb Tide; Blossoms on Broadway; Thrill of a Lifetime; Dangerous to Know; Big Broadcast of 1938.* 1938: *Her Jungle Love; College Swing* (GB *Swing, Teacher, Swing*);

Tropic Holiday; Give Me a Sailor; Spawn of the North; Men With Wings; Disbarred; Zaza; Cafe Society; King of Chinatown; Sudden Money; Man of Conquest (+Adele Palmer); *If I Were King; Never Say Die.* 1939: *Invitation to Happiness; Man About Town; Beau Geste; The Magnificent Fraud; Honeymoon in Bali* (GB *Husbands or Lovers*); *The Cat and the Canary; The Great Victor Herbert; Remember the Night; Road to Singapore; The Star Maker.*

1940: *The Ghost Breakers; The Great McGinty; Love Thy Neighbor; The Lady Eve; The Road to Zanzibar; Rhythm on the River.* 1941: *Caught in the Draft; Kiss the Boys Goodbye; Here Comes Mr Jordan; Hold Back the Dawn; Aloma of the South Seas; Skylark; Ball of Fire; Sullivan's Travels; The Lady Has Plans; The Great Man's Lady; This Gun for Hire; Birth of the Blues; New York Town.* 1942: *You Belong to Me* (GB *Good Morning, Doctor*); *Are Husbands Necessary?; The Gay Sisters; The Glass Key; The Major and the Minor; I Married a Witch; The Road to Morocco; Star Spangled Rhythm; They Got Me Covered* (+Adrian); *Young and Willing; Holiday Inn.* 1943: *And the Angels Sing; Lady of Burlesque* (GB *Striptease Lady*) (+Natalie Visart); *Five Graves to Cairo; True to Life; Flesh and Fantasy* (+Vera West); *Ministry of Fear; No Time for Love* (+Irene); *Miracle of Morgan's Creek; Standing Room Only; The Uninvited; Going My Way; Lady in the Dark* (+Raoul Pene du Bois, Mitchell Leisen, Babs Wilomez); *Tender Comrade* (+Renie). 1944: *Double Indemnity; Hail the Conquering Hero; I Love a Soldier; And Now Tomorrow; Here Come the Waves; I'll Be Seeing You; The Affairs of Susan; Rainbow Island.*

1945: *Incendiary Blonde; Out of This World; Christmas in Connecticut* (GB *Indiscretion*) (+Milo Anderson); *You Came Along; Duffy's Tavern* (+Mary K Dodson); *The Lost Weekend; Love Letters; Masquerade in Mexico; Road to Utopia; My Reputation* (+Leah Rhodes); *The Blue Dahlia; The Strange Love of Martha Ivers; The Bride Wore Boots; To Each His Own; The Bells of St. Mary's.* 1946: *Notorious; Blue Skies* (+Waldo Angelo, Karinska); *Cross My Heart; The Perfect Marriage; California* (+Gile Steele); *The Farmer's Daughter; My Favourite Brunette; Ramrod; Blaze of Noon.* 1947: *The Other Love* (+Marion Herwood Keyes); *The Two Mrs Carrolls* (+Milo Anderson); *Welcome Stranger; Dear Ruth; Cry Wolf* (+Travilla); *Variety Girl* (+Dorothy O'Hara, Waldo Angelo); *Desert Fury; Wild Harvest; Where There's Life; Road to Rio; I Walk Alone; The Big Clock; Saigon; So Evil My Love* (+Motley); *The Sainted Sisters; Arch of Triumph* (+Marion Herwood Keyes); *The Trouble With Women.* 1948: *Dream Girl; The Emperor Waltz* (+Gile Steele); *Beyond Glory; A Foreign Affair; Night Has a Thousand Eyes; Sorry, Wrong Number; Isn't it Romantic; Rachel and the Stranger; Miss Tatlock's Millions; June Bride; The Accused; My Own True Love; A Connecticut Yankee in King Arthur's Court* (+Dodson, Steele). 1949: *The Great Gatsby; Red Hot and Blue; My Friend Irma; The Great Lover; The Heiress* (+Gile Steele); *Beyond the Forest; My Foolish Heart* (+Mary Wills); *Samson and Delilah* (+Dorothy Jeakins, Elois Jenssen, Gile Steele, Gwen Wakeling); *Thelma Jordan* (GB *The File on Thelma Jordan*); *Riding High; No Man of Her Own; Manhandled* (+Myrtil).

1950: *Sunset Boulevard; The Furies; Copper Canyon; All About Eve* (+Charles LeMaire); *September Affair; Branded; Payment on Demand* (+Walter Plunkett); *Aaron Slick from Punkin' Creek* (GB *Marshmallow Moon*); *Dark City.* 1951: *Dear Brat; That's My Boy; Here Comes the Groom; A Place in the Sun; Crosswinds; Darling, How Could You!* (GB *Rendezvous*); *Detective Story; The Greatest Show on Earth* (+Miles White, Dorothy Jeakins); *Something to Live For; Denver and Rio Grande; My Favorite Spy; When Worlds Collide.* 1952: *Carrie; Just for You; Somebody Loves Me; The Savage; The Turning Point; Road to Bali; Come Back, Little Sheba; The Stars are Singing; Pony Express; War of the Worlds; Hurricane Smith; Scared Stiff.* 1953: *Shane; The Vanquished; Forever Female; Houdini; The Caddy; The Naked Jungle; Red Garters; Casanova's Big Night* (+Yvonne Wood); *Elephant Walk; Little Boy Lost; Sangaree; Tropic Zone.* 1954: *About Mrs Leslie; Living it Up; Rear Window; Sabrina* (GB *Sabrina Fair*); *White Christmas; Three Ring Circus; The Country Girl; The Bridges at Toko-ri; Run for Cover; Strategic Air Command.*

1955: *The Far Horizons; Hell's Island; The Seven Little Foys; You're Never Too Young; To Catch a Thief; The Desperate Hours; The Trouble With Harry; Lucy Gallant; Artists and Models; The Rose Tattoo; Anything Goes* (+Tom Keogh); *The Court Jester* (+Yvonne Wood); *The Come On; The Birds and the Bees; The Girl Rush.* 1956: *The Scarlet Hour; The Man Who Knew Too Much; The Proud and the Profane; The Leather Saint; That Certain Feeling; Pardners; The Mountain; The Search for Bridey Murphy; The Ten Commandments* (+Ralph Jester, John Jensen, Dorothy Jeakins, Arnold Friberg); *Hollywood or Bust; The Rainmaker; Three Violent People; Fear Strikes Out; Funny Face* (+Hubert de Givenchy). 1957: *Gunfight at the OK Corral; Beau James; Loving You; The Joker*

Gertrude Olmstead in Becky (Andre-Ani)

Patricia Ellis in Here Comes the Groom *(Head)*

Edith Head designs for Hotel

Edith Head Sketch for Airport 1975

is Wild; The Sad Sack; Short Cut to Hell; The Tin Star; Witness for the Prosecution; The Delicate Delinquent; The Devil's Hairpin; Hear Me Good; St Louis Blues. 1958: *Hot Spell; The Matchmaker; Vertigo; Rock-a-bye Baby; As Young as We Are; Houseboat; The Buccaneer* (+Ralph Jester, John Jensen); *Separate Tables* (+Mary Grant); *The Black Orchid; Alias Jesse James; The Geisha Boy; King Creole; Maracaibo.* 1959: *Last Train from Gun Hill; Don't Give Up the Ship; The Five Pennies; A Hole in the Head; But Not for Me; That Kind of Woman; Career; The Jayhawkers; Visit to a Small Planet; Heller in Pink Tights; Teacher's Pet; A Touch of Larceny.*

1960: *The Rat Race; GI Blues; Cinderfella; The Facts of Life* (+Edward Stevenson); *Pepe; All in a Night's Work.* 1961: *On the Double; The Pleasure of His Company; The Ladies' Man; Mantrap; Breakfast at Tiffanys* (+Hubert de Givenchy, Pauline Trigere); *Blue Hawaii; The Errand Boy; Pocketful of Miracles* (+Walter Plunkett); *Summer and Smoke; My Geisha; Too Late Blues; Love in a Goldfish Bowl.* 1962: *The Counterfeit Traitor; The Man Who Shot Liberty Valance; Girls! Girls! Girls!; It's Only Money; A Girl Named Tamiko; Who's Got the Action?; Papa's Delicate Condition; The Birds; Critic's Choice; I Could Go On Singing; My Six Loves; Hatari!.* 1963: *Come Blow Your Horn; Hud; The Nutty Professor; Donovan's Reef; Wives and Lovers; A New Kind of Love* (+Christian Dior, Lanvin-Castillo, Pierre Cardin, Yves St Laurent); *Fun in Acapulco; Who's Minding the Store?; Love With The Proper Stranger; Who's Been Sleeping in My Bed?; Man's Favorite Sport?; What a Way to Go!* (+Moss Mabry). 1964: *The Carpetbaggers; Marnie; The Patsy; A House Is Not a Home; Where Love Has Gone; John Goldfarb, Please Come Home; Roustabout; Thirty-Six Hours; The Disorderly Orderly* (+Devore); *Love Has Many Faces; Sylvia; Sex and the Single Girl* (+Norman Norell); *The Yellow Rolls Royce* (+Pierre Cardin, Castillo of Paris, Coffin, Mendleson).

1965: *The Family Jewels; The Great Race* (+Donfeld); *The Hallelujah Trail; Harlow; The Sons of Katie Elder; Boeing Boeing; Red Line 7000; Inside Daisy Clover* (+Bill Thomas); *The Slender Thread; The Oscar.* 1966: *Last of the Secret Agents; Assault on a Queen; Paradise – Hawaiian Style; This Property is Condemned; Torn Curtain; Waco; Not With My Wife You Don't; Penelope; The Swinger; Hotel* (+Howard Shoup); *Warning Shot; Easy Come, Easy Go.* 1967: *Chuka; Barefoot in the Park; Caper of the Golden Bulls* (GB *Carnival of Thieves*); *El Dorado; The Secret War of Harry Frigg.* 1968: *Blue; What's So Bad About Feeling*

Good?; In Enemy Country; The Pink Jungle; House of Cards; The Hellfighters; Sweet Charity. 1969: *The Lost Man; Winning; Eye of the Cat; Butch Cassidy and the Sundance Kid; Tell Them Willie Boy is Here; Topaz; Airport; Skullduggery.*

1970: *The Forbin Project; Myra Breckinridge* (+Theadora Van Runkle); *Red Sky at Morning.* 1971: *Sometimes a Great Notion* (GB *Never Give an Inch*). 1972: *Pete 'n' Tillie; Hammersmith is Out.* 1973: *A Doll's House* (Dir/Losey) (+John Furness); *The Don is Dead; Ash Wednesday; Showdown.* 1974: *The Sting.* 1975: *Airport 1975; The Great Waldo Pepper; Rooster Cogburn; The Man Who Would Be King.* 1976: *Gable and Lombard; Family Plot; W. C. Fields and Me.* 1977: *Airport 77* (+Burton Miller). 1978: *The Big Fix; Olly, Olly, Oxen Free; Sextette.* 1980: *The Last Married Couple in America.* 1982: *Dead Men Don't Wear Plaid.*

HERSCHEL

American costume designer, real name Herschel McCoy. At Fox Studios from 1936 to 1942, and at M-G-M from 1951 to 1954.

ACADEMY AWARD NOMINATIONS:

1951: *Quo Vadis?* 1953: *Dream Wife* (b&w) (+Helen Rose).

FILMS:

1936: *Pepper; Charlie Chan at the Race Track; Back to Nature; Star For a Night; Thirty-Six Hours To Kill; 15 Maiden Lane; Thank You, Jeeves; Can This Be Dixie?; Career Woman; Charlie Chan at the Opera; Under Your Spell; Crack-Up; The Holy Terror; Laughing at Trouble; Off To the Races; Woman Wise; Time Out For Romance; Fair Warning.* 1937: *Angel's Holiday; Big Business; Midnight Taxi; Think Fast, Mr Moto; Step Lively, Jeeves!; That I May Live; Born Reckless; The Lady Escapes; Sing and Be Happy; The Great Hospital Mystery; One Mile From Heaven; She Had to Eat; Wild and Woolly; Dangerously Yours; Ali Baba Goes To Town* (+Gwen Wakeling); *Borrowing Trouble; Charlie Chan at the Olympics; Charlie Chan on Broadway; Forty-five Fathers; Lancer Spy; Without Warning; Charlie Chan at Monte Carlo; Hot Water; Thank You, Mr Moto; International Settlement; Change of*

PAULETTE DUVAL

ELEANOR BOARDMAN

RENEE ADOREE

NORMA SHEARER

CLAIRE WINDSOR

ALICE TERRY

MAE MURRAY

BLANCHE SWEET

ERTÉ

Erte, surrounded by some of the stars for whom he was to design

Heart; Battle of Broadway. 1938: *Island in the Sky; Inside Story; Keep Smiling; Mr Moto Takes a Chance; Passport Husband; Road Demon; Five of a Kind* (+Helen A Myron); *Meet the Girls; Time Out for Murder; Arizona Wildcat* (+Helen A Myron); *Pardon Our Nerve; Sharpshooters; Danger Island* (GB *Mr Moto on Danger Island*). 1939: *Winner Takes All; Frontier Marshal; Mr Moto Takes a Vacation; Charlie Chan at Treasure Island; Hollywood Cavalcade; City in Darkness; The Escape; 20,000 Men a Year; The Man Who Wouldn't Talk.*

1940: *Manhattan Heartbeat; Earthbound; Sailor's Lady; Street of Memories; Charlie Chan at the Wax Museum; Pier 13; Youth Will Be Served; Michael Shayne, Private Detective; Romance of the Rio Grande; Murder Among Friends.* 1941: *Scotland Yard; The Bride Wore Crutches; Accent on Love; Dance Hall; Dressed to Kill; Private Nurse; Charlie Chan in Rio; Great Guns; Last of the Duanes; Man at Large; We Go Fast; Moon Over Her Shoulder; Small Town Deb; On the Sunny Side.* 1942: *Dr Renault's Secret; Time To Kill; My Friend Flicka.* 1948: *Joan of Arc* (+Dorothy Jeakins, Karinska); *Tulsa.* 1951: *Quo Vadis?* 1952: *Dream Wife* (+Helen Rose); *Julius Caesar.* 1953: *Latin Lovers* (+Helen Rose); *Give a Girl a Break* (+Helen Rose). 1954: *The Prodigal.*

HERWOOD KEYES, MARION

Costume designer at M-G-M in the mid-'40s, mostly as assistant to Irene.

Marion Herwood Keyes sketch for Arch of Triumph

FILMS:

1944: *Gaslight* (GB *Murder in Thornton Square*) (+Irene); *Marriage is a Private Affair* (+Irene); *Mrs Parkington* (+Irene, Valles); *The Thin Man Goes Home* (+Irene). 1945: *Keep Your Powder Dry* (+Irene); *The Picture of Dorian Gray* (+Irene, Valles). 1945: *The Clock* (GB *Under the Clock*) (+Irene); *Without Love* (+Irene); *The Valley of Decision* (+Irene); *Weekend at the Waldorf* (+Irene); *Her Highness and the Bellboy* (+Valles). 1946: *The Hoodlum Saint* (+Irene, Valles). 1947: *The Other Love* (+Edith Head); *Body and Soul; Arch of Triumph* (+Edith Head). 1948: *No Minor Vices.*

HOPKINS, GEORGE 'NEJE'

Designed costumes and also wrote scenarios for Theda Bara at Fox.

FILMS:

1915: *A Fool There Was.* 1917: *Madame Dubarry.*

HOUSTON, GRACE

Costume designer at Universal 1947/48.

FILMS:

1947: *The Senator Was Indiscreet* (GB *Mr Ashton Was Indiscreet*); *The Naked City; All My Sons.* 1948: *Mr Peabody and the Mermaid; Abbott and Costello Meet Frankenstein* (GB *Abbott and Costello Meet the Ghosts*). 1956: *Crime of Passion.*

HUBERT, RENE

Born France 1899. Costume designer who has worked in Berlin, France, England and Hollywood – both in films and theatre. In 1935 was put under contract to Alexander Korda for *Things to Come* and worked for Korda's company, London Films, until 1940. Died 1966.

ACADEMY AWARD NOMINATIONS:

1954: *Desirée* (+Charles LeMaire). 1964: *The Visit* (b&w).

FILMS:

1927: *Frisco Sally Levy; The Callahans and the Murphys; On Ze Boulevard; Twelve Miles Out; Adam and Evil; After Midnight; Foreign Devils; Body and Soul; Quality Street.* 1930: *Those Three French Girls; War Nurse; The Easiest Way; The Temporary Widow; What a Widow.* 1931: *Indiscreet; The Secret Six; Men Call it Love.* 1933: *Perfect Understanding.* 1934: *Servant's Entrance; Marie Galante; Music in the Air; Elinor Norton; Lottery Lover* (+William Lambert).

1935: *It's a Small World; The Farmer Takes a Wife; Spring Tonic; Under the Pampas Moon; The Daring Young Man; Doubting Thomas; Curly Top; Here's to Romance; Orchids to You; Things to Come* (+John Armstrong, The Marchioness of Queensberry); *The Ghost Goes West* (+John Armstong); *Our Little Girl.* 1936: *Men Are Not Gods; Fire Over England; Wings of the Morning; Dark Journey.* 1937: *The Drum* (US *Drums*); *Farewell Again; Under the Red Robe; Dinner at the Ritz; Paradise for Two* (US *The Gaiety Girls*); *The Sky's the Limit; The Return of the Scarlet Pimpernel; The Divorce of Lady X; Break the News.* 1938: *A Yank at Oxford.* 1939: *The Four Feathers* (+Godfrey Brennan); *Over the Moon.*

1940: *The Flame of New Orleans.* 1941: *That Hamilton Woman* (GB *Lady Hamilton*). 1941: *New Wine* (GB *The Great Awakening*). 1942: *Twin Beds* (+Irene); *The Pride of the Yankees; The Powers Girl* (GB *Hello Beautiful*). 1943: *Bomber's Moon; Heaven Can Wait; Sweet Rosie O'Grady; Paris After Dark* (GB *The Night is Ending*); *The Song of Bernadette; Lifeboat; The Lodger; Jane Eyre; The Sullivans; Buffalo Bill; It Happened Tomorrow; Wintertime.* 1944: *Pin Up Girl; Irish Eyes are Smiling; Wilson; Hangover Square* (+Kay Nelson); *A Royal Scandal* (GB *Czarina*).

1945: *Billy Rose's Diamond Horseshoe* (GB *Diamond Horseshoe*) (+Kay Nelson, Sascha Brastoff, Bonnie Cashin); *Captain Eddie; Nob Hill; State Fair; The Spider; Dragonwyck.* 1946: *Centennial Summer; My Darling Clementine; Wake Up and*

Erte design for Gwen Lee in Bright Lights *(working title: "A Little Bit of Broadway")*

Gertrude Olmstead in The Callahans and the Murphys

Patricia Ellis in Paradise For Two *(Rene Hubert)*

Dream; *13 Rue Madelaine*; *The Late George Apley*; *Carnival in Costa Rica*. 1947: *Moss Rose* (+Charles LeMaire); *The Foxes of Harrow* (+Charles LeMaire); *Forever Amber* (+Charles LeMaire). 1948: *Fury at Furnace Creek*; *Green Grass of Wyoming* (+Charles LeMaire); *That Lady In Ermine* (+Charles LeMaire); *When My Baby Smiles at Me* (+Charles LeMaire). 1949: *The Fan* (GB *Lady Windermere's Fan*) (+Charles LeMaire); *The Beautiful Blonde From Bashful Bend*; *Oh, You Beautiful Doll* (+Charles LeMaire).

1950: *Ticket to Tomahawk* (+Charles LeMaire); *Love That Brute*. 1954: *Desirée* (+Charles LeMaire); 1956: *Anastasia*. 1958: *The Journey*.

1961: *The Four Horsemen of the Apocalypse* (+Walter Plunkett, Orry-Kelly). 1963: *The Visit*.

IRENE

Born Irene Lentz, Brookings, South Dakota, 1901. Died 1962. Went to Los Angeles in 1927 and studied at the Wolf School of Design, although her first choice of career had been music. She was persuaded to open a dress shop by her fiancé, Dick Jones. The shop was a success and her first film star customer, Lupe Velez, persuaded other stars to patronise her. Irene closed the shop after the death of her husband and went to Europe, spending most of the time in Paris. She opened a second shop on her return and moved to larger premises in 1933. An executive of the famous store, Bullocks Wilshire, was impressed by the window display and gave her a contract as Head of Bullocks Wilshire Costume Design Salon. It was there that she began designing clothes for stars to wear in pictures. Paramount, RKO, Columbia, United Artists – all used Irene originals for their stars. Louis B Mayer put her under contract at M-G-M in 1942 and she worked there as Executive Designer until 1949. Two years before leaving M-G-M Irene had persuaded Mayer to allow her to open a business as a wholesale designer. It was unusual for a studio to allow any of their departmental heads to divide their loyalties, and even more unusual for the patriachal head of M-G-M to give permission for such a venture. Irene Inc was financed by twenty-five departmental stores throughout the country. This gave them exclusive rights to the Irene styles in their respective cities. She continued to design off-screen clothes for stars after leaving M-G-M, but returned to films to do Doris Day's lavish wardrobe for *Midnight Lace* and costumes for Mary Peach in *A Gathering of Eagles*. Irene appeared as herself in the film *The Great Morgan*.

ACADEMY AWARD NOMINATIONS:
1948: *B F's Daughter* (b&w). 1960: *Midnight Lace*.

FILMS:

1933: *Goldie Gets Along; Flying Down to Rio* (+ Walter Plunkett).
1937: *Merrily We Live* (+ Howard Greer); *Shall We Dance; Topper* (+ Lange). 1938: *Vivacious Lady* (+ Bernard Newman); *Blockade; Algiers* (+ Omar Kiam); *You Can't Take it With You* (+ Bernard Newman); *There Goes My Heart; Service de Luxe* (+ Vera West); *Trade Winds* (+ Helen Taylor); *Topper Takes a Trip* (+ Omar Kiam); *Midnight.* 1939: *Bachelor Mother; In Name Only* (+ Edward Stevenson); *The Housekeeper's Daughter; Intermezzo: a Love Story* (+ Travis Banton); *Eternally Yours* (+ Travis Banton); *Green Hell* (+ Bernard Newman); *Too Many Husbands.*

1940: *The House Across the Bay; Waterloo Bridge* (+ Gile Steele); *He Stayed for Breakfast; Lucky Partners; Hired Wife* (+ Vera West); *Arise My Love; Seven Sinners* (+ Vera West); *This Thing Called Love* (GB *Married But Single*).

1941: *That Uncertain Feeling; Submarine Zone* (GB *Escape to Glory*); *Bedtime Story; The Lady is Willing; To Be or Not to Be.*

1942: *Twin Beds* (+Rene Hubert); *Take a Letter, Darling* (GB *The Green Eyed Woman*) (+Mitchell Leisen); *They All Kissed the Bride; The Talk of the Town; You Were Never Lovelier; The Palm Beach Story; Reunion* (GB *Mademoiselle France*); *Three Hearts for Julia; Cabin in the Sky* (+Howard Shoup, Gile Steele); *Assignment in Brittany* (+Howard Shoup, Gile Steele); *The Human Comedy; Tales of Manhattan* (+ Tree, B Newman, Wakeling, Cassini); *Slightly Dangerous; The Youngest Profession* (+ Shoup).

1943: *Dubarry Was a Lady* (+Howard Shoup); *Swing Shift Maisie* (GB *The Girl in Overalls*); *Best Foot Forward* (+Gile Steele); *Girl Crazy* (+Irene Sharaff); *The Man from Down Under* (+Gile Steele); *Thousands Cheer; Whistling in Brooklyn; Madame Curie* (+Gile Steele); *No Time for Love* (+ Edith Head); *A Guy Named Joe; The Heavenly Body; Broadway Rhythm* (+Irene Sharaff, Gile Steele).

1944: *White Cliffs of Dover* (+Gile Steele); *Andy Hardy's Blonde Trouble; Meet the People* (+Irene Sharaff); *Two Girls and a Sailor* (+Kay Dean); *Bathing Beauty* (+Kay Dean, Irene Sharaff); *Gaslight* (GB *Murder in Thornton Square*) (+Marion Herwood Keyes); *Three Men in White; An American Romance; Dragon Seed* (+Valles); *The 7th Cross; Kismet; The Thin Man Goes Home* (+Marion Herwood Keyes); *Lost in a Harem* (+Kay Dean, Valles); *Marriage is a Private Affair* (+Marion Herwood Keyes); *Mrs Parkington* (+Marion Herwood Keyes, Valles); *National Velvet* (+Kay Dean, Valles); *Meet Me in St Louis* (+Irene Sharaff); *Thirty Seconds Over Tokyo* (+Kay Dean); *Blonde Fever; Music for Millions* (+Kay Dean); *This Man's Navy* (+ Kay Dean); *Nothing but Trouble.*

1945: *Keep Your Powder Dry* (+Marion Herwood Keyes); *The Picture of Dorian Gray* (+Marion Herwood Keyes, Valles); *The Clock* (GB *Under the Clock*) (+Marion Herwood Keyes); *Without Love* (+Marion Herwood Keyes); *Son of Lassie; The Valley of Decision* (+Marion Herwood Keyes); *Thrill of a Romance* (+Kay Dean); *Twice Blessed* (+Kay Carter); *Anchors Aweigh* (+Kay Dean); *The Hidden Eye* (+Kay Carter); *Our Vines Have Tender Grapes* (+Kay Carter); *Weekend at the Waldorf* (+Marion Herwood Keyes); *Abbott and Costello in Hollywood* (GB *Bud Abbott and Lou Costello in Hollywood*) (+Kay Carter, Valles); *Dangerous Partners* (+Kay Carter), *She Went to the Races; Yolanda and the Thief* (+Irene Sharaff); *What Next, Corporal Hargrove?; Adventure; The Sailor Takes a Wife* (+Kay Carter); *Up Goes Maisie* (GB *Up She Goes*); *Ziegfeld Follies* (+ Helen Rose, Irene Sharaff); *The Harvey Girls* (+ Rose, Valles); *The Hoodlum Saint* (+Marion Herwood Keyes, Valles); *The Green Years* (+ Valles); *The Postman Always Rings Twice* (+ Marion Herwood Keyes).

1946: *Courage of Lassie; Faithful in My Fashion* (+Howard Shoup); *Little Mister Jim* (+Howard Shoup); *Three Wise Fools* (+Valles); *Two Smart People* (+Valles); *Holiday in Mexico* (+Valles); *No Leave, No Love; The Dark Mirror; Undercurrent; My Brother Talks To Horses* (+Walter Plunkett); *The Mighty McGurk* (+Howard Shoup); *Lady in the Lake; Till the Clouds Roll By* (+Helen Rose, Valles); *The Yearling* (+Valles); *Love Laughs at Andy Hardy; The Secret Heart; The Arnelo Affair; The Beginning or the End.*

1947: *High Barbaree; Undercover Maisie; Dark Delusion* (GB

Irene with Liza Minnelli in the M-G-M Wardrobe Department

58

Cynthia's Secret); *Cynthia* (GB *The Rich Full Life*); *Fiesta*; *The Hucksters*; *Living in a Big Way* (+Shirley Barker); *Merton of the Movies* (+Helen Rose); *The Romance of Rosy Ridge* (+Valles); *Song of Love* (+Walter Plunkett, Valles); *Song of the Thin Man* (+Shirley Barker); *The Unfinished Dance* (+Helen Rose); *Desire Me* (+Valles); *Green Dolphin Street* (+Plunkett, Valles); *Cass Timberlane*; *If Winter Comes*; *Tenth Avenue Angel*; *B F's Daughter* (GB *Polly Fulton*); *Three Daring Daughters* (GB *The Birds and the Bees*) (+Shirley Barker); *Summer Holiday* (+Walter Plunkett); *State of the Union* (GB *The World and His Wife*).

1948: *The Pirate* (+Tom Keogh); *On An Island With You*; *Easter Parade* (+Valles); *Julia Misbehaves*; *The Sun Comes Up*; *The Bribe*.

1949: *The Barkleys of Broadway* (+Valles); *In the Good Old Summertime* (+Valles); *Neptune's Daughter*; *Scene of the Crime*; *The Great Sinner* (+Valles); *Malaya* (GB *East of the Rising Sun*); *Key to the City*; *Please Believe Me*.

1960: *Midnight Lace*. 1961: *Lover Come Back*. 1962: *A Gathering of Eagles*.

JEAKINS, DOROTHY

Born California, 1914. Educated at the Otis Art Institute. Theatre credits in California and New York and for the American Shakespeare Festival in Stratford, Connecticut. Also designed costumes for ABC-TV and CBS-TV.

ACADEMY AWARD NOMINATIONS:

1948: **Joan of Arc* (+Karinska). 1950: **Samson and Delilah* (+Edith Head, Elois Jenssen, Gile Steele, Gwen Wakeling). 1952: *The Greatest Show on Earth* (+Edith Head, Miles White); *My Cousin Rachel* (+Charles LeMaire) (b&w). 1956: *The Ten Commandments* (+Edith Head, Ralph Jester, John Jensen, Arnold Friberg). 1961: *The Children's Hour* (GB *The Loudest Whisper*) (b&w). 1962: *The Music Man*. 1964: **The Night of the Iguana* (b&w). 1965: *The Sound of Music*. 1966: *Hawaii*. 1973: *The Way We Were* (+Moss Mabry). 1987: *The Dead*.

FILMS:

1948: *Joan of Arc* (+Karinska, Herschel). 1949: *Samson and Delilah* (+Edith Head, Elois Jenssen, Gile Steele, Gwen Wakeling). 1950: *Cyrano de Bergerac*. 1951: *Outcast of Poker Flats* (+Charles LeMaire); *The Big Sky*; *The Greatest Show on Earth* (+Edith Head, Miles White); 1952: *Belles on their Toes* (+Charles LeMaire); *Titanic* (+Charles LeMaire); *Les Misérables* (+Charles LeMaire); *Lure of the Wilderness* (+Charles LeMaire); *Stars and Stripes Forever* (GB *Marching Along*) (+Charles LeMaire); *My Cousin Rachel* (+Charles LeMaire); *Niagara* (+Charles LeMaire); *Treasure of the Golden Condor*. 1953: *City of Bad Men* (+Charles LeMaire); *White Witch Doctor* (+Charles LeMaire); *Inferno* (+Charles LeMaire); *The Kid From Left Field* (+Charles LeMaire); *Beneath the Twelve Mile Reef* (+Charles LeMaire). 1954: *Three Coins in the Fountain* (+Charles LeMaire); *The Ten Commandments* (+Edith Head, Ralph Jester, John Jensen, Arnold Friberg). 1956: *Friendly Persuasion*. 1957: *South Pacific*. 1958: *Green Mansions*. 1959: *The Unforgiven*. 1960: *Elmer Gantry*; *Let's Make Love*. 1961: *All Fall Down*; *The Children's Hour* (GB *The Loudest Whisper*). 1962: *The Music Man*. 1963: *Ensign Pulver*; *The Best Man*. 1964: *The Night of the Iguana*; *The Sound of Music*. 1965: *The Fool Killer*. 1966: *Any Wednesday* (GB *Bachelor Girl Apartment*); *Hawaii*. 1967: *The Flim-Flam Man* (GB *One Born Every Minute*); *Reflections in a Golden Eye*. 1968: *Finian's Rainbow*; *The Fixer*; *The Stalking Moon*; *True Grit*. 1969: *The Molly Maguires*. 1970: *Little Big Man*. 1972: *Fuzz*; *Fat City*. 1973: *The Way We Were* (+Moss Mabry); *The Iceman Cometh*. 1975: *Young Frankenstein*; *The Hindenburg*; *The Yakuza*. 1977: *Audrey Rose*. 1978: *The Betsy*. 1979: *Love and Bullets*; *North Dallas Forty*. 1981: *On Golden Pond*; *The Postman Always Rings Twice*. 1987: *The Dead*.

JENSSEN, ELOIS

Born in Palo Alto, California, and attended the Westlake School for Girls in Southern California. At the age of thirteen, she was enrolled at the Parson's School of Design in Paris and

Sketch by Irene for Easter Parade

Dolores Del Rio in Flying Down to Rio *(Irene)*

Left: Elois Jenssen design for Hedy Lamarr in Let's Live a Little. *Right: Cecil B DeMille and Elois Jenssen with* Samson and Delilah *sketches*

From left: costume for Marie Windsor in Outpost in Morocco; *Hedy Lamarr in* Dishonored Lady; *gown for Hedy Lamarr in* Dishonored Lady. *All designs by Elois Jenssen*

studied fashion design until World War II interrupted the course. The time spent in Paris was invaluable as visits to the great couture houses were part of the curriculum. The Jenssen family returned to America and Elois took a four-year course at the Chouinard Art Institute. After graduating, she presented herself to Hunt Stromberg, who had just left M-G-M to start his own production company. Natalie Visart had just signed with Stromberg, but needed a sketch artist and assistant. Elois Jenssen worked with her for three years until Miss Visart left to get married. Hedy Lamarr had liked the sketches Miss Jenssen had done for the film *The Strange Lady*, and asked her to design the clothes for the Hunt Stromberg production, *Dishonored Lady*. An argument between Miss Lamarr and Stromberg almost caused the project to abort before it started, but peace was restored, and a very young Miss Jenssen created a stunningly sophisticated series of outfits for Hedy Lamarr. She also received her first screen costume credit for the picture.

After Stromberg closed his production office, Miss Jenssen freelanced for a while, working on another Hedy Lamarr film, *Let's Live a Little*, among others. At the end of 1948, five designers began work on the mammoth task of creating costumes for the Cecil B DeMille religious epic, *Samson and Delilah*. They were Edith Head, Dorothy Jeakins, Elois Jenssen, Gile Steele and Gwen Wakeling, and they all received a 1950 Academy Award for the best colour costume design.

Next came a three-year contract with Fox and, at the end of that, Miss Jenssen was asked to work on the Ann Sothern television series "Private Secretary". She also worked on "I Love Lucy" (with Lucille Ball), "My Living Doll" (with Julie Newmar) and "Bracken's World" (with Evelyn Keyes).

Elois Jenssen is a member of the Costume Designers' Guild, the Academy of Motion Picture Arts and Sciences and The Fashion Group. For several years she taught motion picture and television design at the Chouinard Art Institute.

ACADEMY AWARD NOMINATIONS:
1950: ★*Samson and Delilah* (+ Edith Head, Dorothy Jeakins, Gile Steele, Gwen Wakeling). 1982: *Tron* (+ Rosanna Norton).

FILMS:
1947: *Dishonored Lady*; *Lured* (GB *Personal Column*). 1948: *So This Is New York*; *The Pitfall*; *Let's Live a Little*; *Samson and Delilah* (+Edith Head, Dorothy Jeakins, Gile Steele, Gwen Wakeling). 1949: *Outpost in Morocco*; *A Kiss for Corliss*; *Mrs Mike*. 1950: *The Man Who Cheated Himself*; *The Groom Wore Spurs* (for Joan Davis); *Cry Danger*. 1951: *Phone Call From a Stranger*. 1952: *Deadline, USA* (+Charles LeMaire); *Diplomatic*

Opposite: Howard Greer costume for Trouble With Wives

60

Courier; We're Not Married (+Charles LeMaire); *Something For the Birds* (+Charles LeMaire). 1955: *Forever Darling* (for Lucille Ball). 1982: *Tron* (+Rosanna Norton).

JOHNSTONE, ANNA HILL

Born Greenville, South Carolina, 1913. Extensive theatre credits from 1946. Has designed costumes for many of Elia Kazan's films.

ACADEMY AWARD NOMINATIONS:
1972: *The Godfather.* 1981: *Ragtime.*

SFTA NOMINATION:
1972: *The Godfather.*

FILMS:
1948: *Portrait of Jenny* (GB *Jennie*) (+Lucinda Ballard). 1953: *On the Waterfront.* 1954: *East of Eden.* 1956: *Baby Doll; Edge of the City* (GB *A Man is Ten Feet Tall*). 1957: *A Face in the Crowd.* 1958: *Stage Struck.* 1959: *Odds Against Tomorrow; Wild River.* 1961: *Splendor in the Grass.* 1962: *David and Lisa.* 1963: *America, America* (GB *The Anatolian Smile*); *Fail Safe; Ladybug, Ladybug.* 1964: *The Pawnbroker; Harvey Middleman, Fireman.* 1965: *The Group.* 1967: *Trilogy; Bye Bye Braverman.* 1968: *The Swimmer; The Night They Raided Minsky's.* 1969: *Alice's Restaurant; Truman Capote's Trilogy.* 1970: *Cotton Comes to Harlem; There Was a Crooked Man.* 1971: *Who is Harry Kellerman and Why is He saying Those Terrible Things About Me?* 1972: *The Godfather; Play It Again, Sam; Come Back Charleston Blue; The Effect of Gamma Rays on Man-in-the-Moon Marigolds.* 1973: *Summer Wishes, Winter Dreams; Gordon's War; Serpico.* 1975: *The Taking of Pelham One Two Three; Dog Day Afternoon; Report to the Commissioner* (GB *Operation Undercover*). 1976: *The Last Tycoon; The Next Man.* 1978: *King of the Gypsies.* 1979: *Going in Style.* 1981: *Prince of the City; Ragtime.* 1982: *The Verdict.* 1983: *Daniel; A Night in Heaven.* 1986: *Power.*

KALLOCH, ROBERT

Born in New York City, 1893. Educated at Dwight's Preparatory School and at the New York School of Fine and Applied Art. Like many other American dress designers, Kalloch learned his job at the New York, London and Paris branches of Lucille Ltd, where he began as a sketch artist before World War I. One of Lucille's most famous clients was Mrs Irene Castle, who was so elegant that she made a career of exhibition ballroom dancing seem quite respectable, and Robert Kalloch designed many of her dresses. He also designed for Anna Pavlova, including some of her ballet costumes.

In the early '30s, Kalloch went to Columbia Pictures. In the late '20s this studio had been making low-budget pictures and was unable to attract any major stars for long-term contract. The head of the studio was Harry Cohn and, in an effort to improve the image of Columbia, he persuaded actresses like Irene Dunne, Nancy Carroll, Grace Moore, Lilian Harvey and Fay Wray to star in his films. Robert Kalloch was the first good designer to work at Columbia and, because of Cohn's dislike of period films, was given plenty of opportunity to design sophisticated wardrobes which were always given a lot of publicity in the film magazines. Harry Cohn insisted on checking costume sketches for all his leading ladies to make quite sure that they were dressed "in good taste"

Kalloch stayed at Columbia until 1941 and then moved to M-G-M for two years. After leaving M-G-M, he did occasional freelance work.

FILMS:
1932: *That's My Boy; Hat Check Girl; Air Hostess; The Bitter Tea of General Yen* (+Edward Stevenson); *Child of Manhattan.* 1933: *Parole Girl; The Circus Queen Murder; The Woman I Stole; Lady For a Day; Brief Moment; The Wrecker; My Woman; Master of Men; Fog; Let's Fall in Love; It Happened One Night; Before*

Opposite: Howard Greer among gowns for Forbidden Paradise

Midnight. 1934: *Sisters Under the Skin; One Night of Love; Lady By Choice; The Captain Hates the Sea; I'll Fix It; Most Precious Thing in Life; Fugitive Lady; Mills of the Gods.*

1935: *I'll Love you Always; Let's Live Tonight; Eight Bells; Love Me Forever* (GB *On Wings of Love*). 1936: *Women in Distress; Women of Glamor.* 1937: *Let's Get Married; Racketeers in Exile; The League of Frightened Men; Motor Madness; Venus Makes Trouble; Girls Can Play; The Devil is Driving; History Is Made At Night; A Fight to the Finish; The Frame-Up; The Awful Truth; A Dangerous Adventure; It Happened in Hollywood* (GB *Once a Hero*); *Murder in Greenwich Village; I'll Take Romance; Paid to Dance; The Shadow; It's All Yours; All-American Sweetheart; No Time to Marry; Start Cheering; She Married an Artist; There's Always a Woman; Women in Prison; A Dangerous Adventure; It Can't Last Forever; Life Begins With Love.* 1938: *Holiday* (GB *Free to Live*); *The Lone Wolf in Paris; Who Killed Gail Preston?; Squadron of Honor; Little Miss Roughneck; Golden*

Mary Brian in Fog *(Robert Kalloch)*

Handwritten annotation on the sketch:

Ida Lupino
"Weather or No"

Dove grey two-
piece faille silk
suit —
The frock has a
pencil silhouette-
is sleeveless and
has a self-fabric
belt. the neck is
out lined with a
self-fabric twisted
cord.
The coat — lavishly
trimmed in silver
fox has a swagger
back and elbow-
length sleeves.
self-fabric hat-
off the face — bonnety
look — Stitched
grey fabric shoes.
and bag.

Robert Kalloch sketch for Ida Lupino in Let's Get Married (Weather Or No *was the film's working title*)

Boy; I Am the Law; The Lady Objects; Blondie; The Lone Wolf Spy Hunt (GB The Lone Wolf's Daughter); Let Us Live. 1939: The Lady and the Mob; Blind Alley; Only Angels Have Wings; Good Girls Go to Paris; Blondie Takes a Vacation; Mr Smith Goes to Washington; The Amazing Mr Williams; His Girl Friday; Music in My Heart; The Lone Wolf Strikes.

1940: Island of Doomed Men; The Lone Wolf Meets a Lady; He Stayed for Breakfast; Blondie Has Servant Trouble; Blondie on a Budget; Angels Over Broadway; Blondie Plays Cupid; The Lady in Question. 1941: I'll Wait for You; Shadow of the Thin Man; The People v Dr Kildare (GB My Life is Yours); The Getaway; Ringside Maisie (GB Cash and Carry); Dr Kildare's Wedding Day (GB Mary Names the Day); Life Begins for Andy Hardy; Whistling in the Dark; Honky Tonk (+ Gile Steele); Married Bachelor; H M Pulham Esq; Babes on Broadway; Johnny Eager; You'll Never Get Rich; Tortilla Flat (+ Steele); We Were Dancing (+ Adrian). 1942: Rio Rita (+ Gile Steele); Her Cardboard Lover; I Married an Angel (+ Motley); Mrs Miniver (+ Gile Steele); Pacific Rendezvous; Crossroads; Panama Hattie; The War Against Mrs Hadley; For Me and My Gal; White Cargo; Random Harvest; Somewhere I'll Find

You; Journey for Margaret; Ship Ahoy. 1945: Suspense. 1947: Mr Blandings Builds His Dream House.

KARLICE

Designer on several films made for PRC from 1944 to 1946.

FILMS:

1944: The Town Went Wild. 1945: Mask of Diijon. 1946: Devil Bat's Daughter; Avalanche; Queen of Burlesque; Wild West.

KAUFMAN, RITA

Born in Lincoln, Nebraska and educated at the Convent of the Sacred Heart at Lincoln University. In 1931 she started work

Opposite: Gloria Swanson in Music in the Air *(Rene Hubert)*

Merle Oberon in The Man From the Folies Bérgère *(Kiam)*

An Omar Kiam design for Splendor

at Hattie Carnegie's fashion house in New York, but left shortly afterwards when put under contract to the Fox West Coast Studio as Fashion Creator. During her time at Fox she designed for the top stars at the studio including Janet Gaynor, Clara Bow, Marion Nixon and Helen Vinson, and worked in collaboration with the designers David Cox and Joe Strassner. Rita Kaufman married the actor Edmund Lowe and retired from the film industry.

FILMS:

1932: *Call Her Savage* (+David Cox); *Sherlock Holmes; Me and My Gal* (GB *Pier 13*); *State Fair.* 1933: *Bondage; Hello, Sister; Humanity; Infernal Machine; Adorable; I Loved You Wednesday; The Devil's in Love; Dr Bull; Paddy the Next Best Thing; The Power and the Glory; My Weakness* (+Joe Strassner); *Shanghai Madness; The Worst Woman in Paris?; Hoopla; Mr Skitch; As Husbands Go; I Am Suzanne; Carolina; Coming Out Party.* 1934: *All Men are Enemies; Stand Up and Cheer; Change of Heart; Now I'll Tell* (GB *When New York Sleeps*); *The World Moves On; Grand Canary; Springtime for Henry.*

KAY, KATHLEEN

M-G-M Wardrobe Department from 1925/27. At Fox 1927/28.

FILMS:

1925: *Dance Madness* (+Maude Marsh, Andre-Ani); *The Torrent* (+Maude Marsh, Andre-Ani, Max Ree); *Monte Carlo* (+Maude Marsh, Andre-Ani). 1926: *Money Talks* (+Maude Marsh, Andre-Ani); *Beverly of Graustark* (+Maude Marsh, Andre-Ani); *Brown of Harvard* (+Maude Marsh); *The Boy Friend* (+Maude Marsh, Andre-Ani); *The Gay Deceiver* (Maude Marsh, Andre-Ani); *The Waning Sex* (+Maude Marsh, Andre-Ani); *Love's Blindness* (+Maude Marsh, Andre-Ani); *There You Are!* (+Maude Marsh); *Upstage* (+Maude Marsh, Andre-Ani); *The Fire Brigade* (+Maude March, Andre-Ani). 1927: *Altars of Desire* (+Maude Marsh, Andre-Ani); *Heaven on Earth* (+Maude Marsh, Andre-Ani); *Chain Lightning; Seventh Heaven.* 1928: *Four Sons.*

KIAM, OMAR

Born in Mexico of American parents and educated at Poughkeepsie Military Academy in New York. Started work in a department store in Houston, Texas, and worked his way up to become Head Designer for the Millinery Department. Omar Kiam lived and worked in Paris for some time and returned to work in his own studio in New York. In the '30s he was designing costumes for Broadway plays such as "Dishonored Lady," "Dinner at Eight" and "Reunion in Vienna," but left New York to become Head Designer for all Samuel Goldwyn's productions. Omar Kiam also worked for David Selznick and Hal Roach.

FILMS:

1934: *We Live Again* (GB *Resurrection*); *Kid Millions; The Mighty Barnum; Clive of India; Folies Bérgère* (GB *The Man From the Folies Bérgère*); *The Wedding Night; Cardinal Richelieu.* 1935: *Call Of the Wild; Les Misérables; The Dark Angel; Barbary Coast; Splendor; Strike Me Pink; These Three.* 1936: *One Rainy Afternoon; Dodsworth; Come and Get It; The Gay Desperado; Beloved Enemy.* 1937: *Pick a Star; A Star is Born; Woman Chases Man; Stella Dallas; Dead End; The Hurricane; The Goldwyn Follies; The Adventures of Marco Polo.* 1938: *Algiers* (+Irene); *The Cowboy and the Lady; The Young in Heart; Wuthering Heights; Zenobia.*

KING, MURIEL

American fashion designer whose work appeared in several films between 1935 and 1944.

FILMS:

1935: *Sylvia Scarlet* (+Bernard Newman). 1937: *Stage Door* (inc. fashion show); *Manhattan Merry-Go-Round* (GB *Manhattan Music Box*) (+Eloise). 1940: *Back Street* (+Vera West). 1943: *Cover Girl* (+Travis Banton, Gwen Wakeling). 1944: *Christmas Holiday* (+Howard Greer, Vera West); *Casanova Brown; The Woman in the Window.*

Opposite: Loretta Young in He Stayed for Breakfast *(Irene)*

KOCH, NORMA

American designer, in films from 1951. Often worked for Robert Aldrich. Died 1979.

ACADEMY AWARD NOMINATIONS:

1962: *Whatever Happened to Baby Jane? (b&w). 1964: Hush, Hush, Sweet Charlotte (b&w). 1972: Lady Sings the Blues (+Ray Aghayan, Bob Mackie).

FILMS:

1951: Rose of Cimarron. 1954: Vera Cruz. 1956: Slightly Scarlet. 1957: The She Devil; Sayonara. 1960: Cry for Happy. 1961: The Last Sunset. 1962: Whatever Happened to Baby Jane? 1963: Four For Texas; Kings of the Sun. 1964: Hush, Hush, Sweet Charlotte. 1965: The Flight of the Phoenix. 1967: The Way West. 1969: MacKenna's Gold. 1971: The Grissom Gang. 1972: Lady Sings the Blues (+Ray Aghayan, Bob Mackie).

LAMBERT, WILLIAM

Designer at Fox from 1933–36.

FILMS:

1933: Sailor's Luck; Pleasure Cruise; Berkeley Square. 1934: She Was a Lady; The White Parade; Hell in the Heavens; The County Chairman; Helldorado; Lottery Lover; One More Spring; Under Pressure; The Little Colonel. 1935: In Old Kentucky; Welcome Home; Redheads on Parade; Bad Boy; Thanks a Million; Way Down East; Professional Soldier; Charlie Chan at the Circus; Every Saturday Night; Here Comes Trouble; Little Miss Nobody; The Song and Dance Man; The Gay Deception. 1936: The Country Beyond; The First Baby; Human Cargo; Champagne Charlie; Educating Father; The Crime of Dr Forbes; High Tension.

LANGE, SAMUEL

Costume designer at Columbia 1935/36.

FILMS:

1935: If You Could Only Cook; Don't Gamble with Love; The Lone Wolf Returns; Hell-Ship Morgan; Mr Deeds Goes to Town; Pride of the Marines; You May Be Next (GB Panic On the Air). 1936: And So They Were Married; Devil's Squadron; Roaming Lady; Blackmailer. 1937: Love From a Stranger; Topper (+Irene).

LEHMANN, OLGA

Born in Chile of British parents. Painter, costume designer and set designer. Studied at the Slade School of Fine Art. First work in the film industry as a scenic artist, later designing sets and costumes.

FILMS:

1955: The Gamma People. 1956: Safari; Laughter in Paradise. 1957: Robbery Under Arms. 1958: The Inn of the Sixth Happiness (+Margaret Furse); tom thumb. 1959: The Scapegoat. 1960: The Millionairess. 1961: The Guns of Navarone. 1963: The Victors. 1964: First Men in the Moon. 1969: Captain Nemo and the Underwater City. 1971: Kidnapped.

LEMAIRE, CHARLES

Born Chicago. Started as a vaudeville actor and changed to costume design when he was offered a job at Andre-Sherri in New York. Many Broadway shows in the early '20s including "Ziegfield's Follies", "George White's Scandals" and "Earl Carroll's Vanities", also on and off stage costumes for many Broadway stars. While in New York, Charles LeMaire designed for three films, The Heart of a Siren (1925), George White's Scandals (1934) and The Men in Her Life (1941). In 1943 LeMaire became Executive Designer and Director of Wardrobe for Fox and worked there until 1949, leaving to open his own salon. He retired in 1962 to devote his time to painting and writing. He and his wife had several successful joint exhibitions. Died 1985.

ACADEMY AWARD NOMINATIONS:

1950: *All About Eve (+Edith Head) (b&w). 1951: The Model and the Marriage Broker (+Renie) (b&w); David and Bathsheba (+Edward Stevenson). 1952: My Cousin Rachel (+Dorothy Jeakins) (b&w); With a Song in My Heart. 1953: *The Robe (+Emile Santiago); The President's Lady (b&w); How to Marry a Millionaire (+Travilla). 1954: Desirée (+Rene Hubert); There's No Business Like Show Business (+Travilla, Miles White). 1955: *Love is a Many-Splendored Thing; The Virgin Queen (+Mary Wills). 1956: Teenage Rebel (+Mary Wills) (b&w). 1957: An Affair To Remember. 1958: A Certain Smile (+Mary Wills). 1959: The Diary of Anne Frank (+Mary Wills) (b&w).

FILMS:

1925: Heart of a Siren. 1933: Take a Chance. 1934: George White's 1935 Scandals. 1941: The Men in her Life. 1946: Strange Triangle; The Razor's Edge (+Oleg Cassini); Boomerang (+Kay Nelson).

1947: The Home Stretch (+Kay Nelson); Moss Rose (+Kay Nelson); Miracle on 34th Street (GB The Big Heart) (+Kay Nelson); The Ghost and Mrs Muir (+Eleanor Behm); I Wonder Who's Kissing Her Now? (+Bonnie Cashin); Thunder in the Valley (GB Bob, Son of Battle) (+Eleanor Behm); Mother Wore Tights (+Orry-Kelly); A Kiss of Death; The Foxes of Harrow (+Rene Hubert); Forever Amber (+Rene Hubert); Nightmare Alley (+Bonnie Cashin); Daisy Kenyon; Gentleman's Agreement (+Kay Nelson); Captain From Castile; You Were Meant for Me (+Kay Nelson); Call Northside 777 (+Kay Nelson); Sitting Pretty (+Kay Nelson). 1948: Scudda Hoo! Scudda Hay! (GB Summer Lightning) (+Bonnie Cashin); Green Grass of Wyoming (+Rene Hubert); Give My Regards to Broadway (+Bonnie Cashin); The Iron Curtain (+Bonnie Cashin); The Street With No Name (+Kay Nelson); Deep Waters; The Walls of Jericho (+Kay Nelson); Cry of the City (+Bonnie Cashin); Apartment for Peggy (+Kay Nelson); Road House (+Kay Nelson); The Luck of the Irish (+Bonnie Cashin); Unfaithfully Yours (+Bonnie Cashin); Yellow Sky; The Snake Pit (+Bonnie Cashin); That Lady in Ermine (+Rene Hubert); That Wonderful Urge (+Oleg Cassini); When My Baby Smiles at Me (+Rene Hubert); Chicken Every Sunday; A Letter to Three Wives (+Kay Nelson); Mother is a Freshman (GB Mother Knows Best) (+Kay Nelson); Down To the Sea in Ships.

1949: The Fan (GB Lady Windermere's Fan) (+Rene Hubert); Mr Belvedere Goes to College (+Bonnie Cashin); It Happens Every Spring (+Bonnie Cashin); House of Strangers; Come to the Stable (+Kay Nelson); You're My Everything; Everybody Does it (+Kay Nelson); Thieves' Highway; Pinky; Oh, You Beautiful Doll; Dancing in the Dark (+Travilla); Whirlpool (+Oleg Cassini); When Willie Comes Marching Home (+Travilla); Mother Didn't Tell Me (+Travilla); Three Came Home; Cheaper By the Dozen (+Edward Stevenson); Under My Skin; Wabash Avenue.

1950: The Gunfighter (+Travilla); Ticket to Tomahawk (+Rene Hubert); Panic in the Streets (+Travilla); Where the Sidewalk Ends (+Oleg Cassini); Stella (+Edward Stevenson); Mr 880 (+Travilla); No Way Out (+Travilla); My Blue Heaven; I'll Get By (+Travilla); All About Eve (+Edith Head); Two Flags West (+Kay Nelson); The Jackpot (+Edward Stevenson); American Guerilla in the Philippines (GB I Shall Return) (+Travilla); Halls of Montezuma; I'd Climb the Highest Mountain (+Edward Stevenson); For Heavens Sake; Call Me Mister; The Thirteenth Letter (+Edward Stevenson); You're in the Navy Now; Follow the Sun (+Renie); Rawhide (+Travilla); Bird of Paradise (+Travilla); I Can Get It for You Wholesale (GB This is My Affair); Fourteen Hours (+Edward Stevenson); The House on Telegraph Hill (+Renie).

1951: On The Riviera (+Travilla, Oleg Cassini); The Guy Who Came Back (+Renie); The Frogmen; Secret of Convict Lake (+Edward Stevenson); Take Care of My Little Girl (+Travilla); As Young As You Feel (+Renie); Mr Belvedere Rings the Bell (+Renie); Meet Me After the Show (+Travilla); People Will Talk; David and Bathsheba (+Edward Stevenson); The Day the Earth Stood Still (+Perkins Bailey, Travilla); Love Nest

Opposite: Rita Hayworth in The Lady from Shanghai *(Louis)*

(+Renie); *Let's Make It Legal* (+Renie); *Anne of the Indies* (+Edward Stevenson); *Fixed Bayonets*; *Elopement*; *Golden Girl*; *The Model and the Marriage Broker* (+Renie); *Red Skies of Montana* (+Edward Stevenson); *The Pride of St Louis* (+Travilla); *With a Song in My Heart*; *Return of the Texan* (+Renie); *Viva Zapata!* (+Travilla); *Five Fingers*.

1952: *Deadline, USA* (GB *Deadline*) (+Elois Jenssen); *Belles on Their Toes* (+Dorothy Jeakins); *Outcasts of Poker Flats*; *Wait Til the Sun Shines, Nellie* (+Renie); *Lydia Bailey* (+Travilla); *Les Misérables* (+Dorothy Jeakins); *Were Not Married* (+Elois Jenssen); *Dreamboat* (+Renie); *Don't Bother to Knock* (+Travilla); *What Price Glory* (+Edward Stevenson); *Lure of the Wilderness* (+Dorothy Jeakins); *O Henry's Full House* (GB *Full House*) (+Edward Stevenson); *Monkey Business* (+Travilla); *Snows of Kilimanjaro*; *Bloodhounds of Broadway* (+Travilla). *Night Without Sleep* (+Renie); *Something for the Birds* (+Elois Jenssen); *Way of a Gaucho* (+Mario Vanarelli); *Stars and Stripes Forever* (GB *Marching Along*) (+Dorothy Jeakins); *My Pal Gus*; *My Cousin Rachel* (+Dorothy Jeakins); *Taxi* (+Renie); *Treasure of the Golden Condor* (+Dorothy Jeakins); *Niagara* (+Dorothy Jeakins); *The Silver Whip* (+Edward Stevenson); *Tonight We Sing* (+Renie); *The President's Lady* (+Renie); *Destination Gobi*.

1953: *The Farmer Takes a Wife* (+Travilla); *Down Among the Sheltering Palms* (+Travilla); *Man on a Tightrope* (+Ursula Maes); *Titanic* (+Dorothy Jeakins); *Powder River* (+Travilla); *The Girl Next Door* (+Travilla); *The Desert Rats*; *Pickup on South Street* (+Travilla); *City of Bad Men* (+Dorothy Jeakins); *Gentlemen Prefer Blondes* (+Travilla); *A Blueprint for Murder*; *White Witch Doctor* (+Dorothy Jeakins); *Dangerous Crossing* (+Renie); *Inferno* (+Dorothy Jeakins); *The Kid From Left Field* (+Dorothy Jeakins); *Mr Scoutmaster* (+Renie); *The Robe* (+Emile Santiago); *How to Marry a Millionaire* (+Travilla); *King of the Khyber Rifles* (+Travilla); *Beneath the Twelve Mile Reef* (+Dorothy Jeakins); *Three Young Texans* (+Travilla); *Man in the Attic* (+Travilla); *Hell and High Water* (+Travilla); *Night People* (+Ursula Maes); *Vicki* (+Renie).

1954: *River of No Return* (+Travilla); *Prince Valiant*; *The Siege at Red River* (+Renie); *Three Coins in the Fountain* (+Dorothy Jeakins); *Broken Lance* (+Travilla); *Garden of Evil* (+Travilla); *Demetrius and the Gladiators*; *The Egyptian*; *Woman's World*; *The Black Widow* (+Travilla); *Desiree* (+Rene Hubert); *There's No Business Like Show Business* (+Travilla, Miles White); *Prince of Players* (+Mary Wills); *Untamed* (+Renie); *A Man Called Peter* (+Renie).

1955: *Violent Saturday* (+Kay Nelson); *Daddy Long Legs* (+Kay Nelson, Tom Keogh); *Soldier of Fortune*; *The Seven Year Itch* (+Travilla); *The Virgin Queen* (+Mary Wills); *House of Bamboo*; *How To Be Very, Very Popular* (+Travilla); *The Left Hand of God* (+Travilla); *Love is a Many-Splendored Thing*; *The Tall Men* (+Travilla); *Seven Cities of Gold* (+Adele Balkan);

Jean Louis sketch for It Had To Be You

The Girl in the Red Velvet Swing; *The Rains of Ranchipur* (+Travilla, Helen Rose); *The Bottom of the Bottle* (GB *Beyond the River*) (+Travilla); *The Lieutenant Wore Skirts* (+Travilla); *Carousel* (+Mary Wills); *On the Threshold of Space*; *The Man in the Gray Flannel Suit*; *Yacht on the High Seas* (+Adele Balkan); *The Revolt of Mamie Stover* (+Travilla).

1956: *Twenty Three Paces to Baker Street* (+Travilla); *Hilda Crane*; *D-Day the 6th of June*; *The Proud Ones* (+Travilla); *Bus Stop* (+Travilla); *Bigger Than Life* (+Mary Wills); *The Last Wagon* (+Mary Wills); *The Best Things in Life are Free*; *Between Heaven and Hell* (+Mary Wills); *Teenage Rebel* (+Mary Wills); *The Girl Can't Help It*; *Top Secret Affair* (GB *Their Secret Affair*); *Three Brave Men* (+Adele Balkan); *Oh Men! Oh Women!*

1957: *The Way to the Gold* (+Adele Balkan); *The Wayward Bus* (+Mary Wills); *The Desk Set* (GB *His Other Woman*); *A Hatful of Rain* (+Mary Wills); *Bernardine* (+Mary Wills); *An Affair to Remember*; *The Sun Also Rises* (+Fontana Sisters of Rome); *Three Faces of Eve* (+Renie); *No Down Payment* (+Mary Wills); *Forty Guns* (+Leah Rhodes); *Stopover Tokyo*; *April Love* (+Renie); *The Enemy Below*; *Gift of Love*; *The Long Hot Summer* (+Adele Palmer); *The Young Lions* (+Adele Balkan; *Will Success Spoil Rock Hunter?*; *A Certain Smile* (+Wills).

1958: *Ten North Frederick*; *From Hell to Texas* (GB *Manhunt*) (+Adele Balkan); *The Bravados* (+Adele Balkan); *The Fly* (+Adele Balkan); *The Hunters*; *In Love and War* (+Adele Palmer); *Mardi Gras*; *Rally Round The Flag Boys*; *These Thousand Hills*; *Compulsion* (+Adele Palmer); *Thunder in the Sun*; *The Diary of Anne Frank* (+Mary Wills); *The Fiend Who Walked the West* (+Adele Palmer); *The Remarkable Mr Pennypacker* (+Wills). *Warlock*.

1959: *A Woman Obsessed*; *Say One For Me* (+Adele Palmer); *The Man Who Understood Women*.

1960: *The Marriage-Go-Round*. 1961: *A Walk on the Wild Side*.

LILLIAN

Designer at Fox studio 1934/35.

FILMS:

1934: *Charlie Chan in Paris*. 1935: *Life Begins at Forty*; *$10 Raise* (GB *Mr Faintheart*).

LOUIS, JEAN

Born Paris, 1907, and studied at the Arts Decoratifs. Became a sketch artist at the Paris couture house of Drecol, then went to New York to work for Hattie Carnegie for seven years. Jean Louis worked as Head Designer for Columbia Pictures from 1944 until 1958, when he moved to Universal. He ran his own couture business, Jean Louis Inc, and although not under long term contract to a studio, continued to supply clothes for films.

ACADEMY AWARD NOMINATIONS:

1950: *Born Yesterday* (b&w). 1952: *Affair in Trinidad* (b&w). 1953: *From Here to Eternity* (b&w). 1954: *A Star Is Born* (+Mary Ann Nyberg, Irene Sharaff); *It Should Happen To You* (b&w). 1955: *Queen Bee* (b&w). 1956: **The Solid Gold Cadillac* (b&w). 1957: *Pal Joey*. 1958: *Bell, Book and Candle*. 1961: *Judgement at Nuremburg* (b&w); *Back Street*. 1965: *Ship of Fools* (+Bill Thomas) (b&w). 1966: *Gambit*. 1967: *Thoroughly Modern Millie*.

FILMS:

1944: *Secret Command*; *Strange Affair*; *Together Again*; *Tonight and Every Night* (+Vertes). 1945: *A Thousand and One Nights*; *Over Twenty One*; *Kiss and Tell*; *One Way to Love*; *Tomorrow is Forever*; *The Bandit of Sherwood Forest*; *Gilda*; *Meet Me on Broadway*. 1946: *Renegades*; *Perilous Holiday*; *The Jolson Story*; *The Thrill of Brazil*; *Gallant Journey*; *Dead Reckoning*; *Johnny O'Clock*; *Mr District Attorney*; *Framed* (GB *Paula*); *The Guilt of Janet Ames* (+Travis Banton). 1947: *Down to Earth*; *Her Husband's Affair*; *The Corpse Came COD*; *It Had to Be You*; *The Swordsman*; *Relentless*; *I Love Trouble*; *To the Ends of the Earth*; *The Sign of the Ram*; *The Mating of Millie*. 1948: *The Lady From Shanghai*; *Lulu Belle*; *The Black Arrow* (GB *The Black Arrow Strikes*); *The Fuller Brush Man* (GB *That Mad Mr Jones*); *The Loves of Carmen*; *The Gallant Blade*; *The Return of October*; *You Gotta Stay Happy*; *The Man from Colorado*; *The Dark Past*; *Shockproof*; *Knock on Any Door*; *Slightly French*; *The Undercover Man*; *The Walking Hills*. 1949: *We Were Strangers*;

Opposite: Claire Trevor in Crossroads *(Robert Kalloch)*

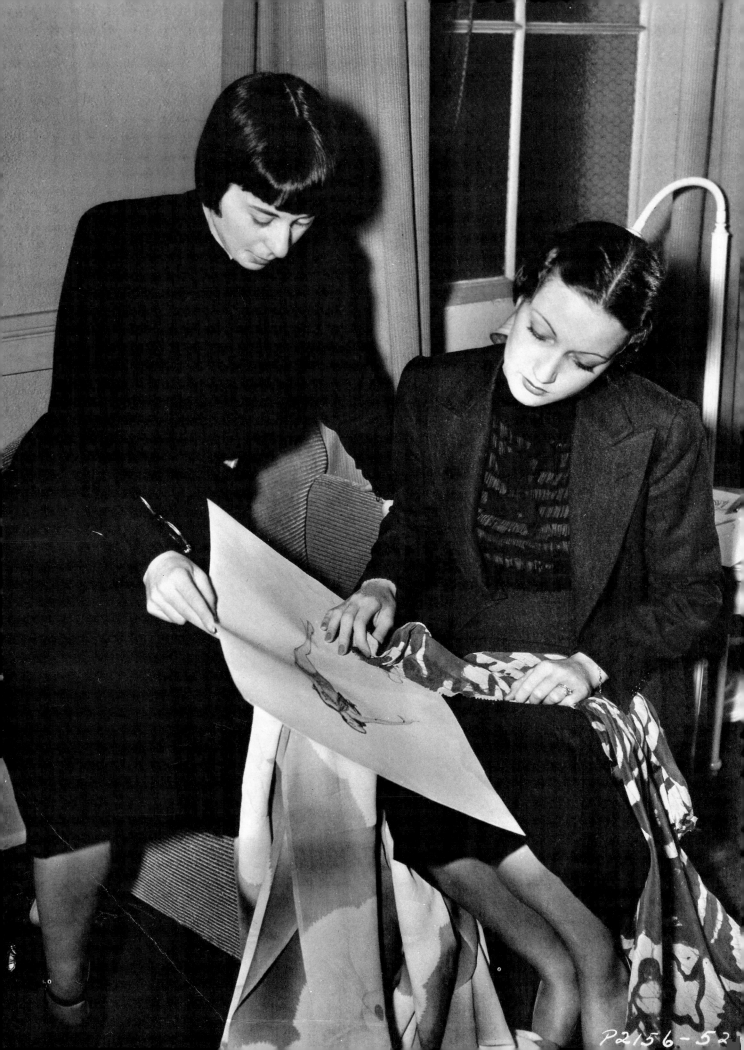

P 2156-52

Designs by Edith Head. Opposite: The designer showing Dorothy Lamour a sketch for Tropic Holiday. *Sketches above, clockwise: for Paulette Goddard in* The Ghost Breakers; *for Paul Newman in* The Sting; *for Carroll Baker in* Harlow; *for Robert Redford in* The Great Waldo Pepper

Jean Louis designs for Rita Hayworth in Pal Joey

Johnny Allegro (GB Hounded); Lust For Gold; Anna Lucasta; Jolson Sings Again; Mr Soft Touch (GB House of Settlement); Miss Grant Takes Richmond (GB Innocence is Bliss); The Reckless Moment; Tokyo Joe; All the King's Men; Tell it to the Judge; And Baby Makes Three; The Travelling Salesman; Father is a Bachelor; A Woman of Distinction.

1950: Cargo to Capetown; Kill the Umpire; No Sad Songs for Me; The Fortunes of Captain Blood; In a Lonely Place; The Good Humor Man; Rogues of Sherwood Forest; The Petty Girl (GB Girl of the Year); Between Midnight and Dawn; The Fuller Brush Girl (GB The Affairs of Sally); He's a Cockeyed Wonder; Born Yesterday; Emergency Wedding (GB Jealousy); The Flying Missile; The Killer That Stalked New York (GB Frightened City); Ten Tall Men. 1951: The Brave Bulls; Lorna Doone; Mask of the Avenger; Two of a Kind; Never Trust a Gambler; Saturday's Hero (GB Idols in the Dust); The Family Secret; The Magic Carpet; The First Time; Scandal Sheet (GB The Dark Page); The Marrying Kind. 1952: Paula (GB The Silent Voice); The Brigand; Affair in Trinidad; Captain Pirate (GB Captain Blood, Fugitive); The Happy Time; The Four Poster; Assignment-Paris; Salome (+Emile Santiago). 1953: The Iron Glove; Serpent of the Nile; Let's Do it Again; The Five Thousand Fingers of Dr T; From Here to Eternity; The Big Heat; A Star is Born (+Mary Ann Nyberg, Irene Sharaff); Bad for Each Other; Miss Sadie Thompson; It Should Happen to You. 1954: The Caine Mutiny; Pushover; Human Desire; Phffft; The Violent Men (GB Rough Company); The Long Gray Line; Three for the Show; Tight Spot.

1955: Five Against the House; My Sister Eileen; Queen Bee; Picnic; Autumn Leaves; The Solid Gold Cadillac; The Eddie Duchin Story; You Can't Run Away From It; Nightfall; Jubal. 1956: Over-Exposed. 1957: The Garment Jungle; The Monte Carlo Story; Jeanne Eagels; The Brothers Rico; 3.10 to Yuma; Pal Joey. 1958: Bell, Book and Candle; The Last Hurrah; Imitation of Life (+Bill Thomas). 1959: Middle of the Night; Pillow Talk (+Thomas); Who Was That Lady?; The Last Angry Man; They Came to Cordura.

Wardrobe test for Judy Garland

74

Jane Wyman in Let's Do it Again *(Jean Louis)*

Jean Louis and Rita Hayworth: Miss Sadie Thompson

1960: *Strangers When We Meet*; *Suddenly Last Summer* (+ Messel, Ellacott, Hartnell); *Portrait in Black*; *The Misfits*; *Song Without End*. 1961: *Back Street*; *Judgement at Nuremberg*. 1962: *If a Man Answers*. 1963: *For Love or Money*; *Thrill of It All*. 1964: *Bedtime Story*; *I'd Rather be Rich*; *Send Me No Flowers*; *Bus Riley's Back in Town* (+ Rosemary Odell); *Strange Bedfellows*.

1965: *Mirage*; *Ship of Fools* (+ Bill Thomas); *That Funny Feeling*; *Madame X*; *A Man Could Get Killed* (+ Dimitri Kritsos). 1966: *Blindfold*; *Gambit*; *Thoroughly Modern Millie*. 1967: *Banning*; *Rosie*; *The Ballad of Josie*; *Guess Who's Coming to Dinner*; *PJ* (GB *New Face in Hell*). 1968: *Don't Just Stand There*; *The Hell with Heroes*. 1969: *Marlowe*. 1972: *Lost Horizon*. 1973: *Forty Carats*.

LUCILLE (LADY DUFF GORDON)

Lucille Ltd was the couture house owned by Lady Duff Gordon, with salons in London and America. Designers Robert Kalloch, Shirley Barker, Howard Greer and Gilbert Clark have all worked for Lucille Ltd.

FILMS:
1916: *The Misleading Lady*; *The Strange Case of Mary Page*. 1918: *Virtuous Wives* (+ O'Kane Cromwell). 1920: *Way Down East* (+ O'Kane Cromwell). 1921: *Heedless Moths*.

LUICK, EARL

Born Michigan 1905. Studied art at the University of Oregon. Started with DeMille Pictures and worked at Warner Brothers from 1928 to 1933. Later at Fox from 1942 to 1943.

FILMS:
1927: *King of Kings* (+ Adrian and Gwen Wakeling). 1928: *On*

Trial; *Conquest*. 1929: *The Desert Song*; *Gold Diggers of Broadway*; *Fifty Million Frenchmen*.

1930: *Bride of the Regiment* (GB *Lady of the Rose*); *Old English*; *Big Boy*; *The Doorway to Hell*; *Illicit*; *Man to Man*; *Other Men's Women*; *Outward Bound*. 1931: *The Public Enemy* (+ Stevenson); *The Maltese Falcon*; *Chances*; *Night Nurse*; *The Last Flight*; *The Reckless Hour*; *Five Star Final*; *The Honor of the Family*; *Her Majesty, Love*; *Blonde Crazy* (GB *Larceny Lane*); *Safe in Hell* (GB *The Lost Lady*); *Union Depot* (GB *Gentleman for a Day*); *The Hatchet Man*; *The Man Who Played God*; *Little Caesar*. 1932: *The Mouthpiece*; *Passport to Hell* (GB *Burnt Offering*); *Weekends Only*; *Chandu the Magician*; *Down to Earth*; *Too Busy to Work*; *Cavalcade*; *Hot Pepper*; *Broadway Bad*; *Wild Girl* (GB *Salomy Jane*). 1933: *Zoo in Budapest*; *The Warrior's Husband*; *Pilgrimage*; *I Loved a Woman*; *Ever in My Heart*; *The World Changes*; *House on 56th Street* (+ Orry-Kelly); *Lady Killer* (+ Orry-Kelly).

1942: *Springtime in the Rockies*; *Orchestra Wives*; *The Black Swan*; *China Girls*; *Life Begins at 8:30* (GB *The Light of Heart*); *Margin for Error*; *The Meanest Man in the World*. 1943: *Crash Dive*; *The Ox-Bow Incident* (GB *Strange Incident*).

LUZA, ALBERTO

Costume designer at Twentieth Century-Fox in 1935.

FILMS:
1935: *Ginger*; *Silk Hat Kid*; *Charlie Chan in Shanghai*; *Your Uncle Dudley*; *Gentle Julia*.

MABRY, MOSS

American designer, mostly at Warners in the '50s, subsequently films for M-G-M, Fox and Columbia.

ACADEMY AWARD NOMINATIONS:

1956: *Giant* (+Marjorie Best). 1964: *What a Way To Go!* (+ Edith Head). 1965: *Morituri* (b&w). 1973: *The Way We Were* (+Dorothy Jeakins).

FILMS:

1951: *Trouble Along the Way.* 1953: *South Sea Woman; Thunder Over the Plains; Three Sailors and a Girl; The Command; Phantom of the Rue Morgue; Dial M for Murder; Lucky Me; Them!* 1954: *The Bounty Hunter; Battle Cry.* 1955: *The Sea Chase; Mr Roberts; Illegal; Rebel Without a Cause; I Died a Thousand Times; Target Zero; Hell on 'Frisco Bay; Tall Man Riding.* 1956: *Santiago* (GB *The Gun Runners*) (+ Marjorie Best); *The Bad Seed; A Cry in the Night; Towards the Unknown* (GB *Brink of Hell*); *The Girl He Left Behind; Giant* (+Marjorie Best).

1960: *Mutiny on the Bounty; The Subterraneans.* 1962: *The Manchurian Candidate.* 1963: *The Ceremony; Move Over Darling; Shock Treatment.* 1964: *Fate is the Hunter; How to Murder Your Wife; Dear Brigitte; What a Way to Go!* (+Edith Head). 1965: *Morituri; The Reward; The Silencers.* 1966: *Three on a Couch; Way . . . Way Out; Murderers' Row.* 1967: *A Guide for the Married Man; The Big Mouth; Tony Rome* (+Elinor Simmons); *Sol Madrid* (GB *The Heroin Gang*); *How to Save a Marriage and Ruin Your Life; Where Angels Go . . . Trouble Follows.* 1968: *The Detective; Lady in Cement; The Wrecking Crew; The Mad Room.* 1969: *The Great Bank Robbery; The Maltese Bippy; Bob & Carol & Ted & Alice; Cactus Flower* (+Guy Verhille).

1970: *How Do I Love Thee?; Doctor's Wives; The Mephisto Waltz; RPM.* 1971: *The Love Machine.* 1972: *Stand Up and Be Counted; Portnoy's Complaint; Butterflies are Free.* 1973: *The Way We Were* (+Dorothy Jeakins). 1975: *The Trial of Billy Jack; Once Is Not Enough.* 1976: *From Noon to Three; King Kong* (+Sylbert); *The Shootist.* 1978: *Casey's Shadow.* 1979: *Sunburn.* 1980: *Touched by Love.* 1981: *Continental Divide.* 1982: *The Toy.*

MACKENZIE, N'WAS

Head of Wardrobe Department at Warner Brothers. Also at Twentieth Century-Fox.

FILMS:

1937: *Missing Witnesses.* 1938: *Penrod and His Twin Brother; Crime School; Penrod's Double Trouble.* 1943: *The Moon is Down; The Dancing Masters;* 1944: *Roger Touhy, Gangster* (GB *The Last Gangster*).

MACKIE, BOB

Early film work in partnership with Ray Aghayan.

ACADEMY AWARD NOMINATIONS:

1972: *Lady Sings the Blues* (+Ray Aghayan, Norma Koch). 1975: *Funny Lady* (+Ray Aghayan). 1981: *Pennies from Heaven.*

Designer Odette Myrtil

FILMS:

1967: *Divorce—American Style* (+ Frances Lear). 1972: *Lady Sings the Blues* (+Ray Aghayan, Norma Koch). 1974: *Funny Lady* (+Ray Aghayan). 1981: *. . . All the Marbles* (GB *California Dolls*); *Pennies from Heaven.* 1983: *Staying Alive.*

MACLEAN, LORRAINE

Studio stylist for Monogram Pictures and Allied Artists.

FILMS:

1945: *Sunbonnet Sue; Allotment Wives* (GB *Woman in the Case*) (+Odette Myrtil). 1946: *Joe Palooka, Champ; Decoy; Gentleman Joe Palooka; Wife Wanted* (GB *Shadow of Blackmail*). 1947: *Violence; Black Gold; Joe Palooka in the Knockout; Song of My Heart; Angel's Alley; Panhandle; Jiggs and Maggie in Society.* 1948: *The Dude Goes West; The Babe Ruth Story; Joe Palooka in Winner Take All* (GB *Winner Take All*); *Joe Palooka in the Big Fight.* 1957: *It Happened on Fifth Avenue.*

MAES, URSULA

Assistant to Charles LeMaire at Fox in 1952, also one picture at Republic.

FILMS:

1952: *Man on a Tightrope* (+Charles LeMaire). 1953: *Night People* (+Charles LeMaire). 1956: *Magic Fire.*

MANN, CATHLEEN

Artist and portrait painter who designed costumes for some British films of the '30s. Her contribution to Alexander Korda's *Things to Come* is credited by her correct title, the Marchioness of Queensberry.

FILMS:

1934: *Chu-chin-chow; Evensong; The Iron Duke.* 1936: *Things To Come* (+John Armstrong, Rene Hubert). 1937: *The Show Goes On.*

MARSH, MAUDE

At M-G-M Wardrobe Department 1925/27.

FILMS:

1925: *Monte Carlo* (+Kathleen Kay, Andre-Ani); *Dance Madness* (+Kathleen Kay, Andre-Ani); *The Torrent* (+Kathleen Kay, Andre-Ani, Max Ree). 1926: *Money Talks* (+Kathleen Kay, Andre-Ani); *Brown of Harvard* (+Kathleen Kay); *Beverly of Graustark* (+Kathleen Kay, Andre-Ani); *The Gay Deceiver* (+Kathleen Kay, Andre-Ani); *The Boy Friend* (+Kathleen Kay, Andre-Ani); *The Waning Sex* (+Kathleen Kay, Andre-Ani); *Love's Blindness* (+Kathleen Kay, Andre-Ani); *There You Are!* (+Kathleen Kay); *Upstage* (+Kathleen Kay, Andre-Ani); *The Fire Brigade* (+Kathleen Kay, Andre-Ani). 1927: *Altars of Desire* (+Kathleen Kay, Andre-Ani); *Heaven on Earth* (+Kathleen Kay, Andre-Ani).

MAYER, MURRAY

Designer at Columbia Pictures in 1935.

FILMS:

1935: *After the Dance; The Black Room; Atlantic Adventure; The Public Menace; A Feather in Her Hat; Crime and Punishment; Grand Exit.*

Opposite: Helen Vinson in As Husbands Go *(Rita Kaufman)*

MENDLESON, ANTHONY

Born London, 1915, and educated at St Pauls School, Hammersmith. Studied art in France and Italy. Designed costumes for theatre and, in 1947, was appointed resident designer and supervisor of costumes at Ealing Studios. Has extensive credits as a freelance since leaving Ealing Studios in 1956.

ACADEMY AWARD NOMINATIONS:
1972: *Young Winston*. 1976: *The Incredible Sarah*.

SFTA NOMINATIONS:
1964: *The Long Ships*; *The Yellow Rolls-Royce*. 1969: *Oh! What a Lovely War*. 1972: **Young Winston*; *Macbeth*; *Alice's Adventures in Wonderland*.

FILMS:
1947: *It Always Rains on Sunday*; *Against the Wind*. 1948: *Scott of the Antarctic*; *Another Shore*. 1949: *Passport to Pimlico*; *Kind Hearts and Coronets*; *Whisky Galore* (US *Tight Little Island*); *Train of Events* (+Victor Stiebel); *A Run for Your Money*; *The Blue Lamp*. 1950: *Dance Hall*; *Cage of Gold*; *The Magnet*; *Pool of London*. 1951: *The Lavender Hill Mob*; *The Man in the White Suit*; *Secret People*; *His Excellency*; *I Believe in You*. 1952: *Mandy* (US *Crash of Silence*); *The Titfield Thunderbolt*. 1953: *The Cruel Sea*; *The Square Ring*; *Meet Mr Lucifer*; *The Maggie* (US *High and Dry*); *The Love Lottery*. 1954: *Lease of Life*; *The Divided Heart*; *Out of the Clouds*. 1955: *The Ship that Died of Shame* (US *PT Raiders*); *Touch and Go*; *The Ladykillers*; *Who Done It?*; *The Feminine Touch* (US *The Gentle Touch*). 1956: *The Long Arm* (US *The Third Key*); *Checkpoint*; *True as a Turtle*; *Fortune is a Woman* (US *She Played With Fire*). 1957: *The Smallest Show on Earth*; *The One That Got Away*; *Chase a Crooked Shadow*. 1958: *Bachelor of Hearts*. 1959: *Follow a Star*; *Left, Right and Centre*; *The Mouse That Roared*.
1960: *Make Mine Mink*; *Man in the Moon*. 1961: *A Matter of Who*. 1962: *Guns of Darkness*; *Billy Budd*; *The Man Who Finally Died*. 1963: *The Mouse on the Moon*; *The Long Ships*. 1964: *The Yellow Rolls-Royce* (+Castillo of Paris, Head, Pierre Cardin, Coffin). 1965: *Thunderball*; *The Fighting Prince of Donegal*. 1967: *Pretty Dolly*. 1968: *The Magus*; *Oh! What a Lovely War*. 1969: *David Copperfield*. 1970: *Jane Eyre*. 1971: *Macbeth*. 1972: *Young Winston*; *Alice's Adventures in Wonderland*. 1974: *Eleven Harrowhouse*. 1976: *A Bridge Too Far*; *The Incredible Sarah*. 1977: *Gulliver's Travels*. 1980: *Rough Cut*.

MESSEL, OLIVER

Born 1904. British costume and set designer with screen credits from 1943 to 1948. Also worked as production designer on *Suddenly Last Summer*. Died 1978.

FILMS:
1934: *The Private Life of Don Juan*. 1935: *The Scarlet Pimpernel* (+John Armstrong). 1936: *Romeo and Juliet* (+Adrian). 1940: *The Thief of Bagdad* (+John Armstrong, Marcel Vertes). 1945: *Caesar and Cleopatra*. 1946: *Carnival*. 1948: *The Queen of Spades*. 1959: *Suddenly Last Summer* (+Louis, Hartnell, Ellacott).

MORLEY, JAY

American costume designer under contract to Universal, 1953/57.

FILMS:
1949: *The Black Book* (GB *Reign of Terror*). 1952: *Face to Face*. 1953: *The Golden Blade*; *Walking My Baby Back Home*; *The Glenn Miller Story*; *Taza, Son of Cochise*. 1954: *Drums Across the River*; *Johnny Dark*; *Dawn at Socorro*; *Four Guns to the Border*; *Six Bridges to Cross*; *Abbott and Costello Meet the Keystone Cops*; *The Far Country*. 1955: *The Man from Bitter Ridge*; *The Second Greatest Sex*; *Tarantula*; *There's Always Tomorrow*; *Red Sundown*; *The Creature Walks Among Us*. 1956: *The Price of Fear*; *Star in the Dark*; *Francis in the Haunted House*; *The Unguarded Moment*; *Written on the Wind* (+Bill Thomas); *The*

Mole People; *Gun for a Coward*; *The Incredible Shrinking Man*; *The Tattered Dress*. 1957: *Interlude*.

MORLEY, RUTH

American costume designer with theatre credits since 1950. Theatre work includes musicals and opera. Some television credits for NBC-TV and CBS-TV.

ACADEMY AWARD NOMINATION:
1962: *The Miracle Worker* (b&w)

SFTA NOMINATION:
1983: *Tootsie*.

FILMS:
1958: *Never Love a Stranger*. 1961: *The Young Doctors*; *The Hustler*. 1962: *The Miracle Worker*; *The Connection*. 1965: *Lilith*; *Young Dillinger*; *A Thousand Clowns*. 1968: *The Brotherhood*. 1970: *Diary of a Mad Housewife*. 1971: *To Find a Man*; *The Hot Rock* (GB *How to Steal a Diamond in Four Uneasy Lessons*). 1974: *Man on a Swing*. 1976: *One Summer of Love*; *Taxi Driver*. 1977: *Annie Hall* (+George Newman, Marilyn Putnam, Ralph Lauren, Nancy McArdle). 1978: *The Brink's Job*; *Slow Dancing in the Big City*. 1979: *Kramer vs Kramer*. 1980: *Little Miss Marker*. 1982: *The Chosen*; *Hammett*; *I Ought to Be in Pictures*; *One from the Heart*; *Tootsie*. 1985: *The Key Exchange*. 1986: *The Money Pit*. 1987: *Hello Again*.

MYERS, RUTH

Independent British costume designer.

FILMS:
1967: *Smashing Time*; *Work is a Four Letter Word*. 1969: *Three Into Two Won't Go*; *All the Right Noises*; *A Nice Girl Like Me*. 1970: *The Twelve Chairs*. 1972: *The Ruling Class* (+Jean Muir). 1973: *A Touch of Class*. 1975: *The Adventure of Sherlock Holmes' Smarter Brother*; *The Romantic Englishwoman*. 1977: *The World's Greatest Lover*. 1978: *Magic*; *The Silver Bears*. 1979: *And Justice for All*; *The Main Event*. 1980: *The Competition*; *In God We Trust*; *It's My Turn*. 1982: *Cannery Row*. 1983: *Something Wicked This Way Comes*. 1985: *Plenty*. 1986: *Haunted Honeymoon*.

MYRON, HELEN A.

Costume designer at Fox from 1935 to 1940.

FILMS:
1935: *Charlie Chan in Egypt*; *This Is the Life*; *Thunder in the Night*; *Paddy O'Day*; *My Marriage*; *Charlie Chan's Secret*. 1936: *Charlie Chan at the Opera*. 1937: *Checkers*; *City Girl*; *Love on a Budget*. 1938: *Mr Moto's Gamble*; *Rascals*; *Speed to Burn*; *A Trip to Paris*; *Always in Trouble*; *Safety in Numbers*; *Down on the Farm*; *Five of a Kind* (+Herschel); *Arizona Wildcat* (+Herschel); *Up the River*; *Charlie Chan in Honolulu*. 1939: *Mr Moto's Last Warning*; *Chasing Danger*; *The Jones Family in Hollywood*; *Stop, Look and Love*; *One Wild Night*; *Everybody's Baby*; *News Is Made at Night*; *Chicken Wagon Family*; *Quick Millions*; *High School*; *Young As You Feel*. 1940: *On Their Own*; *Girl from Avenue A*.

MYRTIL, ODETTE

Born Odette Quignard, Paris, France, 1898. Worked as musician, actress and singer from 1911. From 1930 to 1936 was a dress designer in Beverly Hills. From 1945 to 1948 designed for two Monogram films and some independent productions.

Opposite: Barbara La Marr in Heart of a Siren
(Charles LeMaire)

FILMS:
1945: *Divorce; People Are Funny; Allotment Wives (GB Woman in the Case)* (+Lorraine MacLean). 1948: *The Lucky Stiff; Manhandled* (+Head).

NELSON, KAY

Designer at Twentieth Century-Fox Studios.

ACADEMY AWARD NOMINATION:
1949: *Mother Is a Freshman.*

FILMS:
1943: *Up In Mabel's Room.* 1944: *Take It or Leave It; Something For the Boys* (+Yvonne Wood); *Winged Victory; Sunday Dinner for a Soldier; Hangover Square* (+Rene Hubert). 1945: *Billy Rose's Diamond Horseshoe (GB Diamond Horseshoe)* (+Rene Hubert, Sascha Brastoff, Bonnie Cashin); *Within These Walls; Leave Her to Heaven; Behind Green Lights; Shock; Sentimental Journey.* 1946: *The Dark Corner; Do You Love Me?* (+Edward Stevenson); *Somewhere in the Night; Margie; Boomerang* (+Charles LeMaire). 1947: *Miracle on 34th Street (GB The Big Heart)* (+Charles LeMaire); *Gentleman's Agreement* (+Charles LeMaire); *Call Northside 777* (+Charles LeMaire); *You were Meant for Me* (+Charles LeMaire); *Sitting Pretty* (+Charles LeMaire); *The Home Stretch* (+Charles LeMaire). 1948: *Street With No Name* (+Charles LeMaire); *The Walls of Jericho* (+Charles LeMaire); *Hollow Triumph (GB The Scar); Apartment for Peggy* (+Charles LeMaire); *Road House* (+Charles LeMaire); *A Letter to Three Wives* (+Charles LeMaire); *Mother is a Freshman (GB Mother Knows Best)* (+Charles LeMaire). 1949: *Come to the Stable* (+Charles LeMaire); *Everybody Does It* (+Charles LeMaire); *Father Was a Fullback; Slattery's Hurricane; Thieves Highway* (+Charles LeMaire). 1953: *Blowing Wild* (+Marjorie Best); *A Lion Is in the Streets.* 1954: *Witness to Murder.* 1955: *Violent Saturday* (+Charles LeMaire); *Daddy Long Legs* (+Charles LeMaire; ballet costumes by Tom Keogh). 1959: *Tall Story.*

NEWMAN, BERNARD

Born Joplin, Missouri. Studied at the Art Student's League and in Paris. Worked at Bergdorf Goodman in New York for twelve years, during which time he graduated from window dresser to Head Designer. Went to RKO in 1933 to do the gowns for *Roberta.* Between 1933 and 1936 he worked on over twenty films but left to return to Bergdorf Goodman. He returned to RKO for one assignment in 1937—a Ginger Rogers film called *Vivacious Lady.* At Warner Brothers 1946/47.

FILMS:
1933: *Rafter Romance.* 1934: *Roberta.* 1935: *Star of Midnight; Break of Hearts; The Nitwits; Top Hat; I Dream Too Much; In Person; Sylvia Scarlet* (+Muriel King); *The Lady Consents; Two in the Dark; Follow the Fleet.* 1936: *When You're In Love (GB For You Alone); The Witness Chair; The Bride Walks Out; Swingtime* (+John Harkrider); *Walking on Air; Adventure in Manhattan; Smartest Girl in Town; Theodora Goes Wild; More Than a Secretary; History Is Made at Night.* 1937: *Vivacious Lady* (+Irene). 1938: *You Can't Take It With You* (+Irene). 1939: *Green Hell* (+Irene). 1942: *Tales of Manhattan* (+Irene, Tree, Wakeling, Cassini). 1946: *Deception; Humoresque* (+Adrian). 1947: *Possessed* (+Adrian); *Deep Valley; Dark Passage; Escape Me Never* (+Travilla); *Hazard; The Woman In White.*

NEWMAN, PAULA

British designer at British International Pictures 1933/34, and at Gainsborough Pictures in 1936.

FILMS:
1933: *On Secret Service; Red Wagon.* 1934: *Love at Second Sight (US The Girl Thief).* 1936: *Where There's a Will; Everybody Dance.*

NOVARESE, VITTORIO NINO

Italian costume designer and technical adviser on American and British films since 1949. Also costume credits on many Italian films. Died 1983.

ACADEMY AWARD NOMINATIONS:
1949: *Prince of Foxes* (b&w). 1963: **Cleopatra* (+Renie, Irene Sharaff). 1965: *The Greatest Story Ever Told* (+Marjorie Best); *The Agony and the Ecstasy.* 1970: **Cromwell.*

FILMS:
1949: *Black Magic* (+George Annenkoff); *Prince of Foxes.* 1950: *Shadow of the Eagle.* 1959: *The Greatest Story Ever Told* (+Marjorie Best). 1960: *The Savage Innocents.* 1961: *Francis of Assisi; Cleopatra* (+Renie, Irene Sharaff). 1965: *The Agony and the Ecstasy; The War Lord.* 1967: *The King's Pirate.* 1969: *Cromwell.* 1970: *Zachariah.* 1974: *Blazing Saddles.* 1975: *The Terminal Man.*

NYBERG, MARY ANN

Freelance designer active in films in the mid-'50s. At M-G-M from 1952/53, then films for Fox and United Artists. Died 1979.

ACADEMY AWARD NOMINATIONS:
1953: *The Band Wagon.* 1954: *A Star is Born* (+Jean Louis, Irene Sharaff).

Bernard Newman gown for Roberta

Kay Francis in The House of 56th Street *(Orry-Kelly)*

Kay Francis in Living on Velvet *(Orry-Kelly)*

Leslie Caron with costume sketches for An American in Paris

The Dolly Sisters: *showgirls' costumes by Orry-Kelly*

FILMS:

1952: *Lili.* 1953: *The Band Wagon.* 1954: *A Star is Born* (+Jean Louis, Irene Sharaff); *Carmen Jones.* 1955: *The Man With the Golden Arm.*

O'BRIEN, SHEILA

Born Dallas, Texas and migrated to California in the '30s. Designer often used by Joan Crawford, sometimes without screen credit. Died 1983.

ACADEMY AWARD NOMINATION:

1952: *Sudden Fear* (b&w).

FILMS:

1950: *The Damned Don't Cry; Harriet Craig.* 1951: *Goodbye, My Fancy; This Woman is Dangerous.* 1952: *Sudden Fear.* 1954: *Johnny Guitar.* 1955: *Female on the Beach.* 1965: *Never Too Late.*

ODELL, ROSEMARY

Costume Designer at Universal from 1945 to 1967.

FILMS:

1945: *Easy To Look At.* 1946: *The Time of Their Lives; Michigan Kid.* 1947: *The Vigilantes Return; Brute Force; The Wistful Widow of Wagon Gap* (GB *The Wistful Widow*); *Are You With It?* 1948: *Feudin', Fussin' and a-Fightin'; Larceny* (+Orry-Kelly). *The Life of Riley; Red Canyon; Abbott & Costello Meet the Killer, Boris Karloff.* 1949: *Yes Sir, That's My Baby; Free for All; The Story of Molly X; Francis; Outside the Wall*

1950: *The Fat Man; The Lawless* (GB *The Dividing Line*); *Louisa; Peggy; The Sleeping City; The Milkman; Bedtime For Bonzo.* 1951: *Hollywood Story; Comin' Round the Mountain;*

Bright Victory (GB *Lights Out*); *The Lady From Texas; Reunion in Reno; The Strange Door; Finders Keepers; Bend of the River* (GB *Where the River Bends*); *Here Comes the Nelsons.* 1952: *Has Anybody Seen My Gal?; Sally and St Ann; Scarlet Angel; Son of Ali Baba; Horizons West; The Lawless Breed; Meet Me at the Fair; City Beneath the Sea; Battle of Apache Pass; Seminole; Column South; It Came from Outer Space; Thunder Bay; Francis Covers the Big Town.* 1953: *Abbott and Costello Meet Dr Jekyll and Mr Hyde; All I Desire; Fort Algiers; The Veils of Bagdad; Border River; The Creature From the Black Lagoon; Ride Clear of Diabolo.* 1954: *Yankee Pasha; Tanganyika; The Black Shield of Falworth; Naked Alibi; So This is Paris; Destry; Chief Crazy Horse (Valley of Fury); Man Without a Star.* 1955: *This Island Earth; Abbott and Costello Meet the Mummy; Ain't Misbehavin'; The Square Jungle; Backlash; Francis in the Navy; The Private War of Major Benson.* 1956: *A Day of Fury; Toy Tiger; Outside the Law; Pillars of the Sky* (GB *The Tomahawk and the Cross*); *Showdown at Abilene; Four Girls in Town; Kelly and Me; The Night Runner; Quantez.*

1961: *Tammy, Tell Me True.* 1962: *The Spiral Road; That Touch of Mink; Forty Pounds of Trouble; To Kill a Mockingbird; The Ugly American; Tammy and the Doctor.* 1963: *Captain Newman MD; The Brass Bottle; Island of the Blue Dolphin; Wild and Wonderful* (+Valentino of Rome). 1964: *The Lively Set; Fluffy.* 1965: *Shenandoah; The Rare Breed; The Ghost and Mr Chicken.* 1966: *. . . And Now Miguel; Beau Geste; The Pad (and How to Use It); The Appaloosa* (GB *South West to Sonora*) (+Helen Colvig); *Texas Across the River* (+Helen Colvig); *Ride to Hangman's Tree; Moment to Moment* (+Yves St. Laurent); *The Reluctant Astronaut.* 1967: *Rough Night in Jericho; Nobody's Perfect.* 1968: *Rascal.*

O'NEILL, ALICE

Designer at United Artists and Fox 1927/30, often as assistant to Sophie Wachner.

Opposite: Rita Hayworth in Gilda (Jean Louis)

1927: *The Lady Bird*; *Drums of Love*. 1928: *Tempest*; *Lady of the Pavements* (+Jetta Goudal); 1929: *Fox Movietone Follies of 1929* (GB *Movietone Follies of 1929*) (+Sophie Wachner); *Married in Hollywood* (+Sophie Wachner); *Lummox*; *Puttin' on the Ritz*; *Be Yourself*; *The Bad One*. *The Lottery Bride*; *Just Imagine* (+Sophie Wachner, Dolly Tree).

ORRY-KELLY

Born John Kelly in Kiama, Australia, 1897. Died 1964.
Orry-Kelly studied art in Australia but decided to become an actor and sailed for New York. The acting career never materialised, but he got a job painting murals in a night club and doing sketches of the patrons. This led to a job at the Fox East Coast studios illustrating titles for silent films. He designed costumes and scenery for the Schubert revues and for "George White's Scandals". Ethel Barrymore admired his work and wore clothes designed by him in several stage productions. Katharine Hepburn's wardrobe in her Broadway

Bette Davis in Bordertown *(Orry-Kelly)*

debut, "Death Takes a Holiday" was also designed by Orry-Kelly. Several unsuccessful attempts to run nightclubs during the Depression took him across to the West Coast but, in between the business ventures, he designed for the St Louis Opera Company.

Orry-Kelly arrived in Hollywood in 1932 and started work at the Warner Brothers First National Studios. Cary Grant, an old friend from his New York days, had introduced him to the Head of Wardrobe at Warners and he worked there for the next eleven years. His first important film was a Ruth Chatterton picture, *The Rich Are Always With Us.* He left Warners in 1943, (returning only to work on Bette Davis pictures) and worked at Fox, Universal, RKO and M-G-M.

A designer's work can only be shown to its best advantage if the studio contract players can wear the clothes well. Orry-Kelly was fortunate to be at Warners with Kay Francis, Bette Davis, Veree Teasdale, Dolores Del Rio and Helen Vinson and, as the studio made very few period pictures, his fashion designs for films like *Fashions of 1934, Stolen Holiday* and *First Lady* were used as a major selling point in the publicity campaigns sent out to exhibitors.

Several film musical assignments during the latter part of his

career allowed Orry-Kelly the opportunity to use his earlier experiences with Broadway shows to good effect. He was working on the film *Kiss Me, Stupid* when he died in 1964.

ACADEMY AWARD NOMINATIONS:

1951: *An American in Paris* (+Walter Plunkett, Irene Sharaff). 1957: *Les Girls*. 1959: *Some Like It Hot* (b&w). 1962: *Gypsy*.

FILMS:

1932: *The Rich Are Always With Us*; *So Big*; *Winner Takes All*; *Crooner*; *One Way Passage*; *Tiger Shark*; *Two Against The World* (+Hattie Carnegie); *The Crash*; *Cabin in the Cotton*; *I am a Fugitive from a Chain Gang*; *Three on a Match*; *Scarlet Dawn*; *You Said A Mouthful*; *Lawyer Man*; *The Match King*; *Employees Entrance*; *Frisco Jenny*; *The King's Vacation*; *Parachute Jumper*; *Twenty Thousand Years in Sing Sing*; *42nd Street*; *Hard to Handle*; *Ladies They Talk About*; *Blondie Johnson*; *Grand Slam*; *Mystery of the Wax Museum*; *Central Airport*; *The Keyhole*.
1933: *The Little Giant*; *The Mind Reader*; *The Working Man*; *Ex Lady*; *Gold Diggers of 1933*; *Picture Snatcher*; *Baby Face*; *The Life of Jimmy Dolan* (GB *The Kid's Last Fight*); *Lilly Turner*; *The Mayor of Hell*; *The Narrow Corner*; *The Silk Express*; *Heroes for Sale*; *Mary Stevens MD*; *Private Detective 62*; *She Had To Say Yes*; *Voltaire*; *Captured*; *The Kennel Murder Case*; *The World Changes*; *College Coach*; *Female*; *Convention City*; *House on 56th Street* (+Earl Luick); *Lady Killer* (+Earl Luick); *Son of a Sailor*; *Easy to Love*; *Fashions of 1934*; *Massacre*; *As The Earth Turns*; *Dark Hazard*; *I've Got Your Number*; *Jornal of a Crime*; *Wonder Bar*; *Gambling Lady*; *Harold Teen* (GB *The Dancing Fool*); *Heat Lightning*; *Jimmie the Gent*; *Bedside*.
1934: *A Modern Hero*; *Twenty Million Sweethearts*; *The Adventures of Mark Twain*; *Smarty* (GB *Hit Me Again*); *He Was Her Man*; *The Key*; *Upper World*; *A Very Honorable Guy*; *The Circus Clown*; *Dr Monica*; *Fog Over 'Frisco*; *Here Comes the Navy*; *The Merry Frinks*; *The Merry Wives of Reno*; *Registered Nurse*; *Friends of Mr Sweeney*; *Midnight Alibi*; *Return of the Terror*; *British Agent*; *Dames*; *The Dragon Murder Case*; *Housewife*; *Madame DuBarry*; *The Personality Kid*; *Side Streets*; *Desirable*; *Happiness Ahead*; *The Case of the Howling Dog*; *The Lost Lady*; *Big Hearted Herbert*; *The Firebird*; *Flirtation Walk*; *Gentlemen are Born*; *Kansas City Princess*; *The St Louis Kid* (GB *A Perfect Weekend*); *Babbitt*; *I Sell Anything*; *Border Town*; *I Am a Thief*; *Sweet Adeline*; *The White Cockatoo*; *Devil Dogs of the Air*; *Maybe it's Love*; *The Secret Bride* (GB *Concealment*); *The Right To Live* (GB *The Sacred Flame*); *Sweet Music*; *Gold Diggers of 1935*; *Living on Velvet*; *Travelling Saleslady*; *The Woman in Red*; *Go Into Your Dance* (GB *Casino de Paree*).
1935: *The Case of the Curious Bride*; *The Florentine Dagger*; *G-Men*; *Girl from 10th Avenue* (GB *Men on Her Mind*); *In Caliente*; *Stranded*; *Broadway Gondolier*; *Bright Lights* (GB *Funny Face*); *Page Miss Glory*; *Going Highbrow*; *The Irish in Us*; *The Goose and the Gander*; *'Frisco Kid*; *I Live for Love* (GB *I Live For You*); *Little Big Shot*; *Shipmates Forever*; *I Found Stella Parrish*; *The Pay-Off*; *Stars Over Broadway*; *Broadway Hostess*; *Ceiling Zero*; *The Widow from Monte Carlo*; *Dangerous*; *Miss Pacific Fleet*; *The Petrified Forest*; *Freshman Love* (GB *Rhythm on the River*); *Colleen*; *I Married a Doctor*; *The Singing Kid*; *Snowed Under*; *The Walking Dead*.
1936: *The Golden Arrow*; *Murder in the Big House* (GB *Jailbreak*); *Times Square Playboy*; *Hearts Divided*; *The Law in Her Hands*; *Murder By an Aristocrat*; *The White Angel*; *Give Me Your Heart* (GB *Sweet Aloes*); *Satan Met a Lady*; *China Clipper*; *Polo Joe*; *Stage Struck*; *Cain and Mabel*; *Here Comes Carter* (GB *Voice of Scandal*); *Three Men on a Horse*; *Golddiggers of 1937*; *Isle of Fury*; *Stolen Holiday*; *Green Light*; *The King and the Chorus Girl* (GB *Romance is Sacred*); *Marked Woman*; *Call It a Day*.
1937: *The Go Getter*; *Kid Galahad*; *Another Dawn*; *Ever Since Eve*; *Confession*; *It's Love I'm After*; *The Singing Marine*; *That Certain Woman*; *First Lady*; *Tovarich* (+Adrian); *Hollywood Hotel*; *Jezebel*.
1938: *Women are Like That*; *My Bill*; *Four Daughters*; *Four's a Crowd*; *Angels with Dirty Faces*; *Secrets of an Actress*; *The Sisters*; *Comet Over Broadway*; *King of the Underworld*; *Wings of the Navy*; *Dark Victory*; *The Oklahoma Kid*.
1939: *Juarez*; *Women in the Wind*; *Indianapolis Speedway* (GB *Devil on Wheels*); *The Old Maid*; *When Tomorrow Comes*; *The Private Lives of Elizabeth and Essex*; *On Your Toes*; *Virginia City*.
1940: *'Til we Meet Again*; *All This and Heaven Too*; *My Love*

Opposite: Claudette Colbert in a gown designed by Travis Banton for her personal wardrobe, 1936

Sylvia Sidney in a Travis Banton gown, 1935

Came Back; The Sea Hawk; A Dispatch from Reuters (GB This Man Reuter); No Time for Comedy; The Letter; The Strawberry Blonde.

1941: The Great Lie; Affectionately Yours; Million Dollar Baby; The Bride Came COD; The Little Foxes; The Maltese Falcon; King's Row; The Man Who Came to Dinner; Arsenic and Old Lace.

1942: Edge of Darkness; In This Our Life; Now, Voyager; George Washington Slept Here; The Hard Way; Casablanca.

1943: Mission to Moscow; This is the Army; Watch on the Rhine; Princess O'Rourke; Old Acquaintance.

1944: Mr Skeffington; The Corn is Green.

1945: Conflict; The Dolly Sisters. 1946: A Stolen Life; My Heart Goes Crazy (GB London Town); Temptation; The Shocking Miss Pilgrim. 1947: Ivy; Something in the Wind; Mother Wore Tights (+Charles LeMaire); Night Song; A Woman's Vengeance. 1948: Berlin Express (+Rosemary Odell); One Touch of Venus; For the Love of Mary; Rogue's Regiment; Family Honeymoon. 1949: The Lady Gambles; Johnny Stoolpigeon; Once More My Darling; Undertow; Take One False Step; Woman in Hiding; South Sea Sinner (GB East of Java); One Way Street; Deported.

1950: Harvey; Under the Gun. 1951: An American in Paris (+Irene Sharaff, Walter Plunkett); The Lady Says No. 1952: Pat and Mike; The Star; I Confess. 1953: She Couldn't Say No (GB Beautiful But Dangerous). 1954: Oklahoma! (+Motley).

1957: Les Girls (+Siegal, Irene Sharaff). 1958: Too Much, Too Soon; Auntie Mame; The Hanging Tree (+Marjorie Best); Some Like it Hot; A Majority of One.

1961: The Four Horsemen of the Apocalypse (+Rene Hubert, Walter Plunkett); Sweet Bird of Youth. 1962: Five Finger Exercise; The Chapman Report; Gypsy (+Shoup). Two for the Seesaw; In the Cool of the Day (+Pierre Balmain). 1963: Irma La Douce; Sunday in New York. 1965: Lady L.

PALMER, ADELE

Started as a sketch artist with Vera West at Universal, then as costume designer at Republic from 1938 to 1957. When Republic abandoned the production of films for the cinema, Miss Palmer moved to Fox, where she worked from 1957 to 1959.

ACADEMY AWARD NOMINATION:
1959: The Best of Everything.

FILMS:
1938: My Wife's Relatives. 1939: Man of Conquest (+Edith Head); The Zero Hour; Wolf of New York; Village Barn Dance; Thou Shalt Not Kill; Smuggled Cargo; Main Street Lawyer (GB Small Town Lawyer); Mickey the Kid; She Married a Cop; Should Husbands Work?; Calling All Marines; Sabotage; Jeepers Creepers; The Covered Trailer; Rio Grande.

1940: Forgotten Girls; Dark Command; The Crooked Road; Gangs of Chicago; In Old Missouri; Women in War; Three Faces West; Wagons Westward; Girl from God's Country; Scatterbrain; Earl of Puddlestone (GB Jolly Old Higgins); The Girl from Havana; Grand Ole Opry; Hit Parade of 1941; Friendly Neighbours; Melody Ranch; Meet the Missus; Who Killed Aunt Maggie?; Behind the News; Arkansas Judge (GB False Witness); Bowery Boy; Petticoat Politics.

1941: Ice Capades; Lady From Louisiana; Rookies on Parade; Sis Hopkins; Country Fair; The Gay Vagabond; The Great Train Robbery; Puddin' Head (GB Judy Goes to Town); Hurricane Smith; Rags to Riches; Doctors Don't Tell; The Pittsburgh Kid; Mercy Island; Public Enemies; Sailors on Leave; The Devil Pays Off; Tuxedo Junction (GB The Gang Made Good).

1942: In Old California; Flying Tigers; Johnny Doughboy.

1943: Chatterbox; A Scream in the Dark; O, My Darling Clementine; Casanova in Burlesque; The Fighting Seabees; My Best Gal.

1944: Port of Forty Thieves; Utah; Jamboree; Man from 'Frisco; Three Little Sisters; Atlantic City; Sing, Neighbour, Sing; Strangers in the Night; Earl Carroll Vanities; Flame of Barbary Coast; The Phantom Speaks; Steppin' in Society; The Cheaters; The Man From Oklahoma; Swingin' on a Rainbow; Tell it to a Star; Behind City Lights; A Sporting Chance; Don't Fence Me In; Three's a Crowd; Scotland Yard Investigator; Dakota; Girls of the Big House; Mexicana; The Fatal Witness; The Madonna's Secret (+Howard Greer); Murder in the Music Hall.

1946: The Gay Blades; In Old Sacramento; The Tiger Woman;

Spectre of the Rose; Man From Rainbow Valley; One Exciting Week; Valley of the Zombies; Night Train to Memphis; The Undercover Woman; Earl Carroll Sketchbook (GB Hats Off to Rhythm); Passkey to Danger; Rendezvous with Annie; Affairs of Geraldine; Plainsman and the Lady; Sioux City Sue; That Brennan Girl; The Magnificent Rogue; Out California Way; The Mysterious Mr Valentine; Traffic in Crime; The Pilgrim Lady; Angel and the Badman; Calendar Girl; Trail to San Antone; The Ghost Goes Wild; Hit Parade of 1947.

1947: Northwest Outpost (GB End of the Rainbow); Springtime in the Sierras; That's My Gal; The Trespasser; Wyoming; Exposed; Robin Hood of Texas; On the Old Spanish Trail; Driftwood; The Fabulous Texan; Campus Honeymoon; The Flame; Main Street Kid; Slippy McGee; California Firebrand; Madonna of the Desert.

1948: The Bold Frontiersman; The Inside Story; Lightnin' in the Forest; In Old Los Angeles; Carson City Raiders; The Gallant Legion; Heart of Virginia; I, Jane Doe (GB Diary of a Bride); King of the Gamblers; Secret Service Investigator; Daredevils of the Clouds; Eyes of Texas; Train to Alcatraz; Moonrise; Out of the Storm; Macbeth; Angel in Exile; Wake of the Red Witch; The Red Pony. 1949: The Duke of Chicago; Hideout; Streets of San Francisco; Too Late for Tears; Hellfire; Brimstone; The Fighting Kentuckian; The Kid From Cleveland; Alias the Champ; Down Dakota Way; Flame of Youth; Post Office Investigator; Sands of Iwo Jima; The Blonde Bandit; Belle of Old Mexico; Unmasked; Federal Agent at Large; Tarnished.

1950: Harbor of Missing Men; House by the River; Wagonmas-

Adele Palmer as a sketch artist at Universal, 1938

ter; Trial Without Jury; Prisoners in Petticoats; The Hit Parade of 1951; Surrender; Rio Grande; Belle Le Grande; Missing Women; Cuban Fireball; Insurance Investigator; Oh! Susanna; Trail of Robin Hood.

1951: Fighting Coast Guard; Bullfighter and the Lady; Million Dollar Pursuit; Rodeo King and the Senorita; The Sea Hornet; Honeychile; Street Bandits; The Wild Blue Yonder (GB Thunder Across the Pacific); Pals of the Golden West; Woman in the Dark; Hoodlum Empire.

1952: Gobs and Gals; The Quiet Man; I Dream of Jeannie; Woman of the North Country; Ride the Man Down; Tropical Heatwave; South Pacific Trail; Montana Belle; The Lady Wants Mink; San Antone; The Woman They Almost Lynched.

1953: Fair Wind to Java; The Sun Shines Bright; Perilous Journey; Champ for a Day; Sea of Lost Ships; Flight Nurse; Geraldine; Jubilee Trail; Hell's Half Acre; Sweethearts on Parade; The Fortune Hunter.

1954: Make Haste to Live; Untamed Heiress; The Shanghai Story; The Atomic Kid; Hell's Outpost; Timberjack; The Eternal Sea.

1955: I Cover the Underworld; The Road to Denver; City of Shadows; The Last Command; Double Jeopardy (GB Crooked Ring); A Man Alone; Headline Hunters (GB Deadline Alley); The Twinkle in God's Eye; No Man's Woman; The Vanishing American; The Fighting Chance; Come Next Spring; Jaguar; Santa Fe Passage.

1956: The Maverick Queen; Terror at Midnight (GB And Suddenly You Run); Stranger at My Door; The Man is Armed; Dakota Incident; Lisbon; Thunder Over Arizona; A Stranger Adventure; A Woman's Devotion; When Gangland Strikes.

1957: *Peyton Place; The Long Hot Summer* (+Charles LeMaire).

1958: *Compulsion* (+Charles LeMaire).

1959: *The FBI Story; Say One for Me* (+ Charles LeMaire); *The Best of Everything; Hound Dog Man; The Sound and the Fury*.

PENE du BOIS, RAOUL

Born Raoul-Henri Charles Pene du Bois, New York City, 1914. Scenic and costume designer for Broadway productions since 1934. Designed settings and costumes for several Paramount films in the mid-'40s. Died 1985.

FILMS:

1934: *Ready for Love.* 1941: *Louisiana Purchase.* 1943: *Dixie; Lady in the Dark* (+Edith Head, Mitchell Leisen, Babs Wilomez). 1944: *Frenchman's Creek.* 1945: *Kitty.*

PLUNKETT, WALTER

Born California, 1902. Started his career as an actor, but changed to costume design when asked to design for the dancer Ruth St Denis. In 1926 he became Head of the FBO Studios (which later became RKO). Plunkett was Head of RKO Wardrobe Department until 1930 and again from 1932 to 1935. He then became a designer at the same studios from 1936 to 1939, mainly working on costume pictures. After freelancing at various studios, he began work in 1938 for pro-

Designer Walter Plunkett and Jean Simmons with costume sketches for Young Bess

ducer David Selznick on *Gone With the Wind.* This was Walter Plunkett's most famous film and, in 1976, he recreated one of the dresses worn by Vivien Leigh in this film for a permanent exhibition in a Los Angeles Museum. In 1947 Plunkett was put under contract to M-G-M and worked there until his retirement in 1965. Died 1982.

ACADEMY AWARD NOMINATIONS:

1950: *The Magnificent Yankee* (b&w); *That Forsyte Woman* (GB *The Forsyte Saga*) (+Valles). 1951: *Kind Lady* (+Gile Steele) (b&w); *An American in Paris* (+Orry-Kelly, Irene Sharaff). 1953: *The Actress* (b&w); *Young Bess.* 1957: *Raintree County.* 1958: *Some Came Running.* 1961: *Pocketful of Miracles* (+Edith Head). 1963: *How the West Was Won.*

Renie at RKO in 1945

FILMS:

1927: *Hard Boiled Haggerty.* 1928: *Sinners in Love; The Red Sword; Love in the Desert.* 1932: *Night After Night.* 1933: *The Past of Mary Holmes; Double Harness; Morning Glory; The Right to Romance; Flying Down to Rio* (+ Irene); *Spitfire; Little Women; Son of Kong.* 1934: *Finishing School; Sing and Like It; Where Sinners Meet; The Life of Vergie Winters; Stingaree; Bachelor Bait; Cockeyed Cavaliers; Strictly Dynamite; The Age of Innocence; The Fountain; His Greatest Gamble; We're Rich Again; Down to Their Last Yacht* (GB *Hawaiian Nights*); *The Gay Divorcee* (GB *The Gay Divorce*); *Anne of Green Gables; Kentucky Kernels; The Silver Streak; Wednesday's Child; By Your Leave; Dangerous Corner; The Little Minister; Lightning Strikes Twice; Of Human Bondage.*

1935: *Hooray for Love; The Informer; The Arizonian; Jalna; Alice Adams; Hot Tip; Freckles; His Family Tree; The Three Musketeers; The Rainmaker; To Beat the Band; Hi, Gaucho.* 1936: *Mary of Scotland; The Plough and the Stars; The Soldier and the Lady* (GB *Michael Strogoff*); *Quality Street.* 1937: *The Woman I Love* (GB *The Woman Between*); *A Woman Rebels; Nothing Sacred* (+ Travis Banton); *The Adventures of Tom Sawyer.* 1938: *The Story of Vernon and Irene Castle* (+Stevenson, Irene Castle); *Stagecoach.* 1939: *Allegheny Uprising* (GB *The First Rebel*); *Gone With the Wind; The Hunchback of Notre Dame; Abe Lincoln in Illinois; Vigil in the Night.*

1940: *Captain Caution.* 1941: *Ladies in Retirement; Lydia* (+ Marcel Vertes); *Sundown; Go West, Young Lady; Lady for a Night.* 1943: *In Old Oklahoma* (GB *War of the Wildcats*); *The Heat's On* (GB *Tropicana*); *Knickerbocker Holiday.* 1944: *Can't Help Singing; A Song to Remember* (+ Travis Banton). 1945: *Along Came Jones.* 1947: *Song of Love* (+ Irene, Valles). 1947: *My Brother Talks to Horses; Duel in the Sun; The Sea of Grass.* 1947: *Summer Holiday* (+ Irene); *Green Dolphin Street* (+ Irene, Valles). 1948: *The Three Musketeers; The Kissing Bandit; Little Women.* 1949: *The Secret Garden; Madame Bovary* (+ Valles); *That Forsyte Woman* (GB *The Forsyte Saga*) (+ Valles); *Adam's Rib; Ambush; Black Hand; The Outriders.*

1950: *Annie Get Your Gun* (+Helen Rose); *Devil's Doorway; Father of the Bride* (+Helen Rose); *The Happy Years; Summer Stock* (+Helen Rose); *Toast of New Orleans* (+Helen Rose); *King Solomon's Mines; The Miniver Story* (+Gaston Mallet); *Two Weeks With Love* (+Helen Rose); *The Magnificent Yankee* (GB *The Man With Thirty Sons*); *Payment on Demand* (+Edith Head); *Vengeance Valley; Soldiers Three; Mr Imperium* (GB *You Belong to My Heart*). 1951: *Kind Lady* (+Gile Steele); *Show Boat; The Law and the Lady* (+Gile Steele); *An American in Paris* (+Orry-Kelly, Irene Sharaff); *Across the Wide Missouri; Man with a Cloak* (+Gile Steele); *Westward the Women; Singin' in the Rain.* 1952: *Carbine Williams; Plymouth Adventure; The Prisoner of Zenda; Million Dollar Mermaid* (GB *One Piece Bathing Suit*) (+Helen Rose). 1953: *Young Bess; Scandal at Scourie; Ride, Vaquero; The Actress; All the Brothers Were Valiant; Kiss Me Kate.*

Opposite: Jean Louis design for Evelyn Keyes in The Thrill of Brazil

1954: *Seven Brides for Seven Brothers; The Student Prince; Valley of the Kings; Athena* (+Helen Rose); *Deep in My Heart* (+Helen Rose); *Jupiter's Darling* (+Helen Rose); *The Glass Slipper* (+Helen Rose); *Many Rivers to Cross.*

1955: *Moonfleet; The Scarlet Coat; The King's Thief; Diane; Forbidden Planet* (+Helen Rose); *Tribute to a Bad Man.* 1956: *Lust for Life; The Wings of Eagles.* 1957: *Gun Glory; Raintree County; The Brothers Karamazov; Merry Andrew.* 1958: *The Sheepman; The Law and Jake Wade; Some Came Running.* 1959: *Home From the Hill.*

1960: *Pollyanna; Bells are Ringing; Cimarron.* 1961: *Pocketful of Miracles* (+Edith Head); *The Four Horsemen of the Apocalypse* (+Rene Hubert, Orry-Kelly). 1962: *How the West Was Won; Two Weeks in Another Town* (+Balmain). 1965: *Marriage on the Rocks; Seven Women.*

REE, MAX

Born Denmark. Studied law and philosophy at the Royal University of Copenhagen and also trained as an architect at the Royal Academy of Copenhagen. He worked with Max Reinhardt in Berlin and, between 1922 and 1925, designed sets and costumes for the "Greenwich Village Follies", the "Music Box Revue" and "Earl Carroll's Vanities". In 1925 he went to M-G-M and designed costumes for Greta Garbo in two films – *The Torrent* and *The Temptress*. Between 1927 and 1929 he was Director of Costume Department at First National Studios and, from 1929 to 1931, was supervising art director for Radio Pictures. His association with Reinhardt was renewed in 1935 for the Warners production of *A Midsummer Night's Dream.*

FILMS:

1925: *The Torrent.* 1926: *The Scarlet Letter; The Temptress.* 1927: *Rose of the Golden West; The Private Life of Helen of Troy; The Love Mart.* 1928: *The Yellow Lily; Show Girl; The Whip; The Wedding March; Adoration; The Barker; Weary River; The Divine Lady; Queen Kelly.* 1929: *Hot Stuff; Broadway Babies; Street Girl; The Man and the Moment; Side Street; Hit the Deck.* 1930: *Beau Ideal; Cimarron; The Royal Bed* (GB *The Queen's Husband*); *Bachelor Apartment.* 1931: *High Stakes; Consolation Marriage* (GB *Married in Haste*); *The Lost Squadron.* 1935: *A Midsummer Night's Dream.* 1946: *Carnegie Hall.*

RENIE

Real name Irene Brouillet Conley. Educated at UCLA and Chouinard Art School. Costume and set designer for Fanchon and Marco. From 1935 to 1936, sketch designer at Paramount, then contract with RKO from 1936/1949. At Fox from 1951 onwards, with occasional freelance work for other studios.

ACADEMY AWARD NOMINATIONS:

1951: *The Model and the Marriage Broker* (+Charles LeMaire) (b&w). 1953: *The President's Lady* (+Charles LeMaire) (b&w). 1959: *The Big Fisherman.* 1963: **Cleopatra* (+Irene Sharaff, Vittorio Nino Novarese). 1978: *Caravans.*

FILMS:

1936: *Criminal Lawyer; Don't Tell the Wife.* 1937: *Forty Naughty Girls; Saturday's Heroes; Danger Patrol; Living on Love; High Flyers; Millionaire Playboy; Crashing Hollywood; Double Danger; Quick Money; Night Spot.* 1938: *Go Chase Yourself; Law of the Underworld; Having Wonderful Time* (+Edward Stevenson); *Crime Ring; I'm From the City; Sky Giant; Room Service; Fugitives For a Night; Tarnished Angel; A Man to Remember; Annabel Takes a Tour; The Great Man Votes; The Flying Irishman; Twelve Crowded Hours; The Saint Strikes Back.* 1939: *The Girl From Mexico; The Rookie Cop; The Girl and the Gambler; Career; Conspiracy; The Day the Bookies Wept; The Spellbinder; Two Thoroughbreds; Sued for Libel; Married and In Love; The Marines Fly High; Primrose Path.*

1940: *Little Orvie; One Crowded Night; Wildcat Bus; I'm Still Alive; Stranger On the Third Floor; Kitty Foyle; The Saint In Palm Springs.* 1941: *Footlight Fever; The Devil and Miss Jones; Repent At Leisure; Parachute Battalion; Tom, Dick and Harry; Sing Your Worries Away; The Mayor of 44th Street.* 1942: *The Falcon Takes Over; The Big Street* (+Freddie Wittop); *The Fal-*

con's Brother; *The Navy Comes Through; Seven Days Leave; Cat People; Hitler's Children; The Falcon Strikes Back; This Land is Mine.* 1943: *Mr Lucky; The Sky's the Limit; The Adventures Of a Rookie; The Seventh Victim; Gildersleeve on Broadway; Around the World; The Falcon and the Co-eds; The Falcon Out West; Mexican Spitfire's Blessed Event; Tender Comrade* (+Head). 1944: *Days of Glory; A Night of Adventure; Music in Manhattan; The Master Race; My Pal, Wolf; Girl Rush; None But the Lonely Heart; The Falcon in Hollywood; The Body Snatcher; Pan Americana.* 1945: *Bad Man's Territory; Back to Bataan; Johnny Angel; Cornered; Sing Your Way Home; A Game of Death; Deadline at Dawn.* 1946: *Ding Dong Williams; The Bamboo Blonde; Crack-Up; Step by Step; Genius at Work; Nocturne; Beat the Band.* 1947: *A Likely Story; The Long Night; Riffraff; If You Knew Susie; So Well Remembered* (+Honoria Plesch); *The Miracle of the Bells.* 1948: *Return of the Badmen; Mystery in Mexico; Station West.* 1949: *Roughshod.*

1951: *The House On Telegraph Hill* (+Charles LeMaire); *As Young As You Feel* (+Charles LeMaire); *Mr Belvedere Rings the Bell* (+Charles LeMaire); *Let's Make It Legal* (+Charles LeMaire); *Love Nest* (+Charles LeMaire); *The Model and the Marriage Broker* (+Charles LeMaire); *Return of the Texan* (+Charles LeMaire); *The Guy Who Came Back* (+Charles LeMaire). 1952: *Wait 'Til the Sun Shines, Nellie* (+Charles LeMaire); *Dreamboat* (+Charles LeMaire); *Night Without Sleep* (+Charles LeMaire); *Taxi* (+Charles LeMaire); *Tonight We Sing* (+Charles LeMaire); *The President's Lady* (+Charles LeMaire); 1953: *Dangerous Crossing* (+Charles LeMaire); *Mr Scoutmaster* (+Charles LeMaire); *The Siege at Red River* (+Charles LeMaire); *Gorilla At Large; Vicki* (+LeMaire). 1954: *A Man Called Peter* (+Charles LeMaire); *Untamed* (+Charles LeMaire); 1956: *A King and Four Queens.* 1957: *Three Faces of Eve* (+Charles LeMaire); *The Girl Most Likely.* 1958: *The Big Fisherman.* 1961: *Snow White and the Three Stooges* (GB *Snow White and the Three Clowns*). 1962: *Cleopatra* (+Irene Sharaff, Vittorio Nino Novarese). 1964: *Circus World* (GB *The Magnificent Showman*); *The Pleasure Seekers.* 1966: *The Sand Pebbles.* 1967: *The Legend of Lylah Clare.* 1968: *The Killing of Sister George; Whatever Happened to Aunt Alice?* 1976: *Great Scout and Cathouse Thursday.* 1978: *Caravans.* 1981: *Body Heat.*

RHODES, LEAH

American designer, prolific at Warners in the '40s. Died 1986.

ACADEMY AWARD NOMINATION:

1949: **Adventures of Don Juan* (+Travilla, Marjorie Best).

FILMS:

1941: *The Smiling Ghost.* 1943: *Murder on the Waterfront; Find the Blackmailer; Northern Pursuit; The Desert Song* (+Marjorie Best); *Passage to Marseille.* 1944: *Between Two Worlds; The Conspirators; Experiment Perilous* (+Edward Stevenson); *God Is My Co-pilot; Roughly Speaking* (+Travis Banton); *Hotel Berlin.* 1945: *Confidential Agent; Saratoga Trunk; My Reputation* (+Edith Head). 1946: *Her Kind of Man; Two Guys from Milwaukee* (GB *Royal Flush*); *The Big Sleep; Cloak and Dagger; Never Say Goodbye; Pursued; That Way With Women; Stallion Road* (+Milo Anderson). 1947: *The Voice of the Turtle; My Girl Tisa.* 1948: *Wallflower; Key Largo; Two Guys from Texas* (GB *Two Texas Knights*); *Adventures of Don Juan* (+Travilla, Marjorie Best); *One Sunday Afternoon.* 1949: *Night Unto Night; Colorado Territory; The Girl from Jones Beach; Task Force; White Heat; The Story of Seabiscuit* (GB *Pride of Kentucky*); *Chain Lightning.* 1950: *Bright Leaf; Tea for Two; Three Secrets; The Breaking Point.* 1951: *Strangers on a Train; Mark of the Renegade; Come Fill the Cup; The Golden Horde; Starlift; I'll See you in My Dreams* (+Marjorie Best); *Bugles in the Afternoon; Room for One More* (+Marjorie Best). 1952: *About Face; The Winning Team; April in Paris.* 1953: *Abbott and Costello Go to Mars; Lone Hand; So This is Love* (GB *The Grace Moore Story*). 1957: *Forty Guns* (+Charles LeMaire). 1958: *Kings Go Forth.* 1965: *Tickle Me; Valley of the Giants.* 1966: *Picture Mommy Dead; Good Times.* 1968: *Five Card Stud.*

RICARDO, JOY

Born 1912. Trained as a designer under Patou and Ardance. Entered films in 1944 by designing Deborah Kerr's costumes for *Perfect Strangers.*

Gene Kelly and Jean Hagen in Singin' in the Rain *(Walter Plunkett)*

Leah Rhodes sketch for Doris Day in April in Paris

Helen Rose design for Celeste Holm in High Society

FILMS:

1946: *Take My Life; I See a Dark Stranger (US The Adventuress).*
1948: *One Night With You; Silent Dust (+Rahvis).*

RICKARDS, JOCELYN

Australian born designer for films and theatre, working in London since 1949. Started in films in 1956 on *The Prince and the Showgirl.*

ACADEMY AWARD NOMINATION:

1966: *Morgan – A Suitable Case for Treatment* (b&w).

SFTA NOMINATIONS:

1967: **Mademoiselle; The Sailor from Gibraltar.* 1970: *Ryan's Daughter.*

FILMS:

1959: *Look Back in Anger.* 1960: *The Entertainer.* 1963: *From Russia With Love.* 1964: *Rattle of a Simple Man.* 1965: *The Knack . . . and How to Get It; Morgan – A Suitable Case for Treatment.* 1966: *Mademoiselle; Blow-up.* 1967: *The Sailor From Gibraltar; Interlude.* 1968: *The Bliss of Mrs Blossom; Wonderwall.* 1969: *Alfred the Great; Laughter in the Dark.* 1970: *Ryan's Daughter.* 1971: *Sunday, Bloody Sunday.*

ROSE, HELEN

Studied at the Chicago Academy of Fine Arts before moving to Los Angeles in 1929. First professional job was with Fanchon and Marco, designing for their "Ice Follies". Fanchon and Marco supervised the costumes for the musical sequences in three Fox musicals, *Hello, Frisco, Hello, Coney Island* and *Stormy Weather,* and Helen Rose did the designs for these films. From 1942 she had a contract with M-G-M and worked almost exclusively for them until her retirement. Died 1985.

ACADEMY AWARD NOMINATIONS:

1951: *The Great Caruso* (+Gile Steele). 1952: *The Merry Widow* (+Gile Steele); **The Bad and the Beautiful* (b&w). 1953: *Dream Wife* (+Herschel). 1954: *Executive Suite* (b&w). 1955: **I'll Cry Tomorrow* (b&w); *Interrupted Melody.* 1956: *The Power and the Prize* (b&w). 1959: *The Gazebo* (b&w). 1966: *Mr Buddwing* (GB *Woman Without a Face*) (b&w).

FILMS:

1943: *Hello, Frisco, Hello; Coney Island; Stormy Weather.* 1945: *Ziegfeld Follies* (+Irene, Irene Sharaff); *The Harvey Girls* (+Irene, Valles); *Two Sisters From Boston* (+Valles). 1946: *Till the Clouds Roll By* (+Irene Valles). 1947: *The Unfinished Dance* (+Irene); *Good News* (+Valles); *The Big City; The Bride Goes Wild; Merton of the Movies* (+Irene). 1948: *Homecoming; A Date With Judy; Luxury Liner* (+Valles); *Act of Violence; Words and Music* (+Valles); *Take Me Out to the Ball Game* (GB *Everybody's Cheering*). 1949: *The Stratton Story; That Midnight Kiss; The Red Danube; East Side, West Side; On the Town; Nancy Goes to Rio; The Big Hangover.*

1950: *Annie Get Your Gun* (+Walter Plunkett); *Father of the Bride* (+Walter Plunkett); *Duchess of Idaho; Three Little Words; A Life of Her Own; Right Cross; Toast of New Orleans* (+Walter Plunkett); *Summer Stock* (GB *If You Feel Like Singing*) (+Walter Plunkett); *To Please a Lady; Two Weeks with Love* (+Walter Plunkett); *Grounds for Marriage; Pagan Love Song; Father's Little Dividend.*

1951: *The Great Caruso* (+Gile Steele); *Excuse My Dust* (+Gile Steele); *No Questions Asked; Rich, Young and Pretty; Strictly Dishonorable; The People Against O'Hara; The Strip; Texas Carnival; Too Young to Kiss; The Unknown Man; The Light Touch; Invitation; The Belle of New York* (+Gile Steele); *Love is Better than Ever* (GB *The Light Fantastic*); *The Girl in White* (GB *So Bright the Flame*).

1952: *Skirts Ahoy; Glory Alley; Holiday for Sinners; The Merry Widow* (+Gile Steele); *Washington Story* (GB *Target for Scandal*); *Because You're Mine; Everything I Have Is Yours; Above and Beyond; The Bad and the Beautiful; The Million Dollar Mermaid* (GB *One Piece Bathing Suit*); *Jeopardy; I Love Melvin; Small Town Girl; The Story of Three Loves; Dream Wife* (+Herschel); *Sombrero.*

1953: *The Girl Who Had Everything; Remains To Be Seen;*

Opposite: Irene Dunne in Roberta *(Bernard Newman)*

FASH-127

Designer Helen Rose with Grace Kelly

From left: Elizabeth Taylor in a Helen Rose design for A Date With Judy; Esther Williams in Jupiter's Darling (costume design by Helen Rose and Walter Plunkett); Helen Rose design for Lana Turner in The Merry Widow

Dangerous When Wet; Latin Lovers (+Herschel); Mogambo; Torch Song; Easy To Love; Escape From Fort Bravo; Give a Girl a Break (+Herschel); The Long, Long Trailer; Executive Suite; Rhapsody; Rose Marie.

1954: The Student Prince (+Walter Plunkett); Her Twelve Men; Rogue Cop; Athena (+Walter Plunkett); The Last Time I Saw Paris; Deep In My Heart (+Walter Plunkett); Green Fire; Jupiter's Darling (+Walter Plunkett); Hit the Deck; Interrupted Melody; The Glass Slipper (+Walter Plunkett). 1955: Bedevilled; Love Me or Leave Me; It's Always Fair Weather; The Opposite Sex; The Tender Trap; The Rains of Ranchipur (+Charles LeMaire, Travilla); I'll Cry Tomorrow; Ransom; Meet Me In Las Vegas (GB Viva Las Vegas); Forbidden Planet (+Walter Plunkett); Gaby.

1956: The Swan; High Society; These Wilder Years; The Power and the Prize; Tea and Sympathy; Ten Thousand Bedrooms; Designing Woman; Something of Value.

1957: The Seventh Sin; Silk Stockings; Tip on a Dead Jockey (GB Time for Action); Don't Go Near the Water; The High Cost of Loving; Saddle the Wind.

1958: Cat on a Hot Tin Roof; Party Girl; The Tunnel of Love; The Mating Game.

1959: Count Your Blessings; Ask Any Girl; It Started With a Kiss; The Gazebo; Never So Few; All the Fine Young Cannibals.

1960: Butterfield 8; Go Naked In the World. 1961: Ada; The Honeymoon Machine; Bachelor in Paradise. 1962: The Courtship of Eddie's Father. 1964: Goodbye Charlie. 1965: Made in Paris. 1966: Mr Buddwing (GB Woman Without a Face).

1967: How Sweet It Is!

Note: Anne Baxter's clothes for Bedevilled (1955) were designed by Helen Rose, but they showed too much cleavage and new clothes were supplied by Jean Desses. (The film was being made in France.) Helen Rose presumably had screen credit because of her contract.

ROTH, ANN

American costume designer, mostly theatre work, but occasional film credits from 1963.

ACADEMY AWARD NOMINATION:
1984: Places in the Heart.

SFTA NOMINATION:
1975. *The Day of the Locust.

Bernard Newman design for Ginger Rogers (with Fred Astaire) in Top Hat

Barbra Streisand in Funny Girl *(Irene Sharaff)*

Irene Sharaff design for Funny Girl

FILMS:

1963: *The World of Henry Orient*. 1965: *A Fine Madness*. 1967: *Up the Down Staircase; Sweet November*. 1968: *Pretty Poison*. 1969: *Midnight Cowboy; Jenny*. 1970: *The Owl and the Pussycat; They Might Be Giants; The People Next Door*. 1971: *Klute; The Pursuit of Happiness*. 1972: *The Valachi Papers* (+ Giorgio Desideri). 1975: *Law and Disorder; The Day of the Locust; The Happy Hooker; Mandingo*. 1976: *Murder By Death*. 1977: *The Goodbye Girl*. 1978: *California Suite* (+ Patrick Norris); *Coming Home; Nunzio*. 1979: *Hair; Promises in the Dark*. 1980: *Dressed to Kill; The Island; Nine to Five*. 1981: *Honky Tonk Freeway; Only When I Larf; Rollover*. 1982: *The World According to Garp*. 1983: *The Man Who Loved Women; Silkwood; The Survivors*. 1984: *Places in the Heart*. 1985: *Jagged Edge; Maxie; The Slugger's Wife; Sweet Dreams*. 1986: *Heartburn; The Morning After*.

ROYER

Born Lewis Royer Hastings, Washington DC, 1904. Adviser and stylist for Lord and Taylor and also lecturer in Costume and Interior design at New York University, Columbia University and New York School of Fine and Applied Art. Started at Fox as Studio Stylist in 1933 and worked there until 1939. At the Hal Roach studios from 1940 to 1942.

FILMS:

1933: *Arizona to Broadway; It's Great To Be Alive; The Man Who Dared; Charlie Chan's Greatest Case; Life In the Raw; Walls of Gold; The Mad Game; The Last Trail; Smoky; Olsen's Big Moment; Orient Express; Ever Since Eve; Jimmy and Sally*. 1934: *I Believed In You; Sleepers East; Murder in Trinidad; Three On a Honeymoon; Baby, Take a Bow; Handy Andy; Call It Luck; She Learned About Sailors; Wild Gold; Judge Priest; Charlie Chan in London; Pursued; Love Time; 365 Nights in Hollywood; Bright Eyes; Mystery Woman; The Great Hotel Murder*.

1935: *Black Sheep; Dante's Inferno; Ladies Love Danger*. 1936: *Sins of Man; To Mary, With Love; White Fang; Sing, Baby, Sing; Lloyds of London; Reunion; One in a Million; Stowaway; Fifty Roads To Town; Love is News*. 1937: *Cafe Metropole; This is My Affair (GB His Affair); Slave Ship; You Can't Have Everything; Thin Ice (GB Lovely to Look At); Life Begins in College (GB The Joy Parade); Love and Hisses; Happy Landing; In Old Chicago*. 1938: *Four Men and a Prayer; Kentucky Moonshine; Always Goodbye; Josette; Hold That Co-ed; My Lucky Star; Suez; Jesse James; The Three Musketeers; Wife, Husband and Friend*. 1939: *Rose of Washington Square; Young Mr Lincoln; Stanley and Livingstone; Here I Am a Stranger; Barricade; Swanee River; Daytime Wife; Little Old New York; The Story of Alexander Graham Bell (GB The Modern Miracle); Second Fiddle*.

1940: *Turnabout; Topper Returns*. 1941: *The Shanghai Gesture* (+ Oleg Cassini); *Brooklyn Orchid (GB The McGuerins from Brooklyn)*. 1942: *About Face; Miss Annie Rooney; Friendly Enemies; The Devil With Hitler; Taxi Mister*.

RUSSELL, SHIRLEY

Studied at the Royal Academy of Art. Designed costumes for many of Ken Russell's films.

ACADEMY AWARD NOMINATIONS:
1979: *Agatha*. 1981: *Reds*.

SFTA NOMINATIONS:
1969: *Women in Love*. 1977: *Valentino*. 1979: *Agatha;* ★*Yanks*. 1982: *Reds*. 1987: *Hope and Glory*.

FILMS:
1964: *French Dressing*. 1967: *Billion Dollar Brain*. 1969: *Women in Love*. 1970: *The Music Lovers*. 1971: *The Devils; The Boy Friend*. 1972: *Savage Messiah*. 1973: *Mahler*. 1974: *The Little Prince*. 1975: *Tommy; Lisztomania*. 1976: *Valentino*. 1979: *Agatha; Cuba; Yanks*. 1981: *Lady Chatterley's Lover; Reds*. 1983: *The Return of the Soldier; Wagner*. 1985: *The Bride*. 1987: *Hope and Glory*.

SALTERN, IRENE

Costume designer at Republic Pictures 1937/1938. Worked on some Columbia pictures and for Hal Roach Studios 1940/41.

Opposite: Bette Davis in Fashions of 1934 *(Orry-Kelly)*

Olivia de Havilland with designer Irene Sharaff on The Dark Mirror

FILMS:

1937: *Hollywood Stadium Mystery; King of the Newsboys; Prison Nurse.* 1938: *Call of the Yukon; Invisible Enemy; Under Western Stars; Gangs of New York; Romance on the Run; Army Girl; Ladies in Distress; Desperate Adventure; Tenth Avenue Kid; Night Hawk; Down in Arkansas; I Stand Accused; Storm Over Bengal; Orphans of the Street; Federal Manhunt: Pride of the Navy; The Mysterious Miss X; Woman Doctor; Forged Passport.* 1940: *The Howards of Virginia* (GB *The Tree of Liberty*); *The Westerner; Cheers for Miss Bishop.* 1941: *They Dare Not Love; Time Out For Rhythm; Niagara Falls.*

SANTIAGO, EMILE

American costume designer, first screen credits for Biblical films in the early '50s.

ACADEMY AWARD NOMINATION:

1953: **The Robe* (+Charles LeMaire).

FILMS:

1952: *Androcles and the Lion.* 1953: *Salome* (+Jean Louis); *The Robe* (+Charles LeMaire). 1955: *Strange Lady in Town.* 1958: *The Big Country* (+Yvonne Wood).

SCHIAPARELLI

Italian-born designer with couture houses in Paris and London.

FILMS:

1934: *Brewster's Millions* (+Motley, Norman Hartnell); *Little Friend.* 1935: *The Tunnel* (US *Transatlantic Tunnel*) (+Joe Strassner). 1935: *King of the Damned.* 1936: *Love in Exile; I'd Give My Life* (+Lucille Toray, Lanvin, Morgaleau, Creed, Victor Stiebel). 1937: *Jump for Glory* (US *When Thief Meets Thief*) (+Norman Hartnell); *Every Day's a Holiday.* 1938: *Artists and Models Abroad* (GB *Stranded in Paris*) (+Alix, Lanvin, Maggy Rouff, Paquin, Patou, Lelong, Worth); *Pygmalion* (+Professor L Czettel, Worth). 1952: *Moulin Rouge* (+Marcel Vertes).

SHARAFF, IRENE

Born Boston, Mass. Studied at the New York School of Fine and Applied Arts, the Art Student's League, New York and Grande Chaumière in Paris. Her first job in the theatre was as assistant to Aline Bernstein at the Civic Repertory Theatre Company in New York. Three years later Miss Sharaff designed sets and costumes for their 1932 production of "Alice in Wonderland". Since then she has designed costumes for plays, musicals, ballet and television. Her background in the theatre made her an ideal choice for filmed musicals, and she is one of the few designers who have worked on both stage

Opposite: Vivien Leigh in Gone With the Wind *(Walter Plunkett). Following pages: Barbara La Marr in* Heart of a Siren *(Charles LeMaire)*

shows and their subsequent film versions – including *The King and I*, *West Side Story*, *The Flower Drum Song* and *Funny Girl*.

ACADEMY AWARD NOMINATIONS:

1951: **An American in Paris* (+Orry-Kelly, Walter Plunkett). 1953: *Call Me Madam*. 1954: *Brigadoon*; *A Star is Born* (+Jean Louis, Mary Ann Nyberg). 1955: *Guys and Dolls*. 1956: **The King and I*. 1959: *Porgy and Bess*. 1960: *Can Can*. 1961: **West Side Story*; *The Flower Drum Song*. 1963: **Cleopatra* (+Vittorio Nino Novarese, Renie). 1966: **Who's Afraid of Virginia Woolf?* (b&w). 1967: *The Taming of the Shrew* (+Danilo Donati). 1969: *Hello, Dolly!* 1977: *The Other Side of Midnight*.

SFTA NOMINATION:

1969: *Funny Girl*.

FILMS:

1943: *Girl Crazy* (+Irene); *Broadway Rhythm* (+Irene, Gile Steele). 1944: *Bathing Beauty* (water ballet costumes); *Meet Me in St Louis* (+Irene). 1945: *Yolanda and the Thief* (+Irene). 1946: *The Dark Mirror*; *The Best of Years of our Lives*. 1947: *The Secret Life of Walter Mitty*; *The Bishop's Wife* (+Adrian). 1948: *Every Girl Should Be Married*. 1951: *An American in Paris* (+Orry-Kelly, Walter Plunkett). 1952: *Call Me Madam*. 1954: *Brigadoon*; *A Star is Born* (+Jean Louis, Mary Ann Nyberg). 1955: *Guys and Dolls*; *The King and I*. 1957: *Les Girls* (+Orry-Kelly). 1958: *Porgy and Bess*. 1959: *Can Can*. 1961: *West Side Story*; *The Flower Drum Song*; *Cleopatra* (+Vittorio Nino Novarese, Renie). 1965: *The Sandpiper*. 1966: *The Taming of the Shrew* (+Danilo Donati); *Who's Afraid of Virginia Woolf?* 1968: *Funny Girl*. 1969: *Justine*; *Hello, Dolly!* 1970: *The Great White Hope*. 1977: *The Other Side of Midnight*. 1981: *Mommie Dearest*.

SHOUP, HOWARD

Began his career in 1933 by working for the New York couture house of Hattie Carnegie, then to Bonwit Teller in 1935. Contract at Warner Brothers from 1935 to 1941. After leaving Warners, he went to M-G-M but, after a few months, was called up for military service. After the war, Shoup returned to M-G-M, but left to open a boutique in Beverly Hills, which he ran from 1950 to 1970. After opening the dress shop, he returned to Warners and worked there (with occasional freelance work at other studios) until he retired from the film industry. Shoup was the first President of the Costume Designers Guild and received the Adrian Award from the Guild. Died 1987.

ACADEMY AWARD NOMINATIONS:

1959: *The Young Philadelphians* (b&w). 1960: *The Rise and Fall of Legs Diamond* (b&w). 1961: *Claudelle Inglish* (b&w). 1964: *Kisses For My President* (b&w). 1965: *A Rage To Live* (b&w).

FILMS:

1936: *Her Husband's Secretary*; *Ready Willing and Able*. 1937: *A Family Affair*; *Back in Circulation*; *Marry the Girl*; *The Case of the Stuttering Bishop*; *Talent Scout* (GB *Studio Romance*); *San Quentin*; *Varsity Show*; *Expensive Husbands*; *The Perfect Specimen*; *The Footloose Heiress*; *Over the Goal*; *Love Is On the Air* (GB *Radio Murder Mystery*); *Submarine D-1*; *West of Shanghai*; *Torchy Blane, the Adventurous Blonde*; *Alcatraz Island*; *She Loved a Fireman*; *Swing Your Lady*; *The Daredevil Drivers*; *The Invisible Menace*; *Love, Honor and Behave*; *The Patient in Room 18*; *Sergeant Murphy*; *A Slight Case of Murder*; *Blondes at Work*; *Over the Wall*; *Wine, Women and Horses*. 1938: *Beloved Brat* (GB *A Dangerous Age*); *Gold Diggers in Paris* (GB *The Gay Impostors*); *Men Are Such Fools*; *Mystery House*; *Little Miss Thoroughbred*; *When Were You Born?*; *Mr Chump*; *Broadway Musketeers*; *Girls on Probation*; *Racket Busters*; *Torchy Gets Her Man*; *Going Places*; *Off the Record*; *Torchy Blane in Chinatown*; *Blackwell's Island*; *Secret Service of the Air*. 1939: *On Trial*; *The Kid from Kokomo* (GB *Orphan of the Ring*); *Daughters Courageous*; *Naughty But Nice*; *Each Dawn I Die*; *The Man Who Dared*; *Four Wives*; *No Place to Go*; *Private Detective*; *Calling Philo Vance*; *Enemy Agent* (GB *British Intelligence*); *The Story of Dr Ehrlich's Magic Bullet*; *Castle on the Hudson*.

1940: *It All Came True*; *Brother Orchid*; *Torrid Zone*; *The Man Who Talked Too Much*; *Murder in the Air*; *City for Conquest*; *The Case of the Black Parrot*; *Four Mothers*; *Footsteps in the Dark*. 1941: *Strange Alibi*; *Here Comes Happiness*; *Shining Victory*; *The*

Nurse's Secret; *International Squadron*; *Kisses for Breakfast*; *Navy Blues*; *Nine Lives Are Not Enough*; *All Through the Night*; *Captains of the Clouds*; *Born To Sing* (+Gile Steele); *Fingers at the Window*. 1942: *The Male Animal*; *Grand Central Murder*; *Tarzan's New York Adventure*; *The Affairs of Martha*; *Jackass Mail* (+Gile Steele); *Pierre of the Plains* (+Gile Steele); *Seven Sweethearts*; *Cabin in the Sky* (+Irene, Gile Steele); *Assignment in Brittany* (+Irene, Gile Steele); *The Youngest Profession* (+Irene). 1943: *Presenting Lily Mars*; *Dubarry Was a Lady* (+Irene). 1946: *Faithful In My Fashion* (+Irene); *Little Mister Jim* (+Irene); *The Mighty McGurk* (+Irene).

1952: *Stop, You're Killing Me*; *The Jazz Singer*; *She's Back on Broadway*. 1953: *House of Wax*; *Calamity Jane*; *So Big* (+Milo Anderson); *The Eddie Cantor Story* (+Marjorie Best); *The Boy From Oklahoma*. 1954: *Young at Heart*. 1955: *Serenade*; *The Court Martial of Billy Mitchell* (GB *One Man Mutiny*); *Pete Kelly's Blues*; *Sincerely Yours*. 1956: *Bundle of Joy*. 1957: *The Helen Morgan Story* (GB *Both Ends of the Candle*); *The Deep Six*; *Marjorie Morningstar*; *The Unholy Wife*; *Bombers B-52* (GB *No Sleep Till Dawn*). 1958: *Westbound*; *The Young Philadelphians* (GB *The City Jungle*); *Home Before Dark*; *I Married a Woman*; *Onionhead*; *Island of Lost Women*. 1959: *Cash McCall*; *The Bramble Bush*; *The Rise and Fall of Legs Diamond*.

1960: *Ice Palace*; *The Crowded Sky*; *Ocean's 11*; *Parrish*; *A Fever in the Blood*; *Portrait of a Mobster*. 1961: *Claudelle Inglish* (GB *Young and Eager*); *Susan Slade*; *Rome Adventure* (GB *Lovers Must Learn*). 1962: *Gypsy* (+Orry Kelly). 1963: *A Distant Trumpet*; *A Child is Waiting*; *All of Noise*. 1964: *Kisses For My President*; *Youngblood Hawke*. 1965: *A Rage to Live*. 1966: *An American Dream* (GB *See You In Hell, Darling*); *Hotel* (+Edith Head). 1967: *The Cool Ones*; *Cool Hand Luke*; *Oh Dad, Poor Dad . . .*

SQUIRE, JULIA

Born Surrey, 1926. Trained at Central London School of Art. Entered industry in 1945 as assistant on *London Town*.

FILMS:

1950: *Gone to Earth* (US *The Wild Heart*); *Pandora and the Flying Dutchman* (+Beatrice Dawson). 1951: *The Magic Box*. 1952: *Women of Twilight* (US *Twilight Women*). 1953: *The Heart of the Matter*; *The Captain's Paradise*; *An Inspector Calls*. 1954: *Father Brown* (US *The Detective*); *The Man Who Loved Redheads*. 1955: *Double Cross*; *The End of the Affair*. 1956: *Port Afrique*. 1958: *Beyond This Place* (US *Web of Evidence*).

STEELE, GILE

At M-G-M from 1938 to 1951, but occasional films at Paramount. Specialised in men's costumes. Died 1952.

ACADEMY AWARDS NOMINATIONS:

1948: *The Emperor Waltz* (+Edith Head). 1949: **The Heiress* (+Edith Head) (b&w). 1950: **Samson and Delilah* (+Edith Head, Dorothy Jeakins, Elois Jenssen, Gwen Wakeling). 1951: *Kind Lady* (+Walter Plunkett) (b&w); *The Great Caruso* (+Helen Rose). 1952: *The Merry Widow* (+Helen Rose).

FILMS:

1938: *The Toy Wife* (GB *Frou Frou*) (+Adrian); *Marie Antoinette* (+Adrian). 1939: *Broadway Melody of 1940* (+Adrian); *The Man from Dakota* (+Dolly Tree).

1940: *Twenty Mule Team* (+Dolly Tree); *Florian* (+Adrian); *Edison, the Man* (+Dolly Tree); *Waterloo Bridge* (+Irene); *New Moon* (+Adrian); *Pride and Prejudice* (+Adrian); *The Mortal Storm* (+Adrian); *Boom Town* (+Adrian); *Wyoming* (GB *Bad Man of Wyoming*) (+Dolly Tree); *Strike Up the Band* (+Dolly Tree); *Escape* (+Adrian); *Little Nellie Kelly* (+Dolly Tree); *Bitter Sweet* (+Adrian); *Comrade X* (+Adrian); *Flight Command* (+Dolly Tree); *Go West* (GB *The Marx Brothers Go West*) (+Dolly Tree).

1941: *The Bad Man* (GB *Two Gun Cupid*) (+Dolly Tree); *Billy the Kid* (+Dolly Tree); *A Woman's Face* (+Adrian); *Wild Man of Borneo* (+Dolly Tree); *They Met in Bombay* (+Adrian); *Blossoms in the Dust* (+Adrian); *Dr Jekyll and Mr Hyde* (+Adrian); *Honky Tonk* (+Robert Kalloch); *The Chocolate Soldier* (+Adrian); *H M Pulham Esq* (+Robert Kalloch); *Born to Sing* (+Howard Shoup); *Rio Rita* (+Robert Kalloch); *Smilin' Through* (+Adrian); *Tortilla Flat* (+Kalloch).

1942: *Mrs Miniver* (+Robert Kalloch); *Jackass Mail* (+Howard Shoup); *Pierre of the Plains* (+Howard Shoup); *For Me*

From Reaching for the Moon *(Cox)*

The Boy Friend.

Polly Browne
Room in Bloomsʳ

Shirley Russell sketch for Twiggy in The Boy Friend

and My Gal (+Robert Kalloch); Cabin in the Sky (+Irene, Howard Shoup); Assignment in Brittany (+Irene, Howard Shoup).

1943: Above Suspicion (+Irene); Best Foot Forward (+Irene); The Man from Down Under (+Irene); Madame Curie (+Irene); The Cross of Lorraine; Broadway Rhythm (+Irene, Irene Sharaff); Dubarry Was a Lady (+Irene, Shoup). 1944: White Cliffs of Dover. 1946: California (+Edith Head). 1947: The Imperfect Lady (+Dorothy O'Hara); I Remember Mama (+Edward Stevenson); A Connecticut Yankee in King Arthur's Court (+Head, Dodson). 1948: The Emperor Waltz (+Edith Head): The Paleface (+Mary K Dodson).

1949: The Heiress (+Edith Head). 1951: The Great Caruso (+Helen Rose); Excuse My Dust (+Helen Rose); Kind Lady (+Walter Plunkett); The Law and the Lady (+Walter Plunkett); Man With a Cloak (Walter Plunkett); Lone Star; The Belle of New York (+Helen Rose); Scaramouche; The Merry Widow (+Helen Rose).

STEVENSON, EDWARD

Born Pocatello, Idaho, 1906. Died 1968. On moving to Hollywood in 1922, he met Andre-Ani who taught him fashion illustration. When Andre-Ani went to M-G-M in 1925, Edward Stevenson went with him to work as his sketch artist. In 1927 he became an assistant designer at Fox, but after one

Kay Francis and Basil Rathbone in
A Notorious Affair (Edward Stevenson)

year he moved to First National as head designer, staying there until 1931. Following a short spell at the Hal Roach Studio, he opened his own shop and often supplied clothes to studios without a contract designer. But, anxious to get back into films, Stevenson once more worked as a sketch artist, this time for Bernard Newman on Roberta in 1934. When Newman returned to New York, Stevenson was given a contract at RKO which lasted for thirteen years. Howard Hughes bought RKO in 1949 and Stevenson once again moved to Fox, leaving in 1951. From 1954 until his death he worked with Lucille Ball on her television shows "I Love Lucy" and "Here's Lucy."

ACADEMY AWARD NOMINATIONS:
1951: The Mudlark (b&w) (+Margaret Furse); David and Bathsheba (+Charles LeMaire). 1960: *The Facts of Life (b&w) (+Edith Head).

FILMS:
1929: Smiling Irish Eyes; Sally; Ladies of Leisure. 1930: Murder Will Out; A Notorious Affair; Song of the Flame; Sweethearts and Wives; Father's Son; Kiss Me Again (GB Toast of the Legion); Woman Hungry (GB The Challenge). 1931: Party Husband; Big Business Girl; Men of the Sky; The Public Enemy (+Luick). 1932: The Bitter Tea of General Yen (+Robert Kalloch); Forbidden. 1936: Special Investigator; Grand Jury; Second Wife; We Who Are About to Die; That Girl From Paris; Mummy's Boys; The Plot Thickens (GB The Swinging Pearl Mystery); Night Waitress; We're on the Jury; Sea

Devils; They Wanted to Marry; Too Many Wives. 1937: There Goes My Girl; You Can't Buy Luck; You Can't Beat Love; Super Sleuth; The Toast of New York; The Life of the Party; Fight for Your Lady; Music For Madame; Breakfast For Two; There Goes the Groom; Hitting a New High; Radio City Revels. 1938: Blond Cheat; The Saint in New York; Having Wonderful Time (+Renie); Maid's Night Out; This Marriage Business; Mother Carey's Chickens; Carefree (+Howard Greer); The Mad Miss Manton; Gunga Din; Pacific Liner; Beauty For the Asking; The Story of Vernon and Irene Castle (+Plunkett, Irene Castle). 1939: Sorority House (GB That Girl from College); Panama Lady; Five Came Back; In Name Only (+Irene); Nurse Edith Cavell; Three Sons; Reno; That's Right, You're Wrong; The Swiss Family Robinson; The Joy of Living.

1940: Irene; You Can't Fool Your Wife; Anne of Windy Poplars (GB Anne of Windy Willows); Tom Brown's Schooldays; Dance Girl Dance; They Knew What They Wanted; Too Many Girls; You'll Find Out; Little Men; No, No, Nanette; Play Girl. 1941: Citizen Kane; They Met in Argentina; All that Money Can Buy; My Life with Caroline; Suspicion; Playmates. 1942: Valley of the Sun; Syncopation; Journey Into Fear; The Magnificent Ambersons. 1943: Action in Arabia; The Curse of the Cat People; The Fallen Sparrow; Gangway for Tomorrow; Government Girl; The Ghost Ship; Higher and Higher; Passport to Destiny. 1944: Show Business; Step Lively; Bride By Mistake; Mademoiselle Fifi; Marine Raiders; Experiment Perilous (+Leah Rhodes); What a Blonde; The Enchanted Cottage; Youth Runs Wild.

1945: China Sky; George White's Scandals; Isle of the Dead; Man Alive; The Spanish Main; From this Day Forward. 1946: Do You Love Me? (+Kay Nelson); Bedlam; Lady Luck; It's a Wonderful Life; Sinbad the Sailor (+Dwight Franklin). 1947: Born to Kill (GB Lady of Deceit); Honeymoon; They Won't Believe Me; The Woman on the Beach; The Bachelor and the Bobby-soxer (GB Bachelor Knight); Out of the Past (GB Build My Gallows High); The Judge Steps Out (GB Indian Summer); I Remember Mama (+Gile Steele). 1948: Race Street; Blood on the Moon; A Woman's Secret. 1949: The Big Steal; Easy Living.

1950: Cheaper by the Dozen (+Charles LeMaire); Stella (+Charles LeMaire); The Jackpot (+Charles LeMaire); The Mudlark (+Margaret Furse); I'd Climb the Highest Mountain (+Charles LeMaire); The Thirteenth Letter (+Charles LeMaire); Fourteen Hours (+Charles LeMaire). 1951: Secret of Convict Lake (+Charles LeMaire); David and Bathsheba (+Charles LeMaire); Anne of the Indies (+Charles LeMaire); Red Skies of Montana (+Charles LeMaire); At Sword's Point (GB Sons of the Musketeers). 1952: What Price Glory (+Charles LeMaire); O Henry's Full House (GB Full House) (with Charles LeMaire); Against All Flags; The Silver Whip (+Charles LeMaire); Pony Soldier (GB MacDonald of the Mounties). 1953: War Arrow. 1956: The Magnificent Matador (GB The Brave and the Beautiful); The First Travelling Saleslady; Everything but the Truth. 1960: The Facts of Life (+Edith Head).

Irene Dunne in The Joy of Living (Stevenson)

Ron Talsky design for The Wild Party

Designer Ron Talsky

STRASSNER, JOE

German designer brought from Berlin in 1933 to the Fox Studios in Hollywood by the actress Lilian Harvey. Came to Britain in 1934 and worked in various British studios until 1941.

FILMS:

1933: *Best of Enemies*; *My Weakness* (+Rita Kaufman); *My Lips Betray*. 1934: *Abdul the Damned*; *The Dictator*. 1935: *Escape Me Never*; *Bulldog Jack* (US *Alias Bulldog Drummond*); *The Thirty-Nine Steps*; *Stormy Weather*; *The Clairvoyant*; *First a Girl*; *The Tunnel* (US *Transatlantic Tunnel*) (+Schiaparelli); *The Guv'nor*; *Jack of All Trades*; *Rhodes of Africa*. 1936: *It's Love Again*; *Secret Agent*; *Tudor Rose* (US *Nine days a Queen*); *Everything Is Thunder*; *East Meets West*; *As You Like It* (+John Armstrong); *His Lordship* (US *Man of Affairs*); *Sabotage* (US *The Woman Alone*); *Head Over Heels*. 1937: *Take My Tip*; *Dreaming Lips*. 1938: *We're Going to Be Rich*. 1940: *Under Your Hat*. 1941: *He Found a Star* (+Norman Hartnell).

SYLBERT, ANTHEA

American designer in films from 1967.

ACADEMY AWARD NOMINATIONS:
1974: *Chinatown*. 1977: *Julia*.

SFTA NOMINATIONS:
1974: *Chinatown*. 1978: *Julia*.

FILMS:

1967: *The Tiger Makes Out*. 1968: *Rosemary's Baby*; *The Illustrated Man*. 1969: *Where It's At*; *Some Kind of a Nut*; *John and Mary*. 1970: *A New Leaf*. 1971: *Carnal Knowledge*; *The Cowboys*; *The Steagle*. 1972: *Bad Company*; *The Heartbreak Kid*. 1973: *The Day of the Dolphin*. 1974: *Chinatown*. 1975: *The Fortune*; *Shampoo*. 1976: *King Kong* (+Mabry). 1977: *Julia*. 1978: *F.I.S.T.*

TALSKY, RON

American designer who started with the Western Costume Company after several other jobs in the film industry. Responsible for Raquel Welch's costumes in CBS-TV specials and her films *Kansas City Bomber*, *The Three Musketeers*, *The Four Musketeers* and *The Wild Party*.

ACADEMY AWARD NOMINATION:
1975: *The Four Musketeers* (+Yvonne Blake).

SFTA AWARD NOMINATIONS:
1974: *The Three Musketeers* (+Yvonne Blake). 1975: *The Four Musketeers* (+Yvonne Blake).

FILMS:

1970: *Tell Me That You Love Me, Junie Moon* (+Phyllis Garr, Halston). 1971: *Such Good Friends* (+Hope Bryce Preminger); *The Sporting Club*. 1972: *Kansas City Bomber*; *A Separate Peace*. 1973: *Hit*; *The Three Musketeers* (+Yvonne Blake). 1974: *99 and 44/100% Dead!* (GB *Call Harry Crown*). 1975: *The Four Musketeers* (+Yvonne Blake); *The Wild Party*; *Sheila Levine Is Dead and Living in New York*. 1977: *The Deep*. 1978: *Hot Lead and Cold Feet*. 1979: *Jaguar Lives*; *The Ravagers*. 1980: *Inside Moves*. 1981: *Chu Chu and the Philly Flash*. 1982: *That Championship Season*.

TAYLOR, HELEN

Born Medford, Mass. Educated at Wellesley and schools of art in Boston and New York. Went to Hollywood and appeared in several films. Became assistant to Gwen Wakeling at United Artists. Later became Chief Stylist for Walter Wanger.

FILMS:

1935: *Every Night at Eight*; *Mary Burns, Fugitive*; *The Melody Lingers On*; *Trail of the Lonesome Pine*. 1936: *The Moon's Our Home*; *Big Brown Eyes*; *The Case Against Mrs Ames*; *Fatal Lady*; *Palm Springs* (GB *Palm Springs Affair*); *Spendthrift*; *You Only Live Once*. 1937: *Vogues of 1938* (GB *Walter Wanger's Vogues of 1938*); *Stand-in*; *52nd Street*; *I Met My Love Again*. 1938: *Trade Winds* (+Irene).

Lilian Harvey wearing a Joe Strassner design for My Lips Betray

Joan Bennett in I Met My Love Again *(Helen Taylor)*

Joan Bennett in Vogues of 1938 *(Helen Taylor)*

Helen Taylor design for The Melody Lingers On

Design for Josephine Hutchinson in The Melody Lingers On

1940: *My Son, My Son!* (+William Bridgehouse); 1941: *Pot o' Gold* (GB *The Golden Hour*).

THOMAS, BILL

Born Chicago, 1921. Studied at the Art Centre, Los Angeles. From 1947 to 1948 was assistant costume designer at M-G-M, then to Universal from 1949 to 1959. Also assistant to Irene at Irene Inc. Freelance since 1959.

ACADEMY AWARD NOMINATIONS:

1960: *Seven Thieves* (b&w); **Spartacus* (+Valles). 1961: *Babes in Toyland*. 1962: *Bon Voyage*. 1963: *Toys in the Attic* (b&w). 1965: *Ship of Fools* (+Jean Louis) (b&w); *Inside Daisy Clover* (+Edith

Opposite: Madeleine Carroll in The Case Against Mrs Ames *(Taylor)*

Head). 1967: *The Happiest Millionaire*. 1970: *The Hawaiians* (GB *Master of the Islands*). 1971: *Bedknobs and Broomsticks*.

FILMS:

1950: *Spy Hunt* (GB *Panther's Moon*); *The Desert Hawk*; *Wyoming Mail*; *Mystery Submarine*; *Tomahawk* (GB *Battle of Powder River*); *Undercover Girl*. 1951: *Apache Drums*; *Smuggler's Island*; *The Prince Who Was a Thief*; *The Iron Man*; *Little Egypt* (GB *Chicago Masquerade*); *Thunder on the Hill* (GB *Bonaventure*); *You Never Can Tell* (GB *You Never Know*); *The Lady Pays Off*; *The Raging Tide*; *Flame of Araby*; *Weekend With Father*; *The Cimarron Kid*; *Meet Danny Wilson*; *Flesh and Fury*; *Steel Town*. 1952: *No Room for the Groom*; *The World in His Arms*; *The Duel at Silver Creek*; *Untamed Frontier*; *The Black Castle*; *Bonzo Goes to College*; *Yankee Buccaneer*; *Riders of Vengeance*; *It Grows on Trees*; *Mississippi Gambler*; *Desert Legion*. 1953: *It Happens Every Thursday*; *Take Me To Town*; *The Man from the Alamo*; *The Great Sioux Uprising*; *The Stand at Apache River*; *Wings of the Hawk*; *Back to God's Country*; *The Glass Web*; *Forbidden*; *Saskatchewan* (GB *O'Rourke of the Royal Mounted*). 1954: *Magnificent Obsession*; *Playgirl*; *Black Horse Canyon*; *Sign of the*

Sandra Dee with designer Bill Thomas

Pagan; The Yellow Mountain; Captain Lightfoot; Smoke Signal.
1955: *Never Say Goodbye; The World in My Corner; The Purple Mask; Foxfire; One Desire; All That Heaven Allows; Running Wild; The Benny Goodman Story; The Spoilers.* 1956: *Behind the High Wall; The Rawhide Years; I've Lived Before; Raw Edge; Walk the Proud Land; Written on the Wind* (+ Jay Morley); *The Great Man; Rock, Pretty Baby; Istanbul; Mr Cory; The Night Runner; Girl in the Kremlin; Man Afraid; Battle Hymn.* 1957: *Night Passage; The Midnight Story* (GB *Appointment With a Shadow*); *Man of a Thousand Faces; My Man Godfrey; Slaughter on 10th Avenue; Slim Carter; The Tarnished Angels; Flood Tide* (GB *Above All Things*); *The Lady Takes a Flyer; Touch of Evil; A Time to Love and a Time to Die; Live Fast, Die Young; Man in the Shadow* (GB *Pay the Devil*); *Tammy and the Bachelor.* 1958: *Once Upon a Horse; The Restless Years* (GB *The Wonderful Years*); *Never Steal Anything Small; No Name on the Bullet; Imitation of Life* (+ Jean Louis); *The Female Animal; Kathy O'; Monster on the Campus; The Perfect Furlough* (GB *Strictly for Pleasure*); *The Saga of Hemp Brown; The Thing That Couldn't Die; Twilight for the Gods; Voice in the Mirror; Stranger in My Arms.* 1959: *This Earth Is Mine; Operation Petticoat; Take a Giant Step; Wake Me When It's Over; Seven Thieves; Curse of the Undead; Pillow Talk* (+ Louis); *The Rabbit Trap.*

Opposite: Carole Landis in
Having Wonderful Crime *(Stevenson)*

1960: *The Leech Woman; One Foot in Hell; High Time; Spartacus* (+ Valles); *North to Alaska.* 1961: *The Parent Trap; By Love Possessed; Babes in Toyland; Moon Pilot.* 1962: *Bon Voyage!; Boys' Night Out* (+ Kim Novak); *Son of Flubber.* 1963: *Summer Magic; Toys in the Attic; It's a Mad, Mad, Mad, Mad World; The Prize; A Global Affair.* 1964: *Honeymoon Hotel; Mary Poppins; The Americanization of Emily; Kiss Me Stupid; Those Calloways.*
1965: *Cat Ballou; Ship of Fools* (+ Jean Louis); *That Darn Cat; Inside Daisy Clover* (+ Edith Head). 1966: *Lt Robinson Crusoe, USN; Follow Me, Boys!; Monkeys, Go Home!; The Adventures of Bullwhip Griffin.* 1967. *The Happiest Millionaire; The Gnomemobile; Blackbeard's Ghost; The One and Only Genuine, Original Family Band.* 1968: *Never a Dull Moment; The Horse in the Gray Flannel Suit; The Love Bug.* 1969: *The Gypsy Moths; The Undefeated; The Trouble with Girls.* 1970: *The Hawaiians* (GB *Master of the Islands*); 1971: *The Seven Minutes; Bedknobs and Broomsticks.* 1973: *Oklahoma Crude.* 1974: *The Island at the Top of the World.* 1976: *Logan's Run.* 1977: *Pete's Dragon.* 1979: *The Black Hole.* 1980: *The Formula.*

TOMS, CARL

British designer who has designed sets and costumes for

William Travilla and Sheree North: How To Be Very, Very Popular

theatre, opera, ballet and television. Studied at the Royal College of Art and at the Old Vic School.

FILMS:
1964: *She.* 1966: *One Million Years BC; The Quiller Memorandum; Slave Girls; Jules Verne's Rocket to the Moon* (US *Those Fantastic Flying Fools*). 1967: *The Vengeance of She.* 1968: *The Lost Continent; The Winter's Tale.* 1969: *Moon Zero Two.* 1970: *When Dinosaurs Ruled the Earth.*

TRAVILLA, WILLIAM

American costume designer in films from 1941. At Columbia 1942/43, then three years at Warners from 1946/49. Under contract to Fox from 1949 to 1956 with occasional films for Fox as a freelance designer. Died 1990.

Opposite: Barbra Streisand in Funny Girl *(Irene Sharaff)*

ACADEMY AWARD NOMINATIONS:
1949: **Adventures of Don Juan* (+Leah Rhodes, Marjorie Best). 1953: *How to Marry a Millionaire* (+Charles LeMaire). 1954: *There's No Business Like Show Business* (+Charles LeMaire, Miles White). 1963: *The Stripper* (GB *Woman of Summer*).

FILMS:
1941: *All American Co-ed.* 1942: *Two Yanks in Trinidad.* 1943: *The Desperadoes; Redhead From Manhattan; Two Senoritas from Chicago* (GB *Two Senoritas*). 1946: *The Verdict; The Beast With Five Fingers; Nora Prentiss; Love and Learn.* 1947: *The Unfaithful; Cry Wolf* (+Edith Head); *Escape Me Never* (+Bernard Newman); *That Hagen Girl; Always Together; My Wild Irish Rose.* 1948: *Silver River* (+Marjorie Best); *Good Sam; Two Guys from Texas* (GB *Two Texas Knights*) (+Leah Rhodes); *Adventures of Don Juan* (+Leah Rhodes, Marjorie Best). 1949: *Flamingo Road; Look for the Silver Lining* (+Marjorie Best); *Dancing in the Dark* (+Charles LeMaire); *The Inspector General; When Willie Comes Marching Home* (+Charles LeMaire); *Mother Didn't Tell Me* (+Charles LeMaire).
1950: *The Gunfighter* (+Charles LeMaire); *The Daughter of*

Rosie O'Grady (+Marjorie Best); *Panic in the Streets* (+Charles LeMaire); *No Way Out* (+Charles LeMaire); *Mr 880* (+Charles LeMaire); *I'll Get By* (+Charles LeMaire); *American Guerilla in the Philippines* (GB *I Shall Return*) (+Charles LeMaire); *Rawhide* (+Charles LeMaire); *Woman on the Run*. 1951: *On the Riviera* (+Charles LeMaire, Oleg Cassini); *Take Care of My Little Girl* (+Charles LeMaire); *Meet Me After the Show* (+Charles LeMaire); *The Day the Earth Stood Still* (+Perkins Bailey, Charles LeMaire); *The Pride of St Louis* (+Charles LeMaire); *Viva Zapata!* (+Charles LeMaire). 1952: *She's Working Her Way Through College* (+Marjorie Best); *Lydia Bailey* (+Charles LeMaire); *Don't Bother to Knock* (+Charles LeMaire); *Monkey Business* (+Charles LeMaire); *Bloodhounds of Broadway* (+LeMaire). 1953: *The Farmer Takes a Wife* (+Charles LeMaire); *Down Among the Sheltering Palms* (+Charles LeMaire); *Powder River* (+Charles LeMaire); *Pickup on South Street* (+Charles LeMaire); *The Girl Next Door* (+Charles LeMaire); *Gentlemen Prefer Blondes* (+Charles LeMaire); *How to Marry a Millionaire* (+Charles LeMaire); *King of the Khyber Rifles* (+Charles LeMaire); *Man in the Attic* (+Charles LeMaire); *Hell and High Water* (+Charles LeMaire); *Three Young Texans* (+Charles LeMaire). 1954: *River of No Return* (+Charles LeMaire); *The Rocket Man*; *Princess of the Nile*; *The Raid*; *Garden of Evil* (+Charles LeMaire); *Broken Lance* (+Charles LeMaire); *The Gambler from Natchez*; *The Black Widow* (+Charles LeMaire); *There's No Business Like Show Business* (+Charles LeMaire, Miles White): *White Feather*.

1955: *The Seven Year Itch* (+Charles LeMaire); *How To Be Very, Very Popular* (+Charles LeMaire); *The Left Hand of God* (+Charles LeMaire); *The Tall Man* (+Charles LeMaire); *Gent-*

Arnold Scaasi (who designed the modern costumes for On a Clear Day You Can See Forever) *with Barbra Streisand*

lemen Marry Brunettes (+Christian Dior); *The Rains of Ranchipur* (+Helen Rose); *The Lieutenant Wore Skirts* (+Charles LeMaire); *The Bottom of the Bottle* (GB *Beyond the River*). 1956: *The Revolt of Mamie Stover* (+Charles LeMaire); *Twenty Three Paces to Baker Street* (+Charles LeMaire); *The Proud Ones* (+Charles LeMaire); *Bus Stop* (+Charles LeMaire). 1957: *The Fuzzy Pink Nightgown*.

1960: *From the Terrace*. 1962: *The Stripper* (GB *Woman of Summer*). 1963: *Mary, Mary; Take Her, She's Mine*. 1964: *Signpost to Murder*. 1967: *Valley of the Dolls*. 1968: *The Secret Life of an American Wife*; *The Boston Strangler*; *Daddy's Gone a Hunting*. 1969: *WUSA*.

TREE, DOLLY

American costume designer, real name Dorothy Tree. Before working in films, she was a theatrical designer. Designed for various Broadway musicals, plays and revues in the '20s; also designed the costumes for Mae West's original New York stage production of "Diamond Lil". 1927: designer for Paramount Circuit and Capitol Stage Shows. 1929: Winfield Sheehan put her under contract as "fashion creator" at Fox. 1932: moved to M-G-M where she worked until 1942.

FILMS:

1930: *Just Imagine* (+Sophie Wachner, Alice O'Neill). 1931: *Annabelle's Affairs*; *Bad Girl*; *Wicked*; *Stepping Sisters*; *Business and Pleasure*. 1932: *Almost Married*; *Meet the Baron*. 1933: *The Prizefighter and the Lady* (GB *Every Woman's Man*); *The Chief*. 1934: *Lazy River*; *Viva, Villa*; *Laughing Boy*; *Manhattan Melodrama*; *The Thin Man*; *Stamboul Quest*; *Hide-Out*; *Straight Is the Way*; *Evelyn Prentice*; *The Gay Bride*; *A Wicked Woman*; *David Copperfield*; *The Night Is Young*; *Vanessa, Her Story* (GB *Vanessa*); *West Point of the Air*; *The Casino Murder Case*; *Times Square Lady*.

1935: *Age of Indiscretion*; *One New York Night*; *Public Hero No 1*; *Escapade*; *The Flame Within*; *Mad Love* (GB *The Hands of Orlac*); *Woman Wanted*; *The Bishop Misbehaves*; *Here Comes The Band*; *It's In the Air*; *A Night at the Opera*; *Ah, Wilderness*; *A Tale of Two Cities*; *Riffraff*; *Three Live Ghosts*; *Exclusive Story*; *Whipsaw*; *The Garden Murder Case*; *The Voice of Bugle Ann*; *Wife Versus Secretary*; *Moonlight Murder*; *Petticoat Fever*; *The Robin Hood of Eldorado*; *Three Godfathers*.

1936: *Absolute Quiet*; *Small Town Girl*; *The Unguarded Hour*; *Fury*; *Three Wise Guys*; *We Went To College*; *The Devil-Doll*; *Suzy*; *Sworn Enemy*; *His Brother's Wife*; *Piccadilly Jim*; *Libeled Lady*; *Mad Holiday*; *Sinner Takes All*; *After the Thin Man*; *Dangerous Number*; *The Good Earth*; *Espionage*; *Personal Property* (GB *The Man in Possession*).

1937: *Good Old Soak*; *Night Must Fall*; *Mama Steps Out*; *Song of the City*; *A Day at the Races*; *Saratoga*; *Live, Love and Learn*; *My Dear Miss Aldrich*; *Navy Blue and Gold*; *Thoroughbreds Don't Cry*; *Rosalie*; *The Badman From Brimstone*; *Man Proof*; *Paradise For Three* (GB *Romance For Three*); *The First Hundred Years*; *Of Human Hearts*; *Big City*; *Arsene Lupin Returns*.

Greta Gynt in Mr Emmanuel *(design by Harald)*

Opposite: Barbara Stanwyck in Executive Suite *(Helen Rose)*

Anna Neagle in The Little Damozel: *design by Doris Zinkeisen*

1938: *Four Girls in White; The Girl Downstairs; Stand Up and Fight* (+Valles); *Fast and Loose; Let Freedom Ring* (+Valles); *Ice Follies of 1939* (+Adrian); *Test Pilot; Hold That Kiss; Yellow Jack* (+Gile Steele); *Fast Company; Lord Jeff* (GB *The Boy From Barbados*); *Port of Seven Seas; Woman Against Woman; The Chaser; The Crowd Roars; Rich Man, Poor Girl; Too Hot to Handle; Listen, Darling; Spring Madness.*

1939: *Young Tom Edison* (+Gile Steele); *The Kid From Texas* (+Valles); *Society Lawyer; Within the Law; Bridal Suite; Lucky Night; Tell No Tales; Maisie* (+Valles); *On Borrowed Time; Six Thousand Enemies; Stronger Than Desire; Miracles For Sale; These Glamour Girls; They All Came Out; Babes in Arms; Blackmail; Thunder Afloat* (+Valles); *Another Thin Man; At the Circus* (+Valles); *Bad Little Angel* (+Valles); *Congo Maisie; The Man From Dakota* (+Gile Steele); *Forty Little Mothers; Dancing Co-ed* (GB *Every Other Inch a Lady*).

1940: *Twenty Mule Team* (+Gile Steele); *Two Girls on Broadway* (GB *Choose Your Partner*); *Edison, The Man* (+Gile Steele); *The Captain Is a Lady; We Who Are Young; Andy Hardy Meets Debutante; I Love You Again; Wyoming* (GB *Bad Man of Wyoming*) (+Valles); *Dr Kildare Goes Home; Strike Up the Band* (+Gile Steele); *Gold Rush Maisie; Hullabaloo; Third Finger, Left Hand; The Golden Fleecing; Little Nellie Kelly* (+Gile Steele); *Flight Command* (+Gile Steele); *Go West* (GB *The Marx*

Brothers Go West) (+Gile Steele); *The Penalty; The Trial of Mary Dugan; The Bad Man* (GB *Two Gun Cupid*) (+Gile Steele); *Sporting Blood.*

1941: *Free and Easy; Billy the Kid* (+Gile Steele); *Wild Man of Borneo* (+Gile Steele).

1942: *Two Gentlemen From West Point; The Magnificent Dope; The Loves of Edgar Allan Poe; The Pied Piper; Thunder Birds; Tales of Manhattan* (+Irene, B Newman, Wakeling, Cassini).

URBAN THURLOW, GRETL

Daughter of Joseph Urban, who designed shows for Florenz Ziegfeld. Worked on several films with her father for William Randolph Hearst's Cosmopolitan Pictures.

FILMS:

1922: *When Knighthood was in Flower.* 1923: *Enemies of Women;*

Opposite: Faye Dunaway in Chinatown *(Anthea Sylbert)*

Hedda Hopper in The Snob *(Sophie Wachner)*

Theadora van Runkle design for I Love You, Alice B Toklas

Little Old New York; Under the Red Robe. 1924: *Yolande; Janice Meredith.* 1925: *Zander the Great; Never the Twain Shall Meet.*

VALLES

Full name J Arlington Valles. American costume designer, mostly at M-G-M, who specialised in men's costumes. Usually shared costume credit with Irene, Dolly Tree, Helen Rose or Walter Plunkett, but some solo screen credits. Died 1970.

ACADEMY AWARD NOMINATIONS:

1950: *That Forsyte Woman* (GB *The Forsyte Saga*) (+Walter Plunkett). 1960: **Spartacus* (+Bill Thomas).

FILMS:

1938: *Stand Up and Fight* (+Dolly Tree); *The Adventures of Huckleberry Finn; Let Freedom Ring* (+Dolly Tree). 1939: *The Kid from Texas* (+Dolly Tree); *Maisie* (+Dolly Tree); *Lady of the Tropics* (+Adrian); *Thunder Afloat* (+Dolly Tree); *At the Circus* (+Dolly Tree); *Bad Little Angel* (+Dolly Tree); *Balalaika* (+Adrian). 1944: *Dragon Seed* (+Irene); *Lost in a Harem* (+Irene, Kay Dean); *National Velvet* (+Irene, Kay Dean); *Mrs Parkington* (+Irene, Marion Herwood Keyes); *The Picture of Dorian Gray* (+Irene, Marion Herwood Keyes).

1945: *The Hoodlum Saint* (+Irene, Marion Herwood Keyes); *The Green Years* (+Irene); *Two Sisters from Boston* (+Helen Rose); *Her Highness and the Bellboy* (+Herwood Keyes). 1946: *Three Wise Fools* (+Irene); *Two Smart People* (+Irene); *Holiday in Mexico* (+Irene); *Till the Clouds Roll By* (+Irene, Helen Rose); *The Harvey Girls* (+Rose, Irene). 1947: *Song of Love* (+Irene, Walter Plunkett); *The Romance of Rosy Ridge* (+Irene); *Desire Me* (+Irene); *This Time for Keeps* (+Irene); *Good News* (+Helen Rose); *Green Dolphin Street* (+Irene, Plunkett). 1948: *Easter Parade* (+Irene); *Luxury Liner* (+Helen Rose); *A Southern Yankee* (GB *My Hero*); *Words and Music* (+Helen Rose); *Take Me Out To the Ball Game* (GB *Everybody's Cheering*); *Big Jack*. 1949: *The Barkleys of Broadway* (+Irene); *In the Good Old Summertime* (+Irene); *Madame Bovary* (+Walter Plunkett); *That Forsyte Woman* (GB *The Forsyte Saga*) (+Walter Plunkett); *Malaya* (GB *East of the Rising Sun*) (+Irene).

1950: *Kim*. 1951: *Adventures of Captain Fabian*. 1959: *Spartacus* (+Bill Thomas). 1963: *The Sword in the Stone*.

VAN RUNKLE, THEADORA

American designer whose first film, *Bonnie and Clyde*, spearheaded a nostalgia trend. Has often designed for Faye Dunaway.

ACADEMY AWARD NOMINATIONS:

1967: *Bonnie and Clyde*. 1974: *The Godfather Part II*. 1986: *Peggy Sue Got Married*.

SFTA NOMINATION:

1977: *New York, New York*.

FILMS:

1967: *Bonnie and Clyde*. 1968: *The Thomas Crown Affair; I Love You, Alice B Toklas; The Subject Was Roses; Bullitt*. 1969: *A Place For Lovers; The Arrangement; The Reivers*. 1970: *Myra Breckinridge* (+Edith Head). 1971: *Johnny Got His Gun*. 1973: *Mame; Kid Blue; Ace Eli and Roger of the Skies*. 1974: *The Godfather Part II*. 1976: *Nickelodeon*. 1977: *New York, New York*. 1978: *Heaven Can Wait; Same Time Next Year*. 1979: *The Jerk*. 1981: *Heartbeeps; S.O.B.* 1982: *The Best Little Whorehouse in Texas*. 1986: *Peggy Sue Got Married*.

VERTES, MARCEL

French artist who has contributed work to three British films.

ACADEMY AWARD NOMINATION:

1952: **Moulin Rouge*

Opposite: Virginia Bruce in The First Hundred Years *(Dolly Tree)*

FILMS:

1938: *The Mikado* (sets and costumes). 1940: *The Thief of Bagdad* (+ Oliver Messel, John Armstrong). 1944: *Tonight and Every Night* (+Louis). 1952: *Moulin Rouge* (decor and costumes) (+Schiaparelli).

VISART, NATALIE

American costume designer under contract to Cecil B DeMille. Died 1986.

FILMS:

1936: *The Plainsman* (+Dwight Franklin, Joe de Yong). 1939: *Union Pacific*. 1940: *North-West Mounted Police* (+Joe de Yong); *Meet John Doe*. 1943: *Lady of Burlesque* (GB *Striptease Lady*) (+Edith Head). 1944: *The Story of Dr Wassell*; *Guest in the House*. 1946: *The Strange Woman*.

WACHNER, SOPHIE

Started work as a school teacher in Akron, Ohio, but abandoned her teaching career to work as a costume designer in New York for theatrical producers Charles Dillingham and Florenz Ziegfeld. In 1919 she became Director of Costumes for the Goldwyn Studios which became M-G-M. At Fox from 1924 to 1930.

FILMS:

1923: *Three Weeks* (GB *Romance of a Queen*). 1924: *Dorothy Vernon of Haddon Hall* (+Mitchell Leisen); *His Hour*; *Married Flirts*; *He Who Gets Slapped*; *The Snob*; *The Wife of the Centaur*; *The Great Divide*; *The Dancers*. 1925: *Lady Windermere's Fan*. 1928: *Red Wine*; *Speakeasy*. 1929: *Thru Different Eyes* (GB *Through Different Eyes); Fox Movietone Follies of 1929* (+Alice O'Neill); *Pleasure Crazed*; *Words and Music*; *Big Time*; *Happy Days*; *Married in Hollywood* (+Alice O'Neill); *They Had to See Paris*; *Sunny Side Up*; *Love, Live and Laugh*; *Nix on Dames*; *Romance of the Rio Grande*; *Seven Faces*; *A Song of Kentucky*; *Hot for Paris*; *South Sea Rose*; *Cameo Kirby*; *Lone Star Ranger*; *City*

Alison Lloyd and Chester Morris in Corsair
(Sophie Wachner)

Girl; *Happy Days*; *Song o' My Heart*; *Such Men Are Dangerous*; *The Big Party*; *Crazy that Way*; *The Golden Calf*.
1930: *The Arizona Kid*; *Double Cross Roads*; *High Society Blues*; *Born Reckless*; *Not Damaged*; *On the Level*; *So This is London*; *Women Everywhere*; *One Mad Kiss*; *Wild Company*; *Common Clay*; *Last of the Duanes*; *Man Trouble*; *A Devil with Women*; *Liliom*; *Renegades*; *Scotland Yard*; *Up the River*; *Are You There?*; *Just Imagine* (+Dorothy Tree, Alice O'Neill); *Lightnin'*; *Oh, for a Man!*; *The Princess and the Plumber*; *East Lynne*; *On Your Back*; *Seas Beneath*. 1931: *A Connecticut Yankee* (GB *The Yankee at King Arthur's Court*); *Quick Millions*; *Corsair*. 1936: *Little Lord Fauntleroy*.

Opposite: Marsha Hunt in These Glamour Girls *(Dolly Tree)*

Designer Gwen Wakeling

WAKELING, GWEN

Born Detroit, Michigan, 1901. Discovered by Cecil B DeMille and worked for him both at Pathé and Paramount. Head costume designer at Fox from 1933 to 1942, and from then on has worked regularly in films for Columbia, United Artists, Republic, Warner Brothers and RKO. Miss Wakeling has also done costumes for stage plays, productions at the Los Angeles Civic Light Opera Association and for NBC-TV. Died 1982.

ACADEMY AWARD NOMINATION:

1950: *Samson and Delilah* (+Edith Head, Dorothy Jeakins, Elois Jenssen, Gile Steele).

FILMS:

1927: *King of Kings* (+Earl Luick, Adrian); *The Girl in the Pullman*; *A Harp in Hock*. 1929: *Paris Bound*; *Red Hot Rhythm*; *This Thing Called Love*; *The Racketeer*; *The Grand Parade*; *Officer O'Brien*.
1930: *Swing High*; *Holiday*; *Rich People*; *Her Man*; *Big Money*; *Sin Takes a Holiday*. 1931: *The Common Law*; *Suicide Fleet*; *The Tip Off*. 1932: *Carnival Boat*; *A Woman Commands*. 1933: *Broadway Thru a Keyhole*; *Gallant Lady*; *The House of Rothschild*. 1934: *The Last Gentleman*; *The Affairs of Cellini*; *Bulldog Drummond Strikes Back*; *Born to be Bad*; *The Count of Monte Cristo*; *Transatlantic Merry-go-round*.
1935: *The Littlest Rebel*; *The Man Who Broke the Bank at Monte Carlo*; *King of Burlesque*; *It Had to Happen*; *Prisoner of Shark Island*; *Captain January*; *The Country Doctor*; *Everybody's Old Man*. 1936: *Under Two Flags*; *Half Angel*; *Poor Little Rich Girl*; *Private Number*; *The Road to Glory*; *Girls Dormitory*; *Dimples*; *Ramona*; *Pigskin Parade* (GB *Harmony Parade*); *Ladies in Love*; *White Hunter*; *Banjo on my Knee*; *On the Avenue*; *Nancy Steele is Missing*; *Seventh Heaven*. 1937: *Wake Up and Live*; *Wee Willie Winkie*; *Danger – Love at Work*; *Ali Baba Goes to Town* (+Herschel); *Heidi*; *Second Honeymoon*; *The Baroness and the Butler*; *Sally, Irene and Mary*; *Rebecca of Sunnybrook Farm*; *Love Under Fire*. 1938: *Alexander's Ragtime Band*; *Kidnapped*; *Three Blind Mice*; *I'll Give a Million*; *Little Miss Broadway*; *Gateway*; *Straight, Place and Show* (GB *They're Off*); *Just Around the Corner*; *Submarine Patrol*; *Kentucky*; *Thanks for Everything*; *The Little Princess*; *Tail Spin*; *The Hound of the Baskervilles*. 1939: *Return of the 'Cisco Kid*; *The Gorilla*; *The Adventures of Sherlock Holmes* (GB *Sherlock Holmes*); *Hotel for Women*; *The Rains Came*; *Drums Along the Mohawk*; *The Grapes of Wrath*; *He Married His Wife*.
1940: *Johnny Apollo*; *Young People*; *Brigham Young – Fron-*

Mame *designs by Theadora van Runkle for Lucille Ball (left). Opposite: the designer herself*

tiersman (GB Brigham Young). 1941: *Citadel of Crime*; *Swamp Water* (GB *The Man Who Came Back*); *Weekend in Havana*; *How Green Was My Valley*; *International Lady*; *I Wake Up Screaming* (GB *Hot Spot*); *Confirm or Deny*; *Rise and Shine*; *Son of Fury*; *Roxie Hart*; *Rings on Her Fingers*; *To the Shores of Tripoli*. 1942: *Moontide*; *My Gal Sal*; *This Above All*; *Tales of Manhattan* (+Irene, Tree, B Newman, Cassini). 1943: *Cover Girl* (+Travis Banton, Muriel King). 1947: *Unconquered*; 1949: *Samson and Delilah* (+Edith Head, Dorothy Jeakins, Elois Jenssen, Gile Steele).

1950: *Valentino* (+Travis Banton). 1953: *The High and the Mighty*. 1954: *Silver Lode*; *Passion*; *Track of the Cat*; *Cattle Queen of Montana*. 1955: *Escape to Burma*; *Blood Alley* (+Carl Walker); *Tennessee's Partner*. 1956: *Great Day in the Morning*; *Johnny Concho*; *The River's Edge*. 1961: *The Most Dangerous Man Alive*; 1965: *Frankie and Johnny*.

WALTON, TONY

British designer often responsible for both production and costume design.

ACADEMY AWARD NOMINATIONS:
1964: *Mary Poppins*. 1974: *Murder on the Orient Express*. 1978: *The Wiz*.

SFTA NOMINATION:
1974: *Murder on the Orient Express*.

Designer Clare West

Nita Naldi in The Ten Commandments *(Clare West)*

FILMS:
1964: *Mary Poppins*. 1966: *A Funny Thing Happened on the Way to the Forum*. 1968: *Petulia* (+Arlette Nastat of Real). 1969: *The Seagull*. 1974: *Murder on the Orient Express*. 1977: *Equus*. 1978: *The Wiz*. 1980: *Just Tell Me What You Want*. 1982: *Deathtrap*.

WEST, CLARE

Clare West was one of the first studio designers. Her first important film was *Intolerance*, working for two years on the production. After *Intolerance* she became designer for Cecil B DeMille at a time when he was making sophisticated films with stars like Gloria Swanson, who expected to wear a different gown in every scene and each more lavish than the previous one. In retrospect the clothes worn by the DeMille stars look bizarre but producers didn't care about realism and DeMille's recipe for success was sex, sets and costumes. His films were popular with the general public and the *outré* styles created by Miss West could always guarantee plenty of publicity in the fan magazines.

After leaving the DeMille Studios in 1923 Clare West was put under contract to Norma and Constance Talmadge to design for their films.

FILMS:
1916: *Intolerance*. 1919: *Male and Female* (GB *The Admirable Crichton*).

1920: *Why Change Your Wife?*; *Something to Think About*; *Forbidden Fruit*. 1921: *The Affairs of Anatol*; *Fool's Paradise*; *Saturday Night*. 1922: *Manslaughter*. 1923: *Ashes of Vengeance*; *Hollywood*; *The Ten Commandments*; *Adam's Rib*; *The Golden Bed*; *The Song of Love*; *Secrets*. 1924: *The Goldfish*; *Sherlock Jnr*; *For Sale*; *Flirting With Love*.

1925: *The Road to Yesterday* (+Mitchell Leisen).

WEST, VERA

Educated at Philadelphia School of Design. At Universal from 1928 to 1947, where she became Head Designer.

FILMS:
1928: *The Man Who Laughs* (+David Cox). 1932: *Back Street*; *The Mummy*. 1934: *Gift of Gab*; *Cheating Cheaters*; *The Man Who Reclaimed His Head*; *The Good Fairy*; *Strange Wives*.

1935: *Diamond Jim*; *King Solomon of Broadway*; *Remember Last Night?* (+Ernest Dryden); *The Great Impersonation* (+Brymer); *Magnificent Obsession* (+Brymer); *Next Time We Love*. 1936: *Showboat* (+Doris Zinkeisen); *Postal Inspector*; *As Good as Married*; *Yellowstone*. 1937: *One Hundred Men and a Girl*; *The Westland Case*; *Merry-go-round of 1938*; *Black Doll*.

1938: *Sinners in Paradise*; *Danger on the Air*; *Rage of Paris*; *Letter of Introduction*; *Freshman Year*; *The Road to Reno*; *Youth Takes a Fling*; *The Last Express*; *Service de Luxe* (+Irene); *That Certain Age*; *Little Tough Guys in Society*; *Swing That Cheer*; *Swing, Sister, Swing* (+Kathryn Kuhn); *Son of Frankenstein*; *You Can't Cheat an Honest Man*; *Mystery of the White Room*; *Risky Business*; *Three Smart Girls Grow Up*.

1939: *East Side of Heaven*; *For Love or Money* (GB *Tomorrow at Midnight*); *Inside Information*; *The Sun Never Sets*; *The Forgotten Woman*; *Unexpected Father* (GB *Sandy Takes a Bow*); *They Asked for It*; *I Stole a Million*; *The Under-pup*; *Hawaiian Nights*; *Little Accident*; *Destry Rides Again*; *First Love*; *Hero For a Day*; *Legion of Lost Flyers*; *Tower of London*; *Charlie McCarthy, Detective*; *Laugh it Off* (GB *Lady Be Gay*); *The Invisible Man Returns*; *My Little Chickadee*; *It's a Date*; *House of Fear*; *Black Friday*.

1940: *Enemy Agent* (GB *Secret Enemy*); *Ma! He's Making Eyes at Me*; *If I Had My Way*; *I Can't Give You Anything But Love, Baby*; *Sandy is a Lady*; *Ski Patrol*; *Private Affairs*; *When the Daltons Rode*; *South to Karanga*; *Hired Wife*; *Margie*; *Spring Parade*; *Argentine Nights*; *The Mummy's Hand*; *One Night in the Tropics*; *Seven Sinners* (+Irene); *The Bank Dick* (GB *The Bank Detective*); *Give Us Wings*; *Sandy Gets Her Man*; *Trail of the Vigilantes*; *The Invisible Woman*; *Where Did You Get That Girl?*; *Back Street* (+Muriel King); *Buck Privates*; *Nice Girl?*.

1941: *The Black Cat*; *The Lady from Cheyenne*; *Model Wife* (+Royer); *In the Navy*; *San Antonio Rose*; *Bachelor Daddy*; *Hit*

Opposite: Loretta Young in Born to Be Bad *(Wakeling)*

the Road; Hold That Ghost; Badlands of Dakota; Unfinished Business (+Howard Greer); It Started With Eve; Appointment for Love (+Muriel King); Never Give a Sucker an Even Break (GB What a Man); Keep'em Flying; Hellzappopin'; Melody Lane; The Wolf Man; The Ghost of Frankenstein; Juke Box Jenny; This Woman is Mine; Too Many Blondes; Mob Town.

1942: Mississippi Gambler; The Spoilers; The Strange Case of Dr X; Broadway; Almost Married; Eagle Squadron; Drums of the Congo; Men of Texas (GB Men of Destiny); Invisible Agent; Pardon My Sarong; Between us Girls; Destination Unknown; Nightmare; Pittsburg; Arabian Nights; 'Frisco Lil; Don't Get Personal; Madame Spy; You're Telling Me; Mug Town; Shadow of a Doubt (+Adrian); The Amazing Mrs Holliday; Frankenstein Meets the Wolfman; How's About It?; Keep 'em Slugging; There's One Born Every Minute; Tough as They Come.

1943: Rhythm of the Islands; White Savage; Good Morning Judge; It Ain't Hay (GB Money for Jam); Mr Big; All By Myself; Get Going; Hit the Ice; Two Tickets to London; Hers to Hold (+Adrian); Phantom of the Opera; Always a Bridesmaid; Flesh and Fantasy (+Edith Head); Larceny with Music; Crazy House; Hi'ya, Sailor; The Mad Ghoul; Pursuit to Algiers; The Strange Death of Adolf Hitler; Never a Dull Moment; Son of Dracula; So's Your Uncle; Calling Dr Death; Gung Ho!; His Butler's Sister; Moonlight in Vermont; She's for Me; You're a Lucky Fellow, Mr Smith; Ali Baba and the 40 Thieves; Phantom Lady; Sherlock Holmes and the Spider Woman (GB Spider Woman); Sing a Jingle (GB Lucky Days); Swingtime Johnny; The Impostor; Weekend Pass; Follow the Boys (+Howard Greer); Hat Check Honey; Hi, Good-Lookin'; Ladies Courageous.

1944: Moon Over Las Vegas; Slightly Terrific; Allergic to Love; Pardon My Rhythm; Christmas Holiday (+Muriel King, Howard Greer); Cobra Woman; Ghost Catchers; Her Primitive Man; The Invisible Man's Revenge; South of Dixie; The Mummy's Ghost; Gypsy Wildcat; In Society; The Merry Monahans; The Pearl of Death; The Reckless Age; Babes on Swing Street; The Climax; Dead Man's Eyes; San Diego, I Love You; The Singing Sheriff; Bowery to Broadway; Murder in the Blue Room; Destiny; Enter Arsene Lupin; My Gal Loves Music; Night Club Girl; Hi, Beautiful (GB Pass to Romance); The Suspect; House of Frankenstein; She Gets Her Man; 'Frisco Sal; Her Lucky Night; Sudan; Weird Woman; See My Lawyer; Twilight on the Prairie.

1945: Patrick the Great; Salome, Where she Danced; Swing out, Sister; That's the Spirit; Blonde Ransom; The Frozen Ghost; The Naughty Nineties; Penthouse Rhythm; The Woman in Green; On Stage Everybody (+Mary K Dodson); Men in Her Diary; River Gang (GB Fairy Tale Murder); Shady Lady; That Night With You; The Daltons Ride Again; This Love of Ours (+Travis Banton); House of Dracula; Pillow of Death; Strange Confession; Girl on the Spot; Terror by Night; Smooth as Silk; Honeymoon Ahead; I'll Tell the World.

1946: She Wrote the Book; Danger Woman; Her Adventurous Night; Black Angel; Slightly Scandalous; The Killers; Magnificent Doll (+Travis Banton).

1947: Pirates of Monterey (+Travis Banton).

WHITE, MILES

Born Miles Edgren White, Oakland, California, 1920. Costume designer for theatre, ballet and circus in U.S.A. since 1944.

ACADEMY AWARD NOMINATIONS:

1952: The Greatest Show on Earth. 1954: There's No Business Like Show Business. 1956: Around the World in 80 Days.

FILMS:

1943: Up in Arms. 1946: The Kid From Brooklyn. 1951: The Greatest Show on Earth (+Edith Head, Dorothy Jeakins). 1954: There's No Business Like Show Business (+Charles LeMaire, Travilla). 1955: Around the World in 80 Days.

WILLS, MARY

Costume designer who has worked mainly for Samuel Goldwyn Productions and Twentieth Century-Fox.

ACADEMY AWARD NOMINATION:

1952: Hans Christian Andersen (+Clavé, Karinska). 1954: The Virgin Queen (+Charles LeMaire). 1956: Teenage Rebel (+Charles LeMaire) (b&w). 1958: A Certain Smile (+Charles

LeMaire). 1959: The Diary of Anne Frank (+Charles LeMaire). 1962: ★The Wonderful World of the Brothers Grimm. 1976: The Passover Plot.

FILMS:

1946: Song of the South. 1948: Enchantment. 1949: The Capture; Roseanna McCoy; My Foolish Heart (+Edith Head); Our Very Own. 1950: Edge of Doom (GB Stronger Than Fear). 1951: I Want You. 1952: Hans Christian Andersen (+Clavé). 1954: Prince of Players (+Charles LeMaire). 1955: Carousel (+Charles LeMaire); The Virgin Queen; Good Morning, Miss Dove. 1956: Bigger than Life (+Charles LeMaire); The Last Wagon; Between Heaven and Hell (+Charles LeMaire); Teenage Rebel (+Charles LeMaire); Love Me Tender. 1957: The Wayward Bus (+Charles LeMaire); Bernadine (+Charles LeMaire); A Hatful of Rain (+Charles LeMaire); No Down Payment (+Charles LeMaire); The Proud Rebel; A Certain Smile (+LeMaire); The True Story of Jesse James (GB The James Brothers). 1958: The Diary of Anne Frank (+LeMaire); Fraulein. 1959: The Wonderful Country; The Remarkable Mr Pennypacker (+LeMaire). 1961: Cape Fear. 1962: The Wonderful World of the Brothers Grimm. 1976: The Passover Plot.

WOOD, YVONNE

Born California 1914. Attended Chouinard Art School and started in films as a sketch artist. Four-year contract at Fox from 1941–1945, then a contract at Universal from 1945–1951. Freelance from 1951 to 1960, followed by two years of professional inactivity. Returned to film work in 1963. First film as Costume Designer was the Fox musical The Gang's All Here, starring Carmen Miranda.

FILMS:

1943: The Gang's All Here (GB The Girls He Left Behind); Orchestra Wives; Four Jills in a Jeep. 1944: Molly and Me; The Bermuda Mystery; Tampico; Greenwich Village; Sweet and Lowdown; The Big Noise; Something for the Boys (+Kay Nelson); Circumstantial Evidence; Thunderhead, Son of Flicka.

1945: A Bell For Adano; Don Juan Quilligan; Doll Face (GB Come Back to Me); Johnny Comes Flying Home; Swell Guy; Song of Scheherezade; Buck Privates Come Home (GB Rookies Come Home); White Tie and Tails. 1947: Slave Girl; The Web; Ride the Pink Horse; Black Bart (GB Black Bart, Highwayman); A Double Life (+Travis Banton); Casbah; Fury at Furnace Creek. 1948: Another Part of the Forest; Tap Roots; An Act of Murder; Mexican Hayride; Criss Cross; Live Today for Tomorrow. 1949: Calamity Jane and Sam Bass; Illegal Entry; The Gal Who Took the West; Abandoned; Bagdad; Buccaneers' Girl.

1950: Comanche Territory; Sierra; Winchester 73; Shakedown; Tripoli; Double Crossbones; Frenchie. 1952: The San Francisco Story; Lady in the Iron Mask. 1953: Raiders of the Seven Seas; Fort Algiers; Botany Bay; Casanova's Big Night (+Edith Head). 1955: The Court Jester (+Edith Head); The Conqueror (+Michael Woulfe). 1958: Man of the West; The Big Country (+Emile Santiago). 1959: Li'l Abner; One Eyed Jacks.

1966: Duel at Diablo. 1967: Guns for San Sebastian; Firecreek. 1968: The Good Guys and the Bad Guys. 1969: The Cheyenne Social Club.

1970: Dirty Dingus McGee. 1972: The Life and Times of Judge Roy Bean. 1973: The Outfit.

WOULFE, MICHAEL

Born New York City 1918. Began as sketch artist and assistant designer in the New York garment industry. Went to Hollywood to design costumes for Sylvia Sidney in Blood on the Sun for William Cagney Productions and, as a result, was put under contract. During the three years he was there, Michael Woulfe was loaned out to other studios, including RKO. In 1949 he became Head Designer for RKO and continued to work at the studio until 1955. When Howard Hughes sold his interest in RKO, Michael Woulfe was under contract to Hughes Productions.

FILMS:

1945: Blood on the Sun. 1946: The Searching Wind (+Dorothy O'Hara); The Stranger; Mister Ace; The Locket. 1947: Singapore; Love From a Stranger (GB A Stranger Walked In); Tycoon. 1949: I Married A Communist (GB The Woman on Pier 13); A Dangerous Profession. 1950: The Company She Keeps; Macao; Jet Pilot;

Opposite: Yvonne Wood design for Carmen Miranda

Paul Zastupnevich with sketches for The Towering Inferno

Where Danger Lives. 1951: *The Half-Breed; Split Second; The Thing; Best of the Badmen; The Racket; Roadblock; Two Tickets to Broadway* (+ Balkan); *The Lusty Men.* 1952: *Clash By Night: One Minute to Zero; Angel Face; Blackbeard the Pirate.* 1953: *Dangerous Mission; Second Chance; Devil's Canyon; The French Line* (+ Howard Greer); *She Couldn't Say No; Son of Sinbad.*

1954: *The Conqueror* (+ Yvonne Wood); *Susan Slept Here; Underwater,* 1955: *Bengazi; Glory.* 1971: *Happy Birthday, Wanda June.*

ZASTUPNEVICH, PAUL

Began his professional career in Pittsburgh where he had his own salon. Also designed for the Pittsburgh Civic Ballet. Worked on over 120 productions at the Pasadena Playhouse. Extensive credits for television productions.

ACADEMY AWARD NOMINATIONS:
1972: *The Poseidon Adventure.* 1978: *The Swarm.* 1980: *When Time Ran Out. . . .*

FILMS:
1959: *The Big Circus.* 1960: *The Lost World.* 1961: *Voyage to the Bottom of the Sea.* 1962: *Five Weeks in a Balloon.* 1972: *The Poseidon Adventure.* 1974: *The Towering Inferno.* 1978: *The Swarm.* 1979: *Beyond the Poseidon Adventure.* 1980: *When Time Ran Out. . . .*

ZINKEISEN, DORIS

Painter and costume designer for theatre and films. Designed for Herbert Wilcox productions 1933/38.

FILMS:
1932: *Goodnight Vienna* (US *Magic Night*). 1933: *Bitter Sweet; The Queen's Affair* (US *Runaway Queen*). 1934: *Nell Gwynn.* 1935: *Mimi; Peg of Old Drury.* 1936: *Showboat.* 1938: *Sixty Glorious Years* (US *Queen of Destiny*) (+ Tom Heselwood)

Opposite: Janet Leigh in Jet Pilot *(Michael Woulfe)*

Anna Neagle as the famous actress Peg Woffington in Peg of Old Drury *(this is Peg's costume for the role of Sir Harry Wildair): costume design by Doris Zinkeisen. Overleaf:* Stolen Holiday *(Orry-Kelly)*

Index

BIG TOWN GIRL (36) Herschel
BIKINI BEACH (64) Corso
BILL CRACKS DOWN (36) Eloise
BILLION DOLLAR BRAIN (67) Russell
BILL OF DIVORCEMENT, A (32) De Lima
BILLY BUDD (62) Mendleson
BILLY ROSE'S DIAMOND HORSESHOE (45)
    Nelson, Hubert, *Sascha Brastoff*, Cashin
BILLY ROSE'S JUMBO (62) Haack
BILLY THE KID (30) Cox
BILLY THE KID (41) Tree *m* Steele
BIOGRAPHY OF A BACHELOR GIRL (34)
    Adrian
BIRD OF PARADISE (51) Travilla *wd* LeMaire
BIRDS, THE (62) Head
BIRDS AND THE BEES, THE (47)=THREE
    DARING DAUGHTERS, THE
BIRDS AND THE BEES, THE (55) Head
BISHOP MISBEHAVES, THE (35) Tree
BISHOP MURDER CASE, THE (29) Frazer
BISHOP'S WIFE, THE (47) Sharaff, Adrian
BITTER HARVEST (62) Ellacott
BITTER SWEET (33) Zinkeisen
BITTER SWEET (40) Adrian *m* Steele
BITTER TEA OF GENERAL YEN, THE (32)
    Kalloch, Stevenson
BLACK ANGEL (46) V West
BLACK ARROW, THE (48) Louis
BLACK ARROW STRIKES, THE=BLACK
    ARROW, THE
BLACK BART (47) Wood
BLACK BART, HIGHWAYMAN=BLACK
    BART
BLACKBEARD'S GHOST (67) Thomas
BLACKBEARD THE PIRATE (52) Woulfe
BLACK BIRD, THE (25) Andre-Ani
BLACK BOOK, THE (49) J Morley
BLACK CASTLE, THE (52) Thomas
BLACK CAT, THE (41) V West
BLACK DOLL (37) V West
BLACK FLOWERS FOR THE BRIDE (70) *Florence Klotz*
BLACK GOLD (47) Maclean
BLACK HAND (49) Plunkett
BLACK HORSE CANYON (54) Thomas
BLACK KNIGHT, THE (54) Dawson
BLACK LEGION (36) Anderson
BLACK MAGIC (49) *George Annenkoff*, Novarese
BLACKMAIL (39) Tree
BLACKMAILED (50) Caffin
BLACKMAILER (36) Lange
BLACK NARCISSUS (47) *Hein Heckroth*
BLACK ORCHID, THE (58) Head
BLACKOUT=CONTRABAND
BLACK ROOM, THE (35) Mayer
BLACK SHEEP (35) Royer
BLACK SHIELD OF FALWORTH, THE (54)
    Odell
BLACK SWAN, THE (42) Luick
BLACK TENT, THE (56) Dawson
BLANCHE FURY (47) *Sophie Harris s* M Furse
BLACKWELL'S ISLAND (38) Shoup
BLACK WIDOW, THE (54) Travilla *wd* LeMaire
BLARNEY (26) Andre-Ani
BLAZE OF NOON (46) Head
BLAZING SADDLES (74) Novarese
BLIND ALLEY (39) Kalloch
BLINDFOLD (65) Louis
BLIND GODDESS, THE (48) Caffin
BLISS OF MRS BLOSSOM, THE (68) Rickards
BLITHE SPIRIT (45) *Rahvis*
BLOCKADE (38) Irene
BLOND CHEAT (38) Stevenson
BLONDE BANDIT, THE (49) Palmer
BLONDE CRAZY (31) Luick
BLONDE FEVER (44) Irene
BLONDE RANSOM (45) V West
BLONDES AT WORK (37) Shoup
BLONDE VENUS (32) Banton
BLONDIE (38) Kalloch
BLONDIE GOES LATIN (40) *Monica*
BLONDIE HAS SERVANT TROUBLE (40) Kalloch
BLONDIE JOHNSON (32) Orry-Kelly
BLONDIE OF THE FOLLIES (32) Adrian
BLONDIE ON A BUDGET (40) Kalloch
BLONDIE PLAYS CUPID (40) Kalloch
BLONDIE TAKES A VACATION (39) Kalloch
BLOOD ALLEY (55) Wakeling
BLOOD AND SAND (41) Banton
BLOODHOUNDS OF BROADWAY (52)
    Travilla *wd* LeMaire
BLOOD ON THE MOON (48) Stevenson
BLOOD ON THE SUN (45) Woulfe
BLOSSOMS IN THE DUST (41) Adrian *m* Steele
BLOSSOMS ON BROADWAY (37) Head
BLOWING WILD (53) Nelson, Best
BLOW-UP (66) Rickards
BLUE (68) Head
BLUEBEARD'S EIGHTH WIFE (38) Banton
BLUE DAHLIA, THE (45) Head
BLUE DANUBE, THE (28) Adrian
BLUE DENIM (59) Balkan
BLUE HAWAII (61) Head
BLUE JEANS=BLUE DENIM
BLUE LAMP, THE (49) Mendleson

BLUE MAX, THE (66) Furness
BLUE MURDER AT ST TRINIANS (57) Duse
BLUEPRINT FOR MURDER, A (53) LeMaire
BLUE SKIES (46) Head, *Waldo Angelo*
BLUE VEIL, THE (51) Anderson
BLUFF (24) Chaffin
BOB & CAROL & TED & ALICE (69) Mabry
BOB, SON OF BATTLE=THUNDER IN THE
    VALLEY
BODY AND SOUL (27) Hubert
BODY AND SOUL (47) Herwood Keyes
BODY DISAPPEARS, THE (41) Anderson
BODY SNATCHER, THE (44) Renie
BOEING BOEING (65) Head
BOHEME, LA (25) Erte (for Rene Adoree only)
BOLD CABALLERO (36) Eloise
BOLD FRONTIERSMAN, THE (48) Palmer
BOLERO (33) Banton
BOMBER'S MOON (43) Hubert
BOMBSHELL (33) Adrian
BONAVENTURE=THUNDER ON THE HILL
BONDAGE (33) Kaufman
BOND STREET (48) *Peter McCulloch, Susan
    King-Clark*
BONJOUR TRISTESSE (57) Givenchy
BONNIE AND CLYDE (67) van Runkle
BONNIE PRINCE CHARLIE (48) Benda
BON VOYAGE! (62) Thomas
BONZO GOES TO COLLEGE (52) Thomas
BOOM! (68) *Tiziani of Rome* (for Elizabeth Taylor)
BOOMERANG (46) Nelson *wd* LeMaire
BOOM TOWN (40) Adrian *m* Steele
BORDER RIVER (53) Odell
BORDER TOWN (34) Orry-Kelly
BORN RECKLESS (30) Wachner
BORN RECKLESS (37) Herschel
BORN TO BE BAD (34) Wakeling
BORN TO DANCE (36) Adrian
BORN TO KILL (47) Stevenson
BORN TO SING (41) Shoup *m* Steele
BORN TO SPEED (46) Cassini
BORN YESTERDAY (50) Louis
BORROWING TROUBLE (37) Herschel
BOSTON STRANGLER, THE (68) *s* Travilla
BOTANY BAY (53) Wood
BOTH ENDS OF THE CANDLE=HELEN
    MORGAN STORY, THE
BOTTOM OF THE BOTTLE, THE (55) Travilla
    wd LeMaire
BOUDOIR DIPLOMAT, THE (30) Andre-Ani
BOUNTY HUNTER, THE (54) Mabry
BOWERY BOY (40) Palmer
BOWERY TO BROADWAY (44) V West
BOY, DID I GET A WRONG NUMBER (66)
    Corso
BOY FRIEND, THE (26) Kay, Marsh, Andre-Ani
BOY FRIEND, THE (71) Russell
BOY FROM BARNARDO'S, THE=LORD JEFF
BOY FROM OKLAHOMA, THE (53) Shoup
BOY MEETS GIRL (38) Anderson
BOYS IN BROWN (49) Caffin
BOYS NIGHT OUT (62) Thomas, *Kim Novak* (for
    herself)
BOY WITH GREEN HAIR, THE (48) Balkan
BRAMBLE BUSH, THE (59) Shoup
BRANDED (50) Head
BRASHER DOUBLOON, THE (47) Behm
BRASS BOTTLE, THE (63) Odell
BRAVADOS, THE (58) LeMaire
BRAVE AND THE BEAUTIFUL, THE=MAG-
    NIFICENT MATADOR, THE
BRAVE BULLS, THE (51) Louis
BREAKFAST AT TIFFANY'S (61) Head (Givenchy, *Pauline Trigere* for Audrey Hepburn)
BREAKFAST FOR TWO (37) Stevenson
BREAKING OF BUMBO, THE (70) *Jacqueline
    Charon-Lodwig* (fashion co-ordinator)
BREAKING POINT, THE (50) Rhodes
BREAKING THE ICE (31) *Helen Rachmil*
BREAK OF HEARTS (35) B Newman
BREAK THE NEWS (37) Hubert
BREWSTER'S MILLIONS (34) Schiaparelli, Motley, Hartnell
BREWSTER'S MILLIONS (45) Odette
BRIBE, THE (48) Irene
BRIDAL SUITE, THE (39) Tree
BRIDE BY MISTAKE (44) Stevenson
BRIDE CAME C O D, THE (41) Orry-Kelly
BRIDE COMES HOME, THE (35) Banton
BRIDE GOES WILD, THE (47) Rose
BRIDE OF THE REGIMENT (30) Luick
BRIDE OF VENGEANCE (48) *Mitchell Leisen*,
    Grant
BRIDE WALKS OUT, THE (36) B Newman
BRIDE WORE BOOTS, THE (46) Head
BRIDE WORE CRUTCHES, THE (41) Herschel
BRIDE WORE RED, THE (37) Adrian
BRIDGE OF SAN LUIS REY, THE (29) Adrian
BRIDGES AT TOKO-RI, THE (54) Head
BRIDGE TOO FAR, A (76) Mendleson
BRIEF ENCOUNTER (74) Dawson
BRIEF MOMENT (33) Banton
BRIGADOON (54) Sharaff
BRIGAND, THE (52) Louis
BRIGHAM YOUNG=BRIGHAM YOUNG
    FRONTIERSMAN

BRIGHAM YOUNG FRONTIERSMAN (40)
    Wakeling
BRIGHT EYES (34) Royer
BRIGHT LEAF (50) Rhodes, Best
BRIGHT LIGHTS (25) Erte
BRIGHT LIGHTS (35) Orry-Kelly
BRIGHTON ROCK (47) *Honoria Plesch*
BRIGHT VICTORY (51) Odell
BRIMSTONE (49) Palmer
BRINGING UP BABY (38) Greer
BRINGING UP FATHER (27) Clark
BRINK OF HELL=TOWARDS THE
    UNKNOWN
BRITANNIA MEWS (48) Benda
BRITANNIA OF BILLINGSGATE (33) Conway
BRITISH AGENT (34) Orry-Kelly
BRITISH INTELLIGENCE (39) Shoup
BROADWAY (42) V West
BROADWAY BABIES (29) Ree
BROADWAY BAD (32) Luick
BROADWAY GONDOLIER (35) Orry-Kelly
BROADWAY HOSTESS (35) Orry-Kelly
BROADWAY LTD (41) *Coyla Davies*
BROADWAY MELODY (28) Cox
BROADWAY MELODY OF 1936 (35) Adrian
BROADWAY MELODY OF 1938 (37) Adrian
BROADWAY MELODY OF 1940 (39) Adrian *m*
    Steele
BROADWAY MUSKETEERS (38) Shoup
BROADWAY RHYTHM (43) Irene *a* Sharaff *m*
    Steele
BROADWAY SINGER=TORCH SINGER
BROADWAY THRU A KEYHOLE (33) Wakeling
BROKEN JOURNEY (48) Harris
BROKEN LANCE (54) Travilla *wd* LeMaire
BROOKLYN ORCHID (41) Royer
BROTHERHOOD, THE (68) R Morley
BROTHER JOHN (71) *Guy Verhille*
BROTHERLY LOVE (28) Frazer
BROTHERLY LOVE (69) = COUNTRY DANCE
BROTHER ORCHID (40) Shoup
BROTHER RAT (38) Anderson
BROTHERS KARAMAZOV, THE (57) Plunkett
BROTHERS RICO, THE (57) Louis
BROTHER SUN, SISTER MOON (73) *Danilo
    Donati*
BROWNING VERSION, THE (50) *s* Caffin
BROWN OF HARVARD (26) Kay, Marsh
BRUTE FORCE (47) Odell
BUCCANEER, THE (58) Head, *Ralph Jester, John
    Jensen*
BUCCANEERS' GIRL (49) Wood
BUCK AND THE PREACHER (72) *Guy Verhille*
BUCK PRIVATES (40) V West
BUCK PRIVATES COME HOME (46) Wood
BUD ABBOTT & LOU COSTELLO IN HOL-
    LYWOOD=ABBOTT & COSTELLO IN
    HOLLYWOOD
BUFFALO BILL (43) Hubert
BUGLE CALL, THE (27) Andre-Ani
BUGLES IN THE AFTERNOON (51) Rhodes
BUGSY MALONE (76) *Monica Howe*
BUILD MY GALLOWS HIGH=OUT OF THE
    PAST
BULLDOG DRUMMOND STRIKES BACK
    (34) Wakeling
BULLDOG JACK (35) Strassner
BULLFIGHTER AND THE LADY, THE (51)
    Palmer
BULLFIGHTERS, THE (45) Cashin
BULLFIGHTERS, THE (45) Cashin
BULLITT (68) van Runkle
BUONA SERA, MRS CAMPBELL (68) Haack
BURNING HILLS, THE (56) Best
BURNT OFFERING=PASSPORT TO HELL
BUSHRANGER, THE (28) Coulter
BUSINESS AND PLEASURE (31) Tree
BUS RILEY'S BACK IN TOWN (64) Odell (Louis
    for Ann-Margret)
BUS STOP (56) Travilla *wd* LeMaire
BUTCH CASSIDY AND THE SUNDANCE
    KID (69) Head
BUT NOT FOR ME (59) Head
BUTTERCUP CHAIN, THE (70) *Gabriella Falk*
BUTTERFIELD 8 (60) Rose
BUTTERFLIES ARE FREE (72) Mabry
BUTTONS (27) Clark
BYE BYE BIRDIE (62) Barto
BYE BYE BRAVERMAN (67) Johnstone
BY LOVE POSSESSED (61) Thomas
BY YOUR LEAVE (34) Plunkett

CABARET (72) *Charlotte Flemming*
CABIN IN THE COTTON (32) Orry-Kelly
CABIN IN THE SKY (42) *s* Irene *a* Shoup *m* Steele
CACTUS FLOWER (69) Mabry *m* Guy Verhille*
CADDY, THE (53) Head
CAESAR AND CLEOPATRA (45) Messel
CAFE METROPOLE (37) Royer
CAFE SOCIETY (38) Head
CAGE OF GOLD (50) Mendleson
CAIN AND MABEL (36) Orry-Kelly
CAINE MUTINY, THE (54) Louis
CAIRO (42) Kalloch
CALAMITY JANE (53) Shoup
CALAMITY JANE AND SAM BASS (49) Wood

CALENDAR, THE (48) Harris
CALENDAR GIRL (46) Palmer
CALIFORNIA (27) Andre-Ani
CALIFORNIA (46) Head m Steele
CALIFORNIA FIREBRAND (47) Palmer
CALLAHANS AND THE MURPHYS, THE (27) Hubert
CALL HER SAVAGE (32) Cox s Kaufman
CALLING ALL MARINES (39) Palmer
CALLING DR DEATH (43) V West
CALLING PHILO VANCE (39) Shoup
CALLING THE TUNE (36) L & H Nathan
CALL IT A DAY (36) Orry-Kelly
CALL IT LUCK (34) Royer
CALL ME MADAM (52) Sharaff
CALL ME MISTER (50) LeMaire
CALL NORTHSIDE 777 (47) Nelson wd LeMaire
CALL OF THE BLOOD (47) Haffenden
CALL OF THE FLESH (30) Cox
CALL OF THE RING, THE=DUKE COMES BACK, THE
CALL OF THE WILD (35) Kiam
CALL OF THE YUKON (38) Saltern
CAMELOT (67) John Truscott
CAMEO KIRBY (29) Wachner
CAMILLE (21) Natasha Rambova
CAMILLE (36) Adrian
CAMPUS HONEYMOON (47) Palmer
CANARY MURDER CASE, THE (28) Banton
CAN CAN (59) Sharaff
CANDY (68) Enrico Sabbatini, Fonssagrives & Tiel
CANON CITY (48) Ehren
CAN'T HELP SINGING (44) Plunkett
CAN THIS BE DIXIE? (36) Herschel
CANYON PASSAGE (46) Banton
CAPE FEAR (61) Wills
CAPER OF THE GOLDEN BULLS (67) Head
CAPRICE (66) Aghayan
CAPTAIN BLOOD (35) Anderson
CAPTAIN BLOOD, FUGITIVE=CAPTAIN PIRATE
CAPTAIN BOYCOTT (47) Sophie Harris
CAPTAIN CAREY, USA (49) Dodson
CAPTAIN CAUTION (40) Plunkett
CAPTAIN EDDIE (45) Hubert
CAPTAIN FROM CASTILE (47) LeMaire
CAPTAIN HATES THE SEA, THE (34) Kalloch
CAPTAIN IS A LADY, THE (40) Tree
CAPTAIN JANUARY (35) Wakeling
CAPTAIN LIGHTFOOT (54) Thomas
CAPTAIN NEMO AND THE UNDERWATER CITY (69) Lehmann
CAPTAIN NEWMAN MD (63) Odell
CAPTAIN PIRATE (52) Louis
CAPTAIN SALVATION (27) Andre-Ani
CAPTAIN SINBAD (63) Nathan of London (ballet by Ingrid Winter)
CAPTAIN'S KID, THE (36) Anderson
CAPTAINS OF THE CLOUDS (41) Shoup
CAPTAIN'S PARADISE, THE (53) Squire
CAPTAIN'S TABLE, THE (58) Ellacott
CAPTIVE HEART, THE (46) Mark Luker
CAPTURE, THE (49) Wills
CAPTURED (33) Orry-Kelly
CARAVAN (45) Ernst Stern, Haffenden
CARBINE WILLIAMS (52) Plunkett
CARD, THE (51) Motley (Sophie Harris)
CARDBOARD CAVALIER (48) Abbey
CARDINAL, THE (63) Brooks
CARDINAL RICHELIEU (34) Kiam
CAREER (39) Renie
CAREER (59) Head
CAREER WOMAN (36) Herschel
CAREFREE (38) Stevenson (Greer for Ginger Rogers)
CARELESS LADY (32) Duty
CARGO TO CAPETOWN (50) Louis
CARIBBEAN MYSTERY, THE (45) Cashin
CARMEN JONES (54) Nyberg
CARNAL KNOWLEDGE (71) Sylbert
CARNEGIE HALL (46) Ree
CARNIVAL (46) Messel
CARNIVAL BOAT (32) Wakeling
CARNIVAL IN COSTA RICA (46) Hubert
CARNIVAL OF THIEVES=CAPER OF THE GOLDEN BULLS
CAROLINA (33) Kaufman
CAROUSEL (55) Wills wd LeMaire
CARPETBAGGERS, THE (64) Head
CARRIE (52) Head
CARRINGTON VC (54) Rahvis
CARRY ON AGAIN, DOCTOR (69) Duse
CARRY ON CAMPING (68) Caffin
CARRY ON CLEO (64) Harris
CARRY ON COWBOY (65) Cynthia Tingey
CARRY ON CRUISING (62) Ellacott
CARRY ON JACK (63) Ellacott
CARRY ON SERGEANT (58) Ellacott
CARSON CITY (51) Best
CARSON CITY RAIDERS (48) Palmer
CARVE HER NAME WITH PRIDE (58) Dalton
CASABLANCA (42) Orry-Kelly
CASANOVA BROWN (44) King
CASANOVA IN BURLESQUE (43) Palmer
CASANOVA'S BIG NIGHT (53) Head m Wood
CASBAH (47) Wood

CASE AGAINST MRS AMES, THE (36) Taylor
CASE OF THE BLACK CAT, THE (36) Anderson
CASE OF THE BLACK PARROT, THE (40) Shoup
CASE OF THE CURIOUS BRIDE, THE (35) Orry-Kelly
CASE OF THE HOWLING DOG, THE (34) Orry-Kelly
CASE OF THE STUTTERING BISHOP, THE (37) Shoup
CASH AND CARRY=RINGSIDE MAISIE
CASH McCALL (59) Shoup
CASH ON DELIVERY=TO DOROTHY A SON
CASINO DE PAREE=GO INTO YOUR DANCE
CASINO MURDER CASE, THE (34) Tree
CASINO ROYALE (67) Harris (casino dresses by Guy Laroche, guard girl dresses by Paco Rabanne)
CASS TIMBERLANE (47) Irene
CASTLE KEEP (69) Jacques Fonterey
CAST A DARK SHADOW (55) Harris
CASTLE ON THE HUDSON (39) Shoup
CAT AND THE CANARY, THE (39) Head
CAT AND THE FIDDLE, THE (33) Adrian
CAT BALLOU (65) Thomas
CAT CREEPS, THE (30) Andre-Ani
CATHERINE THE GREAT (33) Armstrong
CAT ON A HOT TIN ROOF (58) Rose
CAT PEOPLE (42) Renie
CATTLE QUEEN OF MONTANA (54) Wakeling
CAUGHT IN THE DRAFT (41) Head
CAUGHT (30) Frazer
CAVALCADE (32) Luick
CEILING ZERO (35) Orry-Kelly
CENTENNIAL SUMMER (46) Hubert
CENTRAL AIRPORT (32) Orry-Kelly
CEREMONY, THE (63) Mabry
CERTAIN SMILE, A (57) Wills, LeMaire
CERTAIN YOUNG MAN, A (28) Clark
CHAD HANNA (40) Banton
CHAINED (34) Adrian
CHAIN LIGHTNING (27) Kay
CHAIN LIGHTNING (49) Rhodes
CHAIRMAN, THE (69) Duse
CHALLENGE, THE=WOMAN HUNGRY
CHALK GARDEN, THE (63) Harris
CHALLENGE TO LASSIE (49) Valles
CHAMPAGNE CHARLIE (36) Lambert
CHAMPAGNE CHARLIE (44) Ernst Stern
CHAMP FOR A DAY (53) Palmer
CHANCES (31) Luick
CHANDU THE MAGICIAN (32) Luick
CHANGE OF HABIT, A (69) Colvig
CHANGE OF HEART (34) Kaufman
CHANGE OF HEART (37) Herschel
CHAPMAN REPORT, THE (62) Orry-Kelly
CHARADE (63) Givenchy
CHARGE AT FEATHER RIVER, THE (53) Best
CHARGE OF THE LIGHT BRIGADE (36) Anderson
CHARGE OF THE LIGHT BRIGADE (68) David Walker
CHARLEY VARRICK (73) Colvig
CHARLEY'S AMERICAN AUNT=CHARLEY'S AUNT
CHARLEY'S AUNT (41) Banton
CHARLIE BUBBLES (67) Blake
CHARLIE CHAN AT MONTE CARLO (37) Herschel
CHARLIE CHAN AT THE CIRCUS (35) Lambert
CHARLIE CHAN AT THE OLYMPICS (37) Herschel
CHARLIE CHAN AT THE OPERA (36) Herschel
CHARLIE CHAN AT THE RACE TRACK (36) Herschel
CHARLIE CHAN AT THE WAX MUSEUM (40) Herschel
CHARLIE CHAN AT TREASURE ISLAND (39) Herschel
CHARLIE CHAN IN EGYPT (35) Myron
CHARLIE CHAN IN HONOLULU (38) Myron
CHARLIE CHAN IN LONDON (34) Royer
CHARLIE CHAN IN PARIS (34) Lillian
CHARLIE CHAN IN RIO (41) Herschel
CHARLIE CHAN IN SHANGHAI (35) Luza
CHARLIE CHAN ON BROADWAY (37) Herschel
CHARLIE CHAN'S GREATEST CASE (33) Royer
CHARLIE CHAN'S SECRET (35) Myron
CHARLIE McCARTHY, DETECTIVE (39) V West
CHASE, THE (65) Donfeld
CHASE A CROOKED SHADOW (57) Mendleson
CHASER, THE (38) Tree
CHASING DANGER (39) Myron
CHASING RAINBOWS (29) Cox
CHATTERBOX (43) Palmer
CHEAPER BY THE DOZEN (49) Stevenson wd LeMaire

CHEATERS, THE (45) Palmer
CHEATERS AT PLAY (31) Cox
CHEATING CHEATERS (34) V West
CHECKERS (37) Myron
CHECKPOINT (56) Mendleson
CHEER BOYS CHEER (39) Ariana
CHEERS FOR MISS BISHOP (40) Saltern
CHEYENNE (47) Anderson
CHEYENNE SOCIAL CLUB, THE (69) Wood
CHICAGO (27) Adrian
CHICAGO, CHICAGO=GAILY, GAILY
CHICAGO DEADLINE (49) Dodson
CHICAGO MASQUERADE=LITTLE EGYPT
CHICKEN EVERY SUNDAY (48) LeMaire
CHICKEN WAGON FAMILY (39) Myron
CHIEF, THE (33) Tree
CHIEF CRAZY HORSE (54) Odell
CHILD IS BORN, A (39) Anderson
CHILD IS WAITING, A (62) Shoup
CHILD OF MANHATTAN (32) Kalloch
CHILDREN OF PLEASURE (30) Cox
CHILDREN'S HOUR, THE (61) Jeakins
CHILTERN HUNDREDS, THE (49) Abbey
CHINA BOUND (29) Cox
CHINA CLIPPER (36) Orry-Kelly
CHINA GIRLS (42) Luick
CHINA SEAS (35) Adrian
CHINA SKY (45) Stevenson
CHINATOWN (74) Sylbert
CHITTY CHITTY BANG BANG (68) Haffenden, Joan Bridge
CHOCOLATE SOLDIER, THE (41) Adrian m Steele
CHOOSE YOUR PARTNER=TWO GIRLS ON BROADWAY
CHRISTMAS HOLIDAY (44) V West (King, Greer for Deanna Durbin)
CHRISTMAS IN CONNECTICUT (45) Anderson (Head for Barbara Stanwyck)
CHRISTOPHER COLUMBUS (49) Haffenden, Ellacott
CHRISTOPHER STRONG (33) Greer
CHU-CHIN-CHOW (34) Mann
CHUKA (67) Head
CHURCH MOUSE, THE (34) Hartnell
CIMARRON (30) Ree
CIMARRON (60) Plunkett
CIMARRON KID, THE (51) Thomas
CINCINNATI KID, THE (65) Donfeld
CINDERFELLA (60) Head
CIPHER BUREAU (38) W H McCrary
CIRCLE, THE (25) Chaffin
CIRCLE OF DANGER (51) Dalton
CIRCLE OF DECEPTION (60) Ellacott
CIRCUMSTANTIAL EVIDENCE (44) Wood
CIRCUS CLOWN, THE (34) Orry-Kelly
CIRCUS GIRL, THE (36) Eloise
CIRCUS QUEEN MURDER, THE (33) Kalloch
CIRCUS ROOKIES (28) Cox
CIRCUS WORLD (64) Renie
CITADEL OF CRIME (41) Wakeling
CITIZEN KANE (41) Stevenson
CITY BENEATH THE SEA (52) Odell
CITY BENEATH THE SEA (70) Zastupnevich
CITY FOR CONQUEST (40) Shoup
CITY GIRL (29) Wachner
CITY GIRL (37) Myron
CITY IN DARKNESS (39) Herschel
CITY JUNGLE, THE=YOUNG PHILADELPHIANS, THE
CITY OF BAD MEN (53) Jeakins wd LeMaire
CITY OF SHADOWS (55) Palmer
CLAIRVOYANT, THE (35) Strassner
CLARENCE (37) Banton
CLASH BY NIGHT (52) Woulfe
CLAUDELLE INGLISH (61) Shoup
CLAUDIA (43) Cashin
CLAUDIA AND DAVID (46) Cashin
CLEOPATRA (61) Novarese, Renie (Sharaff for Elizabeth Taylor)
CLIMAX, THE (44) V West
CLIMBING HIGH (38) Hartnell
CLIVE OF INDIA (34) Kiam
CLOAK AND DAGGER (46) Rhodes
CLOCK, THE (45) s Irene a Herwood Keyes
CLOCKWORK ORANGE, A (71) Milena Canonero
CLOUDED YELLOW, THE (50) Harris
CLUNY BROWN (46) Cashin
COBRA (25) Adrian
COBRA WOMAN (44) V West
COCKEYED CAVALIERS (34) Plunkett
COLLEEN (35) Orry-Kelly
COLLEGE COACH (33) Orry-Kelly
COLLEGE HOLIDAY (36) Head
COLLEGE HUMOR (33) Banton
COLLEGE SWING (37) Head
COLORADO TERRITORY (49) Rhodes
COLUMN SOUTH (53) Odell
COMANCHEROS, THE (61) Best
COMANCHE TERRITORY (50) Wood
COME AND GET IT (36) Kiam
COME BACK CHARLESTON BLUE (72) Johnstone
COME BACK, LITTLE SHEBA (52) Head
COME BACK TO ME=DOLL FACE

COME BLOW YOUR HORN (63) Head
COME CLOSER, FOLKS (36) Dryden
COMEDIANS, THE (67) *Tiziani of Rome*
COMEDY OF TERRORS, THE (63) Corso
COME FILL THE CUP (51) Rhodes
COME FLY WITH ME (40) Adrian
COME LIVE WITH ME (40) Adrian
COME NEXT SPRING (55) Palmer
COME ON, THE (55) Head
COME SEPTEMBER (61) Haack
COME TO THE STABLE (49) Nelson *wd*
   LeMaire
COMET OVER BROADWAY (38) Orry-Kelly
COMIC THE (69) *Guy Verhille*
COMING OUT PARTY (33) Kaufman
COMIN' ROUND THE MOUNTAIN (51) Odell
COMMAND, THE (53) Mabry
COMMON CLAY (30) Wachner
COMMON LAW, THE (31) Wakeling
COMPANY SHE KEEPS, THE (50) Woulfe
COMPULSION (58) Palmer *wd* LeMaire
COMRADE X (40) Adrian *m* Steele
CONCEALMENT=SECRET BRIDE, THE
CONEY ISLAND (43) Rose *s* Fanchon
CONFESSION (37) Orry-Kelly
CONFESSIONS OF A NAZI SPY (39) Anderson
CONFESSIONS OF A QUEEN (25) Chaffin
CONFIDENTIAL AGENT (45) Rhodes
CONFIRM OR DENY (41) Wakeling
CONFLICT (45) Orry-Kelly
CONGO MAISIE (39) Tree
CONGRESS DANCES (31) *Ernst Stern*
CONNECTICUT YANKEE, A (31) Wachner
CONNECTICUT YANKEE IN KING
   ARTHUR'S COURT, A (48) Head, Dodson
   m Steele
CONQUEROR, THE (54) Woulfe *m* Wood
CONQUERORS, THE (32) de Lima
CONQUEST (28) Luick
CONQUEST (37) Adrian
CONSOLATION MARRIAGE (31) Ree
CONSPIRACY (39) Renie
CONSPIRACY OF HEARTS (59) Caffin
CONSPIRATORS, THE (44) Rhodes
CONSTANT HUSBAND, THE (55) Duse
CONSTANT NYMPH, THE (33) Conway
CONTACT MAN=ALIAS NICK BEALE
CONTEST GIRL=BEAUTY JUNGLE, THE
CONTINENTAL EXPRESS=SILENT BAT-
   TLE, THE
CONTRABAND (40) *Rahvis*
CONVENTION CITY (33) Orry-Kelly
COOGAN'S BLUFF (68) Colvig
COOL HAND LUKE (67) Shoup
COOL ONES, THE (67) Shoup
COPPER CANYON (50) Head
COQUETTE (29) Greer
CORNERED (45) Renie
CORN IS GREEN, THE (44) Orry-Kelly
CORPSE CAME C O D, THE (47) Louis
CORRIDOR OF MIRRORS (47) *Hyde-Clarke*
CORSAIR (31) Wachner
COSSACKS, THE (28) Cox
COTTON COMES TO HARLEM (70) Johnstone
COUNTERFEIT (36) Anthony
COUNTERFEIT (60) *Anne Klein of Junior Sophisti-*
   cates
COUNTERFEIT TRAITOR, THE (62) Head
COUNTESS OF MONTE CRISTO, THE (34)
   Billy Livingston
COUNT OF MONTE CRISTO, THE (34) Wake-
   ling
COUNTRY BEYOND, THE (36) Lambert
COUNTRY DANCE (69) Blake
COUNTRY DOCTOR, THE (27) Adrian
COUNTRY DOCTOR, THE (35) Wakeling
COUNTRY FAIR (41) Palmer
COUNTRY GENTLEMEN, THE (36) Eloise
COUNTRY GIRL, THE (54) Head
COUNTY CHAIRMAN, THE (34) Lambert
COUNT YOUR BLESSINGS (59) Rose
COURAGE OF LASSIE (46) *s* Irene
COURAGE OF BLACK BEAUTY (57) *wd*
   Norma
COURAGEOUS DR CHRISTIAN (40)
   Bridgehouse
COURT JESTER, THE (55) Head, Wood
COURT MARTIAL OF BILLY MITCHELL,
   THE (55) Shoup
COURTSHIP OF EDDIE'S FATHER, THE (62)
   Rose
COURTSHIP OF MILES STANDISH, THE (23)
   Mitchell Leisen
COVERED TRAILER, THE (39) Palmer
COVER GIRL (43) Banton, Wakeling, King
COWBOY AND THE LADY (38) Balmain
COWBOY FROM BROOKLYN (38) Anderson
COWBOY QUARTERBACK (39) Anderson
COWBOYS, THE (71) Sylbert
CRACK IN THE MIRROR (60) Givenchy
CRACK-UP (36) Herschel
CRACK-UP (46) Renie
CRADLE SONG (33) Banton
CRAIG'S WIFE (36) Royer
CRASH, THE (32) Orry-Kelly
CRASH DIVE (43) Luick

CRASH DONOVAN (36) Brymer
CRASHING HOLLYWOOD (37) Renie
CRASH OF SILENCE=MANDY
CRAZY HOUSE (43) V West
CRAZY THAT WAY (29) Wachner
CREATURE FROM THE BLACK LAGOON,
   THE (53) Odell
CREATURE WALKS AMONG US, THE (55) J
   Morley
CRIME AND PUNISHMENT (35) Mayer
CRIME OF DR FORBES, THE (36) Lambert
CRIME OF PASSION (56) Houston
CRIME OF THE CENTURY, THE (32) Banton
CRIME RING (38) Renie
CRIME SCHOOL (38) Mackenzie
CRIMINAL LAWYER (36) Renie
CRIMSON PIRATE, THE (52) M Furse
CRISS CROSS (48) Wood
CRITIC'S CHOICE (62) Head
CROMWELL (69) Novarese
CROOKED RING=DOUBLE JEOPARDY
CROOKED ROAD, THE (40) Palmer
CROONER (32) Orry-Kelly
CROSS MY HEART (46) Head
CROSS OF LORRAINE, THE (43) Steele
CROSSROADS (42) Kalloch
CROSSWINDS (51) Head
CROWDED SKY, THE (60) Shoup
CROWD ROARS, THE (38) Tree
CRUEL SEA, THE (53) Mendleson
CRUSADES, THE (35) Banton
CRY DANGER (50) Jenssen
CRY FOR HAPPY (60) Koch
CRY IN THE NIGHT, A (56) Mabry
CRY OF THE CITY (48) Cashin *wd* LeMaire
CRY WOLF (47) Travilla (Head for Barbara Stan-
   wyck)
CUBAN FIREBALL (50) Palmer
CUCKOO ON THE NEST (33) Conway
CURE FOR LOVE, THE (49) *Honoria Plesch*
CURLY TOP (35) Hubert
CURSE OF THE CAT PEOPLE, THE (43)
   Stevenson
CYNARA (32) Anderson
CYNTHIA (47) *s* Irene
CYNTHIA'S SECRET=DARK
   DELUSION
CYRANO DE BERGERAC (50) Jeakins
CZARINA=ROYAL SCANDAL, A

DADDY'S GONE A-HUNTING (68) Travilla
DADDY LONG LEGS (54) Nelson *wd* LeMaire
   (ballet by *Tom Keogh*)
DAISY KENYON (47) LeMaire
DAISY MILLER (75) Furness
DAKOTA (45) Palmer
DAKOTA INCIDENT (56) Palmer
DAKOTA LIL (49) *Norma*
DALLAS (50) Best
DALTONS RIDE AGAIN, THE (45) V West
DAMES (34) Orry-Kelly
DAMNED DON'T CRY, THE (50) O'Brien
DANCE GIRL DANCE (40) Stevenson
DANCE, FOOLS, DANCE (31) Adrian
DANCE HALL (41) Herschel
DANCE HALL (50) Mendleson
DANCE LITTLE LADY (54) *Doris Lee*
DANCE MADNESS (25) Kay, Marsh, Andre-Ani,
   Erte
DANCE OF LIFE, THE (29) Banton
DANCE OF THE VAMPIRES, THE (66) *Sophie*
   Devine
DANCERS, THE (24) Wachner
DANCING FOOL, THE=HAROLD TEEN
DANCING IN THE DARK (49) Travilla *wd*
   LeMaire
DANCING LADY (33) Adrian
DANCING MASTERS, THE (43) Mackenzie
DANCING YEARS, THE (49) *Dorothy Sinclair*
DANGER ISLAND (38) Herschel
DANGER—LOVE AT WORK (37) Wakeling
DANGER ON THE AIR (38) V West
DANGEROUS (35) Orry-Kelly
DANGEROUS ADVENTURE, A (37) Kalloch
DANGEROUS AGE, A=BELOVED BRAT
DANGEROUS CORNER (34) Plunkett
DANGEROUS CROSSING (53) Renie *wd*
   LeMaire
DANGEROUS HOLIDAY (37) Eloise
DANGEROUSLY YOURS (37) Herschel
DANGEROUS MISSION (53) Woulfe
DANGEROUS MOONLIGHT (41) Beaton
DANGEROUS NUMBER (36) Tree
DANGEROUS PARTNERS (45) *s* Irene *a* Kay
   Carter
DANGEROUS PROFESSION, A (49) Woulfe
DANGEROUS TO KNOW (37) Head
DANGEROUS WHEN WET (53) Rose
DANGER PATROL (37) Renie
DANGER ROUTE (67) Caffin
DANGER SIGNAL (45) Anderson
DANGER WOMAN (46) V West
DANNY BOY (41) *Christabel Russell Ltd*
DANTE'S INFERNO (35) Royer
DARBY'S RANGERS (57) Best
DAREDEVIL DRIVERS, THE (37) Shoup

DAREDEVILS OF THE CLOUDS (48) Palmer
DARING YOUNG MAN, THE (35) Hubert
DARK ANGEL, THE (35) Kiam
DARK AT THE TOP OF THE STAIRS, THE
   (60) Best
DARK AVENGERS, THE (55) Haffenden
DARK COMMAND (40) Palmer
DARK CORNER, THE (46) Nelson
DARK DELUSION (47) *s* Irene
DARK HAZARD (33) Orry-Kelly
DARK JOURNEY (36) Hubert
DARK PAGE, THE=SCANDAL SHEET
DARK PASSAGE (47) B Newman
DARK PAST, THE (48) Louis
DARK VICTORY (38) Orry-Kelly
DARLING . . . (65) Harris
DARLING, HOW COULD YOU! (51) Head
DARLING LILI (69) Brooks
DATE WITH JUDY, A (48) Rose
DAUGHTER OF ROSIE O'GRADY, THE (50)
   Best (Travilla for June Haver)
DAUGHTERS COURAGEOUS (39) Shoup
DAVID AND BATHSHEBA (51) Stevenson *wd*
   LeMaire
DAVID AND LISA (62) Johnstone
DAVID COPPERFIELD (34) Tree
DAVID COPPERFIELD (69) Mendleson
DAVY (57) Haffenden
DAWN AT SOCORRO (54) J Morley
DAY AT THE RACES, A (37) Tree
DAYBREAK (46) *Dorothy Sinclair*
DAY OF FURY, A (56) Odell
DAYS OF GLORY (44) Renie
DAY OF THE JACKAL, THE (73) Haffenden,
   Joan Bridge, Rosine Delamare
DAYS OF WINE AND ROSES (62) Donfeld
DAY THE BOOKIES WEPT, THE (39) Renie
DAY THE EARTH CAUGHT FIRE, THE (61)
   Dawson
DAY THE EARTH STOOD STILL, THE (51)
   Travilla *wd* LeMaire (Perkins Bailey for
   Klaatuw)
DAYTIME WIFE (39) Royer
D-DAY THE 6TH OF JUNE (56) LeMaire
DEAD END (37) Kiam
DEADFALL (67) Harris
DEADLIER THAN THE MALE (66) *Cynthia*
   Tingey
DEADLINE=DEADLINE USA
DEADLINE ALLEY=HEADLINE HUNTERS
DEADLINE AT DAWN (45) Renie
DEADLINE USA (52) Jenssen *wd* LeMaire
DEADLY AFFAIR, THE (66) *Cynthia Tingey*
DEADLY ROULETTE (68) Colvig
DEAD MAN'S EYES (44) V West
DEAD OF NIGHT (45) *Bianca Mosca*
DEAD RECKONING (46) Louis
DEAD RINGER (63) Donfeld
DEAR BRAT (51) Head
DEAR BRIGITTE (64) Mabry
DEAR HEART (64) Donfeld
DEAR MR PROHACK (49) Dawson, Brierley
DEAR MURDERER (46) Caffin
DEAR RUTH (47) Head
DEAR WIFE (49) Dodson
DEATH AT BROADCASTING HOUSE (34)
   Colin Beck
DEATH OF A GUNFIGHTER (68) Colvig
DEATH TAKES A HOLIDAY (33) Banton
DECEPTION (46) B Newman
DECISION OF CHRISTOPHER BLAKE, THE
   (48) Anderson
DECLINE AND FALL . . . OF A BIRD-
   WATCHER! (67) Duse (Harris for
   Genevieve Page)
DECOY (46) Maclean
DEEP BLUE SEA, THE (55) Balmain, Duse
DEEP IN MY HEART (54) Rose *m* Plunkett
DEEP SIX, THE (57) Shoup
DEEP VALLEY (47) B Newman
DEEP WATERS (48) LeMaire
DELICIOUS (31) Duty
DEMETRIUS AND THE GLADIATORS (54)
   LeMaire
DEMI-BRIDE, THE (27) Andre-Ani
DEMI-PARADISE, THE (43) Hartnell, *Molyneux,*
   Digby Morton, Bianca Mosca, Charles Creed,
   Peter Russell
DENVER AND RIO GRANDE (51) Head
DEPORTED (50) Orry-Kelly
DESERT FURY (47) Head
DESERT HAWK, THE (50) Thomas
DESERT LEGION (53) Thomas
DESERT NIGHTS (29) Frazer
DESERT RATS, THE (53) LeMaire
DESERT RIDER, THE (29) Coulter
DESERT SONG, THE (29) Luick
DESERT SONG, THE (43) Rhodes, Best
DESIGN FOR LIVING (33) Banton
DESIGNING WOMAN (56) Rose
DESIRABLE (34) Orry-Kelly
DESIRE (35) Banton
DESIREE (54) Hubert *wd* LeMaire
DESIRE ME (47) *s* Irene *m* Valles
DESK SET, THE (57) LeMaire
DESPERADOES, THE (43) Travilla

DESPERATE ADVENTURE (38) Saltern
DESPERATE HOURS, THE (55) Head
DESPERATE JOURNEY (42) Anderson
DESPERATE MOMENT (52) Harris
DESTINATION GOBI (52) LeMaire
DESTINATION UNKNOWN (42) V West
DESTINY (44) V West
DESTRY (54) Odell
DESTRY RIDES AGAIN (39) V West
DETECTIVE, THE (68) Mabry
DETECTIVES (28) Cox
DETECTIVE STORY (51) Head
DEVIL AND MISS JONES, THE (41) Renie
DEVIL BAT'S DAUGHTER (46) Karlice
DEVIL DOGS OF THE AIR (34) Orry-Kelly
DEVIL DOLL (36) Tree
DEVIL IS A WOMAN, THE (35) Banton
DEVIL IS DRIVING, THE (37) Kalloch
DEVIL-MAY-CARE (29) Adrian
DEVIL ON WHEELS=INDIANAPOLIS
    SPEEDWAY
DEVIL PAYS OFF, THE (41) Palmer
DEVILS, THE (71) Russell
DEVIL'S CANYON, (53) Woulfe
DEVIL'S DOORWAY (50) Plunkett
DEVIL'S IN LOVE, THE (33) Kaufman
DEVIL'S PLAYGROUND (36) Dryden
DEVIL'S SQUADRON (36) Lange
DEVIL WITH HITLER, THE (42) Royer
DEVIL WITH WOMEN, A (30) Wachner
DEVOTION (46) Anderson
DIAL M FOR MURDER (54) Mabry
DIAMOND CITY (49) Doris Lee
DIAMOND HANDCUFFS (28) Cox
DIAMOND HEAD (62) Pat Barto
DIAMOND HORSESHOE=BILLY ROSE'S
    DIAMOND HORSESHOE
DIAMOND JIM (35) V West
DIAMONDS FOR BREAKFAST (68) Dinah Greet
DIANE (55) Plunkett
DIARY OF A BRIDE=I, JANE DOE
DIARY OF A CHAMBERMAID, THE (45) Mme
    Barbara, Karinska
DIARY OF A MAD HOUSEWIFE (70) R Morley
DIARY OF A MADMAN (63) Corso
DIARY OF ANNE FRANK, THE (58) Wills,
    LeMaire
DICTATOR, THE (34) Strassner
DIMPLES (36) Wakeling
DING DONG WILLIAMS (46) Renie
DINNER AT EIGHT (33) Adrian
DINNER AT THE RITZ (37) Hubert
DIPLOMATIC COURIER (52) Jenssen
DIRTY DINGUS McGEE (70) Wood
DISBARRED (38) Head
DISGRACED! (33) Banton
DISHONOURED (31) Banton
DISHONOURED LADY (47) Jenssen
DISORDERLY CONDUCT (32) Duty
DISORDERLY ORDERLY. THE (64) Head
DISPATCH FROM REUTERS, A (40) Orry-
    Kelly
DISTANT DRUMS (51) Best
DISTANT TRUMPET, A (63) Shoup
DIVIDED HEART, THE (54) Mendleson
DIVIDING LINE, THE=LAWLESS, THE
DIVINE LADY, THE (28) Ree
DIVORCE (45) Myrtil
DIVORCE–AMERICAN STYLE (67) Mackie,
    Frances Lear
DIVORCEE, THE (30) Adrian
DIVORCE OF LADY X, THE (37) Hubert
DIXIE (43) Pene du Bois
DOCTOR AT LARGE (56) Caffin
DOCTOR AT SEA (55) Ellacott
DR BULL (33) Kaufman
DR DOLITTLE (66) Aghayan
DOCTOR IN CLOVER (65) Caffin
DOCTOR IN DISTRESS (63) Caffin
DOCTOR IN THE HOUSE (53) Caffin
DR JEKYLL AND MR HYDE (31) Banton
DR JEKYLL AND MR HYDE (41) Adrian m
    Steele
DR KILDARE GOES HOME (40) Tree
DR KILDARE'S WEDDING DAY (41) Kalloch
DR MONICA (34) Orry-Kelly
DR RENAULT'S SECRET (42) Herschel
DR RHYTHM (38) Jeakins
DOCTORS DIARY (37) Bridgehouse
DOCTOR'S DILEMMA (59) Beaton
DOCTORS DON'T TELL (41) Palmer
DOCTORS' WIVES (70) Mabry
DOCTOR ZHIVAGO (65) Dalton
DODGE CITY (39) Anderson
DODSWORTH (36) Kiam
DOLL FACE (45) Wood
DOLL'S HOUSE, A (73) Furness (Head for Jane
    Fonda)
DOLLY SISTERS, THE (45) Orry-Kelly
DON JUAN QUILLIGAN (45) Wood
DO NOT DISTURB (65) Aghayan
DONOVAN'S REEF (63) Head
DON'T BET ON BLONDES (35) Anderson
DON'T BOTHER TO KNOCK (52) Travilla wd
    LeMaire

DON'T BOTHER TO KNOCK (61) Dior,
    Michael
DON'T DRINK THE WATER (69) Coffin
DON'T EVER LEAVE ME (49) Ellacott
DON'T FENCE ME IN (45) Palmer
DON'T GAMBLE WITH LOVE (35) Lange
DON'T GET PERSONAL (41) V West
DON'T GIVE UP THE SHIP (59) Head
DON'T GO NEAR THE WATER (57) Rose
DON'T JUST STAND THERE (68) Louis
DON'T LOSE YOUR HEAD (66) Emma Selby-
    Walker
DON'T MAKE WAVES (67) Donfeld
DON'T TELL THE WIFE (36) Renie
DOOMED CARGO=SEVEN SINNERS
DOOMSDAY (27) Banton
DOORWAY TO HELL, THE (30) Luick
DOROTHY VERNON OF HADDON HALL
    (24) Mitchell Leisen (Wachner for Mary
    Pickford)
DOUBLE BUNK (61) Cynthia Tingey
DOUBLE CROSS (55) Squire
DOUBLE CROSSBONES (50) Wood
DOUBLE CROSSROADS (30) Wachner
DOUBLE DANGER (37) Renie
DOUBLE HARNESS (33) Plunkett
DOUBLE INDEMNITY (44) Head
DOUBLE JEOPARDY (55) Palmer
DOUBLE LIFE, A (47) Wood, Banton
DOUBLE MAN, THE (67) Courtney Elliott (Dior
    for Moira Lister)
DOUBLE OR NOTHING (37) Head
DOUBLE TROUBLE (66) Donfeld
DOUBLE WEDDING (37) Adrian
DOUBTING THOMAS (35) Hubert
DOUGHGIRLS, THE (44) Anderson
DOWN AMONG THE SHELTERING PALMS
    (53) Travilla wd LeMaire
DOWN ARGENTINE WAY (40) Banton
DOWN DAKOTA WAY (49) Palmer
DOWN IN ARKANSAS (38) Saltern
DOWN ON THE FARM (38) Myron
DOWN THE STRETCH (36) Anderson
DOWN TO EARTH (32) Luick
DOWN TO EARTH (47) Louis
DOWN TO THEIR LAST YACHT (34) Plunkett
DOWN TO THE SEA IN SHIPS (48) LeMaire
DO YOU LOVE ME? (46) Nelson, Cashin
    (Stevenson for Maureen O'Hara)
DRAEGERMAN COURAGE (37) Anderson
DRAG NET (28) Banton
DRAGON MURDER CASE, THE (34) Orry-
    Kelly
DRAGON SEED (44) s Irene m Valles
DRAGONWYCK (45) Hubert
DRAMATIC SCHOOL (38) Adrian
DREAMBOAT (52) Renie wd LeMaire
DREAM GIRL (48) Head
DREAMING LIPS (37) Strassner
DREAM OF LOVE (28) Adrian
DREAM WIFE (52) Rose m Herschel
DRESSED TO KILL (41) Herschel
DRESSED TO THRILL (35) Greer
DRESSMAKER FROM PARIS, THE (24) Banton
DRESS PARADE (27) Adrian
DRIFTWOOD (47) Palmer
DROP DEAD DARLING (66) Haffenden, Joan
    Bridge (Balmain for Rosanna Schiaffino's
    dinner and nightclub gowns)
DRUM, THE (37) Hubert
DRUMS=DRUM, THE
DRUMS ACROSS THE RIVER (54) J Morley
DRUMS ALONG THE MOHAWK (39) Wake-
    ling
DRUMS OF LOVE (27) O'Neill
DRUMS OF THE CONGO (42) V West
DUBARRY WAS A LADY (43) Irene a Shoup m
    Steele
DUCHESS OF IDAHO (50) Rose
DUDE GOES WEST, THE (48) Maclean
DUEL AT DIABLO (66) Wood
DUEL AT SILVER CREEK, THE (52) Thomas
DUEL IN THE SUN (46) Plunkett
DUFFY (68) Blake
DUFFY'S TAVERN (45) Head (for Dorothy
    Lamour, Betty Hutton), Dodson (for
    Paulette Goddard)
DUKE COMES BACK, THE (37) Eloise
DUKE OF CHICAGO, THE (49) Palmer
DUKE STEPS OUT, THE (29) Cox
DULCY (40) Adrian
DUST BE MY DESTINY (39) Anderson
DYNAMITE (29) Adrian
DYNAMITE MAN FROM GLORY JAIL=
    FOOL'S PARADE

EACH DAWN I DIE (39) Shoup
EAGLE, THE (25) Adrian
EAGLE IN A CAGE (70) David Walker
EAGLE SQUADRON (42) V West
EARL CARROLL SKETCHBOOK (46) Palmer
EARL CARROLL VANITIES (45) Palmer
EARL OF PUDDLESTONE (40) Palmer
EARTHBOUND (40) Herschel
EASIEST WAY, THE (30) Hubert
EASTER PARADE (48) Irene m Valles

EAST LYNNE (30) Wachner
EAST MEETS WEST (36) Strassner
EAST OF EDEN (54) Johnstone
EAST OF JAVA=SOUTH SEA SINNER
EAST OF THE RISING SUN=MALAYA
EAST SIDE OF HEAVEN (39) V West
EAST SIDE, WEST SIDE (49) Rose
EASY COME, EASY GO (66) Head
EASY LIVING (37) Banton
EASY LIVING (49) Stevenson
EASY MONEY (48) Ellacott
EASY TO LOOK AT (45) Odell
EASY TO LOVE (33) Orry-Kelly
EASY TO LOVE (53) Rose
EBB TIDE (37) Head
EDDIE CANTOR STORY, THE (53) Shoup, Best
EDDY DUCHIN STORY, THE (56) Louis
EDGE OF DARKNESS (42) Orry-Kelly
EDGE OF THE CITY (56) Johnstone
EDISON, THE MAN (40) Tree m Steele
EDUCATING FATHER (36) Lambert
EDUCATION OF SONNY CARSON, THE (75)
    Coffin
EFFECT OF GAMMA RAYS ON MAN-IN-
    THE-MOON MARIGOLDS, THE (72)
    Johnstone
EGG AND I, THE (46) Banton
EGYPTIAN, THE (54) LeMaire
EIGHT BELLS (35) Kalloch
EL CID (60) Veniero Colasanti, John Moore
EL DORADO (67) Head
ELEPHANT WALK (53) Head
ELEVEN HARROWHOUSE (74) Mendleson
ELINOR NORTON (34) Hubert
ELMER GANTRY (60) Jeakins
ELOPEMENT (51) LeMaire
EMERGENCY WEDDING (50) Louis
EMMA (31) Adrian
EMPEROR'S CANDLESTICKS, THE (37)
    Adrian
EMPEROR WALTZ, THE (48) Head, Steele
EMPLOYEES ENTRANCE (32) Orry-Kelly
ENCHANTED COTTAGE, THE (44) Stevenson
ENCHANTMENT (48) Wills
ENCORE (51) Harris
ENDLESS NIGHT (71) Furness
END OF THE RAINBOW=NORTHWEST
    OUTPOST
ENEMIES OF WOMEN, THE (23) Urban Thur-
    low, Paul Poiret
ENEMY, THE (27) Clark
ENEMY AGENT (39)=BRITISH INTELLIG-
    ENCE
ENEMY AGENT (40) V West
ENEMY BELOW, THE (57) LeMaire
ENGLAND MADE ME (73) Furness
ENSIGN PULVER (63) Jeakins
ENTER ARSENE LUPIN (44) V West
ENTER MADAM (34) Banton
ENTERTAINER, THE (60) Rickards
ERRAND BOY, THE (61) Head
ERMINE AND RHINESTONE (25) furs by Hick-
    son of Fifth Avenue
ESCAPADE (35) Tree
ESCAPE, THE (39) Herschel
ESCAPE (40) Adrian m Steele
ESCAPE BY NIGHT (37) Eloise
ESCAPE FROM CRIME (42) Anderson
ESCAPE FROM FORT BRAVO (53) Rose
ESCAPE IN THE DESERT (45) Anderson
ESCAPE ME NEVER (35) Strassner
ESCAPE ME NEVER (47) B Newman (Ballet by
    Travilla)
ESCAPE TO BURMA (55) Wakeling
ESCAPE TO GLORY=SUBMARINE ZONE
ESCAPE TO HAPPINESS=INTERMEZZO: A
    LOVE STORY
ESPIONAGE (36) Tree
ETERNALLY YOURS (39) Banton (Irene for
    Loretta Young)
ETERNAL SEA, THE (55) Palmer
EVELYN PRENTICE (34) Tree
EVENINGS FOR SALE (32) Banton
EVENSONG (34) Mann
EVE OF ST MARK, THE (44) Cashin
EVER IN MY HEART (33) Luick
EVER SINCE EVE (33) Royer
EVER SINCE EVE (37) Orry-Kelly
EVERYBODY DANCE (36) P Newman
EVERYBODY DOES IT (49) Nelson wd LeMaire
EVERYBODY'S BABY (38) Myron
EVERYBODY'S CHEERING=TAKE ME OUT
    TO THE BALL GAME
EVERYBODY'S OLD MAN (36) Wakeling
EVERYDAY'S A HOLIDAY (37) Schiaparelli
EVERY GIRL SHOULD BE MARRIED (48)
    Sharaff
EVERY NIGHT AT EIGHT (35) Taylor
EVERY SATURDAY NIGHT (35) Lambert
EVERYTHING BUT THE TRUTH (56) Steven-
    son
EVERYTHING I HAVE IS YOURS (52) Rose
EVERYTHING IS THUNDER (36) Strassner
EVERY WOMAN'S MAN=PRIZEFIGHTER
    AND THE LADY, THE
EXCESS BAGGAGE (28) Cox

EXCLUSIVE STORY (35) Tree
EXCUSE MY DUST (51) Rose *m* Steele
EXECUTIONER, THE (70) Caffin
EXECUTIVE SUITE (53) Rose
EXIT SMILING (26) Andre-Ani
EX-LADY (33) Orry-Kelly
EX-MRS BRADFORD, THE (36) B Newman
EXODUS (60) *Rudi Gernreich* (for Eva Marie Saint)
EXPENSIVE HUSBANDS (37) Shoup
EXPERIMENT PERILOUS (44) Stevenson (Rhodes for Hedy Lamarr)
EXPOSED (46) Palmer
EXPRESSO BONGO (59) Dawson (Balmain for Yolande Donlan)
EXQUISITE SINNER, THE (25) Andre-Ani
EYE OF THE CAT (69) Head
EYE OF THE DEVIL (66) Harris, Furness
EYES OF TEXAS (48) Palmer
EYE WITNESS (49)=YOUR WITNESS

FABULOUS TEXAN, THE (47) Palmer
FACE IN THE CROWD, A (57) Johnstone
FACE IN THE SKY (32) Cox
FACES IN THE DARK (59) Dawson
FACE TO FACE (52) J Morley
FACTS OF LIFE, THE (60) Head, Stevenson
FACTS OF LOVE, THE=29 ACACIA AVENUE
FAHRENHEIT 451 (66) Blake
FAIL SAFE (63) Johnstone
FAIR CO-ED, THE (27) Clark
FAIR WARNING (36) Herschel
FAIR WIND TO JAVA (53) Palmer
FAIRY TALE MURDER=RIVER GANG
FAITHFUL HEART (32) Conway
FAITHFUL IN MY FASHION (46) Shoup *s* Irene
FAITHLESS (32) Adrian
FALCON AND THE CO-EDS, THE (43) Renie
FALCON IN HOLLYWOOD, THE (44) Renie
FALCON'S BROTHER, THE (42) Renie
FALCON STRIKES BACK, THE (42) Renie
FALCON TAKES OVER, THE (42) Renie
FALCON OUT WEST, THE (43) Renie
FALLEN ANGEL (45) Cashin
FALLEN SPARROW, THE (43) Stevenson
FALLING FOR YOU (33) Conway
FALL OF THE HOUSE OF USHER, THE (60) Corso
FALSE WITNESS=ARKANSAS JUDGE
FAME IS THE SPUR (47) *Honoria Plesch*
FAMILY AFFAIR, A (37) Shoup
FAMILY HONEYMOON (48) Orry-Kelly
FAMILY JEWELS, THE (65) Head
FAMILY SECRET, THE (51) Louis
FAN, THE (49) LeMaire, Hubert
FANNY (61) *Anne-Marie Marchand*
FANNY BY GASLIGHT (44) Haffenden
FAR COUNTRY, THE (54) J Morley
FAREWELL AGAIN (37) Hubert
FAREWELL, MY LOVELY (44)=MURDER, MY SWEET
FAREWELL TO ARMS, A (32) Banton
FAREWELL TO ARMS, A (57) *Veniero Colasanti*
FAR HORIZONS, THE (55) Head
FARMER'S DAUGHTER, THE (46) Head
FARMER TAKES A WIFE, THE (35) Hubert
FARMER TAKES A WIFE, THE (53) Travilla *wd* LeMaire
FASHIONS FOR WOMEN (27) Banton
FASHIONS OF 1934 (33) Orry-Kelly
FAST AND LOOSE (38) Tree
FAST AND LOOSE (53) Ellacott
FAST LADY, THE (62) Harris
FAST LIFE (32) Adrian
FAST COMPANY (38) Tree
FATAL LADY (36) Taylor
FATAL WITNESS, THE (45) Palmer
FAT CITY (72) Jeakins
FATE IS THE HUNTER (64) Mabry
FATHER BROWN (54) Squire
FATHER CAME TOO (63) Harris
FATHER GOOSE (64) Aghayan
FATHER IS A BACHELOR (49) Louis
FATHER OF THE BRIDE (50) Rose *m* Plunkett
FATHER'S LITTLE DIVIDEND (50) Rose
FATHER'S SON (30) Stevenson
FATHER'S SON (40) Anderson
FATHER WAS A FULLBACK (49) Nelson
FATHOM (67) *Kiki Byrne*
FAT MAN, THE (50) Odell
FBI STORY, THE (59) Palmer
FEAR STRIKES OUT (56) Head
FEATHER IN HER HAT, A (35) Mayer
FEDERAL AGENT AT LARGE (50) Palmer
FEDERAL MANHUNT (38) Saltern
FEMALE ON THE BEACH (55) O'Brien
FEMININE TOUCH, THE (56) Mendleson
FEUDIN' FUSSIN' AND A-FIGHTIN' (48) Odell
FEMALE (33) Orry-Kelly
FEVER IN THE BLOOD, A (60) Shoup
FIDDLER ON THE ROOF (71) Haffenden, *Joan Bridge*
FIEND WHO WALKED THE WEST, THE (58) Balkan *wd* LeMaire
FIESTA (47) *s* Irene
15 MAIDEN LANE (36) Herschel

FIFTY-FIVE DAYS AT PEKING (62) *Veniero Colasanti, John Moore*
FIFTH AVENUE GIRL (39) Greer
FIFTY-FIFTY GIRL, THE (27) Banton
FIFTY MILLION FRENCHMEN (29) Luick
FIFTY ROADS TO TOWN (36) Royer
FIFTY-SECOND STREET (37) Taylor
FIGHT FOR YOUR LADY (37) Stevenson
FIGHTING CHANCE, THE (55) Palmer
FIGHTING COAST GUARD (51) Palmer
FIGHTING EAGLE, THE (27) Adrian
FIGHTING FATHER DUNNE (47) Balkan
FIGHTING KENTUCKIAN, THE (49) Palmer
FIGHTING O'FLYNN (48) *G E Calthrop*
FIGHTING PRINCE OF DONEGAL, THE (65) Mendleson
FIGHTING SEABEES, THE (43) Palmer
FIGHT TO THE FINISH, A (37) Kalloch
FIG LEAVES (26) Adrian
FILE ON THELMA JORDAN, THE=THELMA JORDAN
FINAL HOUR, THE (36) Dryden
FINDERS KEEPERS (51) Odell
FINDERS KEEPERS (66) *Cynthia Tingey*
FIND THE BLACKMAILER (43) Rhodes
FINE AND DANDY=WEST POINT STORY, THE
FINE MADNESS, A (65) Roth
FINGERS AT THE WINDOW (41) Shoup
FINIAN'S RAINBOW (68) Jeakins
FINISHING SCHOOL (34) Plunkett
FIREBIRD, THE (34) Orry-Kelly
FIRE BRIGADE, THE (26) Kay, Marsh, Andre-Ani
FIRECREEK (67) Wood
FIRE DOWN BELOW (57) Balmain
FIREFLY, THE (37) Adrian
FIRE OVER ENGLAND (36) Hubert
FIRERAISERS, THE (33) Conway
FIRST A GIRL (35) Strassner
FIRST BABY, THE (36) Lambert
FIRST GENTLEMAN, THE (47) Haffenden
FIRST HUNDRED YEARS, THE (37) Tree
FIRST LADY (37) Orry-Kelly
FIRST LOVE (39) V West
FIRST MAN INTO SPACE (58) *Anne Selby-Walker*
FIRST MEN ON THE MOON (64) Lehmann
FIRST REBEL, THE=ALLEGHENY UPRISING
FIRST TIME, THE (51) Louis
FIRST TRAVELLING SALESLADY, THE (56) Stevenson
FIRST YEAR, THE (32) Cox
FITZWILLY (67) Donfeld
FITZWILLY STRIKES BACK=FITZWILLY
FIVE AGAINST THE HOUSE (55) Louis
FIVE CAME BACK (39) Stevenson
FIVE CARD STUD (68) Rhodes
FIVE FINGER EXERCISE (62) Orry-Kelly
FIVE FINGERS (51) LeMaire
FIVE GOLDEN HOURS (60) *Sartoria Sorelle*
FIVE GRAVES TO CAIRO (43) Head
FIVE OF A KIND (38) Herschel, Myron
FIVE PENNIES, THE (59) Head
FIVE STAR FINAL (31) Luick
FIVE THOUSAND FINGERS OF DR T, THE (53) Louis
FIVE WEEKS IN A BALLOON (62) Zastupnevich
FIXED BAYONETS (51) LeMaire
FIXER, THE (68) Jeakins
FLAME, THE (47) Palmer
FLAME IN THE STREETS (61) Caffin
FLAME OF ARABY (51) Thomas
FLAME OF THE BARBARY COAST (44) Palmer
FLAME OF NEW ORLEANS, THE (40) Hubert
FLAME OF YOUTH (49) Palmer
FLAME WITHIN, THE (35) Tree
FLAMING FOREST, THE (26) Andre-Ani
FLAMINGO ROAD (49) Travilla
FLAMING STAR, THE (60) Balkan
FLEDGLINGS (64) *Caroline Charles*
FLESH AND FANTASY (43) V West (Head for Barbara Stanwyck)
FLESH AND FURY (51) Thomas
FLESH AND THE DEVIL (26) Andre-Ani
FLIGHT COMMAND (40) Tree *m* Steele
FLIGHT FOR FREEDOM (42) Adrian
FLIGHT NURSE (53) Palmer
FLIGHT OF THE PHOENIX, THE (65) Koch
FLIM-FLAM-MAN, THE (67) Jeakins
FLIRTATION WALK (34) Orry-Kelly
FLIRTING WITH LOVE (24) C West
FLOODS OF FEAR (58) Ellacott
FLOOD TIDE (57) Thomas
FLORIAN (40) Adrian *m* Steele
FLORADORA GIRL, THE (30) Adrian
FLORENTINE DAGGER, THE (35) Orry-Kelly
FLOWER DRUM SONG, THE (61) Sharaff
FLUFFY (64) Odell
FLY, THE (58) Balkan *wd* LeMaire
FLYING DOWN TO RIO (33) Plunkett (Irene for Dolores del Rio)
FLYING FLEET, The (28) Cox
FLYING IRISHMAN, THE (38) Renie
FLYING MISSILE, THE (50) Louis
FLYING TIGERS (42) Palmer

FOG (33) Kalloch
FOG OVER 'FRISCO (34) Orry-Kelly
FOLIES BERGERE (34) *Arthur M Levy* (Kiam for Merle Oberon)
FOLLOW A STAR (59) Mendleson
FOLLOW ME (72) Harris
FOLLOW ME, BOYS! (66) Thomas
FOLLOW THE BOYS (43) V West (Greer for Vera Zorina)
FOLLOW THE FLEET (35) B Newman
FOLLOW THE SUN (51) Renie *wd* LeMaire
FOLLOW THRU (30) Banton
FOLLOW YOUR HEART (36) Eloise
FOOLISH WIVES (21) *Western Costume Co*
FOOL KILLER, THE (65) Jeakins
FOOLS FOR SCANDAL (37) Anderson (Banton for Carole Lombard)
FOOL'S PARADE (71) *Guy Verhille*
FOOL'S PARADISE (21) C West
FOOLS RUSH IN (49) *Sheila Graham*
FOOL THERE WAS, A (15) Hopkins
FOOTLIGHT FEVER (41) Renie
FOOTLIGHT PARADE (33) Anderson
FOOTLOOSE HEIRESS, THE (37) Shoup
FOOTSTEPS IN THE DARK (40) Shoup
FOOTSTEPS IN THE FOG (55) Dawson, Haffenden
FOR ALIMONY ONLY (26) Adrian
FORBIDDEN (53) Thomas
FORBIDDEN CARGO (53) Ellacott
FORBIDDEN FRUIT (20) C West (*Mitchell Leisen, Natasha Rambova* for Cinderella Ball Sequence)
FORBIDDEN HEAVEN (35) *Lettie Lee*
FORBIDDEN PARADISE (24) Greer
FORBIDDEN PLANET (55) *m* Plunkett (Rose for Anne Francis)
FORBIDDEN STREET=BRITANNIA MEWS
FORBIDDEN WOMAN, THE (27) Adrian
FORBIN PROJECT, THE (70) Head
FOREIGN AFFAIR, A (48) Head
FOREIGN CORRESPONDENT (40) *I Magnin & Co*
FOREIGN DEVILS (27) Hubert
FOREIGN INTRIGUE (56) Balmain
FOREVER AMBER (47) Hubert *wd* LeMaire
FOREVER, DARLING (55) Jenssen
FOREVER FEMALE (53) Head
FORGED PASSPORT (38) Saltern
FORGOTTEN GIRLS (40) Palmer
FORGOTTEN WOMAN, THE (39) V West
FOR HEAVEN'S SAKE (50) LeMaire
FOR LOVE OR MONEY (39) V West
FOR LOVE OR MONEY (63) Louis
FOR ME AND MY GAL (42) Kalloch *m* Steele
FORSAKING ALL OTHERS (34) Adrian
FOR SALE (24) C West
FORSYTE SAGA, THE=THAT FORSYTE WOMAN
FORT ALGIERS (53) Wood
FOR THE LOVE OF MARY (48) Orry-Kelly
FOR THEM THAT TRESPASS (48) *Dorothy Sinclair*
FORTUNE HUNTER, THE (53) Palmer
FORTUNE IS A WOMAN (56) Mendleson
FORTUNES OF CAPTAIN BLOOD, THE (50) Louis
FORTY-FIVE FATHERS (37) Herschel
FORTY GUNS (57) Rhodes, LeMaire
FORTY LITTLE MOTHERS (40) Tree
FORTY NAUGHTY GIRLS (37) Renie
FORTY POUNDS OF TROUBLE (62) Odell
42ND STREET (32) Orry-Kelly
FOR YOU ALONE=WHEN YOU'RE IN LOVE
FOUNTAIN, THE (34) Plunkett
FOUNTAINHEAD, THE (49) Anderson
FOUR DAUGHTERS (38) Orry-Kelly
FOUR FEATHERS, THE (39) *Godfrey Brennan*, Hubert
FOUR FOR TEXAS (63) Koch
FOUR FRIGHTENED PEOPLE (33) Anderson
FOUR GIRLS IN TOWN (56) Odell
FOUR GIRLS IN WHITE (38) Tree
FOUR GUNS TO THE BORDER (54) J Morley
FOUR HORSEMEN OF THE APOCALYPSE, THE (61) Hubert, Plunkett (Orry-Kelly for Ingrid Thulin)
FOUR JILLS IN A JEEP (43) Wood
FOUR JUST MEN, THE (39) *Ariana*
FOUR MEN AND A PRAYER (38) Royer
FOUR MOTHERS (40) Shoup
FOUR MUSKETEERS, THE (75) Blake, Talsky
FOUR POSTER, THE (52) Louis
FOUR'S A CROWD (38) Orry-Kelly
FOUR SONS (28) Kay
FOUR SONS (40) Banton
FOURTEEN HOURS (50) Stevenson *wd* LeMaire
FOUR WALLS (28) Cox
FOUR WIVES (39) Shoup
FOXES OF HARROW, THE (47) Hubert *wd* LeMaire
FOXFIRE (55) Thomas
FOX MOVIETONE FOLLIES OF 1929 (29) Wachner, O'Neill
FRAGMENT OF FEAR (70) Dalton
FRAMED (46) Louis
FRAME-UP, THE (37) Kalloch

FRANCIS (49) Odell
FRANCIS COVERS THE BIG TOWN (53) Odell
FRANCIS IN THE HAUNTED HOUSE (56) J Morley
FRANCIS OF ASSISI (61) Novarese
FRANKENSTEIN MEETS THE WOLFMAN (43) V West
FRANKIE AND JOHNNY (65) Wakeling
FRECKLES (35) Plunkett
FREE AND EASY (30) Cox
FREE AND EASY (41) Tree
FREE FOR ALL (49) Odell
FREE SOUL, A (31) Adrian
FREE TO LIVE=HOLIDAY (38)
FRENCH DRESSING (64) Russell
FRENCHIE (50) Wood
FRENCH LINE, THE (53) Woulfe (and Greer for Jane Russell)
FRENCHMAN'S CREEK (44) Pene du Bois
FRENCH WITHOUT TEARS (39) Worth
FRESHMAN LOVE (35) Orry-Kelly
FRESHMAN YEAR (38) V West
FRIDAY THE THIRTEENTH (33) Conway
FRIEDA (47) *Bianca Mosca*
FRIENDLY ENEMIES (42) Royer
FRIENDLY NEIGHBOURS (40) Palmer
FRIENDLY PERSUASION (56) Jeakins
FRIENDS OF MR SWEENEY (34) Orry-Kelly
FRIGHTENED CITY=KILLER THAT STALKED NEW YORK, THE
FRISCO JENNY (32) Orry-Kelly
FRISCO KID (35) Orry-Kelly
'FRISCO LIL (41) V West
'FRISCO SAL (44) V West
FRISCO SALLY LEVY (27) Hubert
'FRISCO WATERFRONT (35) *Lettie Lee*
FROGMEN, THE (51) LeMaire
FROM HELL TO HEAVEN (33) Banton
FROM HELL TO TEXAS (58) Balkan *wd* LeMaire
FROM HERE TO ETERNITY (53) Louis
FROM RUSSIA WITH LOVE (63) Rickards
FROM THE TERRACE (60) Travilla
FROM THIS DAY FORWARD (46) Stevenson
FRONTIER MARSHAL (39) Herschel
FRONTIERSMAN, THE (27) Andre-Ani
FRONT PAGE WOMAN (35) Anderson
FROU FROU=TOY WIFE, THE
FROZEN GHOST, THE (45) V West
FUGITIVE IN THE SKY (36) Anderson
FUGITIVE LADY (34) Kalloch
FUGITIVE LADY (51) *Irene Galitzine*
FUGITIVES FOR A NIGHT (38) Renie
FULLER BRUSH GIRL, THE (50) Louis
FULLER BRUSH MAN, THE (48) Louis
FULL HOUSE=O HENRY'S FULL HOUSE
FULL TREATMENT, THE (60) Dawson
FUN IN ACAPULCO (63) Head
FUNNY FACE (35)=BRIGHT LIGHTS
FUNNY FACE (56) Head (Givenchy for Audrey Hepburn's Paris Wardrobe)
FUNNY GIRL (68) Sharaff
FUNNY LADY (74) Aghayan, Mackie
FUNNY THING HAPPENED ON THE WAY TO THE FORUM, A (66) Walton
FURIES, THE (50) Head
FURY (36) Tree
FURY AT FURNACE CREEK (48) Hubert
FURY AT SMUGGLERS BAY (61) Dalton
FUZZ (72) Jeakins
FUZZY PINK NIGHTGOWN, THE (57) Travilla

GABY (55) Rose
GAIETY GEORGE (46) *Matilda Etches*
GAIETY GIRLS, THE=PARADISE FOR TWO
GAILY, GAILY (69) Aghayan
GALLANT BLADE, THE (48) Louis
GALLANT JOURNEY (46) Louis
GALLANT LADY (33) Wakeling
GALLANT LEGION, THE (48) Palmer
GALLANT SONS (40) Adrian
GALLOPING MAJOR, THE (50) Ellacott
GAL WHO TOOK THE WEST, THE (49) Wood
GAMBIT (66) Louis
GAMBLER, THE (75) *Albert Wolsky*
GAMBLER FROM NATCHEZ, THE (54) Travilla
GAMBLING (34) *Hattie Carnegie*
GAMBLING LADY (33) Orry-Kelly
GAME OF DEATH, A (45) Renie
GAMES (67) Haack (visual consultant)
GAMMA PEOPLE, THE (55) Lehmann
GANG MADE GOOD, THE=TUXEDO JUNCTION
GANG'S ALL HERE, THE (43) Wood
GANGS OF CHICAGO (40) Palmer
GANGS OF NEW YORK (38) Saltern
GANGSTER, THE (47) Norma
GANGWAY (37) *P L Czettel*
GANGWAY FOR TOMORROW (43) Stevenson
GARDEN MURDER CASE, THE (35) Tree
GARDEN OF ALLAH, THE (36) Dryden
GARDEN OF EVIL (54) Travilla *wd* LeMaire
GARMENT JUNGLE, THE (57) Louis
GASLIGHT (44) *s* Irene *a* Herwood Keyes
GATEWAY (38) Wakeling
GATHERING OF EAGLES, A (62) Irene

GAY ADVENTURE, THE=GOLDEN ARROW
GAY BLADES, THE (46) Palmer
GAY BRIDE, THE (34) Tree
GAY DECEIVER, THE (26) Kay, Marsh, Andre-Ani
GAY DECEPTION, THE (35) Lambert
GAY DESPERADO, THE (36) Kiam
GAY DIVORCE, THE=GAY DIVORCÉE, THE
GAY DIVORCÉE, THE (34) Plunkett
GAY IMPOSTORS, THE=GOLD DIGGERS IN PARIS
GAY INTRUDERS, THE (48) *Helen Ruth*
GAY LADY=TROTTIE TRUE
GAY MRS TREXEL, THE=SUSAN AND GOD
GAY SISTERS, THE (42) Head
GAY VAGABOND, THE (41) Palmer
GAZEBO, THE (59) Rose
GENERAL DIED AT DAWN, THE (36) Banton
GENGHIS KHAN (64) *Cynthia Tingey*
GENIUS AT WORK (46) Renie
GENTLE JULIA (35) Luza
GENTLEMAN FOR A DAY=UNION DEPOT
GENTLEMAN'S AGREEMENT (47) Nelson *wd* LeMaire
GENTLEMAN JIM (42) Anderson
GENTLEMAN JOE PALOOKA (46) Maclean
GENTLEMEN ARE BORN (34) Orry-Kelly
GENTLEMEN MARRY BRUNETTES (55) Travilla (Dior for "Loot" sequence)
GENTLEMEN PREFER BLONDES (53) Travilla *wd* LeMaire
GENTLE TOUCH, THE=FEMININE TOUCH, THE
GEORDIE (55) Duse
GEORGE WASHINGTON SLEPT HERE (42) Orry-Kelly
GEORGE WHITE'S 1935 SCANDALS (34) LeMaire
GEORGE WHITE'S SCANDALS (45) Stevenson
GEORGY GIRL (66) *Mary Quant*
GERALDINE (53) Palmer
GET-AWAY, THE (41) Kalloch
GET GOING (43) V West
GETTING GERTIE'S GARTER (45) *Odette*
GHOST AND MRS MUIR, THE (47) Behm *wd* LeMaire
GHOST BREAKERS, THE (40) Head
GHOST CATCHERS (44) V West
GHOST GOES WEST, THE (35) Hubert (Armstrong for Robert Donat)
GHOST GOES WILD, THE (46) Palmer
GHOST OF FRANKENSTEIN, THE (41) V West
GHOST SHIP, THE (43) Stevenson
GIANT (56) Best (Mabry for Elizabeth Taylor)
G I BLUES (60) Head
GIDGET GOES TO ROME (63) Barto
GIFT OF GAB (34) V West
GIFT OF LOVE (57) LeMaire
GIGI (57) Beaton
GIGOLO (26) Adrian
GILDA (45) Louis
GILDED LILY, THE (34) Banton
GILDERSLEEVE ON BROADWAY (43) Renie
GINGER (35) Luza
GIRL AND THE GAMBLER, THE (39) Renie
GIRL CAN'T HELP IT, THE (56) LeMaire
GIRL CRAZY (43) *s* Irene *a* Sharaff
GIRL DOWNSTAIRS, THE (38) Tree
GIRL FROM AVENUE A (40) Myron
GIRL FROM GOD'S COUNTRY (40) Palmer
GIRL FROM HAVANA, THE (40) Palmer
GIRL FROM JONES BEACH, THE (49) Rhodes
GIRL FROM MAXIMS (36) *Jean Oberle*
GIRL FROM MEXICO, THE (39) Renie
GIRL FROM MISSOURI, THE (34) Adrian
GIRL FROM 10TH AVENUE (35) Orry-Kelly
GIRL HE LEFT BEHIND, THE (56) Mabry
GIRL IN OVERALLS, THE=SWING SHIFT MAISIE
GIRL IN THE KREMLIN (57) Thomas
GIRL IN THE PAINTING=PORTRAIT FROM LIFE
GIRL IN THE PULLMAN, THE (27) Wakeling
GIRL IN THE RED VELVET SWING, THE (55) LeMaire
GIRL IN THE SHOW, THE (30) Cox
GIRL IN WHITE, THE (51) Rose
GIRL MOST LIKELY, THE (57) Renie
GIRL NAMED TAMIKO, A (62) Head
GIRL NEXT DOOR, THE (53) Travilla *wd* LeMaire
GIRL OF THE GOLDEN WEST, THE (37) Adrian
GIRL OF THE NIGHT (60) Aldredge
GIRL OF THE YEAR=PETTY GIRL, THE
GIRL ON THE BOAT, THE (61) *David Ffolkes*
GIRL ON THE SPOT (45) V West
GIRL RUSH (44) Renie
GIRLS ABOUT TOWN (31) Banton
GIRL SAID NO, THE (30) Cox
GIRLS CAN PLAY (37) Kalloch
GIRLS DORMITORY (36) Wakeling
GIRLS! GIRLS! GIRLS! (62) Head
GIRLS HE LEFT BEHIND, THE=GANG'S ALL HERE, THE

GIRLS OF THE BIG HOUSE (45) Palmer
GIRLS ON PROBATION (37) Shoup
GIRL THIEF, THE=LOVE AT SECOND SIGHT
GIRL WAS YOUNG, A=YOUNG AND INNOCENT
GIRL WHO HAD EVERYTHING, THE (53) Rose
GIRL WITHOUT A ROOM (33) Banton
GIVE A GIRL A BREAK (53) Rose *m* Herschel
GIVE HER A RING (34) Hartnell
GIVE ME A SAILOR (38) Head
GIVE ME YOUR HEART (36) Orry-Kelly
GIVE MY REGARDS TO BROADWAY (48) Cashin *wd* LeMaire
GIVE US THIS DAY (49) Brierley
GIVE US WINGS (40) V West
GLASS BOTTOM BOAT, THE (65) Aghayan
GLASS KEY, THE (42) Head
GLASS SLIPPER, THE (54) Rose, Plunkett
GLASS WEB, THE (53) Thomas
GLENN MILLER STORY, THE (53) J Morley
GLOBAL AFFAIR, A (63) Thomas
GLORIFYING THE AMERICAN GIRL (29) Harkrider
GLORY (55) Woulfe
GLORY ALLEY (52) Rose
G-MEN (35) Orry-Kelly
GNOME-MOBILE, THE (67) Thomas
GO-BETWEEN, THE (70) Furness
GOBS AND GALS (52) Palmer
GO CHASE YOURSELF (38) Renie
GODFATHER, THE (72) Johnstone
GODFATHER PART II, THE (75) van Runkle
GOD IS MY CO-PILOT (44) Rhodes
GODLESS GIRL, THE (28) Adrian
GO GETTER, THE (37) Orry-Kelly
GOING HIGHBROW (35) Orry-Kelly
GOING HOLLYWOOD (33) Adrian
GOING MY WAY (44) Head
GOING PLACES (38) Shoup
GOIN' TO TOWN (35) Banton
GO INTO YOUR DANCE (34) Orry-Kelly
GOLD DIGGERS IN PARIS (38) Shoup
GOLD DIGGERS OF BROADWAY (29) Luick
GOLD DIGGERS OF 1933 (33) Orry-Kelly
GOLD DIGGERS OF 1935 (34) Orry-Kelly
GOLD DIGGERS OF 1937 (36) Orry-Kelly
GOLDEN ARROW THE (36) Orry-Kelly
GOLDEN ARROW (49) *William Chappell, Germaine le Comte*
GOLDEN BED, THE (24) Greer, C West
GOLDEN BLADE, THE (53) J Morley
GOLDEN BOY (38) Kalloch
GOLDEN CALF, THE (29) Wachner
GOLDEN EARRINGS (47) Dodson
GOLDEN FLEECING (40) Tree
GOLDEN GIRL (51) LeMaire
GOLDEN HORDE, THE (51) Rhodes
GOLDEN HOUR, THE=POT O'GOLD
GOLDEN MASK, THE=SOUTH OF ALGIERS
GOLDFISH, THE (24) C West
GOLDIE GETS ALONG (33) Irene
GOLD IS WHERE YOU FIND IT (37) Anderson
GOLD RUSH MAISIE (40) Tree
GOLDWYN FOLLIES, THE (37) Kiam
GO NAKED IN THE WORLD (60) Rose
GONE TO EARTH (50) Squire
GONE WITH THE WIND (39) Plunkett
GOODBYE AGAIN (33) Anderson
GOODBYE AGAIN (61) Dior
GOODBYE CHARLIE (64) Rose
GOODBYE COLUMBUS (68) Coffin
GOODBYE MR CHIPS (69) Harris
GOODBYE, MY FANCY (51) O'Brien
GOOD COMPANIONS, THE (32) Conway
GOOD EARTH, THE (36) Tree
GOOD FAIRY, THE (34) V West
GOOD GIRLS GO TO PARIS (39) Kalloch
GOOD GUYS AND THE BAD GUYS, THE (68) Wood
GOOD HUMOUR MAN, THE (50) Louis
GOOD MORNING, DOCTOR=YOU BELONG TO ME
GOOD MORNING JUDGE (43) V West
GOOD NEIGHBOUR SAM (63) *Micheline, Jacqueline*
GOOD NEWS (30) Cox
GOOD NEWS (47) Rose *m* Valles
GOOD OLD SOAK (37) Tree
GOOD SAM (48) Travilla
GOOD TIME GIRL (48) *s* Harris
GOOD TIMES (66) Rhodes
GOOSE AND THE GANDER, THE (35) Orry-Kelly
GORGEOUS HUSSY, THE (36) Adrian
GORILLA, THE (39) Wakeling
GORILLA AT LARGE (53) Renie
GO TO BLAZES (62) *Frank Usher*
GOVERNMENT GIRL (43) Stevenson
GO WEST (40) Tree *m* Steele
GO WEST, YOUNG LADY (41) Plunkett
GRACE MOORE STORY, THE=SO THIS IS LOVE
GRADUATE, THE (67) *Patricia Zipprodt*
GRAND CANARY (34) Kaufman
GRAND CENTRAL MURDER (42) Shoup

GRAND DUCHESS AND THE WAITER, THE (25) Banton
GRAND EXIT (35) Mayer
GRAND HOTEL (32) Adrian
GRAND JURY (36) Stevenson
GRAND NATIONAL NIGHT (53) Dawson
GRAND OLE OPRY (40) Palmer
GRAND PARADE, THE (29) Wakeling
GRAND SLAM (32) Orry-Kelly
GRANNY GET YOUR GUN (39) Anderson
GRAPES OF WRATH, THE (39) Wakeling
GRASS IS GREENER, THE (61) Dior (for Jean Simmons), Hardy Amies (for Deborah Kerr)
GREAT ADVENTURE, THE=ADVENTURERS, THE (50)
GREAT AMERICAN BROADCAST, THE (41) Banton
GREAT AWAKENING, THE=NEW WINE
GREAT BANK ROBBERY, THE (69) Mabry
GREAT CARUSO, THE (51) Rose m Steele
GREAT CATHERINE (67) M Furse
GREAT DAY IN THE MORNING (56) Wakeling
GREAT DIVIDE, THE (24) Wachner
GREATEST SHOW ON EARTH, THE (51) Head, Jeakins (circus by White)
GREATEST STORY EVER TOLD, THE (59/65) Novarese, Best
GREAT EXPECTATIONS (46) Sophie Harris, M Furse
GREAT FLIRTATION, THE (34) Banton
GREAT GABBO, THE (29) Andre-Ani
GREAT GATSBY, THE (49) Head
GREAT GATSBY, THE (73) Aldredge
GREAT GARRICK, THE (37) Anderson
GREAT GOD GOLD (35) Lettie Lee
GREAT GUNS (41) Herschel
GREAT HOSPITAL MYSTERY, THE (37) Herschel
GREAT HOTEL MURDER, THE (34) Royer
GREAT IMPERSONATION, THE (35) V West, Brymer
GREAT LIE, THE (41) Orry-Kelly
GREAT LOVER, THE (49) Head
GREAT MAN, THE (56) Thomas
GREAT MANHUNT, THE=STATE SECRET
GREAT MAN'S LADY, THE (41) Head
GREAT MAN VOTES, THE (38) Renie
GREAT McGINTY, THE (40) Head
GREAT NORTHFIELD MINNESOTA RAID, THE (71) Colvig
GREAT O'MALLEY, THE (36) Anderson
GREAT RACE, THE (65) Donfeld (Head for Natalie Wood)
GREAT RUPERT, THE (50) Helen Rachmil
GREAT ST TRINIAN'S TRAIN ROBBERY, THE (65) Honoria Plesch
GREAT SINNER, THE (49) Irene m Valles
GREAT SIOUX UPRISING, THE (53) Thomas
GREAT TRAIN ROBBERY, THE (41) Palmer
GREAT VICTOR HERBERT, THE (39) Head
GREAT WALTZ, THE (38) Adrian
GREAT WALTZ, THE (72) David Walker
GREAT WHITE HOPE, THE (70) Sharaff
GREAT ZIEGFELD, THE (36) Adrian
GREEN DOLPHIN STREET (47) Plunkett s Irene m Valles
GREEN-EYED WOMAN, THE = TAKE A LETTER DARLING
GREEN FINGERS (46) Rahvis
GREEN FIRE (54) Rose
GREEN FOR DANGER (46) Rahvis
GREENGAGE SUMMER, THE (60) Harris
GREEN GRASS OF WYOMING (48) Hubert wd LeMaire
GREEN HELL (39) Irene, B Newman
GREEN LIGHT (36) Orry-Kelly
GREEN MAN, THE (56) Duse
GREEN MANSIONS (58) Jeakins
GREEN PASTURES (36) Anderson
GREENWICH VILLAGE (44) Wood
GREEN YEARS, THE (45) Valles s Irene
GREYFRIARS BOBBY (60) M Furse
GRISSOM GANG, THE (71) Koch
GROOM WORE SPURS, THE (50) Jenssen (for Joan Davis), Jacie (for Ginger Rogers)
GROUNDS FOR DIVORCE (25) Banton
GROUNDS FOR MARRIAGE (50) Rose
GROUP, THE (65) Johnstone
GUARDSMAN, THE (31) Adrian
GUESS WHO'S COMING TO DINNER? (67) Louis
GUEST IN THE HOUSE (44) Visart
GUIDE FOR THE MARRIED MAN, A (67) Mabry
GUILT OF JANET AMES, THE (46) Louis, Banton
GUINEA PIG, THE (48) Honoria Plesch
GUNFIGHT AT THE OK CORRAL (57) Head
GUNFIGHTER, THE (50) Travilla wd LeMaire
GUNFIGHT IN ABILENE (67) Colvig
GUN FOR A COWARD (56) J Morley
GUNGA DIN (38) Stevenson
GUN GLORY (57) Plunkett
GUN RUNNERS, THE=SANTIAGO
GUNS FOR SAN SEBASTIAN (67) Wood
GUNS OF DARKNESS (62) Mendleson

GUNS OF NAVARONE, THE (61) Lehmann
GUNS OF THE TIMBERLAND (59) Best
GUV'NOR, THE (35) Strassner
GUY NAMED JOE, A (43) Irene
GUYS AND DOLLS (55) Sharaff
GUY WHO CAME BACK, THE (51) Renie wd LeMaire
GYPSY (62) Orry-Kelly, Shoup
GYPSY AND THE GENTLEMAN, THE (57) Harris
GYPSY MOTHS, THE (69) Thomas
GYPSY WILDCAT (44) V West

HAIL THE CONQUERING HERO (44) Head
HALF ANGEL (36) Wakeling
HALF A SIXPENCE (67) Haffenden, Joan Bridge
HALF-BREED, THE (51) Woulfe
HALF SHOT AT SUNRISE (30) Ree
HALFWAY HOUSE, THE (43) Bianca Mosca
HALLELUJAH! (29) Frazer
HALLELUJAH, I'M A BUM (32) Anderson
HALLELUJAH, I'M A TRAMP=HALLELUJAH, I'M A BUM
HALLELUJAH TRAIL, THE (65) Head
HALLS OF MONTEZUMA (50) LeMaire
HAMLET (47) R Furse
HAMMERSMITH IS OUT (72) Head
HANDS ACROSS THE TABLE (35) Banton
HANDS OF ORLAC, THE=MAD LOVE
HANDY ANDY (34) Royer
HANGING TREE, THE (58) Best (Orry-Kelly for Maria Schell)
HANGMEN ALSO DIE! (42) Behm
HANGOVER SQUARE (44) Hubert, Nelson
HANNIE CAULDER (71) Aghayan
HANS CHRISTIAN ANDERSON (52) Wills (ballet by Clavé)
HAPPENING, THE (66) Coffin (Jason Silverstein for Faye Dunaway)
HAPPIDROME (43) Honoria Plesch
HAPPIEST DAYS OF YOUR LIFE, THE (49) Ellacott
HAPPIEST MILLIONAIRE, THE (67) Thomas
HAPPINESS AHEAD (34) Orry-Kelly
HAPPY BIRTHDAY, WANDA JUNE (71) Woulfe
HAPPY DAYS (29) Wachner
HAPPY GO LUCKY (36) Eloise
HAPPY GO LOVELY (50) Duse
HAPPY LANDING (37) Royer
HAPPY ROAD, THE (56) Balmain
HAPPY TIME, THE (52) Louis
HAPPY YEARS, THE (50) Plunkett
HARBOR OF MISSING MEN (50) Palmer
HARD BOILED HAGGERTY (27) Plunkett
HARD DAY'S NIGHT, A (64) Harris
HARD TO GET (38) Anderson
HARD TO HANDLE (32) Orry-Kelly
HARD WAY, THE (42) Orry-Kelly
HARLOW (65) Head
HARMONY PARADE=PIGSKIN PARADE
HAROLD TEEN (33) Orry-Kelly
HARP IN HOCK, A (27) Wakeling
HARRIET CRAIG (50) O'Brien
HARRY AND TONTO (75) Albert Wolsky
HARVEY (50) Orry-Kelly
HARVEY GIRLS, THE (45) Rose s Irene m Valles
HARVEY MIDDLEMAN, FIREMAN (64) Johnstone
HAS ANYBODY SEEN MY GAL? (52) Odell
HATARI! (63) Head
HAT CHECK GIRL (32) Kalloch
HAT CHECK HONEY (43) V West
HATCHET MAN, THE (31) Luick
HATFUL OF RAIN, A (57) Wills wd LeMaire
HATS OFF (36) Anthony
HATS OFF TO RHYTHM=EARL CARROLL SKETCHBOOK
HAUNTED PALACE, THE (63) s Corso
HAUNTING, THE (62) Mary Quant
HAVING WONDERFUL CRIME (44) Stevenson
HAVING WONDERFUL TIME (38) Stevenson, Renie
HAWAII (66) Jeakins
HAWAIIAN NIGHTS (34)=DOWN TO THEIR LAST YACHT
HAWAIIAN NIGHTS (39) V West
HAWAIIANS, THE (70) Thomas
HAZARD (47) B Newman
HEADLINE HUNTERS (55) Palmer
HEAD OVER HEELS (36) Strassner
HEARTBEAT (46) Greer
HEARTBREAK KID, THE (72) Sylbert
HEART IS A LONELY HUNTER, THE (68) Albert Wolsky
HEART OF A SIREN (24) LeMaire
HEART OF THE MATTER (53) Squire
HEART OF THE NORTH (38) Anderson
HEART OF THE ROCKIES (50) Palmer
HEART OF VIRGINIA (48) Palmer
HEARTS DIVIDED (36) Orry-Kelly
HEAT LIGHTNING (33) Orry-Kelly
HEAT'S ON, THE (43) Plunkett
HEAVEN CAN WAIT (43) Hubert
HEAVEN KNOWS, MR ALLISON (57) Haffenden

HEAVENLY BODY, THE (43) s Irene
HEAVEN ON EARTH (27) Kay, Marsh, Andre-Ani
HEEDLESS MOTHS (21) Lucille
HE FOUND A STAR (41) Strassner, Hartnell
HEIDI (37) Wakeling
HEIRESS, THE (49) Head m Steele
HE LEARNED ABOUT WOMEN (32) Banton
HELEN MORGAN STORY, THE (57) Shoup
HELL AND HIGH WATER (53) Travilla wd LeMaire
HELLDORADO (34) Lambert
HELLER IN PINK TIGHTS (59) Head
HELLFIGHTERS, THE (68) Head
HELLFIRE (49) Palmer
HELL IN THE HEAVENS (34) Lambert
HELL IS SOLD OUT (51) Nina Margo s Brierley
HELLO BEAUTIFUL=POWERS GIRL, THE
HELLO, DOLLY! (69) Sharaff
HELLO, FRISCO, HELLO (43) Rose
HELL ON 'FRISCO BAY (55) Mabry
HELLO SISTER (32) Kaufman
HELL'S ANGELS (28) Greer
HELL'S HALF ACRE (53) Palmer
HELL-SHIP MORGAN (35) Lange
HELL'S ISLAND (55) Head
HELL'S KITCHEN (39) Anderson
HELL'S OUTPOST (54) Palmer
HELLZAPOPPIN' (41) V West
HELP! (65) Harris
HELTER SKELTER (49) Ellacott
HE MARRIED HIS WIFE (39) Wakeling
HEMINGWAY'S ADVENTURES OF A YOUNG MAN (62) Donfeld
HENRY V (44) R Furse, M Furse
HENRY VIII AND HIS SIX WIVES (72) John Bloomfield
HER ADVENTUROUS NIGHT (46) V West
HER CARDBOARD LOVER (42) Kalloch
HERE COMES CARTER! (36) Orry-Kelly
HERE COMES HAPPINESS (41) Shoup
HERE COMES MR JORDAN (41) Head
HERE COMES THE BAND (35) Tree
HERE COMES THE GROOM (51) Head
HERE COMES THE NAVY (34) Orry-Kelly
HERE COMES TROUBLE (35) Lambert
HERE COME THE NELSONS (51) Odell
HERE COME THE WAVES (44) Head (non-military costumes)
HERE I AM A STRANGER (39) Royer
HERE IS MY HEART (34) Banton
HERE'S TO ROMANCE (35) Hubert
HER HUSBAND LIES (36) Banton, Head
HER HUSBAND'S AFFAIRS (47) Louis
HER HUSBAND'S SECRETARY (36) Shoup
HER JUNGLE LOVE (38) Head
HER KIND OF MAN (46) Rhodes
HER LAST AFFAIRE (35) Clark
HER LUCKY NIGHT (44) V West
HER MAJESTY, LOVE (31) Luick
HER MAN (30) Wakeling
HEROES FOR SALE (33) Orry-Kelly
HERO FOR A DAY (39) V West
HEROIN GANG, THE=SOL MADRID
HER PRIMITIVE MAN (44) V West
HER SISTER FROM PARIS (25) Adrian
HERS TO HOLD (43) V West (Adrian for Deanna Durbin)
HER TWELVE MEN (54) Rose
HE'S A COCKEYED WONDER (50) Louis
HE STAYED FOR BREAKFAST (40) Kalloch (Irene for Loretta Young)
HE WAS HER MAN (34) Orry-Kelly
HE WHO GETS SLAPPED (24) Wachner
HI, BEAUTIFUL (44) V West
HIDDEN EYE, THE (45) Irene a Kay Carter
HIDDEN HAND, THE (42) Anderson
HIDE-OUT (34) Tree
HIDEOUT (49) Palmer
HI DIDDLE DIDDLE (43) Adrian
HI, GAUCHO (35) Plunkett
HIGH AND DRY=MAGGIE, THE
HIGH AND THE MIGHTY, THE (53) Wakeling
HIGH BARBAREE (47) s Irene
HIGH BRIGHT SUN, THE (64) Caffin
HIGH COMMAND, THE (37) Arnulf Viberacker
HIGH COST OF LOVING, THE (57) Rose
HIGHER AND HIGHER (43) Stevenson
HIGH FLYERS (37) Renie
HIGHLY DANGEROUS (50) Harris
HIGH SCHOOL (39) Myron
HIGH SIERRA (40) Anderson
HIGH SOCIETY (56) Rose
HIGH SOCIETY BLUES (30) Wachner
HIGH STAKES (31) Ree
HIGH TENSION (36) Lambert
HIGH TIDE AT NOON (56) Ellacott
HIGH TIME (60) Thomas
HIGH, WIDE AND HANDSOME (37) Banton
HIGH WINDOW, THE=BRASHER DOUBLOON, THE
HI, GOOD-LOOKIN' (43) V West
HILDA CRANE (56) LeMaire
HILLS OF HOME (48) Valles
HINDENBURG, THE (75) Jeakins
HIRED WIFE (40) Irene, V West

HIRELING, THE (73) Dalton
HIS AFFAIR=THIS IS MY AFFAIR
HIS BROTHER'S WIFE (36) Tree
HIS BUTLER'S SISTER (43) V West (Adrian for
Deanna Durbin)
HIS DOG (27) Adrian
HIS EXCELLENCY (51) Mendleson
HIS FAMILY TREE (35) Plunkett
HIS GIRL FRIDAY (39) Kalloch
HIS GLORIOUS NIGHT (29) Cox
HIS GREATEST GAMBLE (34) Plunkett
HIS HOUR (24) Wachner
HIS KIND OF WOMAN (51) Greer
HIS LORDSHIP (36) Strassner
HIS MAJESTY O'KEEFE (52) Best
HIS NIGHT OUT (34) Brymer
HIS OTHER WOMAN=DESK SET, THE
HIS SECRETARY (25) Andre-Ani
HIS TIGER LADY (28) Banton
HISTORY IS MADE AT NIGHT (36) Kalloch, B
Newman
HIT (73) Talsky
HITLER'S CHILDREN (42) Renie
HIT ME AGAIN=SMARTY
HIT PARADE, THE (37) Eloise
HIT PARADE OF 1941 (40) Palmer
HIT PARADE OF 1947 (46) Palmer
HIT PARADE OF 1951 (50) Palmer
HIT THE DECK (29) Ree
HIT THE DECK (54) Rose
HIT THE ICE (43) V West
HIT THE ROAD (41) V West
HITTING A NEW HIGH (37) Stevenson
HI'YA SAILOR (43) V West
H M PULHAM ESQ (41) Kalloch m Steele
HOBSON'S CHOICE (53) Armstrong s Squire
HOLD BACK THE DAWN (41) Head
HOLD THAT CO-ED (38) Royer
HOLD THAT GHOST (41) V West
HOLD THAT KISS (38) Tree
HOLD YOUR MAN (33) Adrian
HOLE IN THE HEAD, A (59) Head
HOLIDAY (30) Wakeling
HOLIDAY (38) Kalloch
HOLIDAY AFFAIR (49) Greer
HOLIDAY CAMP (47) Harris
HOLIDAY FOR SINNERS (52) Rose
HOLIDAY IN MEXICO (46) Irene m Valles
HOLLOW TRIUMPH (48) Nelson
HOLLYWOOD (23) C West
HOLLYWOOD CANTEEN (44) Anderson
HOLLYWOOD CAVALCADE (39) Herschel
HOLLYWOOD HOTEL (37) Orry-Kelly
HOLLYWOOD OR BUST (56) Head
HOLLYWOOD PARTY (34) Adrian
HOLLYWOOD REVUE OF 1929, THE (29) Cox,
Frazer, Joe Rapf
HOLLYWOOD SPEAKS (32) Greer
HOLLYWOOD STADIUM MYSTERY, THE
(37) Saltern
HOLLYWOOD STORY (51) Odell
HOLY TERROR, THE (36) Herschel
HOMBRE (66) Donfeld
HOMECOMING (48) Rose
HOME FROM THE HILL (59) Plunkett
HOME IN INDIANA (44) Cashin
HOME STRETCH, THE (47) Nelson wd LeMaire
HOME SWEET HOMICIDE (46) Nelson
HONEYCHILE (51) Palmer
HONEYMOON (29) Frazer
HONEYMOON (47) Stevenson
HONEYMOON AHEAD (45) V West
HONEYMOON HOTEL (64) Thomas
HONEYMOON IN BALI (39) Head
HONEYMOON MACHINE, THE (61) Rose
HONKY TONK (41) Kalloch m Steele
HONOLULU (38) Adrian
HONOR OF THE FAMILY, THE (31) Luick
HOODLUM EMPIRE, THE (51) Palmer
HOODLUM SAINT, THE (45) s Irene a Herwood
Keyes m Valles
HOOK, LINE AND SINKER (30) Ethel Smallwood
HOOPLA (33) Kaufman
HOORAY FOR LOVE (35) Plunkett
HORIZONS WEST (52) Odell
HORSE IN THE GRAY FLANNEL SUIT, THE
(68) Thomas
HORSEMASTERS, THE (60) M Furse
HOTEL (66) Head a Shoup
HOTEL BERLIN (44) Rhodes
HOTEL FOR WOMEN (39) Wakeling
HOTEL SAHARA (51) Harris
HOT ENOUGH FOR JUNE (63) Caffin
HOT FOR PARIS (29) Wachner
HOT MILLIONS (68) Germinal Rangel
HOT PEPPER (32) Luick
HOT ROCK, THE (71) R Morley
HOT SPELL (58) Head
HOT SPOT=I WAKE UP SCREAMING
HOT STUFF (29) Ree
HOT TIP (35) Plunkett
HOT WATER (37) Herschel
HOUDINI (53) Head
HOUNDED=JOHNNY ALLEGRO
HOUND OF THE BASKERVILLES, THE (38)
Wakeling

HOUSE ACROSS THE BAY, THE (40) Irene
HOUSEBOAT (58) Head
HOUSE BY THE RIVER (50) Palmer
HOUSE IN THE SQUARE, THE (51) M Furse
HOUSE IS NOT A HOME, A (64) Head
HOUSEKEEPER'S DAUGHTER, THE (39) Irene
HOUSE OF BAMBOO (55) LeMaire
HOUSE OF CARDS (68) Head
HOUSE OF DRACULA (45) V West
HOUSE OF FRANKENSTEIN (44) V West
HOUSE OF ROTHSCHILD, THE (33) Wakeling
HOUSE OF SECRETS (56) Harris
HOUSE OF SETTLEMENT=MR SOFT
TOUCH
HOUSE OF STRANGERS (49) LeMaire
HOUSE OF WAX (53) Shoup
HOUSE ON 56TH STREET (33) Orry-Kelly,
Luick
HOUSE ON 92ND STREET, THE (45) Cashin
HOUSE ON TELEGRAPH HILL, THE (51)
Renie wd LeMaire
HOUSEWIFE (34) Orry-Kelly
HOWARDS OF VIRGINIA, THE (40) Saltern
HOW DO I LOVE THEE? (70) Mabry
HOW GREEN WAS MY VALLEY (41) Wakeling
HOW'S ABOUT IT? (42) V West
HOW SWEET IT IS! (67) Rose
HOW THE WEST WAS WON (62) Plunkett
HOW TO BE VERY, VERY POPULAR (55)
Travilla wd LeMaire
HOW TO MARRY A MILLIONAIRE (53)
Travilla wd LeMaire
HOW TO MURDER YOUR WIFE (64) Mabry
HOW TO SAVE A MARRIAGE AND RUIN
YOUR LIFE (67) Mabry
HOW TO STEAL A DIAMOND IN FOUR
UNEASY LESSONS=HOT ROCK,
THE
HOW TO STEAL A MILLION (66) Givenchy
HOW TO SUCCEED IN BUSINESS WITH-
OUT REALLY TRYING (66) Micheline
HUCKLEBERRY FINN (74) Donfeld
HUCKSTERS, THE (47) s Irene
HUD (63) Head
HUDSON'S BAY (40) Banton
HUGGETTS ABROAD, The (48) s Caffin
HULLABALOO (40) Tree
HUMAN CARGO (36) Lambert
HUMAN COMEDY, THE (42) s Irene
HUMAN DESIRE (54) Louis
HUMANITY (33) Kaufman
HUMORESQUE (46) B Newman (Adrian for Joan
Crawford)
HUNCHBACK OF NOTRE DAME, THE (39)
Plunkett
HUNGRY HILL (46) Abbey
HUNTERS, THE (58) LeMaire
HURRICANE, THE (37) Kiam
HURRICANE SMITH (41) Palmer
HURRICANE SMITH (52) Head
HURRY SUNDOWN (66) Estevez
HUSBANDS OR LOVERS=HONEYMOON
IN BALI
HUSH, HUSH, SWEET CHARLOTTE (64) Koch
HUSTLER, THE (61) R Morley

I ACCUSE! (57) Haffenden
I AM A FUGITIVE FROM A CHAIN GANG (32)
Orry-Kelly
I AM A FUGITIVE FROM THE CHAIN
GANG=I AM A FUGITIVE FROM A
CHAIN GANG
I AM A THIEF (34) Orry-Kelly
I AM SUZANNE (33) Kaufman
I AM THE LAW (38) Kalloch
I BELIEVED IN YOU (34) Royer
I BELIEVE IN YOU (51) Mendleson
I CAN GET IT FOR YOU WHOLESALE (51)
LeMaire
I CAN'T GIVE YOU ANYTHING BUT LOVE,
BABY (40) V West
ICE CAPADES (41) Palmer
ICE FOLLIES OF 1939 (38) Adrian (for Joan Craw-
ford), Tree (Ice Follies)
ICE PALACE (60) Shoup
I CONFESS (52) Orry-Kelly
I COULD GO ON SINGING (62) Head
I COVER THE UNDERWORLD (55) Palmer
IDEAL HUSBAND, AN (47) Beaton
I'D CLIMB THE HIGHEST MOUNTAIN (50)
Stevenson wd LeMaire
I'D GIVE MY LIFE (36) Mlle Lucille Toray,
Schiaparelli, Lanvin, Morgaleau, Creed, Vic-
tor Stiebel
I DIDN'T DO IT (45) Dorothy Broomham
I DIED A THOUSAND TIMES (55) Mabry
IDIOT'S DELIGHT (38) Adrian
IDLE RICH, THE (29) Cox
IDOL, THE (65) Blake
IDOL OF PARIS, THE (47) Honoria Plesch
IDOLS IN THE DUST=SATURDAY'S HERO
I'D RATHER BE RICH (64) Louis
I DREAM OF JEANIE (52) Palmer
I DREAM TOO MUCH (35) B Newman
IF A MAN ANSWERS (62) Louis

IF I HAD MY WAY (40) V West
IF I'M LUCKY (46) Behm (Sascha Brastoff for Car-
men Miranda)
IF MARRIAGE FAILS (25) Andre-Ani
I FOUND STELLA PARRISH (35) Orry-Kelly
IF WINTER COMES (47) Irene
IF YOU COULD ONLY COOK (35) Lange
IF YOU FEEL LIKE SINGING=SUMMER
STOCK
IF YOU KNEW SUSIE (47) Renie
I, JANE DOE (48) Palmer
I LIVED WITH YOU (33) Louis Brooks)
I LIVE FOR LOVE (35) Orry-Kelly
I LIVE FOR YOU=I LIVE FOR LOVE
I LIVE MY LIFE (35) Adrian
I'LL BE SEEING YOU (44) Head
I'LL BE YOURS (46) Banton
I'LL CRY TOMORROW (55) Rose
ILLEGAL (55) Mabry
ILLEGAL DIVORCE=SECOND HAND WIFE
ILLEGAL ENTRY (49) Wood
I'LL FIX IT (34) Kalloch
I'LL GET BY (50) Travilla wd LeMaire
I'LL GIVE A MILLION (38) Wakeling
ILLICIT (30) Luick
I'LL LOVE YOU ALWAYS (35) Kalloch
I'LL NEVER FORGET YOU=HOUSE IN THE
SQUARE, THE
I'LL SEE YOU IN MY DREAMS (51) Rhodes,
Best
I'LL TAKE ROMANCE (37) Kalloch
I'LL TELL THE WORLD (45) V West
I'LL WAIT FOR YOU (41) Kalloch
ILLUSTRATED MAN, THE (68) Sylbert
I LOVE A SOLDIER (44) Head
I LOVED A WOMAN (33) Luick
I LOVED YOU WEDNESDAY (33) Kaufman
I LOVE MELVIN (52) Rose
I LOVE MY WIFE (70) Colvig
I LOVE TROUBLE (47) Louis
I LOVE YOU AGAIN (40) Tree
I LOVE YOU ALICE B TOKLAS (68) van Runkle
I MARRIED A COMMUNIST (49) Woulfe
I MARRIED A DOCTOR (35) Orry-Kelly
I MARRIED AN ANGEL (42) Motley, Kalloch
I MARRIED A WITCH (42) Head
I MET A MURDERER (39) Motley
I MET HIM IN PARIS (37) Banton
I MET MY LOVE AGAIN (37) Taylor
I'M FROM THE CITY (38) Renie
IMITATION OF LIFE (34) Banton
IMITATION OF LIFE (58) Thomas (Louis for
Lana Turner)
I'M NO ANGEL (33) Banton
IMPERFECT LADY, THE (47) Dorothy O'Hara m
Steele
IMPORTANCE OF BEING EARNEST, THE
(52) Dawson
IMPOSTOR, THE (43) West
I'M STILL ALIVE (40) Renie
IN A LONELY PLACE (50) Louis
IN CALIENTE (35) Orry-Kelly
INCENDIARY BLONDE (45) Head
INCIDENT AT PHANTOM HILL (65) Colvig
INCREDIBLE SHRINKING MAN, THE (56) J
Morley
INDIANAPOLIS SPEEDWAY (39) Orry-Kelly
INDIAN SUMMER=JUDGE STEPS OUT, THE
INDISCREET (31) Hubert
INDISCREET (58) Dior
INDISCRETION=CHRISTMAS IN CON-
NECTICUT
INDISCRETION OF AN AMERICAN WIFE=
STAZIONE TERMINI
IN ENEMY COUNTRY (68) Head
I NEVER SANG FOR MY FATHER (67)
Aldredge
INFERNAL MACHINE (33) Kaufman
INFERNO (53) Jeakins wd LeMaire
INFORMER, THE (35) Plunkett
INFORMERS, THE (63) Caffin
IN GAY MADRID (30) Adrian
IN LIKE FLINT (66) Aghayan
IN LOVE AND WAR (58) Palmer wd LeMaire
IN NAME ONLY (39) Stevenson (Irene for Carole
Lombard)
INNOCENCE IS BLISS=MISS GRANT TAKES
RICHMOND
INNOCENTS, THE (61) Motley
INN OF THE SIXTH HAPPINESS (58) M Furse,
Lehmann
IN OLD CALIFORNIA (42) Palmer
IN OLD CHICAGO (37) Royer
IN OLD KENTUCKY (27) Clark
IN OLD KENTUCKY (35) Lambert
IN OLD MISSOURI (40) Palmer
IN OLD OKLAHOMA (43) Plunkett
IN OLD SACRAMENTO (46) Palmer
IN PERSON (35) B Newman
IN SEARCH OF THE CASTAWAYS (62) M
Furse
INSIDE DAISY CLOVER (65) Thomas (Head for
Natalie Wood)
INSIDE INFORMATION (39) V West
INSIDE STORY (38) Herschel
INSIDE STORY, THE (48) Palmer

IN SOCIETY (44) V West
INSPECTOR CALLS, AN (53) Squire
INSPECTOR GENERAL, THE (49) Travilla
INSPIRATION (30) Adrian
INSURANCE INVESTIGATOR (50) Palmer
INTELLIGENCE MEN, THE (64) Dawson
INTERLUDE (57) J Morley
INTERLUDE (67) Rickards
INTERMEZZO: A LOVE STORY (39) Irene, Banton
INTERNATIONAL HOUSE (33) Banton
INTERNATIONAL LADY (41) Wakeling
INTERNATIONAL SETTLEMENT (37) Herschel
INTERNATIONAL SQUADRON (41) Shoup
INTERNS CAN'T TAKE MONEY (37) Banton
INTERRUPTED MELODY (54) Rose
IN THE COOL OF THE DAY (63) Orry-Kelly (for Jane Fonda) Balmain (for Constance Cummings)
IN THE FRENCH STYLE (62) Phillippe Venet
IN THE GOOD OLD SUMMER TIME (49) Irene m Valles
IN THE MEANTIME, DARLING (44) Cashin
IN THE NAVY (41) V West
IN THIS CORNER (48) Ehren
IN THIS OUR LIFE (42) Orry-Kelly
INTOLERANCE (16) C West
INVISIBLE AGENT (42) V West
INVISIBLE ENEMY (38) Saltern
INVISIBLE MAN RETURNS, THE (39) V West
INVISIBLE MAN'S REVENGE, THE (44) V West
INVISIBLE MENACE, THE (37) Shoup
INVISIBLE RAY, THE (35) Brymer
INVISIBLE STRIPES (39) Anderson
INVISIBLE WOMAN, THE (40) V West
INVITATION (51) Rose
INVITATION TO HAPPINESS (39) Head
INVITATION TO THE DANCE (56) Haffenden, Rolf Gerard
I REMEMBER MAMA (47) Stevenson m Steele
IRENE (26) Cora MacCreachy
IRENE (40) Stevenson
IRISH EYES ARE SMILING (44) Hubert
IRISH IN US, THE (35) Orry-Kelly
IRMA LA DOUCE (63) Orry-Kelly
IRON CURTAIN, THE (48) Cashin wd LeMaire
IRON DUKE, THE (34) Mann
IRON GLOVE, THE (53) Louis
IRON MAN, THE (51) Thomas
IRON PETTICOAT, THE (56) Caffin
I SEE A DARK STRANGER (46) Ricardo
I SELL ANYTHING (34) Orry-Kelly
I SHALL RETURN=AMERICAN GUERILLA IN THE PHILIPPINES
ISLAND AT THE TOP OF THE WORLD, THE (74) Thomas
ISLAND IN THE SKY (38) Herschel
ISLAND IN THE SUN (57) Dalton
ISLAND OF DOOMED MEN (40) Kalloch
ISLAND OF LOVE (63) Donfeld
ISLAND OF THE BLUE DOLPHINS (64) Odell
ISLAND RESCUE=APPOINTMENT WITH VENUS
ISLE OF DESTINY (40) Bridgehouse
ISLE OF FURY (36) Orry-Kelly
ISLE OF THE DEAD (45) Stevenson
ISN'T IT ROMANTIC (48) Head
ISN'T LIFE WONDERFUL! (53) Duse
ISTANBUL (56) Thomas
I STAND ACCUSED (38) Saltern
I STOLE A MILLION (39) V West
IT AIN'T HAY (43) V West
I TAKE THIS WOMAN (39) Adrian
IT ALL CAME TRUE (40) Shoup
IT ALWAYS RAINS ON SUNDAY (47) Mendleson
IT CAME FROM OUTER SPACE (53) Odell
IT CAN'T LAST FOR EVER (37) Kalloch
IT COULD HAPPEN TO YOU (37) Eloise
IT GROWS ON TREES (52) Thomas
IT HAD TO BE YOU (47) Louis
IT HAD TO HAPPEN (36) Wakeling
I THANK A FOOL (62) Haffenden
IT HAPPENED IN HOLLYWOOD (37) Kalloch
IT HAPPENED ONE NIGHT (33) Kalloch
IT HAPPENED ON FIFTH AVENUE (56) Maclean
IT HAPPENED TOMORROW (43) Hubert
IT HAPPENS EVERY SPRING (49) Cashin wd LeMaire
IT HAPPENS EVERY THURSDAY (53) Thomas
IT'S A BOY (33) Conway
IT'S A DATE (39) V West
IT'S A GREAT FEELING (49) Anderson
IT'S A GREAT LIFE (29) Cox
IT'S A JOKE, SON (46) Cassini
IT'S ALL YOURS (37) Kalloch
IT'S ALWAYS FAIR WEATHER (55) Rose
IT'S A MAD, MAD, MAD, MAD WORLD (63) Thomas
IT'S A SMALL WORLD (35) Hubert
IT'S A WONDERFUL LIFE (46) Stevenson
IT'S A WONDERFUL WORLD (39) Adrian
IT'S A WONDERFUL WORLD (56) Harris

IT'S GREAT TO BE ALIVE (33) Royer
IT'S HARD TO BE GOOD (48) Abbey
IT SHOULD HAPPEN TO YOU (53) Louis
IT SHOULDN'T HAPPEN TO A DOG (46) Behm
IT'S IN THE AIR (35) Tree
IT'S LOVE AGAIN (36) Strassner
IT'S LOVE I'M AFTER (37) Orry-Kelly
IT'S MAGIC=ROMANCE ON THE HIGH SEAS
IT'S NOT CRICKET (48) s Caffin
IT'S ONLY MONEY (62) Head
IT STARTED IN PARADISE (52) Sheila Graham
IT STARTED WITH A KISS (59) Rose
IT STARTED WITH EVE (41) V West
IVANHOE (52) R Furse
I'VE GOT YOUR NUMBER (33) Orry-Kelly
I'VE LIVED BEFORE (56) Thomas
IVY (47) Orry-Kelly
I WAKE UP SCREAMING (41) Wakeling
I WALK ALONE (47) Head
I WAS A SPY (33) Conway
I WONDER WHO'S KISSING HER NOW? (47) Cashin wd LeMaire

JACKASS MAIL (42) Shoup m Steele
JACK OF ALL TRADES (35) Strassner
JACKPOT, THE (50) Stevenson wd LeMaire
JACQUELINE (56) Abbey
JAGUAR (55) Palmer
JAILBREAK=MURDER IN THE BIG HOUSE
JALNA (35) Plunkett
JAMBOREE (44) Palmer
JANE EYRE (43) Hubert
JANE EYRE (70) Mendleson
JANICE MEREDITH (24) Urban Thurlow
JASSY (47) Haffenden
JAYHAWKERS, THE (59) Head
JAZZ SINGER, THE (52) Shoup
JEALOUSY=EMERGENCY WEDDING
JEANNE EAGELS (57) Louis
JEEPERS CREEPERS (39) Palmer
JENNIE=PORTRAIT OF JENNY
JEOPARDY (52) Rose
JESSE JAMES (38) Royer
JESUS CHRIST, SUPERSTAR (73) Blake
JET PILOT (50) Woulfe
JEZEBEL (37) Orry-Kelly
JIGGS AND MAGGIE IN SOCIETY (47) Maclean
JIM HANVEY, DETECTIVE (37) Eloise
JIMMY THE GENT (33) Orry-Kelly
JIMMY AND SALLY (33) Royer
JOANNA (68) Sue West, Virginia Hamilton Keane
JOAN OF ARC (48) Jeakins, Karinska, Herschel
JOE PALOOKA, CHAMP (46) Maclean
JOE PALOOKA IN THE BIG FIGHT (49) Maclean
JOE PALOOKA IN THE KNOCKOUT (47) Maclean
JOE PALOOKA IN WINNER TAKE ALL (48) Maclean
JOHN AND MARY (69) Sylbert
JOHN GOLDFARB, PLEASE COME HOME (64) Head
JOHN LOVES MARY (48) Anderson
JOHN MEADE'S WOMAN (36) Head, Bridgehouse
JOHNNY ALLEGRO (49) Louis
JOHNNY ANGEL (45) Renie
JOHNNY APOLLO (40) Wakeling
JOHNNY BELINDA (48) Anderson
JOHNNY COMES FLYING HOME (45) Wood
JOHNNY CONCHO (56) Wakeling
JOHNNY DARK (54) J Morley
JOHNNY DOUGHBOY (42) Palmer
JOHNNY EAGER (41) Kalloch
JOHNNY GOT HIS GUN (71) van Runkle
JOHNNY GUITAR (54) O'Brien
JOHNNY O'CLOCK (46) Louis
JOHNNY STOOLPIGEON (49) Orry-Kelly
JOHN PAUL JONES (58) Dalton
JOIN THE MARINES (36) Eloise
JOKER IS WILD, THE (57) Head
JOKERS, THE (67) Tony Armstrong
JOLLY OLD HIGGINS=EARL OF PUDDLESTONE
JOLSON SINGS AGAIN (49) Louis
JOLSON STORY, THE (46) Louis
JONES FAMILY IN HOLLYWOOD, THE (39) Myron
JOSETTE (38) Royer
JOURNAL OF A CRIME (33) Orry-Kelly
JOURNEY, THE (58) Hubert
JOURNEY INTO FEAR (42) Stevenson
JOY IN THE MORNING (64) Donfeld
JOY OF LIVING, THE (38) Stevenson
JOY PARADE, THE=LIFE BEGINS IN COLLEGE
JUAREZ (39) Orry-Kelly
JUBILEE TRAIL (53) Palmer
JUDGMENT AT NUREMBERG (61) Louis
JUDGE PRIEST (34) Royer
JUDGE STEPS OUT, THE (47) Stevenson
JUDITH (65) Blake
JUDY GOES TO TOWN=PUDDIN' HEAD
JUKE BOX JENNY (41) V West

JULES VERNE'S ROCKET TO THE MOON (66) Toms
JULIA MISBEHAVES (48) Irene
JULIUS CAESAR (52) Herschel
JUMP FOR GLORY (37) Schiaparelli, Hartnell
JUMPING FOR JOY (55) Ellacott
JUNE BRIDE (48) Head
JUNIOR BONNER (72) Pat Barto
JUNIOR MISS (45) Cashin
JUPITER'S DARLING (54) Rose, Plunkett
JUST AROUND THE CORNER (38) Wakeling
JUST FOR FUN (62) Shubette of London, John Stephens
JUST FOR YOU (52) Head
JUST IMAGINE (30) Wachner, Tree, O'Neill
JUSTINE (69) Sharaff
JUST LIKE A WOMAN (66) Caroline Mott
JUST SMITH (33) Conway
JUST WILLIAM'S LUCK (47) Dorothy Sinclair

KALEIDOSCOPE (66) Sally Tuffin, Marion Foale
KANSAS CITY BOMBER (72) Talsky
KANSAS CITY PRINCESS (34) Orry-Kelly
KEEP 'EM FLYING (41) V West
KEEP 'EM SLUGGING (42) V West
KEEPER OF THE FLAME (42) Adrian
KEEP SMILING (38) Herschel
KEEP YOUR POWDER DRY (45) Irene, Herwood Keyes
KELLY AND ME (56) Odell
KENNEL MURDER CASE, THE (33) Orry-Kelly
KENTUCKIAN, THE (54) Norma
KENTUCKY (38) Wakeling
KENTUCKY KERNELS (34) Plunkett
KENTUCKY MOONSHINE (38) Royer
KEY, THE (34) Orry-Kelly
KEY, THE (58) Dawson
KEYHOLE, THE (33) Orry-Kelly
KEY LARGO (48) Rhodes
KEYS OF THE KINGDOM (44) Cashin
KEY TO THE CITY (49) Irene
KID FOR TWO FARTHINGS, A (55) Duse
KID FROM BROOKLYN, THE (46) White
KID FROM CLEVELAND, THE (49) Palmer
KID FROM KOKOMO, THE (39) Shoup
KID FROM LEFT FIELD, THE (53) Jeakins wd LeMaire
KID FROM SPAIN, THE (32) Anderson
KID FROM TEXAS, THE (39) Tree m Valles
KID GALAHAD (37) Orry-Kelly
KID MILLIONS (34) Kiam
KIDNAPPED (38) Wakeling
KIDNAPPED (60) M Furse
KIDNAPPED (71) Lehmann
KIDNAPPERS, The (53) Ellacott
KID NIGHTINGALE (39) Anderson
KID'S LAST FIGHT, THE=LIFE OF JIMMY DOLAN, THE
KILLERS, THE (46) V West
KILLERS, THE (64) Colvig
KILLER THAT STALKED NEW YORK, THE (50) Louis
KILLING OF SISTER GEORGE, THE (68) Renie
KILL OR CURE (62) Haffenden, Joan Bridge
KILL THE UMPIRE (50) Louis
KIM (50) Valles
KIND HEARTS AND CORONETS (49) Mendleson
KIND LADY (51) Plunkett m Steele
KING AND FOUR QUEENS, A (56) Renie
KING AND I, THE (55) Sharaff
KING AND THE CHORUS GIRL, THE (36) Orry-Kelly
KING OF BURLESQUE (35) Wakeling
KING OF CHINATOWN (38) Head
KING OF KINGS (27) Adrian, Luick, Wakeling
KING OF KINGS (60) George Wakhevitch
KING OF THE DAMNED (35) Schiaparelli
KING OF THE GAMBLERS (48) Palmer
KING OF THE KHYBER RIFLES (53) Travilla wd LeMaire
KING OF THE LUMBERJACKS (40) Anderson
KING OF THE NEWSBOYS (37) Saltern
KING OF THE TURF (38) Bridgehouse
KING OF THE UNDERWORLD (38) Orry-Kelly
KING RICHARD AND THE CRUSADERS (54) Best
KINGS GO FORTH (58) Rhodes
KINGS OF THE SUN (63) Koch
KING SOLOMON OF BROADWAY (35) V West
KING SOLOMON'S MINES (37) Marianne
KING SOLOMON'S MINES (50) Plunkett
KING'S PIRATE, THE (67) Novarese
KING'S RHAPSODY (54) Anthony Holland
KING'S ROW (41) Orry-Kelly
KING STEPS OUT, THE (36) Dryden
KING'S THIEF, THE (55) Plunkett
KING'S VACATION, THE (32) Orry-Kelly
KIPPS (41) Beaton
KISMET (44) s Irene
KISMET (55) Tony Duquette
KISS, THE (29) Adrian
KISS AND MAKE UP (34) Banton
KISS AND TELL (45) Louis

LORNA DOONE (22) *Milton Menasco*
LORNA DOONE (51) Louis
LOSS OF INNOCENCE=GREENGAGE SUMMER, THE
LOST (55) Caffin
LOST CONTINENT, THE (68) Toms
LOST HORIZON (36) Dryden
LOST HORIZON (72) Louis
LOST IN A HAREM (44) Irene *a* Dean *m* Valles
LOST LADY, THE (31)=SAFE IN HELL
LOST LADY, THE (34) Orry-Kelly
LOST MAN, THE (69) Head
LOST MOMENT, THE (47) Banton
LOST SQUADRON, THE (31) Ree
LOST WEEKEND, THE (45) Head
LOST WORLD, THE (60) Zastupnevich
LOTTERY BRIDE, THE (30) O'Neill
LOTTERY LOVER (34) Hubert, Lambert
LOUDEST WHISPER, THE=CHILDREN'S HOUR, THE
LOUISA (50) Odell
LOUISIANA PURCHASE (41) Pene du Bois
LOVE (27) Clark
LOVE AFFAIR (39) Greer
LOVE AND HISSES (37) Royer
LOVE AND LEARN (47) Travilla
LOVE AND PAIN AND THE WHOLE DAMN THING (73) *Germinal Rangel*
LOVE AT SECOND SIGHT (34) P Newman
LOVE BEFORE BREAKFAST (34) Brymer (Banton for Carole Lombard)
LOVE BUG, THE (68) Thomas
LOVED ONE, THE (65) *Rouben Ter-Arutunian*
LOVE FROM A STRANGER (37) Lange
LOVE FROM A STRANGER (47) Woulfe
LOVE GOD?, THE (69) Colvig
LOVE HAS MANY FACES (64) Head
LOVE, HONOR AND BEHAVE (37) Shoup
LOVE IN EXILE (36) Schiaparelli
LOVE IN LAS VEGAS=VIVA LAS VEGAS
LOVE IN THE AFTERNOON (57) Givenchy
LOVE IN THE DESERT (29) Plunkett
LOVE IN THE ROUGH (30) Cox
LOVE IS A HEADACHE (37) Adrian
LOVE IS A MANY SPLENDORED THING (55) LeMaire
LOVE IS BETTER THAN EVER (51) Rose
LOVE IS NEWS (36) Royer
LOVE IS ON THE AIR (37) Shoup
LOVE LAUGHS AT ANDY HARDY (46) *s* Irene
LOVE LETTERS (45) Head
LOVE, LIVE AND LAUGH (29) Wachner
LOVELORN, THE (27) Clark
LOVE LOTTERY, THE (53) Mendleson
LOVELY TO LOOK AT (37)=THIN ICE
LOVELY TO LOOK AT (52) Adrian (including fashion show), *Tony Duquette* (chorus costumes)
LOVE MACHINE, THE (71) Mabry
LOVE MART, THE (27) Ree
LOVE ME FOREVER (35) Kalloch
LOVE ME OR LEAVE ME (55) Rose
LOVE ME TENDER (56) Wills
LOVE ME TONIGHT (32) Banton
LOVE NEST (51) Renie *wd* LeMaire
LOVE NEVER DIES (21) Wachner
LOVE ON A BUDGET (37) Myron
LOVE ON THE RUN (36) Adrian
LOVE ON WHEELS (32) Conway
LOVE PARADE, THE (29) Banton
LOVER COME BACK (46) Banton
LOVER COME BACK (61) Irene
LOVERS? (27) Andre-Ani
LOVERS AND OTHER STRANGERS (70) *Albert Wolsky*
LOVERS MUST LEARN=ROME ADVENTURE
LOVE'S BLINDNESS (26) Kay, Marsh, Andre-Ani
LOVES OF CARMEN (48) Louis
LOVES OF EDGAR ALLAN POE, THE (42) Tree
LOVE STORY (44) Haffenden
LOVE THAT BRUTE (50) Hubert
LOVE THY NEIGHBOUR (40) Head
LOVE TIME (34) Royer
LOVE UNDER FIRE (37) Wakeling
LOVE WITH THE PROPER STRANGER (63) Head
LOVEY MARY (26) Coulter
LOVING YOU (57) Head
L-SHAPED ROOM, THE (62) Dawson
LUCK OF THE IRISH, THE (48) Cashin *wd* LeMaire
LUCKY CISCO KID (40) Myron
LUCKY DAYS=SING A JINGLE
LUCKY ME (53) Mabry
LUCKY NIGHT (39) Tree
LUCKY NUMBER, THE (33) Conway
LUCKY PARTNERS (40) Irene
LUCKY STIFF (48) Myrtil
LUCY GALLANT (55) Head
LULLABY=SIN OF MADELON CLAUDET, THE
LULU BELLE (48) Louis
LUMMOX (29) O'Neill
LURED (47) Jenssen

LURE OF THE WILDERNESS (52) Jeakins *wd* LeMaire
LUST FOR GOLD (49) Louis
LUST FOR LIFE (56) Plunkett
LUTHER (74) Haffenden
LUV (67) Donfeld
LUXURY LINER (32) Banton
LUXURY LINER (48) Rose *m* Valles
LYDIA (41) Vertes, Plunkett
LYDIA BAILEY (52) Travilla *wd* LeMaire

MACAO (50) Woulfe
MACBETH (48) Palmer
MACBETH (60) Dawson
MACBETH (71) Mendleson
MACKENNA'S GOLD (69) Koch
MAD ABOUT MEN (54) Ellacott
MAD ABOUT MUSIC (37) V West (Head for Deanna Durbin)
MADAME BOVARY (49) Plunkett *m* Valles
MADAME CURIE (43) Irene *m* Steele
MADAME DUBARRY (17) Hopkins
MADAME DUBARRY (34) Orry-Kelly
MADAME LOUISE (51) Ellacott
MADAME PIMPERNEL=PARIS UNDERGROUND
MADAME SPY (42) V West
MADAME X (29) Cox
MADAME X (37) Tree
MADAME X (65) Louis
MADAM SATAN (30) Adrian
MADE FOR EACH OTHER (38) Banton
MADE IN HEAVEN (52) Harris
MADE IN PARIS (65) Rose
MADELAINE (49) M Furse
MADEMOISELLE (66) Rickards
MADEMOISELLE FIFI (44) Stevenson
MADEMOISELLE FRANCE=REUNION
MADE ON BROADWAY (33) Adrian
MAD GAME, THE (33) Royer
MAD GHOUL, THE (43) V West
MAD HOLIDAY (36) Tree
MAD LOVE (35) Tree
MAD MISS MANTON, THE (38) Stevenson
MADNESS OF THE HEART (49) *Rahvis*
MADONNA OF THE DESERT (47) Palmer
MADONNA'S SECRET, THE (45) Palmer (Greer for Gail Patrick)
MAD ROOM, THE (68) Mabry
MADWOMAN OF CHAILLOT, THE (69) *Rosine Delamare*
MAGGIE, THE (53) Mendleson
MAGIC BOW, THE (46) Haffenden
MAGIC BOX, THE (51) Squire
MAGIC CARPET, THE (51) Louis
MAGIC FIRE (55) Maes
MAGIC TOWN (47) Anderson
MAGNET, THE (50) Mendleson
MAGNIFICENT DOLL (46) Banton, V West
MAGNIFICENT DOPE, THE (42) Tree
MAGNIFICENT FRAUD, THE (39) Head
MAGNIFICENT MATADOR, THE (56) Stevenson
MAGNIFICENT OBSESSION (35) V West, Brymer
MAGNIFICENT OBSESSION (54) Thomas
MAGNIFICENT ROGUE, THE (46) Palmer
MAGNIFICENT SHOWMAN, THE=CIRCUS WORLD
MAGNIFICENT TWO, THE (66) Duse
MAGNIFICENT YANKEE, THE (50) Plunkett
MAGUS, THE (68) Mendleson
MA! HE'S MAKING EYES AT ME (40) V West
MAHLER (73) Russell
MAID OF SALEM (36) Banton
MAID'S NIGHT OUT (38) Stevenson
MAIN EVENT, THE (27) Adrian
MAIN STREET KID (47) Palmer
MAIN STREET LAWYER (39) Palmer
MAIN STREET TO BROADWAY (52) *Hattie Carnegie*
MAISIE (39) Tree *m* Valles
MAISIE GETS HER MAN (42) Kalloch
MAJOR AND THE MINOR, THE (42) Head
MAJOR BARBARA (41) Beaton
MAJORITY OF ONE, A (61) Orry-Kelly
MAKE A WISH (37) Brymer
MAKE HASTE TO LIVE (54) Palmer
MAKE MINE MINK (60) Mendleson
MAKE YOUR OWN BED (44) Anderson
MALAYA (49) Irene *m* Valles
MALE AND FEMALE (19) C West
MALE ANIMAL, THE (42) Shoup
MALTESE BIPPY, THE (69) Mabry
MALTESE FALCON, THE (31) Luick
MALTESE FALCON, THE (41) Orry-Kelly
MAMA STEPS OUT (37) Tree
MAME (73) van Runkle
MAN ABOUT THE HOUSE, A (47) Benda
MAN ABOUT TOWN (32) Cox
MAN ABOUT TOWN (39) Head
MAN AFRAID (57) Thomas
MAN ALIVE (45) Stevenson
MAN ALONE, A (55) Palmer
MAN AND THE MOMENT, THE (29) Ree
MAN AT LARGE (41) Herschel

MAN BEHIND THE GUN, THE (52) Anderson
MAN BETRAYED, A (36) Eloise
MAN CALLED GANNON, A (69) Colvig
MAN CALLED PETER, A (54) Renie *wd* LeMaire
MANCHURIAN CANDIDATE, THE (62) Mabry
MAN COULD GET KILLED, A (65) Louis (for Sandra Dee), *Dimitri Kritsos* (for Melina Mercouri)
MANDARIN MYSTERY, THE (36) Eloise
MAN DETAINED (61) Dalton
MANDRAGOLA (65) *Danilo Donati*
MANDY (52) Mendleson
MAN FOR ALL SEASONS, A (66) Haffenden, *Joan Bridge*
MAN FROM BITTER RIDGE, THE (55) J Morley
MAN FROM COLORADO, THE (48) Louis
MAN FROM DAKOTA, THE (39) Tree *m* Steele
MAN FROM DOWN UNDER, THE (43) Irene *m* Steele
MAN FROM 'FRISCO (44) Palmer
MAN FROM OKLAHOMA (45) Palmer
MAN FROM RAINBOW VALLEY (46) Palmer
MAN FROM THE ALAMO, THE (53) Thomas
MAN FROM THE DINERS' CLUB, THE (62) *Pat Barto*
MAN FROM THE FOLIES BERGERE, THE=FOLIES BERGERE
MAN FROM YESTERDAY (32) Banton
MANHATTAN HEARTBEAT (40) Herschel
MANHATTAN MELODRAMA (34) Tree
MANHATTAN MERRY-GO-ROUND (37) Eloise (King for Tamara Geva)
MANHATTAN MUSIC BOX=MANHATTAN MERRY-GO-ROUND
MANHUNT (41) Banton
MANHUNT (58)=FROM HELL TO TEXAS
MANIACS ON WHEELS=ONCE A JOLLY SWAGMAN
MAN I LOVE, THE (28) Banton
MAN I LOVE, THE (46) Anderson
MAN I MARRIED, THE (40) Banton
MAN IN POSSESSION, THE=PERSONAL PROPERTY
MAN IN THE ATTIC (53) Travilla *wd* LeMaire
MAN IN THE GRAY FLANNEL SUIT, THE (55) LeMaire
MAN IN THE IRON MASK, THE (39) Bridgehouse
MAN IN THE MOON (60) Mendleson
MAN IN THE WHITE SUIT, THE (51) Mendleson
MAN IS ARMED, THE (56) Palmer
MAN IS TEN FEET TALL, A=EDGE OF THE CITY
MAN-MADE WOMAN (28) Adrian
MANNEQUIN (37) Adrian
MAN OF A THOUSAND FACES (57) Thomas
MAN OF CONQUEST (39) Palmer (Head for Gail Patrick)
MAN OF THE MOMENT (55) Ellacott
MAN OF THE WEST (58) Wood
MAN ON A SWING (74) R Morley
MAN ON A TIGHTROPE (52) Maes, LeMaire
MAN ON THE EIFFEL TOWER, THE (49) *Robert Piguet, Jacque Griffe*
MANPOWER (41) Anderson
MAN PROOF (37) Tree
MAN'S FAVOURITE SPORT? (63) Head
MANSLAUGHTER (22) C West
MAN'S MAN, A (29) Cox
MAN TO MAN (30) Luick
MAN TO REMEMBER, A (38) Renie
MANTRAP (61) Head
MAN TROUBLE (30) Wachner
MAN WHO BROKE THE BANK AT MONTE CARLO, THE (35) Wakeling
MAN WHO CAME BACK, THE=SWAMP WATER
MAN WHO CAME TO DINNER, THE (41) Orry-Kelly
MAN WHO CHANGED HIS MIND, THE (36) *Molyneux*
MAN WHO CHEATED HIMSELF, THE (50) Jenssen
MAN WHO COULD WORK MIRACLES, THE (36) Armstrong
MAN WHO DARED, THE (33) Royer
MAN WHO DARED, THE (39) Shoup
MAN WHO FINALLY DIED, THE (62) Mendleson
MAN WHO HAUNTED HIMSELF, THE (69) Dawson
MAN WHO KNEW TOO MUCH, THE (55) Head, Dalton
MAN WHO LAUGHS, THE (28) Cox, V West
MAN WHO LIVED AGAIN, THE=MAN WHO CHANGED HIS MIND, THE
MAN WHO LOVED REDHEADS, THE (54) Squire
MAN WHO PLAYED GOD, THE (31) Luick
MAN WHO RECLAIMED HIS HEAD, THE (34) V West
MAN WHO SHOT LIBERTY VALANCE, THE (62) Head

MAN WHO TALKED TOO MUCH, THE (40) Shoup
MAN WHO WOULDN'T TALK, THE (39) Herschel
MAN WITH A CLOAK (51) Plunkett m Steele
MAN WITH A MILLION=MILLION POUND NOTE, THE
MAN WITHIN, THE (47) Haffenden
MAN WITHOUT A STAR (54) Odell
MAN WITH THE GOLDEN ARM, THE (55) Nyberg
MAN WITH THIRTY SONS, THE=MAGNIFICENT YANKEE, THE
MAN, WOMAN AND SIN (27) Clark
MANY RIVERS TO CROSS (54) Plunkett
MARA MARU (52) Anderson
MARCH HARE, THE (56) Harris
MARCHING ALONG=STARS AND STRIPES FOREVER
MARDI GRAS (58) LeMaire
MARGIE (40) V West
MARGIE (46) Nelson
MARGIN FOR ERROR (42) Luick
MARIANNE (29) Adrian
MARIE ANTOINETTE (38) Adrian m Steele
MARIE GALANTE (34) Hubert
MARIE WALEWSKA=CONQUEST
MARIGOLD (38) Motley
MARINE RAIDERS (44) Stevenson
MARINES FLY HIGH, THE (39) Renie
MARJORIE MORNINGSTAR (57) Shoup
MARKED WOMAN (36) Orry-Kelly
MARK OF CAIN, THE (47) Abbey
MARK OF THE RENEGADE (51) Rhodes
MARK OF THE VAMPIRE (34) Adrian
MARK OF ZORRO, THE (40) Banton
MARLOWE (69) Louis
MARNIE (64) Head
MAROC 7 (67) Clive of London (for Cyd Charisse and the models in the photographic sequences), Luca Sabetelli (for Elsa Martinelli)
MARRIAGE-GO-ROUND, THE (60) LeMaire
MARRIAGE IS A PRIVATE AFFAIR (44) s Irene a Herwood Keyes
MARRIAGE ON THE ROCKS (65) Plunkett
MARRIED AND IN LOVE (39) Renie
MARRIED BACHELOR (41) Kalloch
MARRIED BUT SINGLE=THIS THING CALLED LOVE
MARRIED FLIRTS (24) Wachner
MARRIED IN HASTE=CONSOLATION MARRIAGE
MARRIED IN HOLLYWOOD (29) Wachner, O'Neill
MARRYING KIND, THE (51) Louis
MARRY THE GIRL (37) Shoup
MARSHMALLOW MOON=AARON SLICK FROM PUNKIN' CREEK
MARTY (54) Norma
MARX BROTHERS GO WEST, THE=GO WEST
MARY BURNS, FUGITIVE (35) Taylor
MARYLAND (40) Banton
MARY, MARY (63) Travilla
MARY NAMES THE DAY=DR KILDARE'S WEDDING DAY
MARY OF SCOTLAND (36) Plunkett
MARY POPPINS (64) Walton
MARY, QUEEN OF SCOTS (71) M Furse
MARY STEVENS MD (33) Orry-Kelly
MASK OF DIIJON (45) Karlice
MASK OF FU MANCHU, THE (32) Adrian
MASK OF THE AVENGER (51) Louis
MASKS OF THE DEVIL, THE (28) Adrian
MASQUERADE (64) Dawson
MASQUERADE IN MEXICO (45) Head
MASQUERADER, THE (32) Anderson
MASSACRE (33) Orry-Kelly
MASTER OF BALLANTRAE (53) M Furse
MASTER OF LASSIE=HILLS OF HOME
MASTER OF MEN (33) Kalloch
MASTER OF THE ISLANDS=HAWAIIANS, THE
MASTER RACE, THE (44) Renie
MATA HARI (31) Adrian
MATCH KING, THE (32) Orry-Kelly
MATCHMAKER, THE (58) Head
MATING GAME, THE (58) Rose
MATING OF MILLIE, THE (47) Louis
MATING SEASON, THE (50) Cassini
MATTER OF WHO, A (61) Mendleson
MAVERICK QUEEN, THE (56) Palmer
MAYBE IT'S LOVE (34) Orry-Kelly
MAYERLING (68) Marcel Escoffier
MAYOR OF 44TH STREET, THE (41) Renie
MAYOR OF HELL, THE (33) Orry-Kelly
MAYTIME (36) Adrian
MAYTIME IN MAYFAIR (44) Kitty Foster, Hardy Amies, Charles Creed, Mattli, Molyneux, Digby Morton, Bianca Mosca, Peter Russell, Victor Stiebel, Worth of London (wedding gown by Hartnell)
McCONNELL STORY, THE (55) Shoup
McGUERINS FROM BROOKLYN, THE= BROOKLYN ORCHID
McHALE'S NAVY (64) Colvig

ME AND MY GAL (32) Kaufman
MEANEST MAN IN THE WORLD, THE (42) Luick
MEET DANNY WILSON (51) Thomas
MEET JOHN DOE (40) Visart
MEET ME AFTER THE SHOW (51) Travilla wd LeMaire
MEET ME AT DAWN (46) R Gower Parks
MEET ME AT THE FAIR (52) Odell
MEET ME IN LAS VEGAS (55) Rose
MEET ME IN ST LOUIS (44) Sharaff s Irene
MEET ME ON BROADWAY (45) Louis
MEET ME TONIGHT (52) M Furse
MEET MR LUCIFER (53) Mendleson
MEET NERO WOLF (36) Anthony
MEET THE BARON (32) Tree
MEET THE BOYFRIEND (37) Eloise
MEET THE GIRLS (38) Herschel
MEET THE MISSUS (40) Palmer
MEET THE PEOPLE (44) s Irene a Sharaff
ME, GANGSTER (28) Harry Collins
MELBA (53) Sophie Harris
MELODY FOR TWO (36) Anderson
MELODY LANE (41) V West
MELODY LINGERS ON, THE (35) Taylor
MELODY RANCH (40) Palmer
MENACE (34) Banton
MEN ARE NOT GODS (36) Hubert
MEN ARE SUCH FOOLS (38) Shoup
MEN CALL IT LOVE (31) Hubert
MEN IN HER DIARY (45) V West
MEN IN HER LIFE, THE (41) LeMaire
MEN IN WHITE (33) Adrian
MEN MUST FIGHT (32) Adrian
MEN OF DESTINY=MEN OF TEXAS
MEN OF TEXAS (42) V West
MEN OF THE SKY (31) Stevenson
MEN OF TWO WORLDS (46) Dorothy Broomham
MEN ON HER MIND=GIRL FROM 10TH AVENUE
MEN WITH WINGS (38) Head
MEPHISTO WALTZ (70) Mabry
MERCY ISLAND (41) Palmer
MERRILY WE LIVE (37) Greer (for Billie Burke), Irene (for Constance Bennett)
MERRY ANDREW (57) Plunkett
MERRY FRINKS, THE (34) Orry-Kelly
MERRY-GO-ROUND OF 1938 (37) V West
MERRY MONAHANS, THE (44) V West
MERRY WIDOW, THE (34) Adrian
MERRY WIDOW, THE (52) Rose m Steele
MERRY WIVES OF GOTHAM=LIGHTS OF OLD BROADWAY
MERRY WIVES OF RENO, THE (34) Orry-Kelly
MERTON OF THE MOVIES (47) Rose s Irene
METROPOLITAN (35) Arthur M Levy
MEXICANA (45) Palmer
MEXICAN HAYRIDE (48) Wood
MEXICAN SPITFIRE'S BLESSED EVENT (43) Renie
MICHAEL AND MARY (31) Conway
MICHAEL O'HALLERAN (37) Eloise
MICHAEL SHAYNE, PRIVATE DETECTIVE (40) Herschel
MICHIGAN KID (46) Odell
MICKEY (48) Ehren
MICKEY ONE (65) Domingo Rodrigues
MICKEY THE KID (39) Palmer
MIDDLE OF THE NIGHT (59) Louis
MIDNIGHT (38) Irene
MIDNIGHT ALIBI (34) Orry-Kelly
MIDNIGHT CLUB (33) Banton
MIDNIGHT COURT (36) Anderson
MIDNIGHT COWBOY (69) Roth
MIDNIGHT LACE (60) Irene
MIDNIGHT MADNESS (28) Adrian
MIDNIGHT MARY (33) Adrian
MIDNIGHT STORY, THE (57) Thomas
MIDNIGHT TAXI (37) Herschel
MIDSUMMER NIGHT'S DREAM, A (35) Ree
MIGHTY BARNUM, THE (34) Kiam
MIGHTY JOE YOUNG (49) Balkan
MIGHTY McGURK, THE (46) Shoup s Irene
MIKADO, THE (38) Vertes
MILDRED PIERCE (45) Anderson
MILKMAN, THE (50) Odell
MILLIONAIRE PLAYBOY (37) Renie
MILLIONAIRESS, THE (60) Lehmann
MILLION DOLLAR BABY (41) Orry-Kelly
MILLION DOLLAR MERMAID (52) Plunkett (musical sequences by Rose)
MILLION DOLLAR PURSUIT (51) Palmer
MILLION DOLLAR WEEKEND (48) Barbara Barondess McLean
MILLION POUND NOTE, THE (53) M Furse
MILL ON THE FLOSS, THE (36) Mlle Segalla, Bermans
MILLS OF THE GODS (34) Kalloch
MIMI (35) Zinkeisen
MIND READER, THE (33) Orry-Kelly
MINE OWN EXECUTIONER (47) Alan Haines
MINIVER STORY, THE (50) Gaston Mallet (Plunkett for Greer Garson)
MINISTRY OF FEAR (43) Head
MINNIE AND MOSKOVITCH (71) Colvig

MINSTREL BOY (37) Revillon Freres, Eve Valere, Bivall
MIRACLE, THE (59) Best
MIRACLE IN SOHO (57) Harris
MIRACLE IN THE RAIN (55) Anderson
MIRACLE OF MORGAN'S CREEK (43) Head
MIRACLE OF THE BELLS, THE (47) Renie
MIRACLE ON 34TH STREET (47) Nelson wd LeMaire
MIRACLES FOR SALE (39) Tree
MIRACLE WORKER, THE (62) R Morley
MIRAGE (65) Louis
MIRANDA (47) Caffin
MISERABLES, LES (35) Kiam
MISERABLES, LES (52) Jeakins wd LeMaire
MISFITS, THE (60) Louis
MISLEADING LADY, THE (16) Lucille
MISS ANNIE ROONEY (42) Royer
MISS BREWSTER'S MILLIONS (26) Banton
MISS GRANT TAKES RICHMOND (49) Louis
MISSING WITNESSES (37) Mackenzie
MISSING WOMEN (50) Palmer
MISSION TO MOSCOW (43) Orry-Kelly
MISSISSIPPI GAMBLER (42) V West
MISSISSIPPI GAMBLER (52) Thomas
MISS PACIFIC FLEET (35) Orry-Kelly
MISS SADIE THOMPSON (53) Louis
MISS TATLOCK'S MILLIONS (48) Head
MISTER ACE (46) Woulfe
MR ASHTON WAS INDISCREET=SENATOR WAS INDISCREET, THE
MR BELVEDERE GOES TO COLLEGE (49) Cashin wd LeMaire
MR BELVEDERE RINGS THE BELL (51) Renie wd LeMaire
MR BIG (42) V West
MR BLANDINGS BUILDS HIS DREAM HOUSE (47) Kalloch
MR BUDDWING (66) Rose
MR CHUMP (38) Shoup
MR CORY (56) Thomas
MR DEEDS GOES TO TOWN (35) Lange
MR DISTRICT ATTORNEY (46) Louis
MR DODD TAKES THE AIR (37) Anderson
MR DRAKE'S DUCK (50) Harris
MR 880 (50) Travilla wd LeMaire
MISTER EMMANUEL (44) Harald
MR FAINTHEART=$10 RAISE
MR HOBBS TAKES A VACATION (62) Donfeld
MR IMPERIUM (51) Plunkett
MR LUCKY (43) Renie
MR MOTO ON DANGER ISLAND=DANGER ISLAND
MR MOTO'S GAMBLE (38) Myron
MR MOTO'S LAST WARNING (38) Myron
MR MOTO TAKES A CHANCE (38) Herschel
MR MOTO TAKES A VACATION (39) Herschel
MR PEABODY AND THE MERMAID (48) Houston
MR ROBERTS (55) Mabry
MR SCOUTMASTER (53) Renie wd LeMaire
MR SKEFFINGTON (44) Orry-Kelly
MR SKITCH (33) Kaufman
MR SMITH GOES TO WASHINGTON (39) Kalloch
MR SOFT TOUCH (49) Louis
MR TOPAZE (61) Balmain
MR WU (27) Coulter
MRS FITZHERBERT (47) Eva Melova
MRS MIKE (49) Jenssen
MRS MINIVER (42) Kalloch m Steele
MRS PARKINGTON (44) s Irene a Herwood Keyes m Valles
MRS WIGGS OF THE CABBAGE PATCH (34) Banton
MOBY DICK (56) Haffenden
MOCKERY (27) Clark
MODEL AND THE MARRIAGE BROKER, THE (51) Renie wd LeMaire
MODEL WIFE (41) V West (Royer for Joan Blondell)
MODERN HERO, A (34) Orry-Kelly
MODERN MIRACLE, THE=STORY OF ALEXANDER GRAHAM BELL, THE
MODESTY BLAISE (66) Dawson
MOGAMBO (53) Rose
MOLE PEOPLE, THE (56) J Morley
MOLLY AND ME (44) Wood
MOLLY MAGUIRES, THE (69) Jeakins
MOMENT TO MOMENT (66) Odell, Yves St Laurent
MONEY FOR JAM=IT AIN'T HAY
MONEY TALKS (25) Kay, Marsh, Andre-Ani
MONKEY BUSINESS (52) Travilla wd LeMaire
MONKEYS, GO HOME! (66) Thomas
MONSIEUR BEAUCAIRE (24) Barbier
MONSIEUR BEAUCAIRE (46) Dodson
MONTANA (49) Anderson (Best for Errol Flynn)
MONTANA BELLE (52) Palmer
MONTANA MOON (30) Adrian
MONTE CARLO (25) Kay, Marsh, Andre-Ani
MONTE CARLO OR BUST (69) Furness, Orietta Nasalli-Rocca
MONTE CARLO STORY, THE (57) Louis
MOONFLEET (55) Plunkett
MOON IS BLUE, THE (53) Don Loper
MOON IS DOWN, THE (43) Mackenzie

MOONLIGHT AND MELODY=MOON-
LIGHT AND PRETZELS
MOONLIGHT AND PRETZELS (33) Brymer
MOONLIGHT IN VERMONT (43) V West
MOONLIGHT MURDER (35) Tree
MOON OVER HER SHOULDER (41) Herschel
MOON OVER LAS VEGAS (44) V West
MOON PILOT (61) Thomas
MOONRISE (48) Palmer
MOON'S OUR HOME, THE (36) Taylor
MOONTIDE (42) Wakeling
MOON ZERO TWO (69) Toms
MORE THAN A SECRETARY (36) B Newman
MORGAN—A SUITABLE CASE FOR
TREATMENT (65) Rickards
MORGAN'S LAST RAID (28) Coulter
MORITURI (65) Mabry
MORNING GLORY (33) Plunkett
MOROCCO (30) Banton
MORTAL STORM, THE (40) Adrian m Steele
MOSS ROSE (47) Hubert wd LeMaire
MOST DANGEROUS MAN ALIVE (61) Wakeling
MOST DANGEROUS MAN IN THE WORLD,
THE=CHAIRMAN, THE
MOST PRECIOUS THING IN LIFE (34) Kalloch
MOTHER CAREY'S CHICKENS (38) Stevenson
MOTHER DIDN'T TELL ME (49) Travilla wd
LeMaire
MOTHER IS A FRESHMAN (48) Nelson wd
Le Maire
MOTHER KNOWS BEST=MOTHER IS A
FRESHMAN
MOTHER WORE TIGHTS (47) Orry-Kelly wd
LeMaire
MOTOR MADNESS (37) Kalloch
MOULIN ROUGE (52) Vertes s Squire
(Schiaparelli for Zsa Zsa Gabor)
MOUNTAIN, THE (56) Head
MOUNTAIN JUSTICE (37) Anderson
MOURNING BECOMES ELECTRA (47) Ban-
ton
MOUSE ON THE MOON, THE (63) Mendleson
MOUSE THAT ROARED, THE (59) Mendleson
MOUTHPIECE, THE (32) Luick
MOVE OVER DARLING (63) Mabry
MOZART=WHOM THE GODS LOVE
MUDLARK, THE (50) Stevenson, M Furse
MUG TOWN (42) V West
MUMMY, THE (32) V West
MUMMY'S BOYS (36) Stevenson
MUMMY'S GHOST, THE (44) V West
MUMMY'S HAND, THE (40) V West
MURDER AMONG FRIENDS (36) Herschel
MURDER BY AN ARISTOCRAT (36) Orry-
Kelly
MURDER BY DEATH (75) Roth
MURDERERS' ROW (66) Mabry
MURDER IN GREENWICH VILLAGE (37) Kal-
loch
MURDER IN THE AIR (40) Shoup
MURDER IN THE BIG HOUSE (36) Orry-Kelly
MURDER IN THE BLUE ROOM (44) V West
MURDER IN THE MUSIC HALL (45) Palmer
MURDER IN THORNTON SQUARE=GAS-
LIGHT
MURDER IN TRINIDAD (34) Royer
MURDER MY SWEET (44) Stevenson
MURDER ON THE ORIENT EXPRESS (74)
Walton
MURDER ON ·THE WATERFRONT (43)
Rhodes
MURDER WILL OUT (30) Stevenson
MURDER WITH PICTURES (36) Head
MUSCLE BEACH PARTY (64) Corso
MUSIC FOR MADAME (37) Stevenson
MUSIC FOR MILLIONS (44) s Irene a Dean
MUSIC IN MANHATTAN (44) Renie
MUSIC IN MY HEART (39) Kalloch
MUSIC IN THE AIR (34) Hubert
MUSIC IS MAGIC (35) Rega
MUSIC LOVERS, THE (70) Russell
MUSIC MAN, THE (62) Jeakins
MUTINY ON THE BOUNTY (60/62) Mabry
MY AMERICAN WIFE (36) Banton
MY BEST GAL (43) Palmer
MY BILL (38) Orry-Kelly
MY BLUE HEAVEN (50) LeMaire
MY BROTHER JONATHAN (47) J Gower Parks,
MY BROTHER'S KEEPER (48) Harris
MY BROTHER TALKS TO HORSES (46) Plun-
kett s Irene
MY COUSIN RACHEL (52) Jeakins wd LeMaire
MY DARLING CLEMENTINE (46) Hubert
MY DEAR MISS ALDRICH (37) Tree
MY DREAM IS YOURS (48) Anderson
MY FAIR LADY (64) Beaton
MY FAVOURITE BRUNETTE (46) Head
MY FAVOURITE WIFE (40) Greer
MY FOOLISH HEART (49) Wills, Head
MY FRIEND FLICKA (42) Herschel
MY FRIEND FROM INDIA (28) Adrian
MY FRIEND IRMA (49) Head
MY GEISHA (61) Head
MY GAL LOVES MUSIC (44) V West
MY GAL SAL (42) Wakeling
MY GIRL TISA (47) Rhodes

MY HEART GOES CRAZY=LONDON
TOWN
MY HERO=SOUTHERN YANKEE, A
MY LIFE IS YOURS=PEOPLE VS DR KIL-
DARE, THE
MY LIFE WITH CAROLINE (41) Stevenson
MY LIPS BETRAY (33) Strassner
MY LITTLE CHICKADEE (39) V West
MY LOVE CAME BACK (40) Orry-Kelly
MY LUCKY STAR (38) Royer
MY MAN GODFREY (36) Brymer (Banton for
Carole Lombard)
MY MAN GODFREY (57) Thomas
MY MARRIAGE (35) Myron
MY OWN TRUE LOVE (48) Head
MY PAL GUS (52) LeMaire
MY PAL, WOLF (44) LeMaire
MYRA BRECKINRIDGE (70) van Runkle (Head
for Mae West)
MY REPUTATION (45) Rhodes (Head for Bar-
bara Stanwyck)
MY SISTER AND I (48) Roy Montgomerie
MY SISTER EILEEN (55) Louis
MY SIX LOVES (62) Head
MY SON, MY SON (40) Bridgehouse, Taylor
MYSTERIOUS DOCTOR, THE (43) Anderson
MYSTERIOUS LADY, THE (28) Clark
MYSTERIOUS MISS X, THE (38) Saltern
MYSTERIOUS MR VALENTINE, THE (46)
Palmer
MYSTERY HOUSE (38) Shoup
MYSTERY IN MEXICO (48) Renie
MYSTERY OF MR X (33) Adrian
MYSTERY OF THE WAX MUSEUM (32)
Orry-Kelly
MYSTERY OF THE WHITE ROOM (38) V West
MYSTERY RANCH (32) Cox
MYSTERY SUBMARINE (50) Thomas
MYSTERY WOMAN (34) Royer
MYSTIC, THE (25) Erte, Andre-Ani
MY WEAKNESS (33) Kaufman, Strassner
MY WIFE'S RELATIVES (38) Palmer
MY WILD IRISH ROSE (47) Travilla
MY WOMAN (33) Kalloch

NAKED ALIBI (54) Odell
NAKED CITY, THE (47) Houston
NAKED HEART (50) Michael Whittaker
NAKED JUNGLE, THE (53) Head
NANCY DREW, DETECTIVE (38) Anderson
NANCY GOES TO RIO (49) Rose
NANCY STEELE IS MISSING (36) Wakeling
NARROW CORNER, THE (33) Orry-Kelly
NARROW MARGIN, THE (52) Balkan
NATIONAL VELVET (44) Irene a Dean m Valles
NAUGHTY ARLETTE=ROMANTIC AGE,
THE
NAUGHTY BUT NICE (39) Shoup
NAUGHTY MARIETTE (34) Adrian
NAUGHTY NINETIES, THE (45) V West'
NAVY BLUE AND GOLD (37) Tree
NAVY BLUES (29) Cox
NAVY BLUES (36) Eloise
NAVY BLUES (41) Shoup
NAVY COMES THROUGH, THE (42) Renie
NAZI AGENT (41) Shoup
NEGATIVES (68) Clive Evans
NELL GWYN (34) Zinkeisen
NELSON AFFAIR, THE=BEQUEST TO THE
NATION
NEPTUNE'S DAUGHTER (49) Irene
NEVADA (44) Renie
NEVER A DULL MOMENT (43) V West
NEVER A DULL MOMENT (68) Thomas
NEVER GIVE AN INCH=SOMETIMES A
GREAT NOTION
NEVER GIVE A SUCKER AN EVEN BREAK
(41) V West
NEVER PUT IT IN WRITING (63) Hartnell
NEVER SAY GOODBYE (46) Rhodes
NEVER SAY GOODBYE (56) Thomas
NEVER SO FEW (59) Rose
NEVER STEAL ANYTHING SMALL (58)
Thomas
NEVER THE TWAIN SHALL MEET (25) Urban
Thurlow
NEVER TOO LATE (65) O'Brien
NEVER TRUST A GAMBLER (51) Louis
NEW CENTURIONS, THE (72) Guy Verhille
NEW FACE IN HELL=P J
NEW FACES (53) Thomas Becker (Norma for Eartha
Kitt)
NEW KIND OF LOVE, A (63) Head (Dior,
Lanvin-Castillo, Pierre Cardin, Yves St Laur-
ent for fashion show sequence)
NEW LEAF, A (70) Sylbert
NEW MOON (40) Adrian m Steele
NEWS IS MADE AT NIGHT (39) Myron
NEW WINE (41) Hubert
NEXT TIME WE LOVE (35) V West
NIAGARA (52) Jeakins wd LeMaire
NIAGARA FALLS (41) Saltern
NICE GIRL? (40) V West
NICE GIRL LIKE ME, A (69) Myers

NICHOLAS AND ALEXANDRA (71) Blake
(Antonio Castillo for Janet Suzman and Irene
Worth)
NIGHT AFTER NIGHT (32) Plunkett
NIGHT AND DAY (46) Anderson (dance cos-
tumes by Travilla)
NIGHT AND THE CITY (50) M Furse (Cassini for
Gene Tierney)
NIGHT AT THE OPERA, A (35) Tree
NIGHT BEAT (47) Dawson
NIGHT CLUB GIRL (44) V West
NIGHTFALL (56) Louis
NIGHT HAS A THOUSAND EYES, THE (48)
Head
NIGHT HAWK, THE (38) Saltern
NIGHT IN PARADISE (46) Banton
NIGHT IS ENDING, THE=PARIS AFTER
DARK
NIGHT IS YOUNG, THE (34) Tree
NIGHTMARE (42) V West
NIGHTMARE ALLEY (47) Cashin wd LeMaire
NIGHT MUST FALL (37) Tree
NIGHT MUST FALL (63) Sophie Devine
NIGHT NURSE (31) Luick
NIGHT OF ADVENTURE, A (44) Renie
NIGHT OF THE IGUANA (64) Jeakins
NIGHT PASSAGE (57) Thomas
NIGHT PEOPLE (54) Maes wd LeMaire
NIGHT RUNNER, THE (56) Odell
NIGHT SONG (47) Orry-Kelly
NIGHT SPOT (37) Renie
NIGHT THEY RAIDED MINSKY'S, THE (68)
Johnstone
NIGHT TO REMEMBER, A (58) Caffin
NIGHT TRAIN TO MEMPHIS (46) Palmer
NIGHT UNTO NIGHT (49) Rhodes
NIGHT WAITRESS (36) Stevenson
NIGHT WALKER, THE (64) Cox
NIGHT WITHOUT SLEEP (52) Renie wd LeMaire
NIGHT WITHOUT STARS (51) Harris (Balmain
for Nadia Gray)
NINE LIVES ARE NOT ENOUGH (41) Shoup
99 AND 44/100% DEAD! (74) Talsky
NINOTCHKA (39) Adrian
NITWITS, THE (35) B Newman
NIX ON DAMES (29) Wachner
NOB HILL (45) Hubert
NOBODY LIVES FOREVER (46) Anderson
NOBODY RUNS FOREVER (68) Caffin
NOBODY'S BABY (37) Meinhart
NOBODY'S PERFECT (67) Odell
NOCTURNE (46) Renie
NO DOWN PAYMENT (57) Wills wd LeMaire
NO HIGHWAY (51) M Furse (+ Dior for Dietrich)
NO HIGHWAY IN THE SKY=NO HIGHWAY
NO LEAVE, NO LOVE (46) Irene
NO LOVE FOR JOHNNIE (60) Caffin
NO MAN OF HER OWN (32) Banton
NO MAN OF HER OWN (49) Head
NO MAN'S WOMAN (55) Palmer
NO MINOR VICES (48) Herwood Keyes
NO MORE LADIES (35) Adrian
NO, MY DARLING DAUGHTER (61) Caffin
NO NAME ON THE BULLET (58) Thomas
NONE BUT THE LONELY HEART (44) Renie
NO, NO NANETTE (40) Stevenson
NON-STOP NEW YORK (37) Hartnell
NO ONE MAN (32) Banton
NOOSE (48) Duse
NO PLACE FOR JENNIFER (49) Dorothy Sinclair
NO PLACE TO GO (39) Shoup
NO QUESTIONS ASKED (51) Rose
NORA PRENTISS (46) Travilla
NO ROOM FOR THE GROOM (52) Thomas
NORTHERN PURSUIT (43) Rhodes
NORTH TO ALASKA (60) Thomas
NORTH WEST FRONTIER (59) Caffin (Harris
for Lauren Bacall)
NORTH WEST MOUNTED POLICE (40) Visart
NORTHWEST OUTPOST (47) Palmer
NORTHWEST STAMPEDE (48) Ehren
NO SAD SONGS FOR ME (50) Louis
NOT AS A STRANGER (55) Don Loper
NOT DAMAGED (30) Wachner
NOTHING SACRED (37) Plunkett (Banton for
Carole Lombard)
NO TIME FOR COMEDY (40) Orry-Kelly
NO TIME FOR LOVE (43) Head (Irene for
Claudette Colbert)
NO TIME FOR TEARS (57) Duse
NO TIME TO MARRY (37) Kalloch
NOTORIOUS (46) Head
NOTORIOUS AFFAIR, A (30) Stevenson
NOTORIOUS SOPHIE LANG, THE (34) Banton
NOT SO DUMB (29) Adrian
NOT WITH MY WIFE YOU DON'T (66) Head
NOVEL AFFAIR, A=PASSIONATE STRANGER,
THE
NO WAY OUT (50) Travilla wd LeMaire
NO WAY TO TREAT A LADY (67) Aldredge
NOWHERE TO GO (58) Hartnell
NOW I'LL TELL (34) Kaufman
NOW, VOYAGER (42) Orry-Kelly
NUN AND THE SERGEANT, THE (62) Corso
NUN'S STORY, THE (57) Best
NURSE EDITH CAVELL (39) Stevenson

PHONE CALL FROM A STRANGER (51) Jenssen
PICCADILLY JIM (36) Tree
PICCADILLY THIRD STOP (60) Ellacott
PICK A STAR (37) Kiam
PICKWICK PAPERS, THE (52) Dawson
PICNIC (55) Louis
PICTURE MOMMY DEAD (66) Rhodes
PICTURE OF DORIAN GRAY, THE (44) Irene a
  Herwood Keyes m Valles
PICTURE SNATCHER (33) Orry-Kelly
PICKUP ON SOUTH STREET (53) Travilla wd
  LeMaire
PIED PIPER, THE (42) Tree
PIERRE OF THE PLAINS (42) Shoup m Steele
PIER 13 (32)=ME AND MY GAL
PIER 13 (40) Herschel
PIGSKIN PARADE (36) Wakeling
PILGRIMAGE (33) Luick
PILGRIM LADY, THE (46) Palmer
PILLARS OF THE SKY (56) Odell
PILLOW OF DEATH (45) V West
PILLOW TALK (59) Louis
PILLOW TALK (59) Thomas, Louis
PINK JUNGLE, THE (68) Head
PINK PANTHER, THE (63) Yves St Laurent
PINK STRING AND SEALING WAX (45) Bianca
  Mosca
PINKY (49) LeMaire
PIN UP GIRL (44) Hubert
PIRATE, THE (48) Tom Keogh s Irene
PIRATES OF MONTEREY, THE (47) Banton, V
  West
PIT AND THE PENDULUM, THE (61) Corso
PITFALL, THE (48) Jenssen
PITTSBURGH (42) V West
PITTSBURGH KID, THE (41) Palmer
P J (67) Louis
PLACE FOR LOVERS, A (69) van Runkle
PLACE IN THE SUN, A (51) Head
PLACE OF ONE'S OWN, A (44) Haffenden
PLAINSMAN, THE (36) Visart
PLAINSMAN, THE (66) Colvig
PLAINSMAN AND THE LADY, THE (46)
  Palmer
PLANET OF THE APES (67) Haack
PLANTER'S WIFE, THE (52) Doris Lee
PLAY GIRL (40) Stevenson
PLAYGIRL (54) Thomas
PLAY IT AGAIN, SAM (71) Johnstone
PLAY IT AS IT LAYS (72) Joel Schumacher (Halston
  for Tammy Grimes, Gustave Tassell for
  Ruth Ford)
PLAYMATES (41) Stevenson
PLAY 'MISTY' FOR ME (71) Colvig
PLEASE BELIEVE ME (49) Irene
PLEASE DON'T EAT THE DAISIES (59) Haack
PLEASURE CRAZED (29) Wachner
PLEASURE CRUISE (33) Lambert s Kaufman
PLEASURE OF HIS COMPANY, THE (61) Head
PLEASURE SEEKERS, THE (64) Renie
PLOT THICKENS, THE (36) Stevenson
PLOT TO KILL ROOSEVELT, THE=TEHE-
  RAN
PLOUGH AND THE STARS, THE (36) Plunkett
PLYMOUTH ADVENTURE (52) Plunkett
POCKETFUL OF MIRACLES (61) Head m Plun-
  kett
POET'S PUB (49) Eve Betts Ltd
POLLYANNA (60) Plunkett
POLLY FULTON=B F'S DAUGHTER
POLLY OF THE CIRCUS (31) Adrian
POLO JOE (36) Orry-Kelly
PONY EXPRESS (52) Head
POOL OF LONDON (50) Mendleson
POOR COW (67) Caroline Mott
POOR LITTLE RICH GIRL (36) Wakeling
POPE JOAN (72) Haffenden, Joan Bridge
POPPY (17) Banton
POPPY (36) Head
PORGY AND BESS (58) Sharaff
PORT AFRIQUE (56) Squire
PORTIA ON TRIAL (37) Eloise
PORTNOY'S COMPLAINT (72) Mabry
PORT OF 40 THIEVES (44) Palmer
PORT OF SEVEN SEAS (38) Tree
PORTRAIT FROM LIFE (48) Ellacott
PORTRAIT IN BLACK (60) Louis
PORTRAIT OF A MOBSTER (60) Shoup
PORTRAIT OF CLARE (50) Haffenden
PORTRAIT OF JENNY (48) Johnstone (Ballard
  for Jennifer Jones)
POSEIDON ADVENTURE, THE (72) Zastup-
  nevich
POSSESSED (47) B Newman (Adrian for Joan
  Crawford)
POSTAL INSPECTOR (36) V West
POSTMAN ALWAYS RINGS TWICE, THE (46)
  Irene a Herwood Keyes
POSTMAN DIDN'T RING, THE (42) Herschel
POST OFFICE INVESTIGATOR (49) s Palmer
POT O'GOLD (41) Taylor
POWDER RIVER (53) Travilla wd LeMaire
POWER AND THE GLORY, THE (33) Kaufman
POWER AND THE PRIZE, THE (56) Rose
POWERS GIRL, THE (42) Adrian, Hubert

PRACTICALLY YOURS (44) Greer
PRECINCT 45—LOS ANGELES POLICE=NEW
  CENTURIONS, THE
PREHISTORIC WOMAN=SLAVE GIRLS
PRELUDE TO FAME (50) Molyneux
PREMATURE BURIAL, THE (61) Corso
PRESENTING LILY MARS (43) Shoup
PRESIDENT'S LADY, THE (52) Renie wd
  LeMaire
PRESIDENT'S MYSTERY, THE (36) Eloise
PRETTY POISON (68) Roth
PRETTY POLLY (67) Mendleson
PRICE OF FEAR, THE (56) J Morley
PRIDE AND PREJUDICE (40) Adrian m Steele
PRIDE OF KENTUCKY=STORY OF SEABIS-
  CUIT, THE
PRIDE OF ST LOUIS, THE (51) Travilla wd
  LeMaire
PRIDE OF THE MARINES (35) Lange
PRIDE OF THE MARINES (45) Anderson
PRIDE OF THE NAVY (38) Saltern
PRIDE OF THE YANKEES, THE (42) Hubert
PRIME OF MISS JEAN BRODIE, THE (68) Haf-
  fenden, Joan Bridge
PRIMROSE PATH (39) Renie
PRINCE AND THE PAUPER, THE (37) Ander-
  son
PRINCE AND THE PAUPER, THE (62) M Furse
PRINCE AND THE SHOWGIRL, THE (57)
  Dawson
PRINCE OF ARCADIA (33) Louis Brooks
PRINCE OF FOXES (49) Novarese
PRINCE OF PLAYERS (54) Wills wd LeMaire
PRINCESS AND THE PIRATE, THE (44) Grant
PRINCESS AND THE PLUMBER, THE (30)
  Wachner
PRINCESS CHARMING (34) Hartnell
PRINCESS COMES ACROSS, THE (36) Banton
PRINCESS OF THE NILE (54) Travilla
PRINCESS O'ROURKE (43) Orry-Kelly
PRINCE VALIANT (53) LeMaire
PRINCE WHO WAS A THIEF, THE (51) Thomas
PRISONER OF SHARK ISLAND (35) Wakeling
PRISONER OF ZENDA, THE (37) Dryden
PRISONER OF ZENDA, THE (52) Plunkett
PRISONERS IN PETTICOATS (50) Palmer
PRIVATE AFFAIRS (40) V West
PRIVATE AFFAIRS OF BEL AMI, THE (46)
  Norma
PRIVATE DETECTIVE (39) Shoup
PRIVATE DETECTIVE 62 (33) Orry-Kelly
PRIVATE LIFE OF DON JUAN, THE (34) Mes-
  sel
PRIVATE LIFE OF HELEN OF TROY, THE (27)
  Ree
PRIVATE LIFE OF HENRY VIII, THE (33) Arm-
  strong
PRIVATE LIFE OF SHERLOCK HOLMES, THE
  (70) Harris
PRIVATE LIVES (31) Adrian
PRIVATE LIVES OF ELIZABETH AND ESSEX
  THE (39) Orry-Kelly
PRIVATE NUMBER (36) Wakeling
PRIVATE NURSE (41) Herschel
PRIVATE WORLDS (34) Banton
PRIVILEGE (67) Vanessa Clarke
PRIZE, THE (63) Thomas
PRIZEFIGHTER AND THE LADY, THE (33)
  Tree
PRODIGAL, THE (54) Herschel
PRODUCERS, THE (67) Coffin
PROFESSIONAL SOLDIER (35) Lambert
PROMISE HER ANYTHING (65) Dawson
PROUD AND THE PROFANE, THE (56) Head
PROUD ONES, THE (56) Travilla wd LeMaire
PROUD REBEL, THE (57) Wills
PRUDENCE AND THE PILL (68) Harris
PSYCHE 59 (63) Harris
PSYCHO (60) Colvig
PT RAIDERS=SHIP THAT DIED OF SHAME,
  THE
PUBLIC ENEMIES (41) Palmer
PUBLIC ENEMY, THE (31) Luick, Stevenson
PUBLIC ENEMY'S WIFE (36) Orry-Kelly
PUBLIC EYE, THE=FOLLOW ME
PUBLIC HERO NO 1 (35) Tree
PUBLIC MENACE, THE (35) Mayer
PUDDIN' HEAD (41) Palmer
PULP (72) Gitt Magrini
PUMPKIN EATER, THE (64) Motley
PUPPET ON A CHAIN (70) Blake
PURE HELL OF ST TRINIANS, THE (60) Hon-
  oria Plesch
PURPLE MASK, THE (55) Thomas
PURSUED (34) Royer
PURSUED (46) Rhodes
PURSUIT TO ALGIERS (43) V West
PUSHOVER (54) Louis
PUSSYCAT, PUSSYCAT, I LOVE YOU (70)
  Nikki of Just Men (for Ian McShane), Adriana
  Berselli
PUTTIN' ON THE RITZ (29) O'Neill
PUZZLE OF A DOWNFALL CHILD (70) Terry
  Leong s Jo Ynocencio
PYGMALION (38) Professor L Czettel (also Worth,
  Schiaparelli)

QUALITY STREET (27) Hubert
QUALITY STREET (36) Plunkett
QUANTEZ (56) Odell
QUARTET (48) Harris
QUEEN BEE (55) Louis
QUEEN CHRISTINA (33) Adrian
QUEEN KELLY (28) Ree
QUEEN OF BURLESQUE (46) Karlice
QUEEN OF DESTINY=SIXTY GLORIOUS
  YEARS
QUEEN OF SPADES, THE (48) Messel
QUEEN'S AFFAIR, THE (33) Zinkeisen
QUEEN'S GUARDS, THE (61) Mattli
QUEEN'S HUSBAND, THE (30) Ree
QUICK MILLIONS (31) Wachner
QUICK MILLIONS (39) Myron
QUICK MONEY (37) Renie
QUIET MAN, THE (51) Palmer
QUILLER MEMORANDUM, THE (66) Toms
QUO VADIS (51) Herschel

RACE STREET (48) Stevenson
RACHEL AND THE STRANGER (48) Head
RACKET, THE (51) Woulfe
RACKET BUSTERS (38) Shoup
RACKETEER, THE (29) Wakeling
RACKETEERS IN EXILE (37) Kalloch
RACKETY REX (32) Cox
RADIO MURDER MYSTERY, THE=LOVE IS
  ON THE AIR
RAFFLES (30) Banton
RAGE IN HEAVEN (40) Adrian
RAGE OF PARIS, THE (38) V West
RAGE TO LIVE, A (65) Shoup
RAGING TIDE, THE (51) Thomas
RAGS TO RICHES (41) Palmer
RAID, THE (54) Travilla
RAIDERS, THE=RIDERS OF VENGEANCE
RAIDERS OF THE SEVEN SEAS (53) Wood
RAINBOW OVER TEXAS (46) Palmer
RAINMAKER, THE (56) Head
RAINMAKERS, THE (35) Plunkett
RAINS CAME, THE (39) Wakeling
RAINS OF RANCHIPUR, THE (55) Travilla wd
  LeMaire (Rose for Lana Turner)
RAINTREE COUNTY (57) Plunkett
RAKE'S PROGRESS, THE (45) Caffin
RALLY 'ROUND THE FLAG BOYS (58)
  LeMaire
RAMONA (36) Wakeling
RAMPAGE (62) Cassini
RAMROD (46) Head
RANCHO NOTORIOUS (51) Don Loper
RANDOM HARVEST (42) Kalloch
RANSOM (55) Rose
RARE BREED, THE (65) Odell
RASCAL (68) Odell
RASCALS (38) Myron
RASPUTIN AND THE EMPRESS (32) Adrian
RAT RACE, THE (60) Head
RATTLE OF A SIMPLE MAN (64) Rickards
RAW EDGE (56) Thomas
RAWHIDE (50) Travilla wd LeMaire
RAWHIDE YEARS, THE (56) Thomas
RAZOR'S EDGE, THE (46) LeMaire (Cassini for
  Gene Tierney)
REACH FOR THE SKY (56) Harris
REACHING FOR THE MOON (30) Cox
READY FOR LOVE (34) Pene du Bois
READY, WILLING AND ABLE (36) Shoup
REAR WINDOW (54) Head
REBECCA OF SUNNYBROOK FARM (37)
  Wakeling
REBEL, THE (60) Alan Sievewright
REBEL WITHOUT A CAUSE (55) Mabry
RECKLESS (35) Adrian
RECKLESS AGE (44) V West
RECKLESS HOUR, THE (31) Luick
RECKLESS MOMENT, THE (49) Louis
RECOIL, THE (24) Drecol
RED BERET, THE (53) Harris
RED CANYON (48) Odell
RED DANUBE, THE (49) Rose
REDEMPTION (30) Adrian
RED ENSIGN (33) Conway
RED GARTERS (53) Head
RED HAIR (28) Banton
REDHEAD FROM MANHATTAN (43) Travilla
REDHEADS ON PARADE (35) Lambert
RED HOT AND BLUE (49) Head
RED HOT RHYTHM (29) Wakeling
RED LINE 7000 (65) Head
RED MILL, THE (26) Andre-Ani
RED PONY, THE (48) Palmer
RED SHOES, THE (47) Hein Heckroth
RED SKIES OF MONTANA (51) Stevenson wd
  LeMaire
RED SKY AT MORNING (70) Head
RED SUNDOWN (55) J Morley
RED SWORD, THE (28) Plunkett
RED WAGON (33) P Newman
RED WINE (28) Wachner
REFLECTIONS IN A GOLDEN EYE (67) Jeakins
REGISTERED NURSE (34) Orry-Kelly
REIGN OF TERROR=BLACK BOOK, THE
REIVERS, THE (69) van Runkle

SEARCHING WIND, THE (46) Woulfe (for Sylvia Sidney), *Dorothy O'Hara* (for Ann Richards)
SEAS BENEATH (30) Wachner
SECOND CHANCE (53) Woulfe
SECOND GREATEST SEX, THE (55) J Morley
SECOND HAND WIFE (32) Cox
SECOND HONEYMOON (37) Wakeling
SECOND TIME AROUND, THE (61) Donfeld
SECOND WIFE (36) Stevenson
SECRET AGENT (36) Strassner
SECRET BEYOND THE DOOR (47) Banton
SECRET BRIDE, THE (34) Orry-Kelly
SECRET CEREMONY (68) *Marc Bohan of Dior*
SECRET COMMAND (44) Louis
SECRET ENEMIES (42) Anderson
SECRET ENEMY=ENEMY AGENT
SECRET FOUR, THE=FOUR JUST MEN, THE
SECRET GARDEN, THE (49) Plunkett
SECRET HEART, THE (46) *s* Irene
SECRET LIFE OF AN AMERICAN WIFE, THE (68) Travilla
SECRET LIFE OF WALTER MITTY, THE (47) Sharaff
SECRET OF CONVICT LAKE (51) Stevenson *wd* LeMaire
SECRET OF MY SUCCESS, THE (65) *John Cavanagh*
SECRET PEOPLE (51) Mendleson
SECRETS (23) C West
SECRETS (32) Adrian
SECRET SERVICE INVESTIGATOR (48) Palmer
SECRET SERVICE OF THE AIR (38) Shoup
SECRET SIX, THE (31) Hubert
SECRETS OF AN ACTRESS (38) Orry-Kelly
SECRET WAR OF HARRY FRIGG, THE (67) Head
SEEKERS, THE (54) Harris
SEE MY LAWYER (44) V West
SEE YOU IN HELL, DARLING=AMERICAN DREAM, AN
SEMINOLE (52) Odell
SENATOR WAS INDISCREET, THE (47) Houston
SEND ME NO FLOWERS (64) Louis
SENSATIONS OF 1945 (44) Behm
SENTIMENTAL JOURNEY (45) Nelson
SEPARATE BEDS (63) *Norman Norell*
SEPARATE TABLES (58) Grant (Head for Rita Hayworth)
SEPTEMBER AFFAIR (50) Head
SEPT FOIS FEMME=MODERN TIMES SEVEN
SERENADE (39) Adrian *m* Valles
SERENADE (55) Shoup
SERGEANT MURPHY (37) Shoup
SERGEANT ROUTLEDGE (60) Best
SERPENT OF THE NILE (53) Louis
SERVANT, THE (63) Dawson
SERVANTS' ENTRANCE (34) Hubert
SERVICE DE LUXE (38) V West (Irene for Constance Bennett)
SEVEN BRIDES FOR SEVEN BROTHERS (54) Plunkett
SEVEN CITIES OF GOLD (55) Balkan *wd* LeMaire
SEVEN DAYS LEAVE (42) Renie
SEVEN DAYS TO NOON (50) *Honoria Plesch*
SEVEN FACES (29) Wachner
SEVEN LITTLE FOYS, THE (54) Head
SEVEN MINUTES, THE (71) Thomas
SEVEN SINNERS (36) Molyneux
SEVEN SINNERS (40) V West (Irene for Marlene Dietrich)
SEVEN SWEETHEARTS (42) Shoup
1776 (72) *Patricia Zipprodt*
7TH CROSS, THE (44) *s* Irene
SEVENTH HEAVEN (27) Kay
SEVENTH HEAVEN (36) Wakeling
SEVENTH SIN, THE (57) Rose
SEVENTH VEIL, THE (45) *Dorothy Sinclair*
SEVENTH VICTIM, THE (43) Renie
SEVEN THUNDERS (57) Harris
SEVEN WOMEN (65) Plunkett
SEVEN YEAR ITCH, THE (55) Travilla *wd* LeMaire
SHADOW, THE (37) Kalloch
SHADOW OF A DOUBT (42) V West (Adrian for Teresa Wright)
SHADOW OF BLACKMAIL=WIFE WANTED
SHADOW OF DOUBT (35) Tree
SHADOW OF THE EAGLE (50) Novarese
SHADOWS OF THE THIN MAN (41) Kalloch
SHADOWS OF THE NIGHT (28) Coulter
SHADOWS OVER SHANGHAI (38) *W H McCrary*
SHADY LADY (45) V West
SHAKEDOWN (50) Wood
SHALAKO (68) *Cynthia Tingey* (*Patrick Donahue* for Brigitte Bardot)
SHALL WE DANCE (37) Irene
SHANE (53) Head
SHANGHAI EXPRESS (32) Banton
SHANGHAI GESTURE, THE (41) Royer (for Ona Munson), Cassini (for Gene Tierney)
SHANGHAI MADNESS (33) Kaufman

SHANGHAI STORY, THE (54) Palmer
SHARPSHOOTERS (38) Herschel
SHE (35) Bernstein
SHE (64) Toms
SHE COULDN'T SAY NO (53) Orry-Kelly, Woulfe
SHE DEVIL, THE (57) Koch
SHED NO TEARS (48) Anthony
SHEEPMAN, THE (58) Plunkett
SHE GETS HER MAN (44) V West
SHE GOT HER MAN=MAISIE GOT HER MAN
SHE HAD TO EAT (37) Herschel
SHE HAD TO SAY YES (33) Orry-Kelly
SHEIK STEPS OUT, THE (37) Eloise
SHE KNEW WHAT SHE WANTED (36) *Jill Casson*
SHE LEARNED ABOUT SAILORS (34) Royer
SHE LOVED A FIREMAN (37) Shoup
SHE MARRIED A COP (39) Palmer
SHE MARRIED AN ARTIST (37) Kalloch
SHENANDOAH (65) Odell
SHE PLAYED WITH FIRE=FORTUNE IS A WOMAN
SHERIFF OF FRACTURED JAW, THE (58) Harris
SHERLOCK HOLMES (32) Kaufman
SHERLOCK HOLMES (39)=ADVENTURES OF SHERLOCK HOLMES, THE
SHERLOCK HOLMES AND THE SPIDER WOMAN (43) V West
SHERLOCK JNR (24) C West
SHE'S BACK ON BROADWAY (52) Shoup
SHE'S FOR ME (43) V West
SHE'S WORKING HER WAY THROUGH COLLEGE (52) Travilla, Best
SHE WAS A LADY (34) Lambert
SHE WENT TO THE RACES (45) Irene
SHE WROTE THE BOOK (46) V West
SHINE ON HARVEST MOON (43) Anderson
SHINING HOUR, THE (38) Adrian
SHINING VICTORY (41) Shoup
SHIP COMES IN, A (28) Adrian
SHIP FROM SHANGHAI, THE (30) Greer
SHIPMATES FOREVER (35) Orry-Kelly
SHIP OF FOOLS (65) Thomas (Louis for Vivien Leigh)
SHIPS WITH WINGS (41) *Digby Morton, Lachasse, Maison Arthur, Molyneux, Hartnell, Peter Russell, Victor Stiebel, Dorothy Broomham*
SHIP THAT DIED OF SHAME, THE (55) Mendleson
SHIRALEE, THE (56) Haffenden
SHOCK (45) Nelson
SHOCKING MISS PILGRIM, THE (46) Orry-Kelly
SHOCKPROOF (48) Louis
SHOCK TREATMENT (63) Mabry
SHOES OF THE FISHERMAN, THE (68) *Orietta Nasalli-Rocca*
SHOOT-OUT AT MEDICINE BEND (56) Best
SHOPWORN ANGEL, THE (38) Adrian
SHORT CUT TO HELL (57) Head
SHOT IN THE DARK, A (41) Anderson
SHOT IN THE DARK, A (64) M Furse
SHOULD HUSBANDS WORK? (39) Palmer
SHOULD LADIES BEHAVE? (33) Adrian
SHOW, THE (27) Coulter
SHOWBOAT (36) Zinkeisen, V West
SHOW BOAT (51) Plunkett
SHOW BUSINESS (44) Stevenson
SHOWDOWN AT ABILENE (56) Odell
SHOW GIRL (28) Ree
SHOW GOES ON, THE (37) Mann
SHOW PEOPLE (28) Frazer
SH! THE OCTOPUS (37) Mackenzie
SHUTTERED ROOM, THE (66) *Caroline Mott* (*Hylan Baker* for Carol Lynley)
SIDE STREET (29) Ree
SIDE STREETS (34) Orry-Kelly
SIDEWALKS OF LONDON=ST MARTIN'S LANE
SIEGE AT RED RIVER, THE (53) Renie *wd* LeMaire
SIERRA (50) Wood
SIGN OF THE CROSS, THE (32) Banton
SIGN OF THE PAGAN (54) Thomas
SIGN OF THE RAM, THE (47) Louis
SIGNPOST TO MURDER (64) Travilla
SILENCERS, THE (65) Mabry
SILENT BATTLE, The (39) *Rahvis*
SILENT DUST (48) Ricardo (for Sally Gray and Beatrice Campbell), *Rahvis* (for Maria Vahr)
SILENT VOICE, THE=PAULA (52)
SILENT WATCHER, THE (24) *Eve Roth*
SILENT WITNESS, THE (31) Duty
SILK EXPRESS, THE (33) Orry-Kelly
SILK HAT KID (35) Luza
SILK STOCKINGS (57) Rose
SILVER CHALICE, THE (54) *Rolf Gerard*
SILVER DOLLAR (32) Orry-Kelly
SILVER LODE (54) Wakeling
SILVER RIVER (48) Travilla (for Anne Sheridan) *m* Best
SILVER STREAK, THE (34) Plunkett

SILVER WHIP, THE (52) Stevenson *wd* LeMaire
SIMBA (54) *Doris Lee*
SIMON AND LAURA (55) Harris
SINBAD THE SAILOR (46) Stevenson
SINFUL DAVY (68) M Furse
SING A JINGLE (43) V West
SING AND BE HAPPY (37) Herschel
SING AND LIKE IT (34) Plunkett
SINGAPORE (47) Woulfe
SING AS YOU SWING (37) *Renee Granville*
SING, BABY, SING (36) Royer
SINGER NOT THE SONG, THE (60) Caffin
SINGING KID, THE (35) Orry-Kelly
SINGING MARINE, THE (37) Orry-Kelly
SINGING SHERIFF, THE (44) V West
SINGIN' IN THE RAIN (51) Plunkett
SINGLE MAN, A (28) Adrian
SINGLE STANDARD, A (29) Adrian
SING ME A LOVE SONG (36) Anderson
SING, NEIGHBOUR, SING (44) Palmer
SING YOUR WAY HOME (45) Renie
SING YOUR WORRIES AWAY (41) Renie
SINNERS IN LOVE (28) Plunkett
SINNERS IN PARADISE (38) V West
SINNERS IN THE SUN (32) Banton
SINNER TAKES ALL (36) Tree
SIN OF ABBY HUNT=SONG OF SURRENDER
SIN OF MADELON CLAUDET, THE (31) Adrian
SINS OF MAN (36) Royer
SINS OF RACHEL CADE, THE (60) Best
SINS OF THE CHILDREN (30) Cox
SIN TAKES A HOLIDAY (30) Wakeling
SIOUX BLOOD (29) Coulter
SIOUX CITY SUE (46) Palmer
SIS HOPKINS (41) Palmer
SISTER KENNY (46) Banton
SISTERS, THE (38) Orry-Kelly
SISTERS UNDER THE SKIN (34) Kalloch
SITTING PRETTY (47) Nelson *wd* LeMaire
SIX BRIDGES TO CROSS (54) J Morley
SIX HOURS TO LIVE (32) Cox
SIX THOUSAND ENEMIES (39) Tree
SIXTY GLORIOUS YEARS (38) Zinkeisen, *Tom Heslewood*
SKIDOO (68) *Rudi Gernreich*
SKI PATROL (40) V West
SKIRTS AHOY (52) Rose
SKULLDUGGERY (69) Head
SKY GIANT (38) Renie
SKYLARK (41) Head
SKYSCRAPER (28) Adrian
SKY'S THE LIMIT, THE (37) Hubert
SKY'S THE LIMIT, THE (43) Renie
SLATTERY'S HURRICANE (49) Nelson
SLAUGHTER ON TENTH AVENUE (57) Thomas
SLAVE GIRL (47) Wood
SLAVE GIRLS (66) Toms
SLAVE SHIP (37) Royer
SLEEPERS EAST (34) Royer
SLEEPING CITY, THE (50) Odell
SLENDER THREAD, THE (65) Head
SLEUTH (73) Furness
SLIDE, KELLY, SLIDE (27) Andre-Ani
SLIGHT CASE OF MURDER, A (37) Shoup
SLIGHTLY FRENCH (48) Louis
SLIGHTLY HONORABLE (39) Banton
SLIGHTLY SCANDALOUS (46) *s* V West
SLIGHTLY SCARLET (56) Koch
SLIGHTLY TERRIFIC (44) V West
SLIM CARTER (57) Thomas
SLIPPER AND THE ROSE, THE (75) Harris
SLIPPY McGEE (47) *s* Palmer
SMALLEST SHOW ON EARTH, THE (57) Mendleson
SMALL TOWN DEB (41) Herschel
SMALL TOWN GIRL (36) Tree
SMALL TOWN GIRL (52) Rose
SMALL TOWN LAWYER=MAIN STREET LAWYER
SMART BLONDE (36) Anderson
SMARTEST GIRL IN TOWN (36) B Newman
SMART SET, THE (27) Cox
SMART WOMAN (47) Adrian
SMARTY (34) Orry-Kelly
SMASHING BIRD I USED TO KNOW, THE (68) *Riki Reed*
SMASHING THE MONEY RING (39) Anderson
SMASHING TIME (67) Myers
SMILING GHOST, THE (41) Rhodes
SMILING IRISH EYES (29) Stevenson
SMILIN' THROUGH (32) Adrian
SMOKE SIGNAL (54) Thomas
SMOKY (33) Royer
SMOOTH AS SILK (45) V West
SMUGGLED CARGO (39) Palmer
SMUGGLERS, THE=MAN WITHIN, THE
SMUGGLERS' ISLAND (51) Thomas
SNAKE PIT, THE (48) Cashin *wd* LeMaire
SNOWBOUND (47) Ellacott
SNOWS OF KILIMANJARO, THE (52) LeMaire
SNOB, THE (24) Wachner
SNOWED UNDER (35) Orry-Kelly

SNOW WHITE AND THE THREE CLOWNS
=SNOW WHITE AND THE THREE
STOOGES
SNOW WHITE AND THE THREE STOOGES
(61) Renie
SO BIG (32) Orry-Kelly
SO BIG (53) Anderson, Shoup
SO BRIGHT THE FLAME=GIRL IN WHITE,
THE
SOCIETY GIRL (32) Cox
SOCIETY LAWYER (39) Tree
SO EVIL MY LOVE (48) *Sophie Harris* (Head for
Ann Todd and Geraldine Fitzgerald)
SOFIA (48) *Don Loper*
SOFT BEDS, HARD BATTLES (74) Furness
SO GOES MY LOVE (46) Banton, V West
SOLDIER AND THE LADY, THE (36) Plunkett
SOLDIER OF FORTUNE (55) LeMaire
SOLDIERS THREE (50) Plunkett
SOLID GOLD CADILLAC, THE (56) Louis
SOLITAIRE MAN, THE (33) Adrian
SO LITTLE TIME (51) Harris
SOL MADRID (67) Mabry
SO LONG AT THE FAIR (50) Haffenden
SOMBRERO (52) Rose
SOMEBODY LOVES ME (52) Head
SOME CAME RUNNING (58) Plunkett
SOME GIRLS DO (68) Caffin, *Clive of London*
SOME KIND OF A NUT (69) Sylbert
SOME LIKE IT HOT (58) Orry-Kelly
SOMETHING ALWAYS HAPPENS (34) *Louis
Brooks*
SOMETHING FOR THE BIRDS (52) Jenssen *wd*
LeMaire
SOMETHING FOR THE BOYS (44) Nelson,
Wood
SOMETHING IN THE WIND (47) Orry-Kelly
SOMETHING MONEY CAN'T BUY (52) Harris
SOMETHING OF VALUE (56) Rose
SOMETHING TO LIVE FOR (51) Head
SOMETHING TO THINK ABOUT (20) C West
SOMETIMES A GREAT NOTION (71) Head
SOMEWHERE I'LL FIND YOU (42) Kalloch
SOMEWHERE IN THE NIGHT (46) Nelson
SONG AND DANCE MAN, THE (35) Lambert
SONG IS BORN, A (48) Sharaff
SONG OF BERNADETTE, THE (43) Hubert
SONG OF KENTUCKY, A (29) Wachner
SONG OF LOVE, THE (23) C West
SONG OF LOVE (47) Plunkett *s* Irene *m* Valles
SONG OF MY HEART (47) Maclean
SONG OF SCHEHERAZADE (46) Wood
SONG OF SONGS (33) Banton
SONG OF SURRENDER (49) Dodson
SONG OF THE CITY (37) Tree
SONG OF THE FLAME (30) Stevenson
SONG OF THE THIN MAN (47) Irene, Barker
SONG O' MY HEART (29) Wachner
SONG TO REMEMBER, A (44) Plunkett (Banton
for Merle Oberon)
SON OF ALI BABA (52) Odell
SON OF A SAILOR (33) Orry-Kelly
SON OF DRACULA (43) V West
SON OF FLUBBER (62) Thomas
SON OF FRANKENSTEIN (38) V West
SON OF FURY (41) Wakeling
SON OF LASSIE (45) *s* Irene
SON OF SINBAD (53) Woulfe
SONS AND LOVERS (60) M Furse
SONS OF KATIE ELDER, THE (65) Head
SONS OF THE MUSKETEERS=AT SWORD'S
POINT
SOPHIE LANG GOES WEST (37) Banton, Head
SO RED THE ROSE (35) Banton
SORORITY HOUSE (39) Stevenson
SORRELL & SON (33) *Geene Glenny*
SORROWFUL JONES (48) Dodson
SORRY, WRONG NUMBER (48) Head
SO'S YOUR UNCLE (43) V West
SO THIS IS COLLEGE? (29) Frazer
SO THIS IS LONDON (30) Wachner
SO THIS IS LOVE (53) Rhodes
SO THIS IS NEW YORK (48) Jenssen
SO THIS IS PARIS (54) Odell
SOUL MATES (25) Andre-Ani
SOULS AT SEA (37) Head
SOUND OF MUSIC, THE (64) Jeakins
SOUTHERN MAID, A (33) Hartnell
SOUTHERN STAR, THE (69) Caffin
SOUTHERN YANKEE, A (48) Valles
SOUTH OF ALGIERS (52) Harris
SOUTH OF DIXIE (44) V West
SOUTH OF ST LOUIS (48) Anderson
SOUTH PACIFIC (57) Jeakins
SOUTH PACIFIC TRAIL (52) *s* Palmer
SOUTH SEA ROSE (29) Wachner
SOUTH SEA SINNER (49) Orry-Kelly
SOUTH SEA WOMAN (53) Mabry
SOUTH TO KARANGA (40) V West
SOUTHWEST TO SONORA=APPALOOSA,
THE
SO WELL REMEMBERED (47) *Honoria Plesch*
(Renie for Martha Scott)
SOYLENT GREEN (72) *Pat Barto*
SPANISH DANCER, THE (23) Greer
SPANISH GARDENER, THE (56) M Furse
SPANISH MAIN, THE (45) Stevenson

SPARTACUS (59) Valles (Thomas for Jean Sim-
mons)
SPAWN OF THE NORTH (38) Head
SPEAKEASY (28) Wachner
SPECIAL INVESTIGATOR (36) Stevenson
SPECTRE OF THE ROSE (46) Palmer
SPEED TO BURN (38) Myron
SPEEDWAY (29) Cox
SPELLBINDER, THE (39) Renie
SPELLBOUND (40) *Worth Ltd*
SPELLBOUND (45) Greer (Dream sequence by
Salvador Dali)
SPELL OF AMY NUGENT, THE=SPELL-
BOUND (40)
SPENCER'S MOUNTAIN (62) Best
SPENDTHRIFT (36) Taylor
SPIDER, THE (45) Hubert
SPIDER AND THE FLY, THE (49) Haffenden
SPIDER WOMAN=SHERLOCK HOLMES
AND THE SPIDER WOMAN
SPIRIT OF THE PEOPLE=ABE LINCOLN IN
ILLINOIS
SPIRITUALIST, THE (48) Ehren
SPITE MARRIAGE (28) Cox
SPLENDOR (35) Kiam
SPLINTERS (37) *Morris Angel*
SPLIT SECOND (52) Woulfe
SPIRAL ROAD, THE (62) Odell
SPITFIRE (33) Plunkett
SPLENDOR IN THE GRASS (61) Johnstone
SPOILERS, THE (42) V West
SPOILERS, THE (55) Thomas
SPOILERS OF THE WEST (27) Coulter
SPORTING CHANCE, A (45) Palmer
SPORTING VENUS, THE (25) Chaffin
SPRING FEVER (27) Cox
SPRING MADNESS (38) Tree
SPRING PARADE (40) V West
SPRINGTIME IN THE ROCKIES (42) Luick
SPRINGTIME IN THE SIERRAS (47) Palmer
SPRINGTIME FOR HENRY (34) Kaufman
SPRING TONIC (35) Hubert
SPY HUNT (50) Thomas
SPYLARKS=INTELLIGENCE MEN, THE
SPY SHIP (42) Anderson
SPY WHO CAME IN FROM THE COLD, THE
(65) Motley
SPY WITH A COLD NOSE, THE (66) Blake
SQUADRON OF HONOUR (38) Kalloch
SQUARE JUNGLE, THE (55) Odell
SQUARE PEG, THE (58) Caffin
SQUARE RING, THE (53) Mendleson
STAGECOACH (38) Plunkett
STAGE DOOR (37) King
STAGE FRIGHT (49) Anderson (for Jane Wyman),
Dior (for Marlene Dietrich)
STAGE MOTHER (33) Adrian
STAGE STRUCK (36) Orry-Kelly
STAGE STRUCK (58) Johnstone
STAIRWAY TO HEAVEN=MATTER OF LIFE
AND DEATH, A
STALKING MOON, THE (68) Jeakins
STALLION ROAD (46) Anderson, Rhodes
STAMBOUL QUEST (34) Tree
STAND AND DELIVER (28) Adrian
STAND AT APACHE RIVER, THE (53) Thomas
STAND-IN (37) Taylor
STANDING ROOM ONLY (43) Head
STAND UP AND BE COUNTED (72) Mabry
STAND UP AND CHEER (34) Kaufman
STAND UP AND FIGHT (38) Tree *m* Valles
STANLEY AND LIVINGSTONE (39) Royer
STAR! (68) Brooks
STAR, THE (52) Orry-Kelly
STAR DUST (40) Wakeling
STAR FOR A NIGHT (36) Herschel
STAR IN THE DUST (56) J Morley
STAR IS BORN, A (37) Kiam
STAR IS BORN, A (53) Louis, Nyberg ("Born in a
Trunk" by Sharaff)
STARLIFT (51) Rhodes
STAR OF MIDNIGHT (35) B Newman
STARS AND STRIPES FOREVER (52) Jeakins *wd*
LeMaire
STARS ARE SINGING, THE (52) Head
STARS OVER BROADWAY (35) Orry-Kelly
STAR SPANGLED RHYTHM (42) Head
START CHEERING (38) Kalloch
STATE FAIR (32) Kaufman
STATE FAIR (45) Hubert
STATE FAIR (61) Best
STATE OF THE UNION (47) Irene
STATE SECRET (48) Dawson
STATION WEST (48) Renie
STAZIONE TERMINI (53) Dior
STEEL TOWN (51) Thomas
STELLA (50) Stevenson *wd* LeMaire
STELLA DALLAS (37) Kiam
STEP BY STEP (46) Renie
STEP LIVELY (44) Stevenson
STEP LIVELY, JEEVES! (37) Herschel
STEPPING SISTERS (31) Tree
STEPPIN' IN SOCIETY (45) Palmer
STILETTO (69) Colt (*Stavropoulos* for Britt
Ekland)
STING, THE (75) Head
STINGAREE (34) Plunkett

STOLEN BRIDE, THE (27) Ree
STOLEN HOLIDAY (36) Orry-Kelly
STOLEN HOURS (63) Dawson (*Fabiani* for Susan
Hayward)
STOLEN LIFE, A (46) Orry-Kelly
STOP, LOOK AND LOVE (39) Myron
STOP ME BEFORE I KILL YOU=FULL
TREATMENT, THE
STOPOVER TOKYO (57) LeMaire
STOP PRESS GIRL (49) *Pearl Falconer*
STOP THE WORLD—I WANT TO GET OFF
(66) *Kiki Byrne*
STOP, YOU'RE KILLING ME (52) Shoup
STORM AT DAYBREAK (33) Adrian
STORM OVER BENGAL (38) Saltern
STORMY WEATHER (35) Strassner, *Marianne*
STORMY WEATHER (43) Rose
STORY OF ALEXANDER GRAHAM BELL,
THE (39) Royer
STORY OF DR ERLICH'S MAGIC BULLET,
THE (39) Shoup
STORY OF DR WASSELL, THE (44) Visart
STORY OF ESTHER COSTELLO, THE (57)
Harris (Louis for Joan Crawford)
STORY OF LOUIS PASTEUR, THE (35) Ander-
son
STORY OF MANKIND, THE (57) Best
STORY OF MOLLY X, THE (49) Odell
STORY OF ROBIN HOOD AND HIS MERRY
MEN, THE (51) *Michael Whittaker s* Caffin
STORY OF SEABISCUIT, THE (49) Rhodes
STORY OF THREE LOVES, THE (52) Rose
STORY OF VERNON AND IRENE CASTLE,
THE (38) Plunkett, Stevenson, Irene Castle
STORY OF WILL ROGERS, THE (52) Anderson
STOWAWAY (36) Royer
STRAIGHT IS THE WAY (34) Tree
STRAIGHT, PLACE AND SHOW (38) Wakeling
STRANDED (35) Orry-Kelly
STRANDED IN PARIS=ARTISTS AND MOD-
ELS ABROAD
STRANGE ADVENTURE, A (56) Palmer
STRANGE AFFAIR (44) Louis
STRANGE AFFAIR OF UNCLE HARRY, THE
(45) Banton
STRANGE ALIBI (41) Shoup
STRANGE CARGO (39) Adrian
STRANGE CASE OF DR X, THE (42) V West
STRANGE CASE OF MARY PAGE, THE (16)
Lucille
STRANGE CONFESSION (45) V West
STRANGE DEATH OF ADOLF HITLER, THE
(43) V West
STRANGE DOOR, THE (51) Odell
STRANGE LADY IN TOWN (55) Santiago
STRANGE LOVE OF MARTHA IVERS, THE
(45) Head
STRANGER, THE (46) Woulfe
STRANGER AT MY DOOR (56) Palmer
STRANGER ON THE THIRD FLOOR (40)
Renie
STRANGERS IN THE NIGHT (44) Palmer
STRANGERS MAY KISS (31) Adrian
STRANGERS ON A HONEYMOON (36)
Molyneux
STRANGERS ON A TRAIN (51) Rhodes
STRANGER'S RETURN, THE (33) Adrian
STRANGERS WHEN WE MEET (60) Louis
STRANGER WALKED IN, A=LOVE FROM A
STRANGER
STRANGE TRIANGLE (46) LeMaire
STRANGE WIVES (34) V West
STRANGE WOMAN, THE (46) Visart
STRATEGIC AIR COMMAND (54) Head
STRATTON STORY, THE (49) Rose
STRAWBERRY BLONDE, THE (40) Orry-Kelly
STRAWBERRY ROAN (45) *Lorain and Colin Beck*
STREET BANDITS (51) Palmer
STREETCAR NAMED DESIRE, A (51) Ballard
STREET GIRL (29) Ree
STREET OF CHANCE (30) Banton
STREET OF MEMORIES (40) Herschel
STREET SINGER, THE (37) *David Kidd*
STREETS OF SAN FRANCISCO (49) Palmer
STREET WITH NO NAME, THE (48) Nelson *wd*
LeMaire
STRICTLY DISHONOURABLE (51) Rose
STRICTLY DYNAMITE (34) Plunkett
STRICTLY UNCONVENTIONAL (30) Cox
STRIKE ME PINK (35) Kiam
STRIKE UP THE BAND (40) Tree *m* Steele
STRIP, THE (51) Rose
STRIPPER, THE (62) Travilla
STRIPTEASE LADY=LADY OF BURLESQUE
STRONGER THAN DESIRE (39) Tree
STUDENT PRINCE, THE (54) Rose *m* Plunkett
STUDIO ROMANCE=TALENT SCOUT
STUDY IN TERROR, A (65) Motley
SUBJECT WAS ROSES, THE (68) van Runkle
SUBMARINE D-1 (37) Shoup
SUBMARINE PATROL (38) Wakeling
SUBMARINE ZONE (41) Irene
SUBTERRANEANS, THE (60) Mabry
SUCH GOOD FRIENDS (71) *Hope Bryce Preming-
er*, Talsky
SUCH IS THE LAW (30) *Reville*, Hartnell, *Elspeth
Fox-Pitt*

SUCH MEN ARE DANGEROUS (29) Wachner
SUDAN (44) V West
SUDDEN FEAR (52) O'Brien
SUDDENLY IT'S SPRING (46) Dodson
SUDDENLY LAST SUMMER (60) Ellacott (Louis for Elizabeth Taylor, Hartnell for Katherine Hepburn), Messe¹
SUDDEN MONEY (38) Head
SUED FOR LIBEL (39) Renie
SUEZ (38) Royer
SUICIDE SQUADRON=DANGEROUS MOONLIGHT
SULLIVANS, THE (43) Hubert
SULLIVAN'S TRAVELS (41) Head
SUMMER AND SMOKE (61) Head
SUMMER HOLIDAY (47) Plunkett s Irene
SUMMER HOLIDAY (63) David Gibbs Fashion Group—co-ordinator Cynthia Tingey
SUMMER MAGIC (63) Thomas
SUMMER STOCK (50) Plunkett (Rose for Gloria de Haven)
SUMMER WISHES, WINTER DREAMS (73) Johnstone
SUN ALSO RISES, THE (57) LeMaire (Fontana Sisters of Rome for Ava Gardner)
SUNBONNET SUE (45) Maclean
SUN COMES UP, THE (48) Irene
SUNDAY, BLOODY SUNDAY (71) Rickards
SUNDAY DINNER FOR A SOLDIER (44) Nelson
SUNDAY IN NEW YORK (63) Orry-Kelly
SUNDOWN (41) Plunkett
SUNDOWNERS, THE (60) Haffenden, Joan Bridge
SUN NEVER SETS, THE (39) V West
SUNNY SIDE UP (29) Wachner
SUNRISE AT CAMPOBELLO (60) Best
SUNSET BOULEVARD (50) Head
SUN SHINES BRIGHT, THE (53) Palmer
SUNSHINE SUSIE (31) Conway
SUN VALLEY SERENADE (41) Banton
SUPERNATURAL (33) Banton
SUPER SLEUTH (37) Stevenson
SURRENDER (31) Duty
SURRENDER (50) Palmer
SUSAN AND GOD (40) Adrian
SUSAN LENOX, HER FALL AND RISE (31) Adrian
SUSAN SLADE (61) Shoup
SUSAN SLEPT HERE (54) Woulfe
SUSPECT, THE (44) V West
SUSPENSE (45) Kalloch
SUSPICION (41) Stevenson
SUZY (36) Tree
SWAMP WATER (41) Wakeling
SWAN, THE (56) Rose
SWANEE RIVER (39) Royer
SWEEPSTAKES WINNER (39) Anderson
SWEET ADELINE (34) Orry-Kelly
SWEET ALOES=GIVE ME YOUR HEART
SWEET AND LOWDOWN (44) Wood
SWEET BIRD OF YOUTH (61) Orry-Kelly
SWEET CHARITY (68) Head
SWEETHEARTS (38) Adrian
SWEETHEARTS AND WIVES (30) Stevenson
SWEETHEARTS ON PARADE (53) Palmer
SWEET MUSIC (34) Orry-Kelly
SWEET NOVEMBER (67) Roth
SWEET ROSIE O'GRADY (43) Hubert
SWEET SMELL OF SUCCESS (57) Grant
SWELL GUY (46) Wood
SWIMMER, THE (68) Johnstone
SWINGER, THE (66) Head
SWING HIGH (30) Wakeling
SWING HIGH, SWING LOW (36) Banton
SWINGING PEARL MYSTERY, THE=PLOT THICKENS, THE
SWINGIN' ON A RAINBOW (45) Palmer
SWING OUT SISTER (45) V West
SWING SHIFT MAISIE (43) Irene
SWING, SISTER, SWING (38) V West
SWING, TEACHER, SWING=COLLEGE SWING
SWING THAT CHEER (38) V West
SWINGTIME (36) B Newman (Harkrider for "Bojangles" costumes and Silver Sandal set)
SWINGTIME JOHNNY (43) V West
SWING YOUR LADY (37) Shoup
SWISS FAMILY ROBINSON, THE (39) Stevenson
SWISS FAMILY ROBINSON (60) Harris
SWORD IN THE STONE, THE (63) Valles
SWORD OF MONTE CRISTO (51) Norma
SWORDSMAN, THE (47) Louis
SWORN ENEMY (36) Tree
SYLVIA (64) Head
SYLVIA SCARLET (35) King (for Katharine Hepburn), B Newman (for Natalie Paley)
SYNCOPATION (42) Stevenson

TAILSPIN (38) Wakeling
TAKE A CHANCE (33) LeMaire
TAKE A GIANT STEP (59) Thomas
TAKE A LETTER, DARLING (42) Irene (for Rosalind Russell), Mitchell Leisen (for Constance Moore)
TAKE CARE OF MY LITTLE GIRL (51) Travilla

wd LeMaire
TAKE HER, SHE'S MINE (63) Travilla
TAKE IT OR LEAVE IT (44) Nelson
TAKE ME OUT TO THE BALL GAME (48) Rose m Valles
TAKE ME TO TOWN (53) Thomas
TAKE MY LIFE (46) Ricardo
TAKE MY TIP (37) Strassner
TAKE ONE FALSE STEP (49) Orry-Kelly
TAKING OF PELHAM ONE TWO THREE, THE (74) Johnstone
TALENT SCOUT (37) Shoup
TALE OF TWO CITIES, A (35) Tree
TALES OF HOFFMAN, THE (51) Hein Heckroth
TALES OF MANHATTAN (42) Irene, Tree, B Newman, Wakeling, Cassini
TALK ABOUT JACQUELINE (42) Jacqmar
TALK OF THE TOWN, THE (42) Irene
TALL, DARK AND HANDSOME (40) Banton
TALL MEN, THE (55) Travilla wd LeMaire
TAMAHINE (63) Harris (Guy Laroche for Nancy Kwan)
TAMING OF THE SHREW, THE (66) Danilo Donati (Sharaff for Richard Burton and Elizabeth Taylor)
TAMMY AND THE DOCTOR (62) Odell
TAMMY, TELL ME TRUE (61) Odell
TAMPICO (44) Wood
TANGANYIKA (54) Odell
TANGIER (46) Banton
TAP ROOTS (48) Wood
TARANTULA (55) J Morley
TARGET FOR SCANDAL=WASHINGTON STORY
TARGET ZERO (55) Mabry
TARNISHED (49) Palmer
TARNISHED ANGEL (38) Renie
TARNISHED ANGELS, THE (57) Thomas
TARTU=ADVENTURES OF TARTU
TARZAN AND THE LOST SAFARI (57) Duse
TARZAN AND THE MERMAIDS (48) Norma
TARZAN'S NEW YORK ADVENTURE (42) Shoup
TASK FORCE (49) Rhodes
TATTERED DRESS, THE (56) J Morley
TAXI (52) Renie wd LeMaire
TAXI DANCER, THE (26) Andre-Ani
TAXI DRIVER (76) R Morley
TAXI MISTER (42) Royer
TAZA, SON OF COCHISE (53) J Morley
TEA AND SYMPATHY (56) Rose
TEA FOR THREE (27) Clark
TEA FOR TWO (50) Rhodes
TEENAGE CAVEMAN (58) Corso
TEENAGE REBEL (56) Wills wd LeMaire
TEHERAN (47) Rahvis
TELLING THE WORLD (28) Clark
TELL IT TO A STAR (45) s Palmer
TELL IT TO THE JUDGE (49) Louis
TELL NO TALES (39) Tree
TELL THEM WILLIE BOY IS HERE (69) Head
TEMPEST (28) O'Neill
TEMPTATION (46) Orry-Kelly
TEMPTRESS, THE (26) Andre-Ani, Ree
TEN COMMANDMENTS, THE (23) C West
TEN COMMANDMENTS, THE (54) Head, Ralph Jester, John Jenssen, Jeakins, Arnold Friberg
TENDER IS THE NIGHT (61) Best (Balmain for Jennifer Jones, Joan Fontaine and Jill St John)
TENDER TRAP, THE (55) Rose
$10 RAISE (35) Lillian
TEN GENTLEMEN FROM WEST POINT (42) Tree
TENNESSEE'S PARTNER (55) Wakeling
TEN NORTH FREDERICK (58) LeMaire
TEN TALL MEN (50) Louis
10TH AVENUE ANGEL (47) s Irene
TENTH AVENUE KID (38) Saltern
TEN THOUSAND BEDROOMS (56) Rose
TERMINAL MAN, THE (74) Novarese
TERM OF TRIAL (62) Dawson
TERROR, THE (63) Corso
TERROR ABOARD (33) Banton
TERROR AT MIDNIGHT (56) s Palmer
TERROR BY NIGHT (45) V West
TESHA (28) Reville Ltd
TESS OF THE STORM COUNTRY (32) Cox
TEST PILOT (38) Tree
TEXAS ACROSS THE RIVER (66) Odell, Colvig
TEXAS CARNIVAL (51) Rose
THANKS A MILLION (35) Lambert
THANKS FOR EVERYTHING (38) Wakeling
THANK YOU JEEVES (36) Herschel
THANK YOU, MR MOTO (37) Herschel
THANK YOUR LUCKY STARS (43) Anderson
THAT BRENNAN GIRL (46) Palmer
THAT CERTAIN AGE (38) V West
THAT CERTAIN FEELING (56) Head
THAT CERTAIN WOMAN (37) Orry-Kelly
THAT DARN CAT (65) Thomas
THAT FORSYTE WOMAN (49) Plunkett m Valles
THAT FUNNY FEELING (65) Louis

THAT GIRL FROM COLLEGE=SORORITY HOUSE
THAT GIRL FROM PARIS (36) Stevenson
THAT HAGEN GIRL (47) Travilla
THAT HAMILTON WOMAN=LADY HAMILTON
THAT I MAY LIVE (37) Herschel
THAT KIND OF WOMAN (58) Head
THAT LADY IN ERMINE (48) Hubert 'wd LeMaire
THAT MAN MR JONES=FULLER BRUSH MAN, THE
THAT MIDNIGHT KISS (49) Rose
THAT RIVIERA TOUCH (66) Duse
THAT'S MY GAL (47) Palmer
THAT NIGHT IN RIO (41) Banton
THAT NIGHT WITH YOU (45) V West
THAT'S A GOOD GIRL (33) Eileen Idare Ltd, Hartnell
THAT'S MY BOY (32) Kalloch
THAT'S MY BOY (51) Head
THAT'S RIGHT, YOU'RE WRONG (39) Stevenson
THAT'S THE SPIRIT (45) V West
THAT TOUCH OF MINK (62) Odell
THAT UNCERTAIN FEELING (41) Irene
THAT WAY WITH WOMEN (46) Rhodes
THAT WONDERFUL URGE (48) LeMaire (Cassini for Gene Tierney)
THEIR OWN DESIRE (29) Adrian
THEIR SECRET AFFAIR=TOP SECRET AFFAIR
THELMA JORDAN (49) Head
THEM! (53) Head
THEODORA GOES WILD (36) B Newman
THERE GOES MY GIRL (37) Stevenson
THERE GOES MY HEART (38) Irene
THERE GOES THE GROOM (37) Stevenson
THERE'S A GIRL IN MY SOUP (70) Vangie Harrison
THERE'S ALWAYS A WOMAN (37) Kalloch
THERE'S ALWAYS TOMORROW (54) J Morley
THERE'S NO BUSINESS LIKE SHOW BUSINESS (54) LeMaire, Travilla, White
THERE WAS A CROOKED MAN (70) Johnstone
THERE YOU ARE! (26) Kay, Marsh
THESE GLAMOUR GIRLS (39) Tree
THESE THOUSAND HILLS (58) LeMaire
THESE THREE (35) Kiam
THESE WILDER YEARS (56) Rose
THEY ALL COME OUT (39) Tree
THEY ALL KISSED THE BRIDE (42) Irene
THEY ASKED FOR IT (39) V West
THEY DARE NOT LOVE (41) Saltern
THEY DIED WITH THEIR BOOTS ON (41) Anderson
THEY DRIVE BY NIGHT (40) Anderson
THEY GOT ME COVERED (42) Adrian (Head for Dorothy Lamour)
THEY HAD TO SEE PARIS (29) Wachner
THEY KNEW WHAT THEY WANTED (40) Stevenson
THEY LEARNED ABOUT WOMEN (30) Cox
THEY LIVE BY NIGHT (48) Balkan
THEY MADE HER A SPY (39) Stevenson
THEY MADE ME A CRIMINAL (38) Anderson
THEY MET IN ARGENTINA (41) Stevenson
THEY MET IN A TAXI (36) Anthony
THEY MET IN BOMBAY (41) Adrian m Steele
THEY MIGHT BE GIANTS (70) Roth
THEY'RE OFF=STRAIGHT PLACE AND SHOW
THEY SHOOT HORSES, DON'T THEY? (69) Donfeld
THEY WANTED TO MARRY (36) Stevenson
THEY WERE SISTERS (45) Caffin
THEY WON'T BELIEVE ME (47) Stevenson
THIEF OF BAGDAD, THE (24) Mitchell Leisen (consultant Edward Knoblock)
THIEF OF BAGDAD, THE (40) Messel, Armstrong, Vertes
THIEVES' HIGHWAY (49) Nelson wd LeMaire
THING, THE (51) Woulfe
THINGS HAPPEN AT NIGHT (48) Dorothy Sinclair
THINGS TO COME (36) Armstrong, Hubert, Mann
THIN ICE (37) Royer
THINK FAST, MR MOTO (37) Herschel
THIN MAN, THE (34) Tree
THIN MAN GOES HOME, THE (44) s Irene a Herwood Keyes
THIRD DAY, THE (65) Brooks
THIRD FINGER, LEFT HAND (40) Tree
THIRD KEY, THE=LONG ARM, THE
13 RUE MADELEINE (46) Hubert
THIRTEENTH CHAIR, THE (29) Adrian
THIRTEENTH LETTER, THE (50) Stevenson wd LeMaire
THIRTY DAY PRINCESS (34) Greer
30 IS A DANGEROUS AGE, CYNTHIA (67) Bermans
THIRTY-NINE STEPS, THE (35) Strassner
THIRTY NINE STEPS, THE (58) Caffin
THIRTY SECONDS OVER TOKYO (44) Dean s Irene

THIRTY-SIX HOURS (64) Head
THIRTY SIX HOURS TO KILL (36) Herschel
THIS ABOVE ALL (42) Wakeling
THIS EARTH IS MINE (59) Thomas
THIS GUN FOR HIRE (42) Head
THIS ISLAND EARTH (55) Odell
THIS IS MY AFFAIR (37) Royer
THIS IS MY AFFAIR (51)=I CAN GET IT FOR YOU WHOLESALE
THIS IS MY STREET (63) Caffin
THIS IS THE ARMY (43) Orry-Kelly
THIS IS THE LIFE (35) Myron
THIS LAND IS MINE (42) Renie
THIS'LL MAKE YOU WHISTLE (37) *Kay Norton Glenny*
THIS LOVE OF OURS (45) V West (Banton for Merle Oberon)
THIS MAD WORLD (30) Adrian
THIS MAN IS MINE (46) *Dorothy Broomham*
THIS MAN REUTER=DISPATCH FROM REUTER, A
THIS MAN'S NAVY (45) s Irene a Dean
THIS MARRIAGE BUSINESS (38) Stevenson
THIS MODERN AGE (31) Adrian
THIS PROPERTY IS CONDEMNED (66) Head
THIS SPORTING LIFE (62) *Sophie Devine*
THIS THING CALLED LOVE (29) Wakeling
THIS THING CALLED LOVE (40) Irene
THIS TIME FOR KEEPS (47) s Irene m Valles
THIS WAS A WOMAN (47) *Dorothy Sinclair*
THIS WAY, PLEASE (37) Head
THIS WOMAN IS DANGEROUS (51) O'Brien
THIS WOMAN IS MINE (41) V West
THOMAS CROWN AFFAIR, THE (68) van Runkle
THOROUGHBREDS DON'T CRY (37) Tree
THOROUGHLY MODERN MILLIE (66) Louis
THOSE FANTASTIC FLYING FOOLS=JULES VERNE'S ROCKET TO THE MOON
THOSE MAGNIFICENT MEN IN THEIR FLYING MACHINES (65) *Osbert Lancaster, Diane Greet*
THOSE THREE FRENCH GIRLS (30) Hubert
THOUSAND AND ONE NIGHTS, A (45) Louis
THOUSANDS CHEER (43) s Irene
THOUSAND CLOWNS, A (65) R Morley
THOU SHALT NOT KILL (39) Palmer
THREE BITES OF THE APPLE (67) *Pino Lancetti of Rome*
THREE BLIND MICE (38) Wakeling
THREE BRAVE MEN (56) Balkan wd LeMaire
THREE CAME HOME (49) LeMaire
THREE CHEERS FOR THE IRISH (39) Anderson
THREE COCKEYED SAILORS=SAILORS THREE
THREE COINS IN THE FOUNTAIN (54) Jeakins wd LeMaire
THREE CORNERED MOON (33) Banton
THREE DARING DAUGHTERS (47) Irene, Barker
THREE FACES OF EVE (57) Renie wd LeMaire
THREE FACES WEST (40) Palmer
THREE FOR THE SHOW (54) Louis
THREE GODFATHERS, THE (35) Tree
THREE HATS FOR LISA (65) Caffin
THREE HEARTS FOR JULIA (42) s Irene
365 NIGHTS IN HOLLYWOOD (34) Royer
THREE LITTLE GIRLS IN BLUE (46) Cashin
THREE INTO TWO WON'T GO (69) Myers
THREE LITTLE SISTERS (44) s Palmer
THREE LITTLE WORDS (50) Rose
THREE LIVE GHOSTS (35) Tree
THREE LOVES HAS NANCY (38) Adrian
THREE MEN IN A BOAT (56) *Peter Rice*
THREE MEN IN WHITE (44) s Irene
THREE MEN ON A HORSE (36) Orry-Kelly
THREE MUSKETEERS, THE (35) Plunkett
THREE MUSKETEERS, THE (38) Royer
THREE MUSKETEERS, THE (48) Plunkett
THREE MUSKETEERS, THE (73) Blake, Talsky
THREE ON A COUCH (66) Mabry
THREE ON A HONEYMOON (34) Royer
THREE ON A MATCH (32) Orry-Kelly
THREE RING CIRCUS (54) Head
THREE'S A CROWD (45) Palmer
THREE SAILORS AND A GIRL (53) Mabry
THREE SECRETS (50) Rhodes
THREE SINNERS (28) Banton
THREE SISTERS (70) Dawson
THREE SMART GIRLS (36) Harkrider (also art supervision)
THREE SMART GIRLS GROW UP (38) V West
THREE SONS (39) Stevenson
THREE STRANGERS (45) Anderson
3.10 TO YUMA (57) Louis
THREE VIOLENT PEOPLE (56) Head
THREE WEEKS (23) Wachner
THREE WISE FOOLS (46) Valles s Irene
THREE WISE GUYS (36) Tree
THREE WORLDS OF GULLIVER, THE (60) Abbey
THREE YOUNG TEXANS (53) Travilla wd LeMaire
THRILL OF A LIFETIME (37) Head
THRILL OF A ROMANCE (45) s Irene a Dean
THRILL OF BRAZIL, THE (46) Louis

THRILL OF IT ALL, THE (63) Louis
THROUGH DIFFERENT EYES=THRU DIFFERENT EYES
THRU DIFFERENT EYES (29) Wachner
THUNDER ACROSS THE PACIFIC=WILD BLUE YONDER, THE
THUNDER AFLOAT (39) Tree m Valles
THUNDERBALL (65) Mendleson
THUNDER BAY (53) Odell
THUNDER BIRDS (42) Tree
THUNDERHEAD, SON OF FLICKA (44) Wood
THUNDER IN THE NIGHT (35) Myron
THUNDER IN THE SUN (58) LeMaire
THUNDER IN THE VALLEY (47) Behm wd LeMaire
THUNDER ON THE HILL (51) Thomas
THUNDER OVER ARIZONA (56) Palmer
THUNDER OVER THE PLAINS (53) Mabry
THUNDER ROCK (42) *Honoria Plesch*
TIARA TAHITI (62) Caffin
TICKET TO TOMAHAWK (50) Hubert wd LeMaire
TICKLE ME (65) Rhodes
TIDE OF EMPIRE (28) Cox
TIGER IN THE SKY=McCONNELL STORY, THE
TIGER IN THE SMOKE (56) Ellacott
TIGER MAKES OUT, THE (67) Sylbert
TIGER WOMAN, THE (46) Palmer
TIGER SHARK (32) Orry-Kelly
TIGHT LITTLE ISLAND=WHISKY GALORE
TIGHT SPOT (54) Louis
TILLIE THE TOILER (27) Andre-Ani
TILLIE THE TOILER (41) *Monica*
TILL THE CLOUDS ROLL BY (46) Rose s Irene m Valles
'TIL WE MEET AGAIN (40) Orry-Kelly
TIMBERJACK (54) Palmer
TIME FOR ACTION=TIP ON A DEAD JOCKEY
TIME FOR LOVING, A (71) *Rosine Delamare*
TIME OF THEIR LIVES, THE (46) Odell
TIME OUT FOR MURDER (38) Herschel
TIME OUT FOR ROMANCE (36) Herschel
TIME OUT FOR RHYTHM (41) Saltern
TIME OUT OF MIND (47) Banton
TIMES SQUARE LADY (34) Tree
TIMES SQUARE PLAYBOY (36) Orry-Kelly
TIME, THE COMEDIAN (25) Erte
TIME TO KILL (42) Herschel
TIME TO LOVE AND A TIME TO DIE, A (57) Thomas
TIN HATS (26) Andre-Ani
TIN PAN ALLEY (40) Banton
TIN STAR, THE (57) Head
TIP ON A DEAD JOCKEY (57) Rose
TITANIC (52) Jeakins wd LeMaire
TITFIELD THUNDERBOLT, THE (52) Mendleson
T MEN (47) Ehren
TOAST OF NEW ORLEANS (50) Rose m Plunkett
TOAST OF NEW YORK, THE (37) Stevenson
TOAST OF THE LEGION=KISS ME AGAIN
TO BEAT THE BAND (35) Plunkett
TO BE OR NOT TO BE (41) Irene
TO CATCH A THIEF (55) Head
TODAY WE LIVE (33) Adrian
TO DOROTHY A SON (54) Ellacott
TO EACH HIS OWN (46) Head
TO FIND A MAN (71) R Morley
TO HAVE AND HAVE NOT (44) Anderson
TO KILL A MOCKINGBIRD (62) Odell
TOKYO JOE (49) Louis
TOMAHAWK (50) Thomas
TOMAHAWK AND THE CROSS, THE=PILLARS OF THE SKY
TO MARY—WITH LOVE (36) Royer
TOM BROWN'S SCHOOLDAYS (40) Stevenson
TOM BROWN'S SCHOOLDAYS (51) Dawson
TOM, DICK AND HARRY (41) Renie
TOMMY (75) Russell
TOMORROW AT MIDNIGHT=FOR LOVE OR MONEY
TOMORROW IS ANOTHER DAY (51) Anderson
TOMORROW IS FOREVER (45) Louis
TOMORROW WE LIVE (42) *Rahvis*
TOM THUMB (58) Lehmann
TONIGHT IS OURS (32) Banton
TONIGHT OR NEVER (31) *Chanel*
TONIGHT WE SING (52) Renie wd LeMaire
TONY DRAWS A HORSE (50) Abbey
TONY ROME (67) Mabry, *Elinor Simmons*
TOO BUSY TO WORK (32) Luick
TOO HOT TO HANDLE (38) Tree
TOO LATE BLUES (61) Head
TOO LATE FOR TEARS (49) Palmer
TOO MANY BLONDES (41) V West
TOO MANY GIRLS (40) Stevenson
TOO MANY HUSBANDS (39) Irene
TOO MANY WIVES (37) Stevenson
TOOMORROW (70) *Ronald Paterson*
TOO MUCH, TOO SOON (58) Orry-Kelly
TOO YOUNG TO KISS (51) Rose
TO PARIS WITH LOVE (54) Caffin

TOPAZ (69) Head
TOP BANANA (53) Colt
TOP HAT (35) B Newman
TO PLEASE A LADY (50) Rose
TOP OF THE FORM (52) Ellacott
TOP O' THE MORNING (49) Dodson
TOPPER (37) Lange, Irene
TOPPER RETURNS (40) Royer
TOPPER TAKES A TRIP (38) Irene (for Constance Bennett), Kiam (for Billie Burke)
TOP SECRET AFFAIR (56) LeMaire
TORCH SINGER (33) Banton
TORCH SONG (53) Rose
TORCHY BLANE, THE ADVENTUROUS BLONDE (37) Shoup
TORCHY BLANE IN CHINATOWN (38) Shoup
TORCHY GETS HER MAN (38) Shoup
TORN CURTAIN (66) Head
TORRENT, THE (25) Kay, Marsh, Andre-Ani (Ree for Greta Garbo)
TORRID ZONE (40) Shoup
TO THE ENDS OF THE EARTH (47) Louis
TO THE SHORES OF TRIPOLI (41) Wakeling
TO THE VICTOR (47) Anderson
TOUCH AND GO (55) Mendleson
TOUCH OF CLASS, A (73) Myers
TOUCH OF EVIL (57) Thomas
TOVARICH (37) Orry-Kelly (Adrian for Claudette Colbert)
TOWARD THE UNKNOWN (56) Mabry
TOWERING INFERNO, THE (74) Zastupnevich
TOWER OF LONDON (39) V West
TOWN CALLED BASTARD, A (71) *Ossie Clark, Alice Pollack*
TOWN WENT WILD, THE (44) Karlice
TOYS IN THE ATTIC (63) Thomas
TOY TIGER (56) Odell
TOY WIFE, THE (38) Adrian m Steele
TRACK OF THE CAT (54) Wakeling
TRADE WINDS (38) Irene (for Joan Bennett), Taylor (for Ann Sothern)
TRAFFIC IN CRIME (46) Palmer
TRAILIN' WEST (36) Anderson
TRAIL OF '98, THE (28) Coulter
TRAIL OF THE LONESOME PINE (35) Taylor
TRAIL OF THE VIGILANTES (40) V West
TRAIL TO SAN ANTONE (46) Palmer
TRAIN OF EVENTS (49) Mendleson (Victor Stiebel for Valerie Hobson)
TRAIN TO ALCATRAZ (48) Palmer
TRANSATLANTIC MERRY-GO-ROUND (34) Wakeling
TRANSATLANTIC TUNNEL=TUNNEL, THE
TRAP, THE (66) M Furse
TRAVELLER'S JOY (50) Harris
TRAVELLING SALESLADY (34) Orry-Kelly
TRAVELLING SALESWOMAN, THE (49) Louis
TRAVELS WITH MY AUNT (72) *Anthony Powell* (Rangel for Maggie Smith)
TREASURE ISLAND (50) *Sheila Graham*
TREASURE OF THE GOLDEN CONDOR (52) Jeakins wd LeMaire
TREE GROWS IN BROOKLYN, A (44) Cashin
TREE OF LIBERTY, THE=HOWARDS OF VIRGINIA, THE
TRESPASSER, THE (47) Palmer
TRIAL OF BILLY JACK, THE (74) Mabry
TRIAL OF MARY DUGAN, THE (28) Adrian
TRIAL OF MARY DUGAN, THE (40) Tree
TRIAL OF PORTIA MERRIMAN=PORTIA ON TRIAL
TRIAL WITHOUT JURY (50) Palmer
TRIBUTE TO A BADMAN (55) Plunkett
TRILOGY (67) Johnstone
TRIO (50) Harris
TRIPLE DECEPTION=HOUSE OF SECRETS
TRIPOLI (50) Wood
TRIP TO PARIS, A (38) Myron
TROPICAL HEATWAVE (52) Palmer
TROPICANA=HEAT'S ON, THE
TROPIC HOLIDAY (38) Head
TROTTIE TRUE (49) Dawson
TROUBLE ALONG THE WAY (51) Mabry
TROUBLE IN PARADISE (32) Banton
TROUBLE WITH ANGELS (65) Colvig (Nun's habits by *Sybil Connolly*, who also designed for Hayley Mills)
TROUBLE WITH HARRY, THE (55) Head
TROUBLE WITH WIVES (25) Greer (for Florence Vidor, Esther Ralston), Banton
TROUBLE WITH WOMEN, THE (47) Head
TRUCK BUSTERS (42) Anderson
TRUE AS A TURTLE (56) Mendleson
TRUE CONFESSION (37) Banton
TRUE GRIT (68) Jeakins
TRUE TO LIFE (43) Head
TRUTH ABOUT WOMEN, THE (47) Beaton
TUDOR ROSE (36) Strassner
TULSA (48) Herschel
TUNNEL, THE (35) Schiaparelli, Strassner
TUNNEL OF LOVE, THE (58) Rose
TURNABOUT (40) Royer
TURN BACK THE CLOCK (33) Adrian
TURNED OUT NICE AGAIN (41) *Dorothy Broomham*

TURNING POINT, THE (52) Head
TURN THE KEY SOFTLY (53) Harris
TUXEDO JUNCTION (41) Palmer
TWELVE CROWDED HOURS (38) Renie
TWELVE MILES OUT (27) Hubert
TWENTY MILLION SWEETHEARTS (34) Orry-Kelly
TWENTY MULE TEAM (40) Tree m Steele
29 ACACIA AVENUE (44) Dorothy Sinclair
20,000 MEN IN A YEAR (39) Herschel
23½ HOURS LEAVE (37) Dorothy Beal
TWENTY THREE PACES TO BAKER STREET (56) Travilla wd LeMaire
TWENTY THOUSAND YEARS IN SING SING (32) Orry-Kelly
TWICE BLESSED (45) s Irene a Kay Carter
TWICE TOLD TALES (63) Corso
TWIN BEDS (42) Irene (for Joan Bennett), Hubert (for Glenda Farrell and Una Merkel)
TWINKLE IN GOD'S EYE, THE (55) Palmer
TWISTED NERVE (68) Hazel Graeme
TWISTED ROAD, THE=THEY LIVE BY NIGHT
TWIST OF FATE=BEAUTIFUL STRANGER, THE
TWO AGAINST THE WORLD (32) Orry-Kelly (for Helen Vinson), Hattie Carnegie (for Constance Bennett)
TWO BLACK SHEEP=TWO SINNERS
TWO-FACED WOMAN (41) Adrian
TWO-FISTED (35) Banton
TWO FISTED GENTLEMEN (36) Anthony
TWO FLAGS WEST (50) Nelson wd LeMaire
TWO FOR THE ROAD (66) Ken Scott, Michele Rosier, Mary Quant, Foale & Tuffin, Paco Rabanne for Audrey Hepburn (s Clare Rendelsham)
TWO FOR THE SEESAW (62) Orry-Kelly
TWO GIRLS AND A SAILOR (44) s Irene a Dean
TWO HEARTS IN WALTZ TIME (34) Louis Brooks
TWO GIRLS ON BROADWAY (40) Tree
TWO GUYS FROM MILWAUKEE (48) Rhodes
TWO GUYS FROM TEXAS (48) Rhodes, Travilla
TWO IN THE DARK (35) B Newman
TWO MRS CARROLLS, THE (47) Anderson (Head for Barbara Stanwyck)
TWO MULES FOR SISTER SARA (70) Colvig
TWO OF A KIND (51) Louis
TWO'S COMPANY (36) Hartnell
TWO SENORITAS=TWO SENORITAS FROM CHICAGO
TWO SENORITAS FROM CHICAGO (43) Travilla
TWO SINNERS (35) Lettie Lee
TWO SISTERS FROM BOSTON (45) Rose m Valles
TWO SMART PEOPLE (46) s Irene m Valles
TWO TEXAS KNIGHTS=TWO GUYS FROM TEXAS
TWO THOROUGHBREDS (39) Renie
TWO TICKETS TO LONDON (43) V West
TWO WEEKS IN ANOTHER TOWN (62) Balmain
TWO WEEKS WITH LOVE (50) Rose m Plunkett
TWO WISE MAIDS (36) Eloise
TWO YANKS IN TRINIDAD (42) Travilla
TYCOON (47) Woulfe

UGLY AMERICAN, THE (62) Odell
UNCONQUERED (47) Wakeling
UNDEFEATED, THE (69) Thomas
UNDER CAPRICORN (49) R Furse s Squire
UNDERCOVER MAISIE (47) Irene
UNDERCOVER MAN, THE (48) Louis
UNDERCOVER WOMAN, THE (46) Palmer
UNDERCURRENT (46) Irene
UNDER MY SKIN (49) LeMaire
UNDER PRESSURE (34) Lambert
UNDER-PUP (39) V West
UNDERSTANDING HEART, THE (27) Andre-Ani
UNDER THE BLACK EAGLE (28) Coulter
UNDER THE CLOCK=CLOCK, THE
UNDER THE GUN (50) Orry-Kelly
UNDER THE PAMPAS MOON (35) Hubert
UNDER THE RED ROBE (23) Urban Thurlow
UNDER THE RED ROBE (37) Hubert
UNDER THE YUM-YUM TREE (63) Donfeld
UNDERTOW (49) Orry-Kelly
UNDER TWO FLAGS (36) Wakeling
UNDERWATER (54) Woulfe
UNDER WESTERN STARS (38) Saltern
UNDER YOUR HAT (40) Strassner
UNDER YOUR SPELL (36) Herschel
UNEASY TERMS (48) Rahvis
UNEXPECTED FATHER (39) V West
UNFAITHFUL, THE (47) Travilla
UNFAITHFULLY YOURS (48) Cashin , wd LeMaire
UNFINISHED BUSINESS (41) V West (Greer for Irene Dunne)
UNFINISHED DANCE, THE (47) Rose s Irene
UNFORGIVEN (59) Jeakins
UNGUARDED HOUR, THE (36) Tree

UNGUARDED MOMENT, THE (56) J Morley
UNHOLY NIGHT, THE (29) Adrian
UNHOLY THREE, THE (30) Cox
UNINVITED, THE (43) Head
UNION DEPOT (31) Luick
UNION PACIFIC (39) Visart
UNKNOWN (27) Coulter
UNKNOWN MAN, THE (51) Rose
UNMASKED (49) Palmer
UNSINKABLE MOLLY BROWN, THE (63) Haack
UNSUSPECTED, THE (47) Anderson
UNTAMED (29) Adrian
UNTAMED (54) Renie wd LeMaire
UNTAMED FRONTIER (52) Thomas
UNTAMED HEIRESS (54) Palmer
UP GOES MAISIE (45) Irene
UP IN ARMS (43) White
UP IN CENTRAL PARK (48) Grant
UP IN MABEL'S ROOM (43) Nelson
UPPER WORLD (34) Orry-Kelly
UP SHE GOES=UP GOES MAISIE
UPSTAGE (26) Kay, Marsh, Andre-Ani
UPSTAIRS AND DOWNSTAIRS (59) Ellacott
UP THE CHASTITY BELT (71) Penny Lowe
UP THE DOWN STAIRCASE (67) Roth
UP THE FRONT (72) Zandra Rhodes
UP THE RIVER (30) Wachner
UP THE RIVER (38) Myron
UPTIGHT! (68) Aldredge
UP TO HIS NECK (54) Ellacott
UPTURNED GLASS, THE (47) Mattli
UTAH (44) Palmer

VACATION FROM LOVE (38) Adrian
VAGABOND KING, THE (30) Banton
VAGABOND KING, THE (55) Grant
VALACHI PAPERS, THE (72) Roth, Giorgio Desideri
VALENCIA (26) Andre-Ani
VALENTINO (50) Wakeling, Banton
VALIANT IS THE WORD FOR CARRIE (36) Banton
VALLEY OF DECISION, THE (45) s Irene a Herwood Keyes
VALLEY OF FURY=CHIEF CRAZY HORSE
VALLEY OF GWANGI, THE (69) Furness
VALLEY OF THE DOLLS (67) Travilla
VALLEY OF THE GIANTS (38) Anderson
VALLEY OF THE KINGS (54) Plunkett
VALLEY OF THE SUN (42) Stevenson
VALLEY OF THE ZOMBIES (46) Palmer
VALUE FOR MONEY (55) Harris
VANESSA=VANESSA, HER LOVE STORY
VANESSA, HER LOVE STORY (34) Tree
VANISHING AMERICAN, THE (55) Palmer
VANISHING VIRGINIAN, THE (41) Kalloch m Steele
VANITY (27) Adrian
VANQUISHED, THE (53) Head
VARIETY GIRL (47) Head (production gowns by Dorothy O'Hara, chorus by Waldo Angelo)
VARIETY SHOW (37) Shoup
VEILS OF BAGDAD, THE (53) Odell
VELVET TOUCH, THE (48) Banton
VENGEANCE OF SHE, THE (67) Toms
VENGEANCE VALLEY (50) Plunkett
VENUS MAKES TROUBLE (37) Kalloch
VERA CRUZ (54) Norma
VERDICT, THE (46) Travilla
VERTIGO (58) Head
VERY HONOURABLE GUY, A (34) Orry-Kelly
VERY SPECIAL FAVOUR, A (65) Yves St Laurent
VERY THOUGHT OF YOU, THE (44) Anderson
VICTORS, THE (63) Lehmann
VIGILANTES RETURN, THE (47) Odell
VIGIL IN THE NIGHT (39) Plunkett
VIKING QUEEN, THE (66) Furness
VILLAGE BARN DANCE (39) Palmer
VILLAGE OF DAUGHTERS (61) Haffenden
VILLAGE OF THE GIANTS (65) Rhodes
VINTAGE WINE (34) Louis Brooks
VIOLENCE (47) Maclean
VIOLENT MEN, THE (54) Louis
VIOLENT SATURDAY (55) Nelson wd LeMaire
VIPs, THE (63) Givenchy (for Elizabeth Taylor), Pierre Cardin
VIRGINIA CITY (39) Orry-Kelly
VIRGIN QUEEN, THE (55) Wills, LeMaire
VIRTUOUS WIVES (18) Lucille
VISIT, THE=BESUCH, DER
VISIT TO A SMALL PLANET (59) Head
VIVACIOUS LADY (37) B Newman, Irene
VIVA LAS VEGAS (55)=MEET ME IN LAS VEGAS
VIVA LAS VEGAS (64) Donfeld
VIVA, VILLA (34) Tree
VIVA ZAPATA! (51) Travilla wd LeMaire
VOGUES OF 1938 (37) Taylor
VOICE OF BUGLE ANN (35) Tree
VOICE OF SCANDAL=HERE COMES CARTER
VOICE OF THE TURTLE, THE (47) Rhodes
VOLGA BOATMAN, THE (26) Adrian

VOLTAIRE (33) Orry-Kelly
VOTE FOR HUGGETT (48) Caffin
VOYAGE TO THE BOTTOM OF THE SEA (61) Zastupnevich

WABASH AVENUE (50) LeMaire
WACO (66) Head
WAGONMASTER (50) Palmer
WAGONS ROLL AT NIGHT, THE (41) Anderson
WAGONS WESTWARD (40) Palmer
WAIKIKI WEDDING (36) Head
WAIT 'TIL THE SUN SHINES, NELLIE (52) Renie wd LeMaire
WAKE ME WHEN IT'S OVER (59) Thomas
WAKE OF THE RED WITCH (48) Palmer
WAKE UP AND DREAM (46) Hubert
WAKE UP AND LIVE (37) Wakeling
WALK, DON'T RUN (66) Haack
WALKING BACK (28) Adrian
WALKING DEAD, THE (35) Orry-Kelly
WALKING HILLS, THE (48) Louis
WALKING MY BABY BACK HOME (53) J Morley
WALKING ON AIR (36) B Newman
WALKING STICK, THE (70) Sue Yelland (Fonssagrives & Tiel for Samantha Eggar)
WALK IN THE SPRING RAIN, A (70) Donfeld
WALK ON THE WILD SIDE (61) LeMaire
WALK THE PROUD LAND (56) Thomas
WALLFLOWER (48) Rhodes
WALL OF NOISE (63) Shoup
WALLS OF JERICHO, THE (48) Nelson wd LeMaire
WALLS OF GOLD (33) Royer
WALTER WANGER'S VOGUES OF 1938=VOGUES OF 1938
WALTZ OF THE TOREADORS (61) Dawson
WANING SEX, THE (26) Kay, Marsh, Andre-Ani
WAR AGAINST MRS HADLEY, THE (42) Kalloch
WAR ARROW (53) Stevenson
WAR LORD, THE (65) Novarese
WARNING SHOT (66) Head
WAR OF THE WILDCATS=IN OLD OKLAHOMA
WAR OF THE WORLDS (52) Head
WARRIORS, THE=DARK AVENGERS, THE
WARRIOR'S HUSBAND, THE (33) Luick
WASHINGTON STORY (52) Rose
WATCH ON THE RHINE (43) Orry-Kelly
WATCH YOUR STERN (60) Ellacott
WATERFRONT (39) Anderson
WATERLOO BRIDGE (40) Irene m Steele
WATERLOO ROAD (44) Caffin
WAY DOWN EAST (20) (Prologue) Lucille (O'Kane Cromwell for Lillian Gish)
WAY DOWN EAST (35) Lambert
WAY OF A GAUCHO (52) Mario Vanarelli wd LeMaire
WAY OUT WEST (30) Cox
WAY TO THE GOLD, THE (57) Balkan wd LeMaire
WAY TO THE STARS, THE (45) Virginia Tucker
WAYWARD BUS, THE (57) Wills wd LeMaire
WAY . . . WAY OUT (66) Mabry
WAY WEST, THE (67) Koch
WAY WE WERE, THE (73) Jeakins, Mabry
WE ARE NOT ALONE (39) Anderson
WEARY RIVER (28) Ree
WEB, THE (47) Wood
WEDDING GROUP (36) Haffenden
WEDDING MARCH, THE (28) Ree
WEDDING NIGHT, THE (34) Kiam
WEDNESDAY'S CHILD (34) Plunkett
WEEKEND AT THE WALDORF (45) s Irene a Herwood Keyes
WEEKEND IN HAVANA (41) Wakeling
WEEKEND MILLIONAIRE=ONCE IN A MILLION
WEEKEND PASS (43) V West
WEEKENDS ONLY (32) Luick
WEEKEND WITH FATHER (51) Thomas
WEE WILLIE WINKIE (37) Wakeling
WE GO FAST (41) Herschel
WEIRD WOMAN (44) V West
WE JOINED THE NAVY (62) Harris
WELCOME HOME (35) Lambert
WELCOME STRANGER (46) Head
WE LIVE AGAIN (34) Kiam
WE'RE GOING TO BE RICH (38) Strassner
WE'RE IN THE ARMY NOW=PACK UP YOUR TROUBLES
WE'RE NO ANGELS (55) Grant
WE'RE NOT DRESSING (34) Banton
WE'RE NOT MARRIED (52) Jenssen wd LeMaire
WE'RE ON THE JURY (36) Stevenson
WE'RE RICH AGAIN (34) Plunkett
WESTBOUND (58) Shoup
WESTERNER, THE (40) Saltern
WESTERN UNION (40) Banton
WESTLAND CASE, THE (37) V West
WEST OF SHANGHAI (37) Shoup
WEST OF ZANZIBAR (28) Cox
WEST POINT (27) Clark

Supplement to the Index (1991)

Following pages: the fashion parade from Roberta (Bernard Newman)

Appendix

Oscar Nominations

The Academy of Motion Picture Arts and Sciences (Oscars) inaugurated an award for costume design in 1948. A list of all nominations follows: winners are indicated by a star.

1948
Black & white
B F's Daughter (Irene)
*Hamlet (Roger Furse)
Colour
The Emperor Waltz (Edith Head, Gile Steele)
*Joan of Arc (Dorothy Jeakins, Karinska)

1949
Black & white
*The Heiress (Edith Head, Gile Steele)
Prince of Foxes (Vittorio Nino Novarese)
Colour
*Adventures of Don Juan (Leah Rhodes, Travilla, Marjorie Best)
Mother Is a Freshman (Kay Nelson)

1950
Black & white
*All About Eve (Edith Head, Charles LeMaire)
Born Yesterday (Jean Louis)
The Magnificent Yankee (Walter Plunkett)
Colour
The Black Rose (Michael Whittaker)
*Samson & Delilah (Edith Head, Dorothy Jeakins, Elois Jenssen, Gile Steele, Gwen Wakeling)
That Forsyte Woman (Walter Plunkett, Valles)

1951
Black & white
Kind Lady (Walter Plunkett, Gile Steele)
The Model & the Marriage Broker (Charles LeMaire, Renie)
The Mudlark (Edward Stevenson, Margaret Furse)
*A Place in the Sun (Edith Head)
A Streetcar Named Desire (Lucinda Ballard)
Colour
*An American in Paris (Orry-Kelly, Walter Plunkett, Irene Sharaff)
David and Bathsheba (Charles LeMaire, Edward Stevenson)
The Great Caruso (Helen Rose, Gile Steele)
Quo Vadis? (Herschel McCoy)
Tales of Hoffman (Hein Heckroth)

1952
Black & white
Affair in Trinidad (Jean Louis)
*The Bad & the Beautiful (Helen Rose)
Carrie (Edith Head)
My Cousin Rachel (Charles LeMaire, Dorothy Jeakins)
Sudden Fear (Sheila O'Brien)
Colour
The Greatest Show on Earth (Edith Head, Dorothy Jeakins, Miles White)
Hans Christian Andersen (Clavé, Mary Wills, Madame Karinska)
The Merry Widow (Helen Rose, Gile Steele)
*Moulin Rouge (Marcel Vertes)
With a Song in My Heart (Charles LeMaire)

1953
Black & white
The Actress (Walter Plunkett)
Dream Wife (Helen Rose, Herschel McCoy)
From Here to Eternity (Jean Louis)
The President's Lady (Charles LeMaire, Renie)
*Roman Holiday (Edith Head)
Colour
The Band Wagon (Mary Ann Nyberg)
Call Me Madam (Irene Sharaff)
How to Marry a Millionaire (Charles LeMaire, Travilla)
*The Robe (Charles LeMaire, Emile Santiago)
Young Bess (Walter Plunkett)

1954
Black & white
The Earrings of Madame de (Georges Annenkov, Rosine Delamare)
Executive Suite (Helen Rose)
Indiscretion of an American Wife (Christian Dior)
It Should Happen to You (Jean Louis)
*Sabrina (Edith Head)
Colour
Brigadoon (Irene Sharaff)
Desirée (Charles LeMaire, Rene Hubert)
*Gate of Hell (Sanzo Wada)
A Star is Born (Jean Louis, Mary Ann Nyberg, Irene Sharaff)
There's No Business Like Show Business (Charles LeMaire, Travilla, Miles White)

1955
Black & white
*I'll Cry Tomorrow (Helen Rose)
The Pickwick Papers (Beatrice Dawson)

Queen Bee (Jean Louis)
The Rose Tattoo (Edith Head)
Ugetsu Monogatari (Tadaoto Kainoscho)
Colour
Guys and Dolls (Irene Sharaff)
Interrupted Melody (Helen Rose)
★Love is a Many Splendored Thing (Charles LeMaire)
To Catch a Thief (Edith Head)
The Virgin Queen (Charles LeMaire, Mary Wills)

1956
Black & white
Seven Samurai (Kohei Ezaki)
The Power and the Prize (Helen Rose)
The Proud and the Profane (Edith Head)
★The Solid Gold Cadillac (Jean Louis)
Teenage Rebel (Charles LeMaire, Mary Wills)
Colour
Around the World in 80 Days (Miles White)
Giant (Moss Mabry, Marjorie Best)
★The King and I (Irene Sharaff)
The Ten Commandments (Edith Head, Ralph Jester, John Jensen, Dorothy Jeakins, Arnold Friberg)
War and Peace (Maria de Matteis)

1957
The rules were changed this year to allow for one award only, irrespective of black & white or colour
An Affair to Remember (Charles LeMaire)
Funny Face (Edith Head, Hubert de Givenchy)
★Les Girls (Orry-Kelly)
Pal Joey (Jean Louis)
Raintree County (Walter Plunkett)

1958
Bell, Book and Candle (Jean Louis)
The Buccaneer (Ralph Jester, Edith Head, John Jensen)
A Certain Smile (Charles LeMaire, Mary Wills)
★Gigi (Cecil Beaton)
Some Came Running (Walter Plunkett)

1959
The rules changed back this year to the pre-1957 division between black & white and colour
Black & white
Career (Edith Head)
The Diary of Anne Frank (Charles LeMaire, Mary Wills)
The Gazebo (Helen Rose)

Les Girls (1957): Gwen Verdon

Gigi (1958): Hermione Gingold, Maurice Chevalier

★Some Like it Hot (Orry-Kelly)
The Young Philadelphians (Howard Shoup)

Colour
★Ben-Hur (Elizabeth Haffenden)
The Best of Everything (Adele Palmer)
The Big Fisherman (Renie)
The Five Pennies (Edith Head)
Porgy and Bess (Irene Sharaff)

1960
Black & white
★The Facts of Life (Edith Head, Edward Stevenson)
Never on Sunday (Deni Vachlioti)
The Rise and Fall of Legs Diamond (Howard Shoup)
Seven Thieves (Bill Thomas)
The Virgin Spring (Marik Vos)
Colour
Can-Can (Irene Sharaff)
Midnight Lace (Irene)
Pepe (Edith Head)
★Spartacus (Valles, Bill Thomas)
Sunrise at Campobello (Marjorie Best)

1961
Black & white
The Children's Hour (Dorothy Jeakins)
Claudelle Inglish (Howard Shoup)
Judgment at Nuremberg (Jean Louis)
★La Dolce Vita (Piero Gherardi)
Yojimbo (Yoshiro Muraki)
Colour
Babes in Toyland (Bill Thomas)
Back Street (Jean Louis)
Flower Drum Song (Irene Sharaff)
Pocketful of Miracles (Edith Head, Walter Plunkett)
★West Side Story (Irene Sharaff)

1962
Black & white
Days of Wine and Roses (Donfeld)
The Man Who Shot Liberty Valance (Edith Head)
The Miracle Worker (Ruth Morley)
Phaedra (Deni Vachlioti)
★Whatever Happened to Baby Jane? (Norma Koch)
Colour
Bon Voyage (Bill Thomas)
Gypsy (Orry-Kelly)
The Music Man (Dorothy Jeakins)
My Geisha (Edith Head)
★Wonderful World of the Brothers Grimm (Mary Wills)

1963
Black & white
★Otto e Mezzo (8 ½) (Piero Gherardi)
Love with the Proper Stranger (Edith Head)

Cecil Beaton design for Audrey Hepburn in My Fair Lady *(1964)*

Romeo and Juliet *(1968): Olivia Hussey, Leonard Whiting*

Barry Lyndon *(1975): Marisa Berenson*

The Stripper (Travilla)
Toys in the Attic (Bill Thomas)
Wives and Lovers (Edith Head)
Colour
The Cardinal (Donald Brooks)
★Cleopatra (Irene Sharaff, Vittorio Nino Novarese, Renie)
How the West Was Won (Walter Plunkett)
The Leopard (Piero Tosi)
A New Kind of Love (Edith Head)

1964
Black & white
A House Is Not a Home (Edith Head)
Hush, Hush, Sweet Charlotte (Norma Koch)
Kisses for My President (Howard Shoup)
★Night of the Iguana (Dorothy Jeakins)
The Visit (Rene Hubert)
Colour
Becket (Margaret Furse)
Mary Poppins (Tony Walton)

Camelot *(1967): Richard Harris, Vanessa Redgrave*

★My Fair Lady (Cecil Beaton)
The Unsinkable Molly Brown (Morton Haack)
What a Way to Go! (Edith Head, Moss Mabry)

1965
Black & white
★Darling . . . (Julie Harris)
Morituri (Moss Mabry)
A Rage To Live (Howard Shoup)
Ship Of Fools (Bill Thomas, Jean Louis)
The Slender Thread (Edith Head)
Colour
The Agony and The Ecstasy (Vittorio Nino Novarese)
★Doctor Zhivago (Phyllis Dalton)
The Greatest Story Ever Told (Vittorio Nino Novarese, Marjorie Best)
Inside Daisy Clover (Edith Head, Bill Thomas)
The Sound of Music (Dorothy Jeakins)

1966
Black & white
The Gospel According to St Matthew (Danilo Donati)
Mandragola (Danilo Donati)
Mister Buddwing (Helen Rose)
Morgan, A Suitable Case For Treatment (Jocelyn Rickards)
★Who's Afraid Of Virginia Woolf? (Irene Sharaff)
Colour
Gambit (Jean Louis)
Hawaii (Dorothy Jeakins)
Juliet Of the Spirits (Piero Gherardi)
★A Man For All Seasons (Elizabeth Haffenden, Joan Bridge)
The Oscar (Edith Head)

1967
The rules changed again this year (see 1957)
Bonnie and Clyde (Theodora van Runkle)
★Camelot (John Truscott)
The Happiest Millionaire (Bill Thomas)
The Taming Of The Shrew (Irene Sharaff, Danilo Donati)
Thoroughly Modern Millie (Jean Louis)

1968
The Lion In Winter (Margaret Furse)
Oliver! (Phyllis Dalton)
Planet Of The Apes (Morton Haack)
★Romeo And Juliet (Danilo Donati)
Star! (Donald Brooks)

1969
★Anne Of The Thousand Days (Margaret Furse)
Gaily, Gaily (Ray Aghayan)
Hello, Dolly! (Irene Sharaff)
Sweet Charity (Edith Head)
They Shoot Horses, Don't They? (Donfeld)

1970

Airport (Edith Head)
★Cromwell (Vittorio Nino Novarese)
Darling Lili (Donald Brooks, Jack Bear)
The Hawaiians (Bill Thomas)
Scrooge (Margaret Furse)

1971

Bedknobs And Broomsticks (Bill Thomas)
Death In Venice (Piero Tosi)
Mary Queen Of Scots (Margaret Furse)
★Nicholas and Alexandra (Yvonne Blake, Antonio Castillo)
What's the Matter With Helen? (Morton Haack)

1972

The Godfather (Anna Hill Johnstone)
Lady Sings The Blues (Bob Mackie, Ray Aghayan, Norma Koch)
The Poseidon Adventure (Paul Zastupnevich)
★Travels With My Aunt (Anthony Powell)
Young Winston (Anthony Mendleson)

1973

Cries and Whispers (Greta Johanson)
Ludwig (Piero Tosi)
★The Sting (Edith Head)
Tom Sawyer (Donfeld)
The Way We Were (Dorothy Jeakins, Moss Mabry)

1974

Chinatown (Anthea Sylbert)
Daisy Miller (John Furness)
The Godfather Part II (Theadora van Runkle)
★The Great Gatsby (Theoni V Aldredge)
Murder on the Orient Express (Tony Walton)

1975

★Barry Lyndon (Ulla-Britt Søderlund, Milena Canonero)
The Four Musketeers (Yvonne Blake, Ron Talsky)
Funny Lady (Ray Aghayan, Bob Mackie)
The Magic Flute (Karin Erskine)
The Man Who Would Be King (Edith Head)

*Edith Head design for Robert Redford
in* The Sting *(1973)*

Window display at Selfridge's of London of some of the costumes from The Great Gatsby *(1974)*

1976

Bound for Glory (William Theiss)
★Fellini's Casanova (Danilo Donati)
The Incredible Sarah (Anthony Mendleson)
The Passover Plot (Mary Wills)
The Seven Percent Solution (Allen Barett)

1977

Airport 77 (Edith Head, Burton Miller)
Julia (Anthea Sylbert)
A Little Night Music (Florence Klotz)
The Other Side of Midnight (Irene Sharaff)
★Star Wars (John Mollo)

1978

Caravans (Renie)
Days of Heaven (Patricia Norris)
★Death on the Nile (Anthony Powell)
The Swarm (Paul Zastupnevich)
The Wiz (Tony Walton)

1979

Agatha (Shirley Russell)
★All That Jazz (Albert Wolsky)
Butch and Sundance: The Early Days (William Theiss)
The Europeans (Judy Moorcroft)
La Cage Aux Folles (Piero Tosi, Ambra)

1980

The Elephant Man (Patricia Norris)
My Brilliant Career (Anna Senior)
Somewhere in Time (Jean-Pierre Dorléac)
★Tess (Anthony Powell)
When Time Ran Out . . . (Paul Zastupnevich)

1981

★Chariots of Fire (Milena Canonero)
The French Lieutenant's Woman (Tom Rand)
Pennies from Heaven (Bob Mackie)
Ragtime (Anna Hill Johnstone)
Reds (Shirley Russell)

1982

★Gandhi (John Mollo, Bhanu Athaiya)
La Traviata (Piero Tosi)

Sophie's Choice (Albert Wolsky)
Tron (Elois Jenssen, Rosanna Norton)
Victor/Victoria (Patricia Norris)

1983

Cross Creek (Joe I. Tompkins)
★Fanny and Alexander (Marik Vos)
Heart Like a Wheel (William Theiss)
The Return of Martin Guerre (Anne-Marie Marchand)
Zelig (Santo Loquasto)

1984

★Amadeus (Theodor Pistek)
The Bostonians (Jenny Beavan, John Bright)
A Passage to India (Judy Moorcroft)
Places in the Heart (Ann Roth)
2010 (Patricia Norris)

1985

The Color Purple (Aggie Guerard Rodgers)
The Journey of Natty Gann (Albert Wolsky)
Out of Africa (Milena Canonero)
Prizzi's Honor (Donfeld)
★Ran (Emi Wada)

1986

The Mission (Enrico Sabbatini)
Otello (Anna Anni)
Peggy Sue Got Married (Theodora van Runkle)
Pirates (Anthony Powell)
★A Room with a View (Jenny Beavan, John Bright)

1987

The Dead (Dorothy Jeakins)
Empire of the Sun (Bob Ringwood)
★The Last Emperor (James Acheson)
Maurice (Jenny Beavan)
The Untouchables (Marilyn Vance-Straker)

1988

Coming to America (Deborah Nadoolman)
★Dangerous Liaisons (James Acheson)
A Handful of Dust (Jane Robinson)
Sunset (Patricia Norris)
Tucker: The Man and His Dreams (Milena Canonero)

BAFTA Nominations

The British Academy of Film and Television Arts (BAFTA), formerly The Society of Film and Television Arts (SFTA), inaugurated an award for costume design in 1964. A list of all nominations follows: winners are indicated by a star.

1964
Black & white
Of Human Bondage (Beatrice Dawson)
Psyche 59 (Julie Harris)
★The Pumpkin Eater (Motley)
Colour
★Becket (Margaret Furse)
The Long Ships (Anthony Mendleson)
Woman of Straw (Beatrice Dawson)
The Yellow Rolls-Royce (Anthony Mendleson)

1965
Black & white
No award in this category
Colour
The Amorous Adventures of Moll Flanders (Elizabeth Haffenden, Joan Bridge)
Help! (Julie Harris)
A Shot In The Dark (Margaret Furse)
★Those Magnificent Men In Their Flying Machines (Osbert Lancaster, Dinah Greet)
Young Cassidy (Margaret Furse)

1966
Black & white
No award in this category
Colour
Arabesque (Christian Dior)
The Blue Max (John Furness)
Romeo And Juliet (Nicholas Georgidis)
★The Wrong Box (Julie Harris)

1967
Black & white
★Mademoiselle (Jocelyn Rickards)
The Sailor From Gibraltar (Jocelyn Rickards)
Colour
Casino Royale (Julie Harris)
Far From The Madding Crowd (Alan Barrett)
Half A Sixpence (Elizabeth Haffenden, Joan Bridge)
★A Man For All Seasons (Elizabeth Haffenden, Joan Bridge)

1968
The rules were changed this year to allow for one award only, irrespective of black & white or colour
The Charge Of The Light Brigade (David Walker)
The Lion In Winter (Margaret Furse)
Oliver! (Phyllis Dalton)
★Romeo And Juliet (Danilo Donati)

1969
Funny Girl (Irene Sharaff)
Isadora (Ruth Myers)
★Oh! What A Lovely War (Anthony Mendleson)
Women In Love (Shirley Russell)

1970
Anne Of The Thousand Days (Margaret Furse)
Cromwell (Vittorio Nino Novarese)
Ryan's Daughter (Jocelyn Rickards)
★Waterloo (Maria De Matteis)

1971
★Death In Venice (Piero Tosi)
The Go-Between (John Furness)
Nicholas and Alexandra (Yvonne Blake, Antonio Castillo)
Tales Of Beatrix Potter (Christine Edzard)

1972
Cabaret (Charlotte Flemming)
The Godfather (Anna Hill Johnstone)
★Young Winston, Macbeth, and *Alice's Adventures in Wonderland* (Anthony Mendleson)

1973
Jesus Christ Superstar (Yvonne Blake)
★The Hireling (Phyllis Dalton)
A Doll's House (Beatrice Dawson)
Brother Sun, Sister Moon (Danilo Donati)

1974
Chinatown (Anthea Sylbert)
★ The Great Gatsby (Theoni V Aldredge)
Murder On The Orient Express (Tony Walton)
The Three Musketeers (Yvonne Blake)

1975
The SFTA was re-named The British Academy of Film and Television Arts (BAFTA) this year
Barry Lyndon (Ulla-Britt Søderlund, Milena Canonero)
★The Day Of The Locust (Ann Roth)
The Four Musketeers (Yvonne Blake)
The Man Who Would Be King (Edith Head)

1976

Bugsy Malone (Monica Howe)
★*Die Marquise von O* (Moidele Bickel)
Picnic at Hanging Rock (Judy Dorsman)
The Slipper and the Rose (Julie Harris)

1977

★*Fellini's Casanova* (Danilo Donati)
Joseph Andrews (Michael Annals, Patrick Wheatley)
New York, New York (Theadora van Runkle)
Valentino (Shirley Russell)

1978

★*Death on the Nile* (Anthony Powell)
The Duellists (Tom Rand)
Julia (Anthea Sylbert, Joan Bridge, Anna Lisa Nasalli Rocca)
Star Wars (John Mollo)

1979

Agatha (Shirley Russell)
Alien (John Mollo)
The Europeans (Judy Moorcroft)
★*Yanks* (Shirley Russell)

1980

All That Jazz (Albert Wolsky)
Don Giovanni (Frantz Salieri, Anna Lisa Nasalli Rocca, Jean-François de Pouilly)
Flash Gordon (Danilo Donati)
★*Kagemusha* (Seiichiro Momosawa)

1981

Chariots of Fire (Milena Canonero)
Excalibur (Bob Ringwood)
The French Lieutenant's Woman (Tom Rand)
Tess (Anthony Powell)

1982

★*Blade Runner* (Charles Knode, Michael Kaplan)
The Draughtman's Contract (Sue Blane)
Gandhi (John Mollo, Bhanu Athaiya)
Reds (Shirley Russell)

1983

Fanny and Alexander (Marik Vos)
Heat and Dust (Barbara Lane)
★*La Traviata* (Piero Tosi)
Tootsie (Ruth Morley)

1984

The Bostonians (Jenny Beavan, John Bright)
The Company of Wolves (Elizabeth Waller)
★*Once Upon a Time in America* (Gabriella Pascucci)
Swann in Love (Yvonne Sassinot de Nesle)

1985

Amadeus (Theodore Pistek)
★*The Cotton Club* (Milena Canonero)
Legend (Charles Knode)
A Passage to India (Judy Moorcroft)

1986

The Mission (Enrico Sabbatini)
Out of Africa (Milena Canonero)
Ran (Emi Wada)
★*A Room with a View* (Jenny Beavan, John Bright)

1987

Hope and Glory (Shirley Russell)
Little Dorrit (Sands Films)
★*Radio Days* (Jeffrey Kurland)
The Untouchables (Marilyn Vance-Straker)

1988

The Dressmaker (Judy Moorcroft)
Empire of the Sun (Bob Ringwood)
★*The Last Emperor* (James Acheson)
White Mischief (Marit Allen)

Barbra Streisand in On A Clear Day You Can See Forever *(Cecil Beaton)*